The Journal of Charles Mollet (1742–1819)

A Selection

The Journal of Charles Mollet (1742–1819)

A Selection

Rose-Marie Crossan (ed.)

MÒR MEDIA LIMITED

© Rose-Marie Anne Crossan 2024

All rights reserved. Except as permitted under current legislation, no part of this work may be photocopied, stored in a retrieval system, published, performed in public, adapted, broadcast, transmitted, recorded or reproduced in any form or by any means, without the prior permission of the author.

Rose-Marie Anne Crossan has asserted her right to be identified as the author of this work in accordance with sections 77 and 78 of the Copyright, Designs and Patents Act 1988.

First published 2024

Mòr Media Limited, Benderloch, Argyll, Scotland

www.mormedia.co.uk

ISBN 978-1-0686224-0-3

A catalogue record for this book is available from the British Library.

The publisher has no responsibility for the continued existence or accuracy of URLs for external or third-party internet websites referred to in this book, and does not guarantee that any content on such websites is, or will remain, accurate or appropriate.

Contents

Acknowledgements	vii
Notes on the text	ix
Maps	x
Introduction	15
The journal	15
Demography and economy	17
Language and culture	24
Politics and administration	26
Charles Mollet's background	30
The Journal of Charles Mollet	37
Appendices	415
1. Mollet family tree, ascending	415
2. Mollet family tree, descending	416
3. Composition of principal families associated with Mollet	417
4. Frequently mentioned employees of Mollet's	422
5. Relatedness of Mollet's employees	423
6. Mollet's symbols and codes	424
7. French *émigrés* mentioned by Mollet	427
Bibliography	431
Index	435

Maps

1. Channel Islands and adjacent French and English coasts   x
2. Parishes of Guernsey   xi
3. Detail from 1816 map of Guernsey showing Castel parish   xii
4. Detail from 1787 map of Guernsey showing Charles Mollet's farm and neighbouring properties   xiii

Acknowledgements

This book, which is based on original documents held by Guernsey's Priaulx Library, would not have been possible without the co-operation and assistance of the Library's management and staff, to whom I would like to express my most particular gratitude. I would also like to thank the staff of Guernsey's Greffe and Island Archives Service for their kind help with background research. Among others to whom my thanks are due are Richard Hocart, who has contributed much to my understanding of Georgian Guernsey through his published work and personal communications, and Yan Marquis, who has provided linguistic advice. Last but certainly not least, I am most grateful to Helen Crossan for her indispensable help in preparing my text for publication, and to my husband Jonathan for supporting me through yet another all-consuming three-year project.

Rose-Marie Crossan, MA (Oxon), PhD
Guernsey, February 2024

Notes on the text

1. Currency

Throughout Mollet's life, Guernsey's currency was the French *livre tournois* (divided into 20 *sous* of 12 *deniers* each). Fourteen *livres tournois* were worth £1 sterling by the official London exchange rate, and where sterling equivalents are given here, they are calculated on this basis. Various French coins were in local circulation, the most common of which were gold six-*livre* pieces, silver *écus* and *livres*, copper *sous* and *deniers*.[1] Coins of other nations were also used, including Spanish dollars and British guineas, sovereigns, shillings and pennies. In the 1770s and 1780s, Mollet chiefly used *tournois* coins but increasingly turned to British coins as the French Revolutionary and Napoleonic wars led to local shortages of French specie. His journals juxtapose sums in *tournois* with sums in sterling seemingly haphazardly.

2. Parish names

Charles Mollet always used the French names of Guernsey's country parishes in his diary: *St Sauveur, St André, le Valle, la Forêt, Torteval, St Martin, le Castel, St Samson* and *St Pierre*. Mollet never used the name *St Pierre Port* but invariably referred to the town parish simply as *la ville*. In my translation, I have used the English versions of parish names throughout, and the word 'town' when Mollet wrote *la ville*. When Mollet used the term *St Pierre*, he always meant the country parish sometimes referred to as *St Pierre du Bois* (although he never personally added the *du Bois* element). In English, this parish is known both as St Peter in the Wood and St Peter. Both for consistency and to follow Mollet's practice, I have used the latter form.

3. Blank spaces, omissions and ellipses

Mollet sometimes left blank spaces in his journal entries when he could not immediately recall such things as names, dates, prices or quantities. He apparently intended to fill in these blanks later, but hardly ever did. I have indicated blank spaces within entries by open dotted lines roughly the same length as the spaces left by Mollet. Where I have myself omitted parts of Mollet's text at the beginning or within a journal entry, this is indicated by an ellipsis in square brackets – [...].

---

[1] A French law of 1795 replaced the *livre tournois* with the *franc*, but as the *franc* had by law to have the same metal content as the *livre*, the two were interchangeable. Old *tournois* coins remained in circulation, locally and in France, until well into the nineteenth century. One *écu* was nominally worth six *livres*.

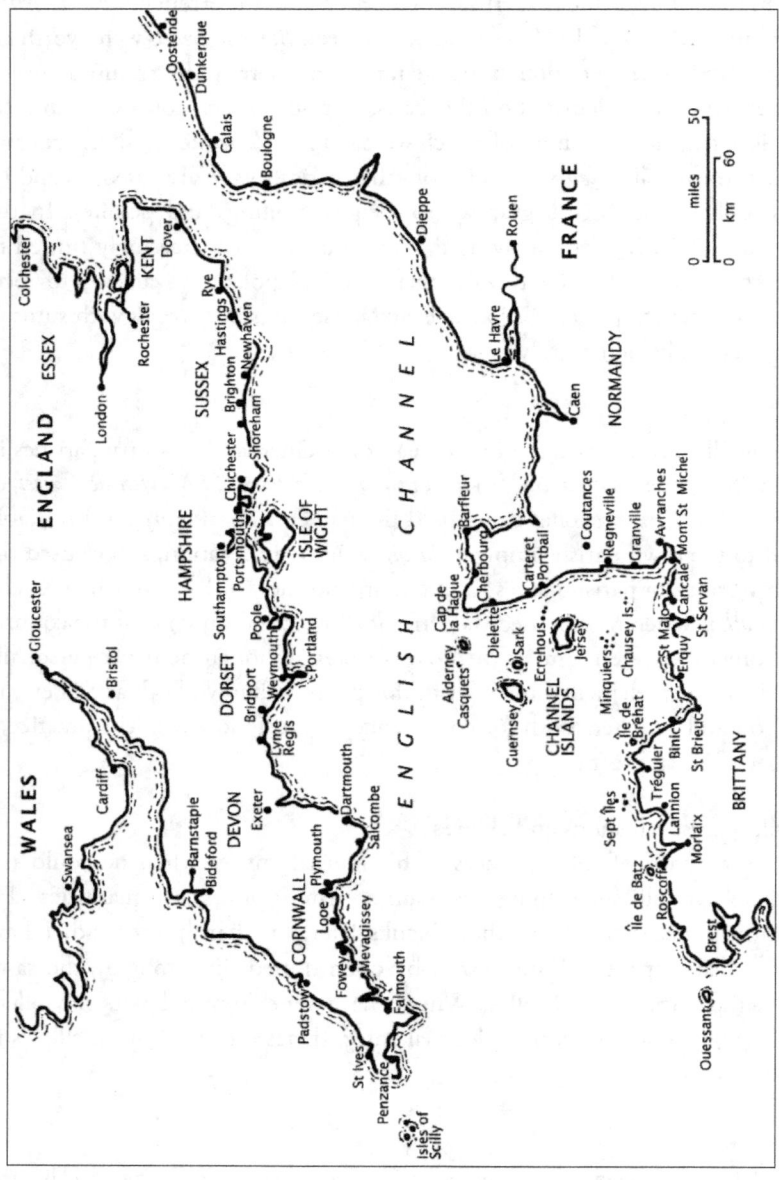

Map 1. Channel Islands and adjacent French and English coasts

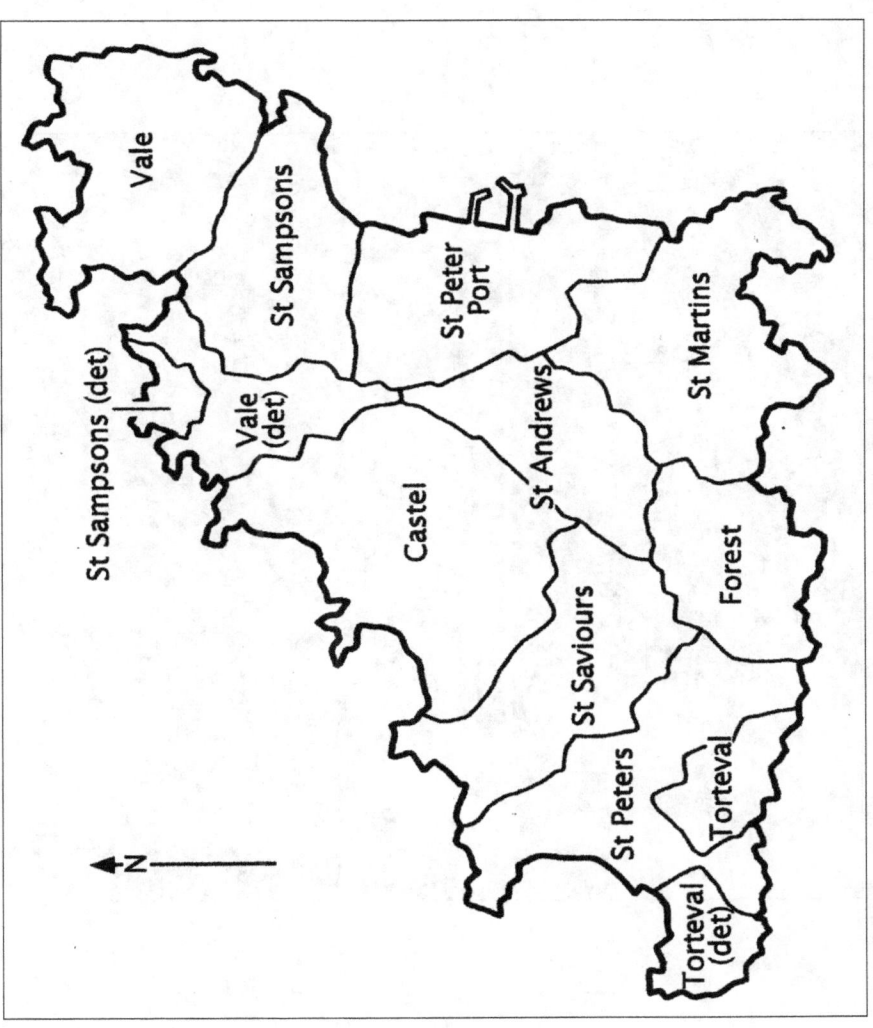

Map 2. Parishes of Guernsey

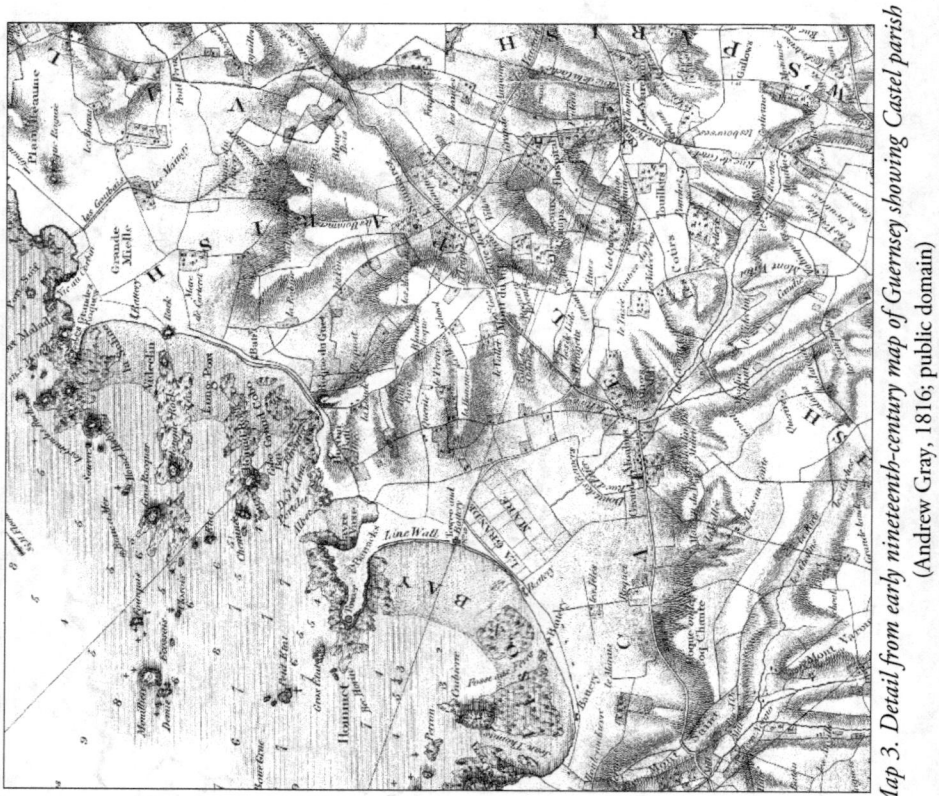

Map 3. Detail from early nineteenth-century map of Guernsey showing Castel parish (Andrew Gray, 1816; public domain)

xiii

Key to principal properties mentioned in Mollet's journal:

486 – Le Moulin de Haut
515 – Le Moulin du Milieu
517 – Le Groignet
520 – Les Grands Moulins
526 – La Porte
528 – La Houguette
533 – Mollet's farm
534 – the 'upper' house
535 – Les Vallées
536 – Les Roussiaux
537 – Les Pelleys
541 – Le Ponchez
544 – La Fontaine
552 – Les Effards
554 – Les Queux
556 – Castel Rectory
558 – Les Covins
1038 – Les Beaucamps de Haut

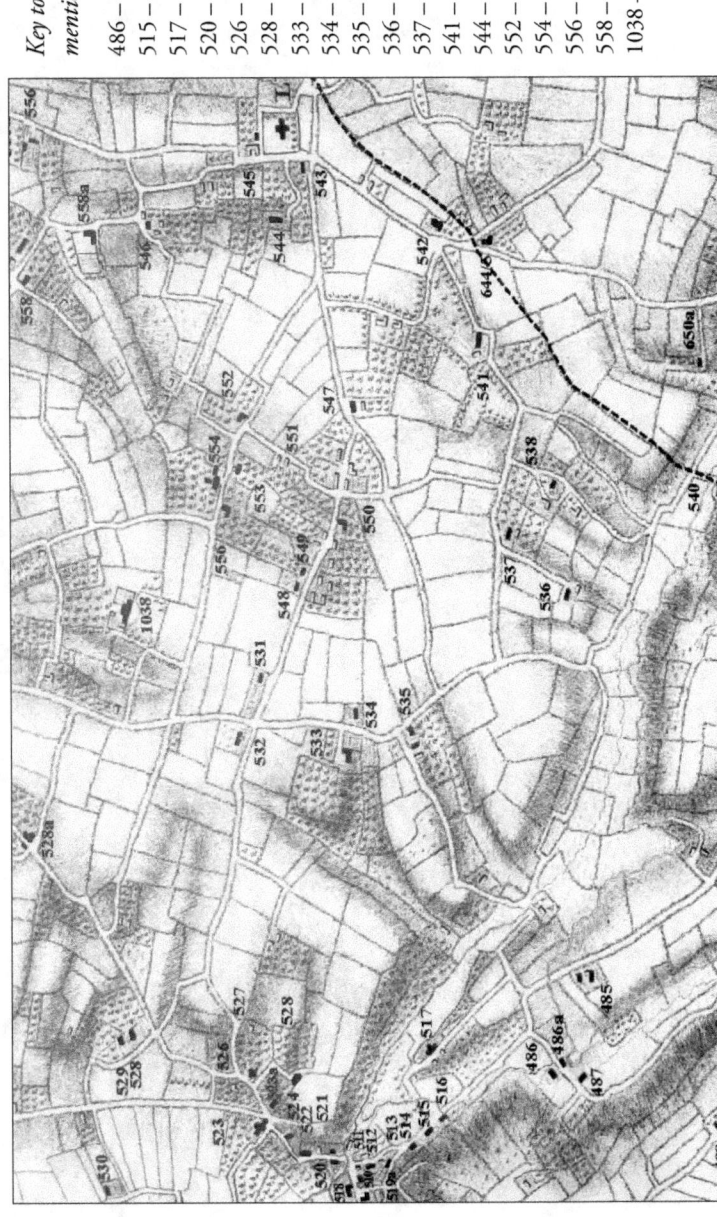

Map 4. Detail from 1787 map of Guernsey showing Charles Mollet's farm and neighbouring properties (Reproduced from J. McCormack, *Channel Island Houses* (Guernsey, 2015) by kind permission of the author)

Introduction

The journal

The six surviving volumes of Charles Mollet's journal were gifted to Guernsey's Priaulx Library in 1951 by Marjorie Barnes of Maiden Newton in Dorset, a distant relative of Charles Mollet's. The first volume begins in 1771 when Mollet was a young man of twenty-eight, and the last ends in 1818, seven months before his death at the age of seventy-six. They document an extraordinary five decades at the junction of the eighteenth and nineteenth centuries characterised both by warfare on an unprecedented scale and rapid and unparalleled change. Other local journals from this period have survived (notably that of Mollet's contemporary Elisha Dobrée),[2] but Mollet's is by far the longest and most detailed. The six extant volumes fill more than 1,500 pages and contain over half a million words.[3]

For all their 1,500 pages, however, the six extant volumes do not represent the entirety of the journal Mollet wrote over the course of his lifetime. There is internal evidence that pre-1771 volumes existed. In addition, two volumes covering intermediate periods are missing (1781–84 and 1812–15). Within the surviving volumes themselves, parts of pages or ranges of pages have also been deliberately excised, the most egregious example falling at the end of Mollet's life, when the final eleven pages (twenty-two sides) have been cut out, leaving only the stubs, with fragments of his writing upon them. Interestingly, Mollet's written entries are complemented throughout with an extensive range of symbols inserted into adjacent margins. It has been impossible to ascertain what these signified, but they form at certain periods almost a parallel narrative to the text.[4]

Mollet was a farmer, and the primary purpose of his diary was to keep track of his agricultural activities. His journal is however infinitely more than

---

[2] Guernsey's Island Archives hold three volumes of Dobrée's journal: AQ 1572/03 (1771–85); AQ 1572/04 (1786–99); AQ 1572/05 (1800–17). Dobrée was fourteen years Mollet's junior but well-known to him.

[3] These volumes are uneven in length. Mollet became more home-focused in his declining years and his diaries grew correspondingly richer in domestic detail. His last volume (1815–18) is almost twice the length of his first (1771–6).

[4] A selection of these are reproduced in Appendix 6.

a farming diary, as he also used it to record his other commercial activities, his public life, his domestic arrangements, his social life, his travels, matters relating to his family, and his observations on external events. For all of these reasons, Mollet's journal affords us a unique insight into late eighteenth-century processes of transformation as they unfolded. It is also unique in a Guernsey context in that it provides singular detail on a hitherto obscure portion of the local community. For although Mollet belonged to Guernsey's upper class, he recorded his dealings with all social strata, thus yielding detail on the characters, lifestyles and behaviours of individuals which does not normally emerge from other historical sources.

Charles Mollet's mother tongue (and that of most of his Guernsey contemporaries) was *guernésiais*, a local variant of Norman French. *Guernésiais* had no written form, so that eighteenth-century islanders normally used standard Parisian French for writing. Mollet, too, used standard French in his journals, but they are nevertheless thoroughly peppered with *guernésiais* vocabulary and heavily influenced by *guernésiais* grammar and syntax. All six of the volumes have been translated into English, and the full translation may be accessed at the Priaulx Library.

Mollet's journal was written in a plain, not to say laconic, style. This neutral language has been replicated in the translation, and there has been no attempt to mimic the style of an eighteenth-century English gentleman. Mollet's spellings, particularly of local words and names, were inconsistent. To give a flavour of the original, all proper nouns have been left precisely as he wrote them. Some of his abbreviations have also been replicated, as has his use of ampersands and figures for numbers. Punctuation has, however, been modernised and many extraneous capital letters eliminated. The excerpts selected for publication here represent between 20 and 25 per cent of the entries in the original journal.

Concurrently with this selection, a companion volume has been published under the title *Charles Mollet and His World: Daily Life in Georgian Guernsey*.[5] This volume contextualises Mollet's diary entries and provides extensive background information on the island as it was in his day. As some background is essential to an understanding of the excerpts, the rest of this Introduction will provide a brief outline of the requisite facts.

---

[5] R.-M. Crossan, *Charles Mollet and His World: Daily Life in Georgian Guernsey* (Benderloch, 2024).

Demography and economy

Guernsey lies about 30 miles off the Normandy coast and 80 miles from the nearest English landfall. Together with the smaller islands of Alderney, Sark, Herm and Jethou, it forms a single semi-autonomous Bailiwick.[6] Jersey, some 27 miles to the south-east, forms a separate Bailiwick of its own. Both of the main Channel Islands are surprisingly small. Jersey's total area is just over 116 square kilometres, and Guernsey's 63.5 square kilometres.[7] This may be contrasted with the Isle of Wight's 380 square kilometres and the Isle of Man's 572 square kilometres. Guernsey's ten parishes are commensurately small, varying in size between 10 and 3 square kilometres.[8] Charles Mollet's home parish, Castel, is the largest in terms of area. Torteval, forming the island's south-west corner, is the smallest. Guernsey's small size notwithstanding, it has for many centuries supported a comparatively large population. This was partly because the island was endowed with the triple advantages of a fertile soil, a benign climate and abundant fish stocks. But it was also in no small measure due to the fact that its only town, St Peter Port, enjoyed a vigorous and substantial maritime trade.

Charles Mollet's lifetime spanned a particularly dynamic phase in Guernsey's demographic history. The population grew from around 12,000 in 1728 to around 21,500 in the second decade of the nineteenth century.[9] At the latter date, St Peter Port alone accommodated at least 13,000 souls, or 61 per cent of the island's population. The majority of these 13,000 were packed into the built-up area around the harbour. The belt of farmland which made up the rest of the parish was considerably less densely populated. St Peter Port's urban area – 'town', as Charles Mollet called it – was always run as an integral part of the parish of St Peter Port and never developed any municipal institutions of its own. However, the size of its late eighteenth- and

---

[6] Note, however, that in the rest of this chapter, the term 'Guernsey' will refer only to the island of Guernsey, and not the whole Bailiwick.
[7] About 1.3 square kilometres were added to Guernsey's land area after 1806, when the Braye du Valle (a tidal channel separating the northern tip of the island from the rest) was reclaimed from the sea.
[8] See Map 2.
[9] These are approximations based on figures reproduced in J.P. Warren, 'Extracts from the diary of Elisha Dobrée', *Transactions of la Société Guernesiaise*, 10 (1929) p. 495, and W. Berry, *History of the Island of Guernsey* (London, 1815), pp. 23–4.

early nineteenth-century population put it firmly on a par with many English provincial towns.[10]

The town of St Peter Port had grown up around a sheltered haven on Guernsey's east coast which was conveniently situated on the main sea route from Biscay into the Channel. It had long been a centre of international trade, the Channel Islands having since the fifteenth century enjoyed the privilege of neutrality during wartime, which permitted Islanders to engage in trade with France while that country was at war with England.[11] This neutrality was brought to an end at the beginning of England's Nine Years War against France in 1689, when an Order in Council confirmed that a prohibition on the import of goods from France should also be observed in the Channel Islands.[12] Although the Order abolished Guernsey's neutrality, it was not resisted by the island's ship-owning elite, some of whom saw it as an opportunity to engage in privateering.[13] The ship-owners who went on to engage in this new enterprise met with a degree of success, and this stimulated local ship-owners and merchants to continue fitting out privateers in all ensuing Franco-British wars until 1815.[14]

Although privateering in itself did not provide a secure foundation for the economy, it did encourage the establishment of St Peter Port as an entrepôt in the Atlantic trade, and thus led to further economic expansion. St Peter Port became an entrepôt almost by default as prize cargoes were brought back to Guernsey by the privateers and stored in the town. Demand for space for

---

[10] In 1801, Canterbury had a population of 9,000; Salisbury 9,114; Reading 9,770; Colchester 11,520; Preston 11,867; and Oxford 12,107 (J. Marshall, *An Analysis and Compendium of All the Returns made to Parliament Relating to the Increase of Population* (London, 1835), pp. 107, 166, 163, 112, 148, 158).

[11] For the historical origin of this privilege, see D.M. Ogier, *The Government and Law of Guernsey* (2005; Guernsey, 2012 edn), p. 181.

[12] For the Channel Islands' political relationship with England (and later the United Kingdom), see section on Politics and administration, below.

[13] Privateering was the practice whereby civilian-owned vessels were permitted to participate in maritime warfare under a commission of war known as a letter of marque. This empowered them to attack enemy vessels and take them and their cargoes as prizes, with the proceeds shared between sponsors, ship-owners, captains, crew, and the issuer of the commission.

[14] Between the Nine Years War and 1815, there were five further major Franco-British conflicts: the War of the Spanish Succession (1701–13), the War of the Austrian Succession (1740–8), the Seven Years War (1756–63), the War of American Independence (1776–83) and the French Revolutionary and Napoleonic Wars (1793–1815).

the wines, spirits, tobacco, tea, etc., was such that, between 1719 and 1747, between twenty and thirty new warehouses were built in St Peter Port.[15] Some of these commodities were re-exported legitimately, but since most were luxury goods subject to high duties in England, they attracted the interest of English smugglers, who started visiting St Peter Port in their small sailing vessels to buy up supplies. In consequence, Guernsey rapidly became one of the main suppliers of contraband to smugglers from southern England.[16] This in turn stimulated local entrepreneurs to set up factories for processing raw tobacco into pipe tobacco and snuff; operations for decanting wine and spirits into portable barrels; and coopers' workshops for manufacturing these small containers.

The smugglers' demand for luxury commodities was by no means limited to periods when the privateers were active, so Guernsey's ship-owners responded by expanding their peacetime fleets to fetch these goods from their places of origin. By the time of Charles Mollet's birth, local ship-owners and merchants were significant participants in the Atlantic trade, bringing in wine, brandy and textiles from France and Iberia; tobacco from Maryland and Virginia; and rum from the West Indies.[17] At around this time, St Peter Port also acquired a parallel role as a depository and bulk-breaker for dutiable commodities destined for legal entry into Britain before the introduction of the bonding system. The historian F.B. Tupper described St Peter Port harbour in the 1790s as 'often crammed to the very mouth', with 'twenty or thirty vessels in the roadstead waiting to enter.'[18]

The success of the entrepôt considerably enriched the mercantile class which formed the top tier of the insular community. This class was predominantly composed of long-established families who could trace their Guernsey pedigrees back to medieval times.[19] As well as dominating ship-

---

[15] G. Stevens Cox, *St Peter Port, 1630–1830: The History of an International Entrepôt* (Woodbridge, 1999), p. 21.
[16] A.G. Jamieson, 'The Channel Islands and smuggling, 1680–1850', in A.G. Jamieson (ed.), *A People of the Sea: The Maritime History of the Channel Islands* (London, 1986), p. 204.
[17] The Acts of Trade and Navigation, by which the shipment of colonial goods direct from the colonies to the Channel Islands was nominally prohibited, were not observed in Guernsey, largely owing to the entrenched opposition of the insular authorities and the fact that no eighteenth-century British administration chose to override this opposition.
[18] F.B. Tupper, *The History of Guernsey and its Bailiwick* (Guernsey, 1854), p. 439.
[19] Charles Mollet knew most of these families. Their names – Bonamy, Carey, De Havilland, De Jersey, De Lisle, De Sausmarez, Gosselin, Le Marchant, Le Mesurier, Maingy, Priaulx – feature frequently in his diaries.

owning and commerce, their members also occupied the highest ranks in Guernsey's militia, and monopolised leading roles in Guernsey's judiciary and administration. The majority of these families were town-based. This privileged class however formed only a tiny fraction of St Peter Port's population. Beneath them were the professional men (doctors, clergymen, etc.) and the large wholesalers and manufactory owners. These in their turn were followed by a stratum of smaller retailers and tradesmen. These three groups comprised between them most of St Peter Port's ratepayers. By the first decade of the nineteenth century, the combined value of their real and personal property as assessed for parish rates stood at around £1,834,400.[20]

At the base of the urban social pyramid, and below the threshold for paying rates, was a large residual class of journeymen artisans, labourers and domestic servants. To begin with, most of these workers were drawn from indigenous town families. However, as economic expansion increased demand for labour, there was a wave of in-migration from the town's rural hinterland. Growing numbers also came from across the sea – some from south-west England, and others (notably Huguenots) from France.[21] The British garrison further swelled the urban population: already comprising about 2,000 officers and men during the American War of Independence, their numbers doubled to around 4,000 at the height of the Napoleonic War, by which time St Peter Port also hosted a Royal Naval squadron.[22] The burgeoning population gave a further boost to the town's economy, increasing demand for housing, food, drink, and services of all kinds.

St Peter Port's rising prosperity brought many improvements to the town during Charles Mollet's lifetime. In the mid-1770s, the two piers of St Peter Port harbour, formerly abutting directly on to the beach, were linked with a solid stone quay. In the mid-1780s, the town acquired a new paved marketplace, furnished on one side by covered *halles* surmounted with a set of elegant Assembly Rooms. In the mid-1790s, a new theatre was added to St Peter Port's amenities.[23] All of these projects were privately financed. In due course, however, increasing rate revenues and growing civic pride led to public funding of improvements. Many of St Peter Port's public thoroughfares were paved and provided with lamps around the turn of the

---

[20] Berry, *Island of Guernsey*, p. 161.
[21] Stevens Cox, *St Peter Port*, pp. 82–5.
[22] Tupper, *History of Guernsey*, pp. 373, 391.
[23] G. Stevens Cox, *Social Life in Georgian Guernsey* (Guernsey, 2014), pp. 3, 31.

nineteenth century. A new courthouse was built in 1799, a new prison in 1811. Finally, during Mollet's last three decades, a wave of private house-building extended the town's built-up area to the west, north and south, as the well-to-do sought modern townhouses and villas away from the overcrowded centre.[24]

St Peter Port operated successfully as an entrepôt for much – but not all – of Charles Mollet's life. In Mollet's penultimate and final decades, the positive trend which had marked his earlier years underwent a series of checks. The first setback, and perhaps the most serious, was the demise of the entrepôt. The initial blow came in 1803, when the introduction of the bonding system in the United Kingdom deprived St Peter Port of its role as a depository for dutiable goods destined for legal re-export.[25] Subsequent blows came in 1805 and 1807 after mounting revenue losses pushed Westminster to extend two stringent anti-smuggling Acts to the Channel Islands, which deprived St Peter Port of its less respectable role as a smugglers' supply-base.[26] These Acts effectively barred St Peter Port's merchants and ship-owners from their most lucrative activity. With the destruction of their trading model, many of them retired, sold their vessels and warehouses, and invested the proceeds in government securities and real estate. The minority who chose not to do so continued to participate in privateering until the end of the Napoleonic War, and some also became active in the 'licence trade', whereby, from 1807, St Peter Port was permitted to become a trading post for the exchange of essential commodities between Britain and France.[27]

Privateering and the licence trade were, however, insufficient in themselves to provide employment to all of St Peter Port's redundant

---

[24] The most extensive residential development was the 'New Town', on the hill to the west of St Peter Port, which was begun in 1792 as a speculative venture and eventually comprised six streets (R. Hocart, 'The building of the New Town', *Transactions of la Société Guernesiaise*, 23 (1992), pp. 342–77).

[25] The bonding system was introduced to the United Kingdom by Westminster's 1803 Warehousing of Goods Act.

[26] The 1805 Smuggling Act banned the import into or export from the Islands of spirits, wines and tobacco in vessels of under 100 tons or in casks of less than 60 gallons or packages of under 450 lb. The 1807 Smuggling Act ordered that all vessels leaving the Islands were to obtain a customs clearance, and forbade vessels coming from the Islands to break bulk or alter cargo during their voyage (Jamieson, 'The Channel Islands and smuggling', p. 209).

[27] The King in Council issued an Order dated 18.12.1807 authorising licences to be issued for trade between Jersey and Guernsey and certain French ports. Imports and exports were held in St Peter Port and then re-shipped.

entrepôt workers. The town's workhouse saw a steep rise in admissions.[28] Some families decided that their fortunes would best be served by leaving the island. In 1806, 1807 and 1810, parties of Guernseymen departed for North America, where they founded Guernsey County in Ohio and Guernsey Cove on Prince Edward Island.

The advent of peace after Waterloo, though welcomed by many, exerted yet further negative effects on St Peter Port's economy. Privateering came to a definitive end. Even more seriously, the garrison was reduced to some 200–300 soldiers. This was a hard blow to St Peter Port's remaining retailers and tradesmen. Problems were then compounded in 1816/17 when Europe-wide harvest failure pushed up food prices to intolerable levels. As Charles Mollet's life came to a close in 1819, a second wave of emigration to North America was well under way.[29]

Although the economy of Guernsey's countryside was very different to that of the town, it too felt the impact of St Peter Port's changing fortunes, not least through the ebb and flow of demand for its produce. The country parishes, almost exclusively agricultural, were covered by hundreds of farms and smallholdings dispersed across a patchwork of enclosed fields.[30] Virtually all of these farms and smallholdings were owned by the families who worked them, since the island had lost the greater part of its large landowners in the thirteenth century.[31] Given the island's modest size and the large number of landowners, holdings were necessarily compact. A census of Guernsey's landholdings was taken in 1817 (in which Mollet himself participated). Only the returns of the Castel have survived, but this is quite fortunate, given that

---

[28] St Peter Port had had a workhouse – the Town Hospital – since 1743. The country parishes had collectively maintained their own workhouse – the Country Hospital – since 1751. For early nineteenth-century admissions, see R.-M. Crossan, *Poverty and Welfare in Guernsey, 1560–2015* (Woodbridge, 2015), pp. 125–6.

[29] A late nineteenth-century newspaper article gave the number of those leaving Guernsey on emigrant ships between 1817 and 1819 as 1,310 (*Comet*, 21.9.1889). We should note that the economy largely recovered in the decade following Mollet's death, stimulated mainly by the advent of new industries, but also partly by the settlement of British half-pay officers and other genteel migrants.

[30] There was some clustering of habitation, particularly around parish churches, but no villages as such. The island's original open fields had been gradually enclosed from the fifteenth century, as generations of landowners consolidated their strips by purchase and exchange to form parcels suited to enclosure.

[31] The reason for this will be explained below.

it was Charles Mollet's home parish.[32] The census counted 240 individual holdings in a parish just over 10 square kilometres in area. Nearly all of them consisted of a dwelling and attached land.[33] The size of each individual holding was recorded, including any land outside the parish boundary which also belonged to the owner. Only 12 per cent of holdings were over 20 acres in size; 70 per cent were under 12 acres; 38 per cent measured just 3 acres or less. In this, the Castel can be considered fairly typical of all the country parishes. Charles Mollet, with his 26⅓ acres, was among the top tenth of insular landowners.[34]

Estimates suggest that an average family needed at least 8 to 14 acres to live entirely off the land,[35] so that only a minority of rural holdings were large enough in themselves to sustain the families which owned them. Country parishioners nevertheless made the utmost use of the land they had. As a commentator observed, 'if it be only a garden, they cultivate fruit and vegetables [...] if they have also a field, they keep a cow and rear poultry,' adding that they consumed their own produce 'most sparingly', saving the bulk of it for market.[36] Like Scottish crofters, Guernsey's country parishioners supplemented the yield from their land with other avocations. Some coastal families clubbed together to buy small boats and fished part-time. Male family members might practise a hereditary trade or craft – tailoring, basket-making, carpentry, thatching, stonemasonry – or they might hire themselves out as day labourers. Female family members invariably worked as servants in better-off neighbours' houses. St Peter Port – and seafaring – also provided important outlets for surplus rural offspring.

In the countryside, the social structure was somewhat flatter than in town. The top tier, to which Mollet himself belonged, was composed of the largest landowners and parish Rectors. Then there were the slightly smaller landowners who nevertheless lived off their land. Next came the smallholding

---

[32] The returns survive at the Island Archives in the form of a copy taken several years later (SG 23/43).
[33] Only eight dwellings in the parish did not have land attached.
[34] By way of comparison, a report for the United Kingdom Board of Agriculture in 1796 deemed 150–200 acres to be typical of 'good middle-sized farms' in Great Britain, and 30–40 acres 'the average of small farms' (T. Robertson, *General Outline of the Report upon the Size of Farms* (Edinburgh, 1796), p. 42).
[35] R. Hocart, *The Country People of Guernsey and their Agriculture, 1640–1840* (Guernsey, 2016), p. 216.
[36] *The Guernsey and Jersey Magazine*, 1 (1836), p. 311.

master tradesmen, and beneath them the smallholding journeymen, fishermen and labourers. Very few non-natives settled permanently in the country parishes owing to the difficulty of acquiring land, which was jealously guarded by its local owners and kept within the same families for generations. The handful who did make their homes in the countryside usually did so by marrying into an established family.

Language and culture

The everyday spoken language of all country parishioners and most lower- and middle-ranking town parishioners was *guernésiais*. As noted above, it was also that of Charles Mollet himself. *Guernésiais* supported a lively oral culture with its own distinctive legends, proverbs and sayings. Aside from *guernésiais*, however, nearly all country-dwellers and most lower- and middle-ranking town parishioners would also have had some knowledge of 'standard' French, in which church services were conducted, which was used in Court records and other official documents, and in which reading and writing were taught in schools. The linguistic situation of urban patricians was slightly different. These were educated to a higher level than the majority of their compatriots and sometimes spent time in France, so that while able to converse fluently in *guernésiais* with servants and tradesmen, they could also speak and write French with greater facility.

The linguistic situation as regarded the upper ranks began perceptibly to change during Mollet's lifetime. Many among this class were merchants who did business with England via the entrepôt. For commercial reasons, therefore, they were obliged to develop a reasonable command of English. In addition to this, almost constant Franco-British warfare from 1778 onwards disrupted longstanding cultural and trading links with France, which cumulatively re-orientated the urban upper ranks squarely towards Britain. Both of these factors motivated increasing numbers of wealthy families to send their children to English boarding schools, or to settle, temporarily or permanently, in England themselves. Such practices ultimately resulted in a language shift among the elite. Charles Mollet's own relatives followed these trends, and his diaries show that his great-nieces and great-nephews were all essentially anglophone.

Mollet also recorded the beginnings of a language shift in urban non-elite ranks. The large cohort of British soldiers and increasing number of economic migrants from south-west England in St Peter Port ensured that English was heard alongside *guernésiais* in every urban shop, street and tavern, with predictable effects. The linguistic position of country-dwellers was, however, more stable – for the time being, at least. This was largely owing to the continuing sparsity of non-natives in the rural parishes, which ensured that it was they who adapted to the prevailing francophone culture, rather than that culture to them. The Mesquêne family, neighbours of Mollet's who descended from a British soldier named McKane, are a case in point.[37]

The francophone heritage of islanders also conditioned the nature of their religious practice and belief. The Protestant Reformation had originally come to Guernsey not from England but from French-speaking Normandy and Geneva. Thus, between the mid-1500s and mid-1600s Guernsey's 'established' religion followed characteristically Continental Calvinistic and Presbyterian norms.[38] The island's Presbyterian regime was however brought to an end in 1662 when Charles II appointed an Anglican Dean with an order to introduce the Anglican liturgy to Guernsey. Although this met with a certain amount of resistance, by 1700 Anglicanism (with its own local characteristics) had by and large replaced Presbyterianism.[39] For several decades thereafter, neither Dissent nor Catholicism had a presence in the island. The first Nonconformists to establish themselves in Guernsey were Quakers, who founded a local congregation in 1782. Next to arrive was Methodism, brought to the island in 1785 by missionaries from England and Jersey. Roman Catholicism came last, reintroduced by *émigrés* fleeing the French Revolution in 1793.[40] As we shall see in the selection from his journal, Charles Mollet had many first-hand contacts with the last two of these denominations.

Guernsey society was strongly hierarchical. This was no exception to the general eighteenth-century norm, but it was perhaps accentuated owing to islanders' physical proximity to one another. Charles Mollet had dealings with members of all ranks, but they occupied quite separate compartments in his life, and he was careful never to mix members of one with members of the others. The way he referred to fellow islanders in his journal reflected the

---

[37] The name appears as Mesquêne in both parish registers and Mollet's own journal.
[38] See D.M. Ogier, *Reformation and Society in Guernsey* (Woodbridge, 1996).
[39] R. Hocart, *Guernsey in the Reign of Charles II* (Guernsey, 2020), pp. 58, 59, 67–8, 174.
[40] J. Jacob, *Annals of some of the British Norman Isles constituting the Bailiwick of Guernsey* (Paris, 1830), pp. 468–74.

gradations into which both he and wider society divided them. Large landowners he often identified by the name of their property, as in Monsieur de St George (Jean Guille) or Monsieur des Touillets (Pierre De Jersey). Other gentlemen he usually referred to as 'Mr', as in Mr Robert Le Marchant or Mr Pierre De Havilland. Smaller farmers he designated *Sieur* ('Sr') and master tradesmen either *Sieur* or *Maître*. His own labourers he normally identified by their forenames only, and other parishioners of humble status by their forename and surname, usually also appending the forename of their father and sometimes also the name of their holding.[41]

The naming of fathers was crucial to correct identification of parishioners owing to the high degree of homonymy in the local community. Not only was there a small stock of forenames, the number of surnames in any given parish was also limited. This arose largely from the expediency of marrying cousins in order to preserve and consolidate property. Mollet's journal is thus confusingly full of characteristically *câtelain* names: Nicolle, Girard, Ozanne, Lihou, Collenette, Le Page, often paired with identical forenames.[42] Cousin marriages were equally prevalent among islanders of Mollet's own rank, and indeed one of his great-nephews married one of his great-nieces, and another great-nephew married a first cousin from the paternal side of the family. A local historian once observed that such inbreeding was highly undesirable because of the significant number of 'handicapped children' produced.[43]

Politics and administration

Geographically, the Channel Islands are offshore islands of France, not of Britain. From the tenth until the early thirteenth century, they belonged to the Duchy of Normandy and were governed as part of it. After Duke John of Normandy, who was also King John of England, lost the Duchy to King Philippe of France in 1204, the Islands were persuaded by various means to

---

[41] Similarly, Mollet referred to women of the non-elite class by their forename and maiden surname, and appended the name of their husband or father. However, references to the wives of large landowners might take the 'Madame des Touillets' form, and other elite women might appear as 'Mrs Robert Le Marchant' or 'Mrs Pierre De Havilland'.
[42] The commonest names for males (in Mollet's diaries, at least) were Pierre, Jean, Nicolas, Etienne and Daniel. For females, they were Marie, Judith, Rachel, Marthe and Anne.
[43] P.J. Girard, 'Country life and some insular enterprises of the late 19th century', *Transactions of la Société Guernesiaise*, 19 (1972), pp. 88-9.

throw in their lot with the English monarchy. Norman tenants-in-chief of insular fiefs were presented with the choice of either subjecting themselves to the English Crown or forfeiting their lands. Since most of these were nobles who also held large estates in France, many opted to abandon their local holdings in order to retain their French domains. This left their numerous humbler sub-tenants in the unusual position of holding their little 'estates' directly of the Crown – which doubtless went some way towards winning their sympathies, especially when complemented by the assurance that they would be allowed to maintain local laws and administrative structures.[44]

Although the Islands' politico-diplomatic status was initially somewhat vague, it was substantially settled in the 1250s, when they were recognised as a personal possession of the English Crown. Whoever thenceforth was king of England was by that fact also lawful sovereign of the Channel Islands.[45] Sovereignty over the Islands gave the English monarch personal authority over them, but they were never politically subsumed into the realm of England, nor, later into the United Kingdom. This meant that they were outside the jurisdiction of the Westminster parliament and unrepresented within it. Over the thirteenth and fourteenth centuries, Jersey and Guernsey evolved into two distinct Bailiwicks. These Bailiwicks grew increasingly apart, and by at least the late fifteenth century, they were politically, legally and administratively quite separate.

At the time of Charles Mollet's birth in 1742, the Crown was represented in both Jersey and Guernsey by Governors. The office of Governor entitled its holder to local Crown revenues,[46] and was usually bestowed on a high-ranking British army officer at the end of his career, as a form of reward for long service. No Governor resided locally or performed his duties in person after the early eighteenth century. These duties were instead delegated to resident Lieutenant-Governors, whom Governors appointed themselves and paid from their own revenues. The responsibilities of Lieutenant-Governors were chiefly military. They were in overall command of both the British garrison and the local militia. In addition, they had specific duties relating to foreigners and security, and acted as conduits for communication between

---

[44] J.A. Everard and J.C. Holt, *Jersey 1204: The Forging of an Island Community* (London, 2004), pp. 79, 94–8, 121–2, 138–9.
[45] J. Loveridge, *The Constitution and Law of Guernsey* (1975; Guernsey, 1997 edn), p. 1.
[46] Crown revenues came principally from dues and tithes on Crown fiefs, which Governors appointed local Receivers to collect in return for a percentage of the sums collected. Towards the end of Mollet's life, these revenues amounted to c.£2,800 annually.

British and insular authorities. At the time of Mollet's birth, the monarch's power over the Channel Islands was chiefly exercised through the Privy Council. After the Home Office was created in 1782, insular affairs were primarily handled by this department, with the Privy Council as intermediary.

As regarded finances, Guernsey was largely self-funding. The British government (which was responsible for the island's defence) limited its spending to the military sphere, paying the expenses of the garrison, partly funding the militia, and contributing towards the construction and upkeep of some (though not all) coastal fortifications. All local domestic needs were met exclusively from local sources: parochial expenses were funded from parish rates, and all-island expenses were funded from a combination of harbour dues, import duties, and island-wide general taxes.[47]

In Mollet's day, Guernsey's government fell into three tiers. Much basic work was done by the island's ten parishes, which exercised civil as well as ecclesiastical functions. Aside from their duties in respect of parish churches and churchyards, they also bore responsibility for parochial policing, parochial poor relief, parochial schools, and parochial roads and sea walls. Each parish possessed a body elected by its *Chefs de Famille* (adult male ratepayers) which was known as the Douzaine.[48] The Douzaine was the parish's governing body. With it lay the power to select and approve the objects of parochial expenditure, and to decide how much should be raised through the rates. It was also the interface between the inhabitants of the parish and higher authorities.

At the apex of parish structure were two *Connétables* or Constables, who were elected by the *Chefs de Famille* and served for a minimum of one year.[49] As well as maintaining public order, these two parish Constables also acted as parochial treasurers and executive officers of their Douzaines, and occupied a

---

[47] There was also a tax on innkeepers from 1780, and, from 1814, a duty on locally sold spirits known as the *impôt*.
[48] Douzeniers were twelve in number in all parishes aside from the Vale, which had sixteen, and St Peter Port, which had twenty. Although service was nominally for life, Douzeniers were allowed by convention to retire at sixty.
[49] From 1736, St Peter Port had an additional four 'assistant constables' chosen annually by the Douzaine from the ranks of shopkeepers and tradesmen, to serve under the parish Constables' direction.

seat in the States.⁵⁰ This made a Guernsey Constable's office highly prestigious, so that parochial Constables were exclusively drawn from the leading families of their parish. Usually elected to this role as young men (as Mollet himself was), many of them were later also elected to the Douzaine.

The Royal Court, which operated at island-wide level, formed the next tier of government. This Court exercised both a judicial and legislative function. It was composed of the Bailiff (who acted as Court president); twelve lay magistrates or Jurats (leading citizens who acted as judges in judicial cases and deliberators in legislative sittings); the Procureur and Comptroller (lawyers who acted as public prosecutors and advisers to the Crown, Court and States); a Greffier (who kept the Court's records); and executive officers known as the Prévôt and the Sergeant. In Mollet's day, the Bailiff, Procureur, Comptroller and Greffier were Crown appointees, and the Sergeant was appointed by the Governor. The Prévôt and Jurats were elected (see below for the electing body). The titles of all of these officers, save the Jurats, were usually prefixed with the designation *du Roi*, as in *le Procureur du Roi*.⁵¹

In its judicial role, the Royal Court had sole cognizance of all criminal matters arising in Guernsey as also sole jurisdiction over most civil matters.⁵² In its legislative role, it promulgated local laws known as *Ordonnances* (Ordinances) at thrice-yearly sessions called *Chefs Plaids* (Chief Pleas). These Ordinances concerned such matters as the regulation of markets, the import and export of produce and livestock, weights and measures, public thoroughfares, taverns, hunting, the foreshore, and much else of routine domestic import. Sometimes they could also be declaratory of existing law and custom.

The States represented the highest tier of local government. This body appears to have arisen in the fifteenth or sixteenth century as an afforcement of the Royal Court convened to deal with matters felt to require a wider measure of consultation than could be achieved by the Court alone. During

---

⁵⁰ States functions are described below. There was only one States seat for each parish, so the two Constables usually took it in turns to attend States meetings, where they voted in accordance with the instructions of their Douzaine, who met to discuss the agenda before the States meeting took place.

⁵¹ Or, later, in English, 'HM Procureur'.

⁵² Some seigneurial courts shared jurisdiction over contractual and landholding matters on their fiefs.

Mollet's lifetime, the States were composed of thirty-two members: the Bailiff (who as well as presiding over the Royal Court, also presided over the States),[53] HM Procureur, the twelve Jurats, ten parish Constables, and eight parish Rectors.[54] During the eighteenth and early nineteenth centuries, the States met a few times each year to deal with such high-level matters as the control of food supplies in times of want, the maintenance of St Peter Port harbour, the initiation and management of public construction projects, and the purchase of arms and equipment for the militia. Most States' decisions were given force by Ordinance of the Royal Court, but any legislation which embodied new taxes, altered the customary law, or made new substantive law had to be submitted for approval by the King in Council (a form of oversight to which Ordinances were not subject). Such legislation was uncommon in Mollet's day.

Aside from its legislative role, the States also had an elective role. In this capacity, its usual thirty-two members were increased to 184 by the addition of both Constables and the entire Douzaines of each parish. In this augmented form, it elected the Jurats of the Royal Court and HM Prévôt.[55]

With this brief summary of Guernsey's politics and administration – important not least because of Mollet's participation at every level – we close our exposition of the broad background against which the diarist lived his life. We shall now narrow our focus to the person of Charles Mollet himself.

Charles Mollet's background

The name 'Mollet', like many other Channel Island names, is French in origin. By the time our diarist was born, there had been Mollets in Guernsey for centuries, and the identities of those who first introduced the name are unknown. Mollets were fairly thick on the ground in the 1700s. An inspection of church register indexes shows that there were around two hundred Mollet baptisms in St Peter Port during the eighteenth century, and the same again in the country parishes.

---

[53] This made the Bailiff Guernsey's *de facto* civic head.
[54] The ten parishes had just eight Rectors between them because St Sampsons /the Vale, and Torteval/the Forest each formed one living.
[55] The elective iteration of the States was later known as the States of Election.

Charles Mollet's branch of the family originated in St Peter Port. His great-grandparents were Pierre Mollet, who worked as a miller in the town parish, and Michelle Ollivier.[56] The couple were married at the Town Church in 1657, and the baptisms of seven children followed between 1658 and 1666. Our Charles Mollet was descended from the couple's second son, also named Charles, who was born in 1660. This Charles, Mollet's grandfather, moved to the Castel parish, where he married Margueritte Henry in 1683 and followed the family occupation as a miller. He had seven children with Margueritte Henry, and after Margueritte died in 1695, a further six children with his second wife Thomasse Le Lacheur. Of these thirteen children, only four daughters and two sons survived into adulthood. The daughters were Margueritte (1686–1757), Rebecca (1688–1732), Marie (1697–1735) and Rachel (1712–46). The two sons, both from the second marriage, were Thomas, born in 1696, and yet another Charles, born in 1706. This Charles was our Charles's father.

In July 1719, our Charles's grandfather died aged fifty-nine (his second wife had died two years previously). As his eldest surviving son, Thomas was his principal heir. In January 1720, the Castel Parish Register recorded twenty-four-year-old Thomas being allocated his *préciput*, or eldership, by the Castel Douzaine.[57] A short time later, the young man acquired a further addition to his patrimony. His father had used some of his profits from milling to put out to loan, and most of these loans were secured on his debtors' personal and real estate. One such loan had been made to James Collenette, the owner of a property in the Castel known as le Déhuzet, and when Collenette's heirs were unable to repay the loan, his property was forfeited to Thomas Mollet.[58]

This property was to remain in the hands of the Mollet family for a century and forms the setting for our Charles Mollet's diaries.[59] Thomas Mollet, however, enjoyed it for only a short time, as he died in January 1739.

---

[56] For a Mollet family tree, see Appendix 1.
[57] 7.1.1720, Castel Parish Register, 1664–1764 (AQ 1083/01, Island Archives). According to Guernsey inheritance law, the eldest son was entitled by way of *préciput* to a single enclosure of about one-sixth of an acre, usually containing the main dwelling, before the rest of the estate was divided between the siblings (two-thirds to males, one-third to females). The Douzaine were responsible for determining the location and extent of the eldership.
[58] 1.3.1720, Amerci en Plaids, Greffe.
[59] For the location and extent of this property (later known as 'Woodlands', though not in the diarist's lifetime), see Maps 3 and 4.

Since Thomas had never married and had no children, his only brother Charles (the diarist's father) inherited the property. At the time of his succession, thirty-three-year-old Charles was living in Jersey. He had perhaps gone to join his sisters Marie and Rachel, who had both married Jerseymen and moved to the larger island.[60] How Charles was earning a living in Jersey is unknown, but it may have been connected to the sea and to trade.

Four years before his brother's death, Charles had married twenty-seven-year-old Marie Le Vavasseur dit Durell at Jersey's Trinity parish church.[61] Marie was one of eight children born to Abraham Le Vavasseur dit Durell and Marie Romeril. The Durell family were well-off and influential in their home island, so this was an advantageous match for the young Guernseyman. Marie probably also brought Charles a sizeable marriage portion.

In November 1736, Charles and Marie Mollet's first child, a daughter also named Marie, was baptised in Jersey's Town Church. This was our Charles's eldest sister. The death of her uncle Thomas when she was two years old evidently brought her father and his household back to Guernsey, as the Mollets' next daughter, Marthe, was baptised at the Castel parish church in the spring of 1740. A son, doubtless much longed for, was also baptised at the Castel church on 25 August 1742. This was our own Charles Mollet. No further Mollet children are recorded.

The infant Charles Mollet's baptismal entry is interesting in that, although his mother is identified as *Dame* Marie Durell, his father is not a *Monsieur* but a *Sieur*. It seems likely that Marie Durell's personal status elevated not only that of her husband but also that of her children, perhaps giving them access to social circles they would not otherwise have entered. Charles's parents secured a prestigious set of godparents for their baby son. These were the siblings Charles, James and Rachel Andros, the adult offspring of Jurat Charles Andros of les Piques, who was one of Guernsey's leading country parishioners.

Returning to the island to take up his Castel estate, Charles Mollet senior was an eminently suitable candidate for parochial office. In January 1741, he was elected a Constable, and the following year a Douzenier.[62] Over the next

---

[60] Marie Mollet married Nicolas De Ste Croix in 1722. Rachel Mollet married Thomas Cartault in 1732.
[61] This marriage, which took place in October 1735, is also recorded in the Castel church register.
[62] 15.1.1741, 12.5.1742, Castel Parish Register, 1664–1764 (AQ 1083/01, Island Archives).

few years, Mollet senior (who was evidently imbued with a strong business sense) added to his assets by putting money out to loan and purchasing *rentes*.[63] By 1762, when our own Charles Mollet came of age, his father was the wealthiest man in the Castel parish. Though still designated a *Sieur*, his property (real and personal) was valued for tax at about £6,200. His nearest rivals were Elizée Le Marchant of la Haye du Puits and Jean Guille of St George, both *Messieurs*, who were assessed at £5,600 and £5,000 respectively.[64] Charles Mollet senior died on 20 May 1770. As well as his Guernsey property, he also left £1,000 in British Government stock.[65]

Before Charles Mollet's father passed away, he had the satisfaction of seeing his two daughters make excellent marriages. In 1754, his elder daughter, Jersey-born Marie, married the St Helier merchant and shipowner Philippe Lerrier. She was to remain in Jersey for the rest of her life and bore her husband thirteen children. A decade later, Mollet's younger daughter Marthe married the St Peter Port merchant and shipowner Peter Mourant. Marthe remained settled in Guernsey, and she and her four children played an important part in our diarist's life.[66] Charles Mollet senior doubtless hoped

---

[63] Several loans and purchases of *rentes* made by Mollet senior are recorded in vol. 34 of Contrats pour Lire et pour la Date at the Greffe. Richard Hocart also mentions a loan of 3,512 *livres tournois* (about £250 stg) made by Mollet senior to Jurat Jean Andros in the 1730s (R. Hocart, *The Country People of Guernsey and their Agriculture, 1640–1840* (Guernsey, 2016), p. 155). The term *rente* requires a detailed explanation, as it will feature elsewhere in this book. *Rentes* derived from the local mode of buying and selling real property in the eighteenth and earlier centuries. When a property was sold, the price was normally converted into a perpetual mortgage expressed in terms of wheat, as most purchasers had insufficient money for a cash purchase. The purchaser undertook to pay an agreed quantity annually at Michaelmas (either in kind, or in cash at a rate set each year by the Royal Court). This was known as a *rente*. The agreement was also binding on a purchaser's heirs and successors in title, and so long as they continued to pay their *rente*, they continued to hold their property as freehold (on a vendor's death, *rentes* originally payable to him became payable to his heirs). The owner of a *rente* could sell it to a third party, or leave it to someone as a bequest. A *rente* could be redeemed at any time in return for money by the person who owed it, but only if the owner of the *rente* agreed to the sale. Alternatively, a property-owner could free himself of a *rente* by purchasing a *rente* of equal value and assigning it to the person to whom he owed the original *rente*. Most eighteenth-century property-owners both owed and owned *rentes*.
[64] Tax List dated 11.2.1762, Castel Parish Register, 1664–1764 (AQ 1083/01, Island Archives).
[65] 26.10.1770 and 4.1.1771, Stock Ledger, 1765–71 (AC27/6731, Bank of England Archives).
[66] For a Lerrier/Mourant family tree, see Appendix 2.

that his only son would also make a felicitous match, but our diarist never married.

Marthe's husband Peter Mourant, although very wealthy, was not from Guernsey's traditional elite. His was a seafaring family which appears to have moved to Guernsey from Jersey two generations before his birth in 1740. His father and at least two of his brothers were sea captains. In 1780, Peter Mourant's assets were valued for tax purposes at around £28,000, making him the fourth wealthiest individual in St Peter Port.[67] In the early 1780s, Peter Mourant used some of his wealth to have a new house built on land which he owned to the north-west of town. This house, which Charles Mollet knew as 'Candie', was also to play a large part in our diarist's life.

The Mourants' family was complete long before they moved into 'Candie'. The couple's eldest child Martha (whom Mollet always called Patty) was born in 1765. Another daughter, Mary (whom Mollet sometimes called Polly), followed in 1767. A third daughter, Anne (to whom Mollet referred as Nancy) was born in 1769, and a son, Peter junior, was born in 1770. Mollet's sister Marthe was only thirty when Peter was born. She went on to have a long and tiring series of stillbirths, all documented in Mollet's diary.

What of Charles Mollet's own childhood? Evidence suggests that he spent frequent holidays in his mother's native Jersey. His later journals recorded ten visits to Jersey from 1771 onwards, during which he interacted with many old friends and acquaintances (the majority of them in high places). Charles Mollet may also have spent part of his school-days in France. Sending children to France for their education seems to have been a common practice in Mollet's Jersey family. His brother-in-law Philippe Lerrier is known to have sent his ward William Chepmell to school in Caen.[68] Although Charles Mollet nowhere mentioned being educated in France, his diary documented four sojourns in Normandy, during which he visited several families with whom he already seemed acquainted.

---

[67] St Peter Port Tax Book, 1797–1803 (AQ 1004/01, Island Archives). For an account of Peter Mourant's commercial activities, see G. Stevens Cox, *The Guernsey Merchants and their World* (Guernsey, 2009), pp. 110–14.

[68] Chepmell, who later moved to Guernsey, was Lerrier's nephew. While in Caen, he was briefly kidnapped by some nuns. This bizarre episode is recounted in C. Ozanne, 'Adventures of a Channel Islander in France in the 18th century', *Transactions of la Société Guernesiaise*, 3 (1928), pp. 275–83.

By 1767, at all events, Charles Mollet was permanently settled on the family farm at le Déhuzet. In December that year, aged twenty-five, he was elected a Churchwarden of the Castel parish, an office which he occupied until 1769.[69] Following his father's death in 1770, Mollet became a landowner and farmer in his own right. His position at the outset of his career could not have been more favourable, for he was a significant figure, not only in his own parish, but in the island as a whole, his father's wealth and mother's rank having placed him in the upper social bracket, and his sisters' marriages having further enhanced his status.

Just seven months after burying his father, Charles Mollet bought himself a small leather-bound volume of blank paper and began to record his daily doings in it. This was the first surviving volume of his journal. It is also the means by which we can – at long last – hear Charles Mollet of le Déhuzet speak for himself. His diary begins on New Year's Day 1771.

---

[69] 23.12.1767, 22.12.1769, Castel Parish Register, 1748–1835 (AQ 1083/3, Island Archives).

The Journal of Charles Mollet

1771

Charles Mollet was twenty-eight at the start of these diaries and lived on his farm in the Castel parish with his sixty-three-year-old widowed mother.

Tues 1 Jan: Mr Migault came in the afternoon.[1] I had some whitecurrants from the Greffier.[2]

Thurs 3 Jan: pressed apples. Drew off cider from No. 2 & No. 3 for the 2nd time.[3] Planted the whitecurrants by the upper gate.

Fri 4 Jan: had 2 cartloads of seaweed. Put one on the kale at le Marquet & the other on the kale in the stackyard.[4] Went to la Haye du Puis in the afternoon. Mr William pressed me to accept the post of Adjutant in his [militia] regiment.[5]

---

[1] André Migault, originally from Normandy, was Rector of the Castel church. He had moved from Jersey to Guernsey in 1753, and returned to Jersey in 1773, employing curates to serve the Castel until 1784 (and St Saviour, where he became Rector in 1784, until his death in 1798). We should note that, at this point, Guernsey was exclusively Anglican.
[2] Joshua (Josué) Gosselin (1739–1813) was Greffier of the Royal Court from 1768 to 1792. He was also a painter and naturalist.
[3] References to 'drawing off', 'pressing', and later to 'layers' relate to different stages of the cider-making process. For a helpful summary of this, see T.F. Priaulx, 'Cider-making, an old-time Guernsey industry', *Transactions of la Société Guernesiaise*, 15 (1953), pp. 286–92.
[4] I have translated Mollet's word *choux* (pl.) as 'kale'. Where Mollet later uses the word *caboche*, I have translated it as 'cabbage'. In his *Dictionnaire Franco-Normand* George Metivier defined *chaou* as a loose-leaved cabbage, and *caboche* as a cabbage with a tight head.
[5] Mollet did not accept the post of Adjutant. 'Mr William' was William Le Marchant (1711–73), who lived at la Haye du Puits, a substantial property not far from Mollet's which was owned by William's eighty-five-year-old father Elizée Le Marchant. When Elizée died in 1779, the property passed to his grandson Josias (Josiah) Le Marchant (1755–1831), with whom Mollet remained associated all his life.

Sun 6 Jan: to church in the morning. Isiah ch. 38, vv. 18 & 19. Richard [Guille] came to dinner.[6]

Weds 9 Jan: to town, dined at my sister's.[7] In the evening I went to la Haye du Puis & to the Rectory. Our servant (Marie Robin) left our service today. It started to snow.

Thurs 10 Jan: to town in the evening. My friend Thos Pipon came to sleep here.[8]

Fri 11 Jan: Mr Migault & Mr Mourant came to dinner. The snow is very deep everywhere – as much as 3 feet in some places.

Sat 12 Jan: yesterday evening, Zacharie [Girard] took Mr Mourant back to town. He had great difficulty getting there. On his return he made a detour by la Haye du Puis thinking that there would be less snow. However, the snow lay so deep in the road that he could advance no further than Nicolas Lihou's house at le Boullion, where he spent the night. He returned here this morning having left the horses at Nicolas Lihou's. He says that the snow was fully 15 feet deep along many stretches of road.

Mon 14 Jan: the weather is unchanged. Zacharie & Etienne [Lihou][9] brought the horses back with much difficulty, taking them over the fields. Before dinner Mr Pipon & I went to le Houmet to fetch Mr Etienne.[10] He dined with us & slept here overnight.

---

[6] The Guilles were also neighbours of Mollet's. Jurat Jean Guille, sen. (1712–78), Seigneur of St George, had five sons, of whom Richard (1745–1818) was the youngest. Richard was at this point training as a surgeon. For more on the composition of the Guille family, see Appendix 3.

[7] The sister mentioned here is Marthe (1740–98). Mollet always referred to her husband, Peter Mourant (1740–1807), as 'Mr Mourant'. For Mollet's sisters and their families, see Appendix 2.

[8] See n. 56, below.

[9] Etienne Lihou (1742–1832) was Charles Mollet's longest-serving day labourer. He was still working for Mollet when the latter died aged seventy-six in 1819.

[10] There was a public house at le Houmet. Pierre Etienne (1743–1825) was a wealthy Guernseyman of English descent. He was also known as Peter Stephens.

Weds 16 Jan: we went to les Moullins before dinner.[11] In the afternoon, we went to la Haye du Puis, as also the Hospital[12] & the Rectory, whence Mr Pipon departed for town. The roads are still full of snow, which – as it is frozen – can now support a person's weight. It is 12 to 15 feet deep in many places. Richard came to dinner.

Fri 18 Jan: I went to town in the afternoon & returned here with Mr Pipon.

Sat 19 Jan: I accompanied Mr Pipon to town in the morning. His ship has left without him. I dismissed Zacharie from my service. He started working here on 19 November. The snow has begun to thaw.

Sun 20 Jan: the two Messrs Mourant,[13] Mr Richard Guille & my sister came to dinner.

Mon 21 Jan: attended Chief Pleas. The farm of the harbour dues remains with Mr Lauga at 3280 *livres* & the King's Weights with Etienne Barbet at 350 *livres*.[14] The Court issued an Ordinance forbidding the holding of parties on Saturday evenings on pain of a 100 *livre* fine to the host & 10 *livres* to those attending.

Tues 22 Jan: I engaged Jean le Messurier (Marie Guillard's son) as a farm servant at 23 *écus* a year.

Thurs 24 Jan: the snow had been thawing since Friday. It drizzled this afternoon. There are still 5 or 6 feet of snow in the road beside le Neuf Courtil & in many other places.

Tues 29 Jan: our house servant [Marie Robin] left us because her mother was ill, & we engaged another, Elizabeth Le Roi, daughter of Daniel. However,

---

[11] There was a public house at les Grands Moulins.
[12] The Country Hospital, a workhouse.
[13] Mollet's brother-in-law Peter Mourant had three brothers, by one of whom he was accompanied here.
[14] For Chief Pleas, see section on Politics and administration in the Introduction. The King's Weights were used to weigh certain goods prior to sale. The farmer of the Weights charged sellers a set fee for each weighing. For the sterling equivalents of currency units used by Mollet, see Notes on Text, above.

my Dear Mother has now dismissed her, not finding her clean. We had two quarters of barley from Sr Thomas Ogier.[15]

Weds 30 Jan: […] Olimpe Girard started here as a house servant at 12 *écus* a year. Dug le Ruquet & began planting potatoes there.[16]

Mon 4 Feb: […] To town in the afternoon. Took 2 barrels of cider to the harbour to load on board Captn Boivin, one for Jacques Hemeri & one for my brother[-in-law].[17]

Fri 8 Feb: planted 100 cabbages at le Marquet. Cut the osier & sent half of it to James Moullin who has been tending it for us.

Sat 9 Feb: pressed our last layer of apples (the 18th). Snow has fallen sufficient to cover the ground.

Sun 10 Feb: received 38 *livres* from Pierre Heaume towards his *rente* for 1770.[18] Gave him a receipt.

Mon 11 Feb: Jean Le Messurier went to his mother's yesterday morning & did not come back until today, when he fetched his clothes & left. It has been snowing again these past two days. There are a good 6 inches on the ground.

Weds 13 Feb: […] I shot a snipe the day before yesterday, & today I took another with a net.

---

[15] A quarter was a measure of volume. Four bushels made one quarter (a bushel was about 1,700 cubic inches). Six denerels made one bushel. Three denerels made one cabot. Five quints made a denerel. The Winchester quarter was approximately two-and-a half times larger than a Guernsey quarter.

[16] All of Mollet's fields had names: le Ruquet, le Marquet, le Carré, le Brulin, le Neuf Courtil, le Courtil Robin, etc.

[17] The elder of Charles Mollet's two sisters, Marie (1736–1809) was married to Jerseyman Philippe Lerrier (1728–1805) and lived in Jersey (see Appendix 2). Mollet always referred to Lerrier as 'my brother'. 'Jacques Hemeri' was probably Jacques Hemery (1746–1831), who became Constable of St Helier in 1773, and served as Jersey's Lieutenant-Bailiff between 1809 and 1814.

[18] For *rente*, see n. 62, Introduction. Since the term has no real English equivalent, I leave it untranslated.

Tues 19 Feb: [...] I took possession of the plot at la Senciere. Jean Trachy paid me [his *rente* arrears]. Abraham & Pierre Collenette started to dig le Courtil de Robin. I will pay them 6 *sous* per perch & expenses for digging & weeding this field.[19]

Weds 20 Feb: planted parsnips (for seed) at the top of le Neuf Courtil, & turnips at le Marquet. Planted a row of raspberries by the upper gate, & 4 peach trees against the wall. [...] Messrs Ozanne, des Valez[20] & Bailleul came to ask me to be Constable, but I declined.

Fri 22 Feb: Mr Wm Le Marchant & Mr Watkins dined with us.[21] Mr Migault & Mr de St George[22] came in the afternoon. Sowed field peas[23] & broad beans at le Marquet (above the entrance to le Ruquet).

Weds 27 Feb: Messrs Gosselin, Henry Mesurier, & Pierre Mesurier of Alderney breakfasted here.[24] There was an election for Constable. Eleven people voted. Srs Pierre Massy, James Ozanne, Pierre La Perre, James Moullin, Nic. Moullin & Jean Bailleul voted for me. Sr Thos Naftel voted for André Cohu. Mr Migault, Mr du Groignet,[25] Sr J. de Jersey of les Pins (sen.) & I voted for Thos de Garis.

Thurs 28 Feb: I went to town in the morning & constituted my cousin James my attorney.[26]

Fri 1 Mar: sent my luggage to town. Constituted Advocate Coutart my second attorney.[27]

---

[19] A Guernsey *perche* was 49 square yards in area. By 'expenses' Mollet meant food and drink.
[20] 'Mr des Valez' was Nicolas Moullin (1701–72), who lived at les Vallées, a neighbouring farm.
[21] 'Mr Watkins' was Daniel Watkins (–1781), a merchant.
[22] Jean Guille, sen. (see n. 6, above).
[23] Mollet's term for these was *pois sarrasins*. They were for drying rather than eating green.
[24] Peter (Pierre) Le Mesurier (1750–1803) was the son of the Governor of Alderney and would in due course become Governor himself. Henry Le Mesurier (1713–79), his uncle, had relinquished the Governorship to Peter's father in 1743.
[25] 'Mr du Groignet' was Hellier De Jersey of le Groignet, a farm contiguous to Mollet's.
[26] James Le Cheminant (1714–96). James was the son of Mollet's paternal aunt Rebecca who had married Daniel Le Cheminant.
[27] Pierre Coutart (1722–1804).

Sat 2 Mar: I took the Constable's oath, & was granted no-trespassing orders for certain of our lands. I slept in town last night, as I was expecting to leave for Jersey. Hellier Marqui began sleeping at our house in the Castel, where he will continue to sleep during my absence.

Sun 3 Mar: to church in the morning. Text ch. 2 [*sic*], vv. 11 & 12. My cousins Nicolas, James, Marguerite & Pierre dined with us,[28] as also Nicolas's wife, Pierre's wife & his sons Hellier & Thomas.

Tues 5 Mar: to town. Dined at my sister's. Purchased a dozen of the old books which belonged to the deceased Bailiff.[29]

Weds 6 Mar: embarked on board Captn Boivin at 8 o'clock. Arrived in Jersey at two. Found our people in good health.

Thurs 7 Mar: dined & took tea with my Aunts.[30]

Fri 8 Mar: wrote to my Dear Mother. Took tea & supped with Doctor Fergusson.[31]

Sat 9 Mar: went to pay my respects to Major Corbet.[32]

Weds 27 Mar: Mr Richard Guille visited me. He has arrived here from France & is about to leave for Guernsey.

Weds 3 Apr: I have been in bed since Thursday, suffering badly from scarlet fever & an ulcerated sore throat. This morning, I went on board Captn

---

[28] These were all Le Cheminants, siblings of James.
[29] Samuel Bonamy (1708–70).
[30] Mollet's mother had five younger sisters, of whom four (Françoise, Jeanne, Anne and Elizabeth) were still alive.
[31] This was Dr William Fergusson, the Scottish husband of Anne, *née* Lerrier, sister of Mollet's brother-in-law Philippe Lerrier.
[32] Moses Corbet (1728–1814) was a Jersey-born army officer who served as Lieutenant-Governor of Jersey between 1771 and 1781.

Gaudin at 7 & arrived in Guernsey at 11. Mr Billy Dobrée lent me his chaise to return home.[33]

Sun 7 Apr: Mr Mourant & my sister came to dinner. Mr Roche came in the afternoon.[34]

Mon 8 Apr: my health has improved steadily since my return. Today I went downstairs for a while & ventured into the garden. Doctor Saumarez came to see me.[35]

Weds 10 Apr: Mr Andros (sen.)[36] & Mr Watkins came to visit me.

Thurs 11 Apr: Mr Thoume & Mr Bradby came in the afternoon.[37]

Sun 14 Apr: the Greffier, Mr Mourant & my sister came to dinner. Mr Nico Dobrée came in the afternoon.[38]

---

[33] The 'chaise' was probably a two-wheeled gig. There were few horse-drawn carriages in Guernsey in the 1770s, owing to the primitive state of the roads. 'Billy Dobrée' was William Dobrée (1748–84), who became curate of the Castel parish following his ordination a few months later (see 6.10.71). Dobrée went on to serve as Rector of St Saviour between 1782 and 1784. He was the father of Peter Paul Dobrée (1782–1825), a subsequent Professor of Greek at Cambridge.

[34] Mollet was friendly with the Roche family until the end of his life. HM Sergeant Jean Roche had married Mary Dagworthy in the late 1730s, and the couple had produced several children: Marie (born 1740), William (1741), Anne (1743), Peter (1746) and Elizabeth (1750). As Mollet did not supply a forename, it is impossible to know which Mr Roche he was referring to.

[35] Dr Matthew De Sausmarez (1719–78) was the Mollets' family doctor. He was replaced in this role by his son Jean (1755–1832) after perishing tragically on a sea voyage in 1778. For more on this family (with whom Mollet maintained a lifelong association), see Appendix 3.

[36] This was Jurat Charles Andros (1690–1773), the father of Charles Mollet's godparents, Charles, James and Rachel Andros. The elder Mr Andros lived with his son Charles at les Piques in St Saviour.

[37] James Bradby (1738–1809) was a naval officer from Southampton who rose through the ranks to become a Rear-Admiral. He was married to Guernseywoman Mary Thoume. The 'Mr Thoume' mentioned here may have been Mary Thoume's father or brother.

[38] Charles Mollet was friendly with several branches of the Dobrée family. His visitor on this occasion was the wealthy merchant and shipowner Nicolas Dobrée (1732–1800) of 'Bellevue', the father of Nicolas Peter Dobrée (1755–1843), who became Rector of the Castel in 1784. See Appendix 3 for other family members.

Tues 16 Apr: awoke to nearly 4 inches of snow. Advocate & Mrs Coutart & Miss Roche came in the afternoon.[39] The snow melted during the day.

Weds 17 Apr: my sister came in the afternoon. The cow was slaughtered (after being milked again today). We sold her to George for 15 *livres* per 100 lb.[40] Loosened the ground around the kale.

Fri 26 Apr: slaughtered a calf, which we sent to George to sell for us. Stacked the furze from les Parcs (328 bundles). [...] The Douzaine met to raise a tax of 200 *livres* for the Hospital, & to consult about a Court summons we received in relation to our dispute with the Bailiff regarding a contribution towards the cost of his deputation to England.[41]

Mon 29 Apr: I went to collect the tax from the Vingtaine des Moullins & the Vingtaine des Houmets.[42]

Weds 1 May: planted cucumbers & field peas at le Ruquet. Mr Bailleul & I took 200 *livres* to Mr Wm Le Marchant for the Hospital.[43]

Sat 4 May: [...] I went to see Miss Fiott who was married on Thursday evening to Mr Pierre Havilland.[44]

Sun 5 May: to church in the morning. I left after the 2nd Psalm to inspect the public houses. Mr Bailleul & I jointly notified the parishioners (by means of a publication) that they were to remove loose stones from the roads before the 1st of June, or we would have it done at their expense. I also notified them in my own name that I would bring actions against the owners of beasts found in the roads & have them fined according to the Ordinance.

---

[39] Advocate Pierre Coutart was married to Marie, *née* Roche. 'Miss Roche' was probably his sister-in-law, Anne Roche (see nn. 27 and 34, above).
[40] George Fenien, a butcher.
[41] William Le Marchant (1721–1809) was Bailiff between 1771 and 1800. For the outcome of the dispute concerning his deputation, see 18.12.71.
[42] The Castel parish was divided into 'Vingtaines' (originally districts containing twenty households) for administrative purposes. They were the Vingtaines des Moullins, des Houmets, des Queritez and de l'Eglise.
[43] William Le Marchant of la Haye du Puits (for whom, see n. 5, above) was Treasurer of the Country Hospital.
[44] Carterette Fiott (1749–89) had married Pierre (Peter) De Havilland (1747–1821), an Advocate and future Bailiff of Guernsey.

Tues 7 May: to town in the morning. In the afternoon, I went to see Mr Andros with my Dear Mother. I later accompanied the old gentleman to Mr Hurai's in Torteval.[45] The Court was there, having been to Pleinmont for a *vue de justice*.[46]

Weds 8 May: to the Vale Church with Mr & Miss Benest in the morning. Mr Durand preached a charity sermon on Psalm 41, v. 1.[47] Dined at the Rectory. Received a request from the Court to advise them how much grain is required by the parish.[48]

Sat 11 May: to town. [...] An Englishwoman has been arrested on suspicion of having killed her bastard child. Planted some green peas & field peas in the furzebrake, as also some broccoli.

Sun 12 May: to church in the afternoon. [...] Issued a notice to the *Chefs de Famille*[49] to come to the church next Wednesday morning between 10 & 12 to declare how much wheat they have & how much they need.

Weds 15 May: to town in the morning & afterwards to a parish meeting. The Constables were charged with requesting 10 quarters of barley, half of the 20 quarters which are needed.

Sat 18 May: to town in the morning. Spoke to Mr Elizée Tupper who will request 10 quarters of barley on behalf of the parish.[50]

Sun 19 May: attended Communion. Text Acts, ch. 19, vv. 1 & 2. Messrs Charles & Richard Guille came in the afternoon. Charles brought 2 pairs of silk stockings from Barcelona which Nico has sent me as a gift.[51]

---

[45] Mr Le Huray ran a public house.
[46] A special session of the Royal Court at the site of an incident or dispute under adjudication.
[47] François Durand (1714–89), the son of Huguenot refugees, was Vicar of the Vale and Rector of St Sampson.
[48] Grain was in short supply at this time and prices were high. These were emergency supplies destined for the parochial poor.
[49] The adult male ratepayers of the parish.
[50] Elizée Tupper (1720–1802) was a successful merchant and Jurat of the Royal Court.
[51] Charles, Richard and Nicolas Guille were brothers (all sons of Jean Guille, sen. of St George). Nicolas Guille (1742–1807) was established in Barcelona as a merchant. He was a particular friend of Charles Mollet's.

Sat 25 May: to town & to Court. In the afternoon, I took tea at la Mare de Carteret & stayed there for supper.[52] Mr Dobrée, Captn Pascal, Mr Chas Mauger & Josué Gosselin were also there.

Sat 8 Jun: to town & to Court. I & several other Constables applied for a postponement of seaweed-cutting until the 2nd tide following the feast of St John.[53] The Court acceded to this. Nico Messurier of the College & Tom Messurier of Alderney took tea here.[54]

Mon 10 Jun: to Hen. Ozanne's with the other Constables to share out the gunpowder for the Regiment. Repaid my cousin the 600 *livres* he lent me a year ago.

Weds 12 Jun: embarked for Jersey on board Captn Boivin at 8 o'clock in the morning. Landed there at 2 in the afternoon (shortly after the arrival of my Lord Albemarle).[55]

Tues 18 Jun: the States [of Jersey] gave a dinner for my Lord Albemarle. I was invited, but I declined.

Sun 23 Jun: my Lord Albemarle departed this morning. Doctor & Mrs Fergusson & I dined at the Procureur's.[56]

---

[52] There was a hostelry at la Mare de Carteret which was much frequented by Guernsey's upper ranks.

[53] The cutting of seaweed was strictly regulated by the Royal Court. There was a spring cutting which took place between the first spring tide after 2 February and 15 March, and a summer cutting which normally began on the first spring tide after the Feast of St John the Baptist and continued for two subsequent tides.

[54] Nicolas Le Mesurier (1750–97) was the son of Henry Le Mesurier who had transferred the hereditary Governorship of Alderney to his brother Jean in 1743 (see n. 24, above). He had done so in exchange for lands at what was known as the 'Old College', so this branch of the family were henceforth known as the 'College' branch. Thomas Le Mesurier (1756–1822) was the son of Governor Jean Le Mesurier, and thus Nicolas's cousin.

[55] Lord Albemarle (George Keppel, 3rd Earl of Albemarle) was Governor of Jersey between 1761 and 1772.

[56] Jersey's Procureur performed a similar role to Guernsey's (for which, see Introduction). The current incumbent was Thomas Pipon (1736–1801). This man (or perhaps his son) may have been the 'Thos Pipon' Mollet referred to earlier in the year (see 10.1.71, above).

Tues 2 Jul: my Uncle has ceded his property to me under the conditions listed in the contract which we passed today.[57] I have constituted the Procureur & my brother[-in-law] my attorneys in Jersey.

Fri 5 Jul: embarked for Southampton on board Captn Gautier at 6 o'clock in the evening.

Sat 6 Jul: arrived at Southampton at 6 o'clock in the evening.

Weds 10 Jul: left Southampton at 2 o'clock in the afternoon & arrived in Portsmouth at 5 o'clock. Mr Hemery took us to see the shipyard & the Academy (he lives at No. 21 Chapel Row, adjacent to the Common). Captn Bailey of the 33rd Regiment recognised me & came to sup with us. We are lodging with Mr Robinson at the King's Head, Broad Street, in the Point. The crossing by hoy from Southampton costs 6d.

Thurs 11 Jul: Bailey took us on a tour of the ramparts & the new works, & also to Gosport & Haslar Hospital, where I made the acquaintance of young Mr Lind, the son of Doctor Lind, & gave him my address. At 4 o'clock, we departed from the Fighting Cocks (near the meat market) in the Chichester coach. The fare was 3 shillings, which we paid in full even though we went no further than Emsworth, where we lodged with Mr Bean at the Black Dog.

[*Charles Mollet writes his next few entries in English rather than French. These are reproduced as they appear in the journal.*]

Sat 13 Jul: [...] Set out from Emsworth for Chichester on the Portsmouth Stage, fare 18[d?], passing by Nut Bourne & Fish Bourne, between which & near the first is an arm of the sea, vessels coming up very near the road, & the tide coming quite up to it. This place is call'd Basham. The coach sets out from Portsmouth to Chichester on Tuesdays, Thursdays & Saturdays in the morning. Put up at the Dolphin in West Street, an indifferent house. Vessels

---

[57] The uncle in question was Jean Le Vavasseur dit Durell (1720–93), the youngest brother of Mollet's mother, who appears to have had mental health problems. In return for the house, Mollet was to provide his uncle with suitable board, lodging and spending money for the rest of his life.

come up no nearer than 6 miles to this town. Left Charles at Emsworth, at the Revd Mr Le Brocq's.[58]

Mon 15 Jul: set out for London at five o'clock in the Stage (fare 16s). [...] Breakfasted at Mowbrey, 37 miles from London & 18 from Petersfield. Enter'd the Portsmouth Road at Guilford, & as far as Godalmin where we left it to go thro' Effingham, Leatherhead & Epsom, where we din'd, & came directly to London.

[*reverts to French*]

Weds 17 Jul: took lodgings at Mr Johnson, upholsterer, No. 12 Canon Street. Peter Messurier is lodging there. I went to see Mr Ellis, No. 5 Gray's Inn, to whom I was recommended by Mr Gosselin.

[*in English again*]

Fri 19 Jul: been to the Society of Arts & Sciences in the morning. Din'd & spent the afternoon at the Miss Lhonorés.[59]

Sun 21 Jul: to church at the Wallone. Mr Chomette preach'd. Text Acts 17, v. 31.

Tues 23 Jul: to Chelsea with Peter Messurier. Din'd at the Swan. Seen the Hospital & the Physick Garden. Drank tea with Mrs La Serre.[60] Seen Don Saltero's Coffee House.

Weds 24 Jul: seen Westminster Abbey. Din'd at Mr John Perchard's.[61]

---

[58] Charles was Mollet's fifteen-year-old nephew Charles Lerrier, with whom he had travelled from Jersey to Southampton.
[59] The L'Honorés were a family of French origin whom Mollet knew from Jersey.
[60] 'Mrs La Serre' was Elizabeth Perchard (1725–96), the wife of Guernsey doctor Guillaume (William) La Serre (1726–74).
[61] The Perchards, from Guernsey, had settled in London where they traded as silversmiths and acted as banking agents for insular clients. John Perchard (1703–77) was the brother of Matthew Perchard (1702–77, for whom see 27.7.71).

Fri 26 Jul: sold £133 6s 8d of my stock at 87⅞. Commission 3/6. Produce : [£]116 19[s] 10[d]. Been with Peter Messurier to the Pantheon, White Conduit House & Musaeum Gardens. Sup'd at the Lamb.

Sat 27 Jul: Polly Lerrier arrived in Town last night.[62] I din'd at Hackney with Mr Matth. Perchard.

Sun 28 Jul: been to Richmond. [...] Met there (our company) Peter Havilland & wife, Miss Kitty Carey, & Mr & Mrs Ab. Le Messurier.[63] Billy Budd & wife came also from Wansburgh.[64]

Mon 29 Jul: been with Mr Ellis in the morning, & the Musaeum in the evening, as also Bagnage Wells. Peter Messurier is gone for Portsmouth. Mr Matty of the Musaeum, has been extreemly polite to me & has appointed me to go tomorrow morning, to be admitted again without a ticket.

[*Charles Mollet turned twenty-nine during the course of August 1771*]

Thurs 1 Aug: [...] Supped with Nico Ste Croix.[65]

Fri 2 Aug: I have had at diner Mrs La Serre, Mr & Mrs Havilland, Mr Lerrier & Polly Lerrier, Miss Fillette L'Honoré, & Mr Johnson who drest the diner. Been to Mr Astley's (riding performance, &c.).

Sun 4 Aug: set out at 7 o'clock with Mr & Miss Lamy, Miss Fillette L'Honoré, Mr Lerrier & Polly (hir'd a coach in pair for 15s a day from the Swan in Bishopsgate Street). Breakfasted at Kew Green, seen Kew Gardens, very fine, & from the top of the Pagoda a good view of the country finely planted &

---

[62] This was Mollet's Jersey-based sister Marie, whom he sometimes also referred to as 'Manon'.
[63] Abraham Le Mesurier (1748–1830) was a successful merchant and future neighbour of Mollet's.
[64] William Budd (1731–84) was a Guernsey merchant, originally from Wanborough in Surrey. He was married to Mary Le Pelley.
[65] Nicolas De Ste Croix (1751–1816) was Mollet's first cousin once removed (Ste Croix's paternal grandmother, Marie Mollet, was the sister of Mollet's father). Born in Jersey, Ste Croix had lived in England since the death of his own father when he was aged eight. In later life, he traded as a coal merchant in Homerton. Ste Croix acted as a London agent for Mollet and figured frequently in his journals until his death in 1816. He was also related to the Condamine family (see n. 531, below).

inhabited. Been let out by a little gate into Richmond Gardens. Gone to dine at the Star & Garter on Richmond Hill. From thence along Hampton Park, by Bushy Park to Hampton Court where seen the Pallace, the Gardens, & the Maze. [...] Sup'd & slept (about a mile from Walton Bridge) at Shepperton, a pleasant village by the river's side, at the King's Head, Wm King master. A good clean house, very civil people & not dear.

Mon 5 Aug: set out from Shepperton, pass'd thro' Stanes & over the Bridge, thro' Egham, & [...] into Windsor Great Park, where seen the Duke's lodge, pleasantly situated near a fine piece of water (could not see the Garden).

Tues 6 Aug: slept & breakfasted at Mr Girdler's, a good house, people clean & obliging, but dear. [...] Din'd at Brentford at the Castel, a very dirty house. Another time should prefer the 3 Pidgeons. Pass'd near Kew Bridge, thro' Turnham Green (where is the 5 mile stone) & thro' Hammersmith & Kensington, where stop & seen the Gardens, & from thence thro' Hyde Park to London. From Richmond, I have been all the way upon the Coach Box, & found it much more agreeable than in the coach. We have paid for our coach & 2 horses 15 sh. a day, besides 1 sh. a night for the horses, & the coachman's expences.

Tues 13 Aug: been to Mr Williamson's Nursery Gardens, near Kensington's Turnpike, & to his other Garden near the Queen Elm Turnpike, Chelsea. Mr Pratt is his head man there.

Sun 18 Aug: Billy Chepmell has been with me the whole day.[66]

Mon 19 Aug: set [out] from London for Salisbury at 10 in the evening in the Exeter Stage, fare 18 sh.

Tues 20 Aug: [...] Arrived at Salisbury at five o'clock. Been to see Old Sarum, where there are scarse any stones left. Seen also the cathedral.

Thurs 22 Aug: paid 8s for a postchaise to go & see Stonehenge. [...] After diner set [out] in a postchaise for Southampton. [...] Arrived at Southampton

---

[66] William Chepmell (1755–98) had known Mollet since childhood. He was a nephew of Mollet's brother-in-law Philippe Lerrier.

at five. We lodged at Salisbury at the White Hart, a bad house. Lodged at Southampton at Mr Wylde's.

Fri 23 Aug: embark'd for Guernsey at 12 o'clock on board Captn Mourant, with Coll. Irwind, our Governor & his familly.⁶⁷ Got out of the Needles at 10. Left Mr Lerrier behind, who is gone to see Charles.

Sat 24 Aug: arriv'd at Guernsey at noon. Gone home by the Presbyterre & the Haye du Puis. Found all friends well & my Uncle here since a month.

[*reverts to French*]

Sun 25 Aug: to church in the afternoon. Text Ephesians, ch. 2, vv. 4 & 5. Afterwards to St George & thence to les Moullins with Nico & Richard Guille. Nico arrived here two days ago.

Fri 30 Aug: accompanied Nico Guille to dinner at Mr Messurier's of the College. Sowed some mountain ash, shiverwood & yew seed behind the Messire Jean pear tree.

Fri 6 Sep: finished pulling out the barley. Made 200 sheaves.

Sun 8 Sep: […] Paid my Dear Mother for last year, deducting 8 guineas for the watch she gave me.

Tues 10 Sep: had a cartload of seaweed from Nic. de Garis. Grafted.⁶⁸

Thurs 12 Sep: Nico Guille came to breakfast & to say his farewells. The Greffier, who arrived yesterday from Jersey, joined us.

Sun 15 Sep: […] A few days ago, Hellier Le Pelley had some nets stolen after he had set them across the beach. This evening he gave me written leave to search for them, with an indication that they might be in the ammunition

---

[67] 'Coll. Irwind' was Lieutenant-Colonel Paulus Aemilius Irving (1714–96). He was sworn in as Guernsey's new Lieutenant-Governor on 29 August 1771 and served until 1783. Note that Mollet always referred to the Lieutenant-Governor simply as 'the Governor'.

[68] Grafting is a way of propagating new fruit trees using buds or twigs: a 'scion' selected from an existing tree is fused on to a branch or stem of another tree (the 'rootstock') by cutting and binding. Mollet's workmen regularly propagated his fruit trees by this method.

magazine near la Grande Mare. Not having the key (& fearing that some of the ammunition might also have been stolen), I did not wish to force the door without informing the Governor, who told me to call one of the artillery officers if I could not lay my hand on the key. I was unable to find it, so I put the matter off until the morning, & some of the other net-owners agreed on their own initiative to keep watch over the magazine.

Mon 16 Sep: I returned to town in the morning. At noon, the Governor, the Bailiff, Mr Andros the Magistrate,[69] Mr Thos Dobrée & Captn Smith came with me to la Mare, & we ordered the door of the magazine to be forced. We duly found Hellier le Pelley's nets inside & restored them to him. Mr Henry, in his capacity as an artillery officer, was charged to keep an eye on the magazine in future.

Weds 18 Sep: had some chicory from Mr Migault which I planted in the furzebrake & among the lucerne. We started feeding parsnips to the pigs.

Thurs 19 Sep: carted the wheat. There are 400 sheaves on the staddle stones & 330 on the other stack. Put the oats in the barn. Finished tidying up the strawberries.

Thurs 26 Sep: went to the Fair & dined at Henry Ozanne's.[70] There were eleven of us. Carted the wheat from les Eturs & le Ruquet.

Mon 30 Sep: to town & to Chief Pleas. *Rentes* were fixed at 10 *livres*, hens at 30 *sous* & capons at 45 *sous*.[71]

Sat 5 Oct: to town in the morning. In the afternoon, my sister was delivered of a stillborn infant.

Sun 6 Oct: to church in the morning. Mr Massy & I left after the second psalm in order to inspect the public houses. We published a notice to the effect that we would enforce the repair of any roads not repaired within the

---

[69] Jurat Charles Andros. Mollet always referred to Jurats as *Magistrats*, which was the standard Guernsey term for these officers in the eighteenth century.

[70] A quarterly livestock fair was held near the Castel church. Henry Ozanne ran a public house in the vicinity.

[71] *Poulage*, an annual due on dwelling houses, was valued in poultry (and eggs), but could also be paid in cash at the rate fixed by Chief Pleas.

next 8 days. To St George in the afternoon. Received a letter from Nico Ste Croix & a magnifying glass which I had ordered for Jean Guille.[72] Billy Dobrée, who brought it to me, has just taken [holy] orders.[73]

Fri 11 Oct: [...] In the evening of the day before yesterday, a vessel was lost near le Ha-nouel.[74] It is believed to be a Jersey vessel, & people think it must have been coming from Portugal or Spain, as lemons & fresh grapes have been washed ashore.

Sat 12 Oct: to town in the morning. Began gathering cider apples.

Sun 13 Oct: this morning I went to tell the millers not to mill on a Sunday, & I also told Guillaume de la Rue not to shave anyone. To church in the afternoon. Mr du Groignet left the church with me to inspect the public houses. We did not find anyone drinking.

Tues 22 Oct: Mr Bailleul & I spent the whole day on the roads informing the landowners where repairs are required, & taking notes so that we might later inform others.

Fri 25 Oct: Messrs Etienne, Josué Gosselin, Bradby & Tom Andros came to dinner.[75]

Mon 28 Oct: [...] Received my hats from Messrs Fort & Benson, & a parcel of trees from Mr Irwin. Received my wheat from Mme du Ponchez & Mr des Vallez.[76]

Weds 30 Oct: accompanied the Douzaine to approve the roadside boundaries of Sr Abraham Robert's land (opposite his house & around the garden of his

---

[72] This would probably have been Jean Guille, jun. (1733–1820). Mollet always referred to Jean Guille, sen. as 'Mr de St George'.
[73] William Dobrée (see n. 33, above) was shortly to become curate of the Castel parish.
[74] A reef off Guernsey's south-western tip, now referred to as Les Hanois.
[75] The last of these was Thomas Fouaschin Andros (1749–1828).
[76] 'Mme du Ponchez' was Marie Moullin, *née* Tourgis, a widow. 'Mr des Vallez' was Nicolas Moullin (see n. 20, above). The wheat was in payment of *rentes*.

other house at les Landes).[77] We all dined at my cousin Daniel's & set a tax of about 250 *livres* for the Hospital.[78]

Fri 1 Nov: [...] Mr Blondel came to clean the clock. Peaty brought me a new cut wig. Sowed rhubarb at le Carré.

Sun 3 Nov: to church in the morning. Same text as [last] Sunday. I advertised my hats to the Castel parishioners.[79]

Thurs 7 Nov: we had a Douzaine meeting in advance of the States meeting on Saturday to discuss the plans for the market.

Fri 8 Nov: in the morning I went to les Adams for some cabbages, as also to give the readers of St Saviour's & St Andrew's churches the notices regarding my hats. [...] Pierre Ferbrache has been working here these past 4 days, making a small table & mending the box-cart.

Sat 9 Nov: to town for the States meeting. It was resolved that the location of the market should be changed.

Thurs 14 Nov: to the Rectory in the afternoon. Took some wheat to Mr Brock, Mr de la Porte,[80] Matt. Tosdevin, Mr Jersey & Wm Lukis (for Mr Massy). Put 20 bushels of burnt lime on le Prey.[81]

Fri 15 Nov: took 2 cartloads of dung & a cartload of ashes to le Prey.[82] Received some *phillysea* [phacelia?] from Mrs Pelley,[83] which I planted in different places around the gardens.

---

[77] It was the duty of the Constables and at least six Douzeniers to grant *bornements* (approve the boundaries) of people wishing to enclose land along public roads or to make changes in walls abutting on to public roads.
[78] Daniel Le Cheminant kept a public house. He was Mollet's first cousin once removed, the son of an older Daniel Le Cheminant (1712–47),who was the deceased eldest son of Mollet's aunt Rebecca, *née* Mollet, and her husband Daniel Le Cheminant.
[79] 'Advertising' consisted of having a notice read out to parishioners in the churchyard after morning service.
[80] 'Mr de la Porte' was James Ozanne, a neighbour of Mollet's.
[81] For bushel, see n. 15, above.
[82] These were the ashes of burnt seaweed, a valuable local fertiliser.
[83] 'Mrs Pelley' was Susanne, *née* De Beaucamp, widow of Jean Le Pelley, a neighbour of Mollet's.

Fri 29 Nov: received a package of trees, shrubs & flowers (containing more than 130 plants) from Mr Williamson, which cost me £3 13s 3d stg.

Sat 7 Dec: put 5 bushels of wheat in the lime pit.

Tues 10 Dec: sowed wheat at le Brulin.

Weds 11 Dec: […] I went to advise the Douzeniers of a forthcoming meeting, as also to deliver a *Billet d'Etat* to Mr Migault.[84]

Sat 14 Dec: we had a Douzaine meeting at Henry Ozanne's this morning to discuss the *Billet d'Etat* concerning the market.

Sun 15 Dec: […] Turned the calves loose at la Senciere. We had kept them tethered up until now, as also the horses, which we only let loose on the hillside last week. This has conserved our stocks of hay, of which we harvested only 7 cartloads this year. These 7 cartloads will have to feed 9 beasts, viz., 2 horses, 3 cows, 1 ox, 2 two-year-old calves & 1 one-year-old calf.

Weds 18 Dec: to town for the States meeting. […] The Bailiff's request to be paid a guinea a day while away on deputations has been granted. Dined at Etienne Barbet's.

Weds 25 Dec: to church in the morning. Text St Luke, ch. 2, vv. 10 & 11. Mr Mourant, my sister, my cousin James & his wife came to dinner.

Tues 31 Dec: took 15 bushels of our ashes, 29 bushels of Charles [Nicolle]'s ashes & 20 bushels of Abraham Collenette's ashes to the parsnip ground in Pierre Girard's strip at la Senciere. […] Mr Migault & my sister came to see my Dear Mother in the afternoon.

Notes relating to 1771

Before beginning his diary for any particular year, Charles Mollet always left a few blank pages on which he would make notes as the year progressed. His main purpose was to keep a running total of the day labourers and tradesmen he employed and the number of days they worked (although his notes also

---

[84] *Billets d'Etat* contained (and still contain) the agenda for forthcoming States meetings.

concerned other matters). In 1771, as well as one live-in farm servant and one live-in house servant, Mollet employed sixteen day workers at various times through the year. Most of these were farm labourers, but he also gave work to tradesmen such as carpenters, painters and thatchers. These day workers put in a total of 704½ man-days for Mollet. The labourers who regularly performed Mollet's farm work were Charles Nicolle (224 days, year-round), Jean Girard (114½ days), Eleazar Ingrouille (83 days, April–December), Etienne Lihou (52 days, year-round) and Hellier Marquis (46½ days, January–April). Payments to day labourers averaged 7 *sous* per day, the equivalent of about 6½ d stg. Some work, such as digging and weeding, was done for piece-rates – usually 6 *sous* per perch, plus 'expenses' (three meals a day plus cider, a benefit which was shared by day labourers and tradesmen). Mollet's payments to tradesmen averaged about 14 *sous* per day (just over one shilling). In total, Mollet spent 418 *livres tournois* on day labourers and tradesmen in 1771, which equated to about £23 6s stg.

1772

Weds 1 Jan: Doctor Sausmarez came to see my Dear Mother who has not been well this past week.

Thurs 2 Jan: my sister came to dinner, as also my cousin Nicolas [Le Cheminant]. Sowed wheat in Pierre Girard's strip at la Senciere. To town in the evening to have a tooth drawn by Brimble.

Tues 7 Jan: a parish meeting was held at the church to approve Sr Jean Cohu's accounts & choose someone to replace him (he is the *Procureur des Pauvres*).[85] We did neither, Sr Jean Cohu not having produced any regular accounts. He could not even tell us which *rentes* belong to the poor & how much they are worth. To town in the afternoon.

Sat 11 Jan: to town for the States meeting. The market tariff has been set at 35 *sous* for large beasts & 2 *sous* a piece for small meat.

Fri 17 Jan: [...] Paid my Uncle for 26 weeks, from 2 July 1771 to 1 January 1772.

Mon 20 Jan: to Chief Pleas. Mr Jean Toupper [Tupper] was granted the farm of the harbour dues for 4010 *livres*, & Jean Williams & Nicolas Martin had the King's Weights for 430 *livres*.

Thurs 23 Jan: [...] Settled my account with Peaty up to the 27th, & agreed on 10 sh. a year for my Uncle.[86]

Mon 3 Feb: eight chicks have hatched from the clutch I took from a nest on 23 January. They are all doing very well.

Sat 8 Feb: to town. Mr Bailleul & I were actioned by Mr Marchant for the [unpaid] Hospital tax, but we had the cause struck out. Marie Mouton, found guilty of theft, was sentenced to 50 lashes & to deposit security against her future good conduct or quit the Island in 8 days. Ester Bougour, for having

---

[85] The *Procureur des Pauvres* was in charge of parochial poor relief funds.
[86] Peaty was Mollet's barber. The 10 shillings for his uncle was for shaving.

falsely accused Mr Hocar of indecent behaviour towards her, was sentenced to two hours in the cage, as also to deposit security against her future good conduct or quit the Island in 8 days.

Sun 9 Feb: […] Finished paying our house servant Olimpe [Girard] for the year ending 30 December last. She will stay another year for the same wage of 12 *écus*.

Tues 11 Feb: went to collect part of the tax of 30 October.

Sat 15 Feb: went to la Haye du Puis to give Mr William [Le Marchant] the tax money.

Tues 18 Feb: Messrs Harry Mesurier & Jean Careye called here during the morning.[87]

Weds 19 Feb: I went shore-gathering on the spring tide.[88]

Mon 24 Feb: we planted potatoes at the wide end of le Ruquet (using the plough).

Sun 1 Mar: to church in the morning. Text Genesis, ch. 17, v. 1 (the end). I went to the Hospital in the afternoon,[89] after which I called at several places in search of parsnip seed.

Thurs 12 Mar: […] Had about 800 cabbage seedlings which we planted at le Ruquet & le Marquet. Also sowed some onion seed.

Fri 13 Mar: to town in the morning to speak to the Bailiff about the thefts from Mr du Groignet & Mme du Ponchez. I saw the Procureur on the same

---

[87] Jean Carey (1748–1821) was a long-standing friend of Mollet's, visiting him regularly until his retirement to Dijon in 1816. He served as a Jurat between June 1772 and 1777 (see 30.6.72). He was often referred to as Jean Carey of 'Choisi' to distinguish him from his contemporary Jean Carey of 'La Bigoterie', who also served as a Jurat. For more on the Careys of 'Choisi', see Appendix 3.

[88] Mollet was looking for ormers, an edible mollusc plentiful around the low-tide mark on Guernsey's foreshore.

[89] As a parish Constable, Mollet had a seat on the Country Hospital Board, which met on a Sunday.

subject in the afternoon, but he did not think we should undertake any investigations.[90]

Sun 15 Mar: to church in the afternoon. Text Ecclesiastes, ch. 9, v. 2. Took tea at la Houguette.[91]

Tues 24 Mar: inspected the roads. We two Constables & 5 of the Douzeniers dined at Rachel le Geyt's.[92] I sold the brown cow to Thos Fallaize of St Martin.

Mon 30 Mar: began digging le Neuf Courtil garden. Planted a magnolia & a scarlet arbutus in the hollow at the turning. Transplanted my myrtle seedlings to le Marquet, le Carré & the turning.

Thurs 2 Apr: dined at Mr Bailleul's for his Constable's treat. There were about 20 of us.

Mon 6 Apr: Pierre Heaume began to work here as a farm servant at 18 *écus* a year. Made a bed for the melons. Sowed clover seed among the wheat in Pierre Girard's strip at la Senciere.

Sun 12 Apr: to church in the afternoon. Mr Godefroid preached.[93] His text was Philippians, ch. 3, v. 14. Mme du Groignet came here after the sermon to tell me that Mme du Ponchez surrendered le Groignet to Mr du Groignet yesterday, in return for life maintenance.[94]

Tues 21 Apr: to the Fair. Dined at Sr Henry Ozanne's. Ploughed les Eturs in preparation for sowing barley.

---

[90] HM Procureur was Jean De Sausmarez (1706–74), who served this office from 1744 until his death in 1774.
[91] La Houguette was the home of the widowed Judith Ozanne and her two daughters, friends of Mollet and his mother.
[92] Rachel Le Geyt ran a public house.
[93] Jean Godefroid (or Godefroy) was Rector of St Saviour from 1763 to 1782. His father, Julien Godefroid (a Huguenot), had served as Rector of St Martin between 1750 and 1762.
[94] By 'surrendered', Mollet meant sold. Mme du Groignet was Marie De Jersey, *née* Roland. Mme du Ponchez was Marie Moullin, *née* Tourgis (for whom see also 12.9.72). For detail on this episode, see T.F. Priaulx, 'Some 18th century legal tangles and family squabbles involving le Groignet estate', *Transactions of la Société Guernesiaise*, 15 (1954), pp. 401–3).

Sat 25 Apr: […] Mr Wm Le Messurier gravely insulted me & attempted to strike me when I went to notify him that he had to repair the cart-tracks belonging to his wards (at la Porte).

Sun 26 Apr: […] I found Jean Girard's ox in our wheat at la Senciere. He paid me 10 *sous* to release it.

Thurs 30 Apr: there was an election for a new Constable. André Cohu was chosen unanimously to replace Mr Bailleul.

Sun 3 May: to church in the morning. Left early to inspect the public houses. The two Mr Mourants, Mr Bailleul & my sister came to dinner. Mr Migault came in the afternoon.

Sat 9 May: attended the States meeting. It was decided that a loan should be taken out to pay the Bailiff. Commissioners were appointed to examine the harbour accounts. Sr André Cohu took the Constable's oath as the replacement for Mr Bailleul.

Sun 10 May: the Governor, Messrs Char. Andros, Wm Le Marchant, Josué Gosselin & Char. Le Marchant came to dinner.[95]

Mon 11 May: sowed barley at les Eturs.

Tues 26 May: my Dear Mother left for Jersey this morning on board Captn Gautier.

Mon 8 Jun: in the morning I went to les Mielles, where the Castel [militia] Regiment was assembled. In the afternoon, I took tea at la Houguette & accompanied Miss Ozanne & Miss Guille to a party.[96]

Sat 13 Jun: to town. I actioned Thomas Gallienne for keeping his livestock on the public highway. He was fined.

---

[95] Charles Le Marchant (born in 1751) was a merchant and shipowner. For 'the Governor', see n. 67, above.
[96] Miss Ozanne was nineteen-year-old Marie Ozanne of la Houguette. Miss Guille was twenty-one-year-old Rachel Guille, daughter of Jean Guille, sen., of St George (see Appendix 3).

Thurs 18 Jun: went to the church to fetch gunpowder to make cartridges for the muskets.

Fri 19 Jun: shared out the gunpowder among the men of our Regiment.

Sat 20 Jun: we were actioned by Mr Marchant, the Hospital Treasurer, & in our turn actioned Sr Jean Cohu, one of the Collectors, whom the Court adjudged responsible for collecting the taxes for the poor, & also for obtaining permission from the Court for levying such taxes.

Tues 23 Jun: dined at the Governor's. Much company. My Uncle arrived from Jersey.

Tues 30 Jun: there was an election for a Magistrate at which Mr Jean Careye, son of Thomas, was elected by a large majority.[97] I gave him my vote. Dined with the Douzaine at Etienne Touzeau's.[98]

Weds 1 Jul: this is the week appointed for collecting seaweed in a sack.[99]

Sat 18 Jul: to town in the morning. Finished cutting the hay at le Prey. Brought in some of the hay from le Neuf Courtil. Gave Jean Girard a clutch of ten chicks to rear, keeping half for himself.

Weds 22 Jul: to town in the evening to meet my Dear Mother who arrived back from Jersey. Mr Mourant came in the afternoon. Planted a few broccoli at le Carré.

Thurs 23 Jul: dined at Fermains at the invitation of Advocate Coutart.[100] There were 15 of us.

[*Charles Mollet turned thirty during the course of August 1772*]

---

[97] See n. 87, above.
[98] Etienne Touzeau kept a public house.
[99] People too poor to own a horse and cart were given exclusive access to seaweed for a week prior to the main summer cutting season, provided they carried their seaweed up the beach in a sack.
[100] There was a gentlemen's dining club at Fermain (which Mollet always spent with a final 's').

Sun 2 Aug: […] There was a charity sermon & music at Torteval.

Thurs 6 Aug: Mr & Mrs Havilland came to dinner. To town in the afternoon. Miss Judith Ozanne has arrived from England, & I escorted her back to la Houguette.[101]

Mon 24 Aug: put supports under the apple trees. Spent the afternoon with Judith Ozanne.

Tues 25 Aug: dined at Mr William Dobrée's with Mr Marchant the Minister, the Dean, Messrs Migault, Godefroid, Pradon, Pépin & Bernet (all Ministers).

Thurs 3 Sep: I was unwell & stayed in bed. Rain nearly all day.

Sun 6 Sep: to church in the morning. Text 1st Epistle of St John. The two Mr Mourants & my sister came to dinner. Mrs Migault & Mme de la Houguette came in the afternoon.[102]

Mon 7 Sep: […] we had a Douzaine meeting at Rachel [Le Geyt]'s in the afternoon, & afterwards went to taste the cider at several public houses.

Sat 12 Sep: to town. Dined at my sister's. In the evening I attended the wedding of Mme du Ponchez & Richard Moullin, as also that of her sister & Pierre Martel.[103]

Mon 5 Oct: to Chief Pleas. *Rentes* were fixed at 10 *livres* 10 *sous*, hens at 10 *sous* & capons at 45 *sous*. An Ordinance was passed giving Douzeniers the same obligation as Constables to enforce the repair of roads, & making them liable to a fine of 18 *sous* if they fail to attend a meeting to which they have been duly summoned by the Constables.

---

[101] Judith Guille Ozanne, then aged sixteen, was probably returning from boarding school in England.
[102] 'Mme de la Houguette' was Judith, *née* Guille (1723–91), the widow of Jurat Jean Ozanne (1723–63). She was the mother of Marie and Judith Ozanne. See nn. 91, 96 and 101, above.
[103] The widowed Marie Tourgis (aged thirty-two) married Richard Moullin, and her sister Elizabeth married Pierre Martel.

Tues 6 Oct: my brother[-in-law], Polly Lerrier & their son Charles arrived from England.

Mon 19 Oct: in the morning we made a search for some linen which was stolen from Thos Cohu of Saumarez, but we found nothing.

Weds 21 Oct: we assembled for a Douzaine meeting but did not hold it, as Mr des Touillets [Pierre De Jersey] objected to our meeting in the church.[104]

Thurs 22 Oct: went to town twice. Had Mr des Touillets served with a summons for Saturday on account of his opposition, as also Char. Nicolle of la Hougue for the cost of road repairs.

Sat 24 Oct: to town. Mr des Touillets' objection was upheld, but we won our cause against Char. Nicolle.

Weds 28 Oct: [...] There was a parish meeting where it was resolved to request 15 quarters of barley & raise a tax of 700 *livres*. The carpenters finished making & hanging the gate at le Brulin.

Thurs 29 Oct: gathered more haws. We now have about 3 bushels. It has been very windy.

Fri 30 Oct: I was unwell & stayed in bed.

Sat 14 Nov: [...] To town. Dined at my sister's. Mr Mourant has written to Nico Guille to order 20 casks of brandy for me.

Weds 18 Nov: [...] Paid Captn Priaulx 11 guineas for bringing over the 15 quarters of wheat required by the parish. Pressed apples. Bought two French hens. We have 32 fowls besides these.

Sun 22 Nov: [...] Mr Mourant, my sister & Billy Combs came to dinner.[105]

Thurs 26 Nov: Charles le Cras rebuilt the hearth & started making a small oven in the wash-house.

---

[104] Jurat Pierre (Peter) De Jersey (1736–1823) was a Churchwarden.
[105] William Combs (or Combes) was Peter Mourant's nephew and business partner. The Combes were a Jersey family.

Sat 28 Nov: […] Strong winds & heavy rain all this week. On Thursday, a French vessel of about 150 tons coming from Martinique was lost at Hougue a la Perre. There were 200 barrels of sugar & 50 barrels of coffee on board, as well as a quantity of cotton. About 30 barrels of sugar were saved. Losses are estimated at £5000 stg. Pressed apples.

Sat 5 Dec: to town. James Lihou of l'Echelle mill was sworn to keep the peace with Daniel Brouard of les Niots mill.

Sun 6 Dec: […] In the afternoon, we went to search Nic. Martel's premises at le Bouillon in St Andrew for a quint & a sackful of barley which was stolen last night from Daniel Brouard of les Niots.[106] We found nothing.

Weds 9 Dec: I felt unwell.

Sat 12 Dec: […] Sr Jean Cohu actioned my Dear Mother & me for the tax of 4 August, which we are refusing to pay, because it was raised without proper authorisation.[107]

Fri 25 Dec: to church in the morning. Text St Matthew, ch. 2, vv. 1 & 2. In the afternoon, I went to la Houguette, & later to join the festivities at les Cauvins.[108]

Sat 26 Dec: to town in the morning. Received the 15 quarters of barley we ordered for the parish. To la Houguette in the afternoon & later to les Cauvins.

Thurs 31 Dec: to town in the morning. Yesterday we drew off the cider from No. 7 & No. 8.

Notes relating to 1772

Mollet's notes for this year show that he gave occasional or regular work to a total of twenty-five individuals (in addition to his live-in farm servant, Pierre Heaume, and female house servant, Olympe Girard). About ten of the twenty-five were tradesmen; five appear to have been children employed to

---

[106] For quint, see n.15, above.
[107] See 20.6.72, above.
[108] There was a public house at les Cauvins.

gather cider apples in the autumn; and the other ten were day labourers, five of whom were regularly employed all year-round, and the rest at peak times only. The five regulars were Charles Nicolle (242 days), Jean Girard (89 days), James Letocq (85½ days), Eleazar Ingrouille (63½ days), and Etienne Lihou (51 days). In 1772, Mollet did not note payments made to his workers this year.

1773

Fri 1 Jan: Mr Mourant, my sister & Billy Combs came to dinner.

Sat 2 Jan: to town in the morning. In the afternoon I went to la Houguette & later joined the festivities at Nic. Rabey's.[109]

Sun 3 Jan: to church in the morning. André Cohu & I left after the first psalm to inspect the public houses. He dined here, & in the afternoon we both went to church at St Andrew.

Thurs 7 Jan: to town for the farming out of tithes. Mr Wm Le Marchant had those of the Castel for 1600 *livres*.[110] I am to have a quarter of them. Sr André Cohu, Srs Jean & Matth. Carré, & Mr Marchant will also have a quarter each.

Sun 10 Jan: […] My roses have been flowering almost constantly since the summer. Today I picked 2 reasonably good ones. There are already buds on the new shoots.

Mon 18 Jan: […] to Chief Pleas. Mr Jean Toupper has been granted the farm of the harbour dues for 3600 *livres* & Etienne Barbet has the King's Weights for 600 *livres*. Hunting is prohibited from the end of January.

Sat 23 Jan: to town & to the States. The proposal of the gentlemen offering to build a market in the Rectory garden has been accepted.

Thurs 28 Jan: very windy. Peaty & Mr MacCuddy came with their ferrets, & we caught three rabbits.

Sun 31 Jan: to church in the afternoon. Mr Martinault preached.[111]

---

[109] Nicolas Rabey kept a public house.
[110] This was William Le Marchant of la Haye du Puits (see n. 5, above).
[111] René Martineau was a refugee Huguenot minister from Poitou. He was ordained as an Anglican priest at the Chapel Royal, St James's Palace in 1768, and by 1773 was serving as curate of the Castel parish. He married Marie Levrier, daughter of the Minister of Sark, in December 1773. Between 1774 and 1780, and again between 1789 and 1816, he served as Vicar of the Vale and Rector of St Sampson.

Sun 7 Feb: […] I dismissed Pierre Heaume. He has been here ten months.

Mon 8 Feb: bundled the furze from the hillside (75 bundles). Engaged Henri Le Geyt as a farm servant. He will start on Monday.

Weds 10 Feb: to town in the morning. We have had several hard frosts since last Wednesday & there has been snow on the ground since Friday. It snowed again today.

Thurs 11 Feb: […] Mr Wm Le Marchant of la Haye du Puis died yesterday evening.

Mon 22 Feb: […] Gales & heavy rain. An elm came down in the lower garden.

Tues 23 Feb: the bad weather continues.

Fri 26 Feb: weather just as stormy as on Monday. Several of our trees have come down this week.

Weds 3 Mar: had 2 cartloads of sand for the dungheap, & one cartload of seaweed for the old nursery.

Mon 8 Mar: spread …. bushels of ashes on the 50 perches at la Senciere where we grew oats last year & are growing wheat this year. Harrowed the whole field. Planted Hotspur peas in the lower garden.

Weds 10 Mar: to town in the morning. The weather has begun to improve.

Tues 16 Mar: had a Douzaine meeting at Rachel le Geyt's. We accomplished nothing.

Fri 19 Mar: the carpenters have been working here these past 2 days. They are making a salting bench, &c.

Weds 31 Mar: […] Had 3 piglets from Hellier Nicolle at 5 shillings each.

Weds 7 Apr: […] André Cohu & I went to Vazon to oversee the quarrying of stone for the fortifications. André Cohu & Sr Jean Ogier came to dinner.

Tues 13 Apr: […] Mme de la Houguette & Mme Josias le Marchant came here in the afternoon.[112]

Thurs 15 Apr: […] At a quarter to two in the afternoon, the earth shook twice in short succession. I felt only the first tremor, but I heard a noise in the air both times.

Sat 17 Apr: […] Yesterday at four in the morning, the earth shook again, once more accompanied by a noise in the air.

Fri 23 Apr: […] Between two & three in the afternoon the earth shook again, but only slightly. There was another much stronger tremor between eleven & midnight.

Sun 25 Apr: the Greffier & Henry Messurier dined here, after which we went to St Peter's church to hear Mr Vallat preach.[113]

Thurs 6 May: […] André Cohu dined here. Later, I accompanied him to the fortifications, where 11 of our Castel men & three carts were at work.

Sun 9 May: I did not go out. It rained today after a long dry spell.

Thurs 20 May: […] my sister was delivered of a stillborn infant. Put the ox out to graze on the grass.

Sat 22 May: to town in the morning. Made an agreement with Mr Charles Shergold to supply him with as much cider as I can at 28 shillings per barrel.[114] In the afternoon, I bought 2 barrels of cider from Hellier le Pelley at 17 *livres* each [24s 4d stg], 4 barrels from Ch. Nicolle of la Hougue at 24 shillings, & 3 barrels from James Moullin of le Prais [Préel] at 23 shillings, all including the barrels.

---

[112] 'Mme Josias Le Marchant' was Marie, *née* Bonamy, widow of Josias Le Marchant, sen., of la Haye du Puits, who had died in 1768.
[113] Isaac Vallat, originally from Lausanne, served as Rector of Alderney between 1749 and 1772, then as Rector of St Peter from 1772 until his death (in Jersey) in 1785. He was married to Jeanne, *née* Allez, a Guernseywoman.
[114] A barrel (*barrique*) contained 55 gallons.

Sun 6 Jun: to church in the morning. Text Hebrews, ch. 11, v. 6. Mr Mourant dined here, & in the afternoon we accompanied Char. Guille, Billy Carey, the Miss Guilles & the Miss Ozannes on an excursion to St Peter & the Forest, where we stopped to drink tea at le Bourg.

Sat 19 Jun: to town. Dined at the Governor's.

Sun 20 Jun: [...] In the afternoon, Charles Guille, his sister, the Miss Ozannes & I went on an excursion to Torteval & the Forest.

Mon 28 Jun: dined at Fermains at the invitation of Mr Jean la Serre.[115] There were 18 of us.

Weds 30 Jun: Mr & Mrs Migault, Mr & Mrs Jean Guille, Advocate & Mrs Coutart, Mrs Martinault, my sister and Mrs Condomine came to dinner.[116] Weeded the barley at le Courtil Robin.

Sun 4 Jul: to les Mielles in the morning to see the Castel Regiment. My Lord & Lady Northampton were there.[117] To church in the afternoon. Same text as last Sunday.

Mon 12 Jul: borrowed the cart from les Queus to take 4 barrels & 4 pipes of cider to the harbour for Mr Shergold.

Tues 20 Jul: Henri [Le Geyt] & I went to gather samphire.

Thurs 29 Jul: my Dear Mother left for Jersey. Had 22 bushels of lime.

[*Charles Mollet turned thirty-one during the course of August 1773*]

---

[115] There were three individuals named Jean La Serre living in Guernsey at this time: Jean (1682–1774), a surgeon from France; his son Jean (1730–1815); and his grandson Jean (1759–1835). It was probably the second Jean who had issued the invitation. Mollet was to maintain a friendship with the La Serre family all his life.

[116] Marie Condamine, *née* Neel (1732–1808), was the widow of former HM Sergeant Jean-Jacques Condamine (1711–64). Mollet's association with the Condamines (to whom he was distantly related) was life-long. Mollet always spelt the name with a middle 'o'.

[117] Spencer Compton, 8th Earl of Northampton (1738–96), and his wife Jane. Compton was Lord Lieutenant of Northamptonshire.

Sun 8 Aug: the Governor & the Greffier breakfasted here. In the afternoon, Richard Guille, his sister, the Miss Ozannes & I went to church at St Peter & took tea at Mr Le Hurai's.

Mon 9 Aug: I picked our first melon.

Sat 14 Aug: to town. Passed contracts with James Brouard for his house.

Thurs 19 Aug: [...] There was a storm last night which caused great damage to the grain crop.

Sun 29 Aug: to church in the afternoon. Mr Pradon preached.[118]

Sun 12 Sep: to church in the morning. Mr Godefroid preached. Notified parishioners that the tithe collection will begin tomorrow. I engaged Nicolas Brouard as a farm servant.

Mon 13 Sep: collected tithe with my cousin James [Le Cheminant] & Charles Nicolle. Had one cartload.

Tues 14 Sep: collected tithe with my cousin & Etienne Lihou.

Mon 20 Sep: finished collecting tithe in the district of les Hougues.[119] We went out eleven times with the cart.

Thurs 23 Sep: [...] Mr [Charles] Andros, the other [tithe] farmers & I dined at les Cauvins, where we settled our accounts for the tithe collection.[120]

Sun 26 Sep: [...] I renewed Pierre Guillard's lease on les Monts de Vaux for 6 years.[121]

---

[118] Antoine-Charles-Frédéric Gounon dit Pradon (1713–78), a refugee Huguenot minister who served as Rector of St Andrew from 1774 until his death in 1778.

[119] The Castel parish was divided into seven tithe collection districts (*quêtes*): les Hougues, les Grantez, le Nanage, les Vallées, le Villocq, les Houmets and le Grand Fil.

[120] Charles Andros (jun.) was not listed as one of the farmers of the Castel tithes when they were first mentioned on 7 January 1773; however, he appears to have taken over from William Le Marchant, who had died on 10 February. Andros's role is corroborated by an entry Mollet made in his diary on 26 February 1785, which mentions 'Mr Andros' as the farmer of the Castel tithes.

[121] Mollet owned two fields at le Mont d'Aval, about half a mile from his farm.

Weds 29 Sep: went to town to fetch my Dear Mother on her return from Jersey.

Weds 13 Oct: I left for Jersey with Nicolas [Brouard] on board Jean Horman & arrived in the afternoon.

Mon 18 Oct: dined at Rozel.[122]

Tues 19 Oct: dined at Mr David Patriarche's.[123]

Mon 25 Oct: [...] Bought a mare from Mr Edouard le Maitre for 40 *écus*.

Weds 27 Oct: [...] Bought a mare from Mr Chesnel for 200 *livres*.

Sun 31 Oct: [...] visited Mr & Mrs Migault who arrived from Guernsey yesterday.

Mon 8 Nov: loaded my two horses on board ship.

Weds 17 Nov: Nicolas [Brouard] & I left for Guernsey in Laurens du Feu's sloop at eleven in the morning. We arrived at seven in the evening.

Fri 19 Nov: I learned on arriving that Henri le Geyt left our service on 20 October. The red cow calved.

Tues 30 Nov: to town. Dined at my sister's. I took possession of James Brouard's house.[124]

Fri 3 Dec: Mr [Charles] Andros [sen.] died this morning. [...] Stabled the horses in J. Brouard's house for the night. We are keeping the big cow indoors.

Sat 25 Dec: Mr Mourant, my sister, Billy Combs, my cousin James [Le Cheminant] & his wife came to dinner. In the evening, I inspected the public houses.

---

[122] Rozel Manor was the seat of Charles Lemprière (1714–1806), who served as Lieutenant-Bailiff of Jersey between 1750 and 1781.
[123] The Patriarche family were linked to the Le Vavasseur dit Durells (Mollet's mother's family) through a seventeenth-century ancestor. David Patriarche (1737–84) served as a Jersey Jurat between 1771 and 1782.
[124] Mollet later referred to this house as 'la Daumaillerie'.

Sun 26 Dec: Mr Cohu & I left church after the first psalm to inspect the public houses.

Mon 27 Dec: Nicolas [Brouard] returned to his home as he is feeling unwell.

Fri 31 Dec: to town. Dined at my sister's. […] Began pulling out the turnips in the lower garden.

Notes relating to 1773

Charles Mollet gave work to a total of twenty-nine people in 1773 (aside from his live-in servants). About half were tradesmen, and the other half day labourers. Of the labourers, only three worked for Mollet regularly. The remainder (some of whom had worked upwards of 80 days for Mollet the previous year) worked only for short spells. Charles Nicolle was Mollet's principal day labourer in 1773, working for Mollet on 252 days. The two other regulars were Etienne Lihou (77 days) and Jean Girard (64 days). The reduced requirement for day labour was due to Mollet's employment of two full-time farm servants for part of the year.

1774

Sat 1 Jan: Mr Mourant, my sister & Billy Combs came to dinner.

Tues 4 Jan: frosts these past 2 or 3 nights.

Weds 5 Jan: Pierre Girard & I measured my plot at la Grande Senciere: 1 vergee & 37 perches, including the roads, earthbanks & offset.[125]

Fri 7 Jan: Nicolas Brouard came to fetch his clothes & take his leave of us, his mother being unable to spare him. Planted some English & Guernsey cabbages at le Marquet.

Sat 15 Jan: to town in the morning. Jean Cateline began working here.

Mon 17 Jan: to town & to Chief Pleas. Mr Pierre Tupper has kept the harbour dues for 3300 *livres*.[126] Etienne Barbet & Nicolas Martin will share the King's Weights for 600 *livres*.

Tues 8 Feb: to town in the afternoon. Started target practice.

Weds 23 Feb: accompanied the Douzaine to approve the roadside boundaries of Wm Carré's land, as also those of Sr Pierre le Roi of le Friquet & Sr Matth. Carré. Dined at les Cauvins.

Thurs 24 Feb: sold about half the osier to the Le Fevres of Sark for 19 *livres*.

Sat 26 Feb: to town. Hellier Le Cornu was sentenced to an hour in the pillory for using a false measure.

Thurs 3 Mar: finished dunging les Eturs. Planted about 70 grafts in the nursery at the turning (beside the path). Pulled out the rest of the turnips.

Sat 5 Mar: to town. Danl Brouard was arrested for forging a note, but he escaped in the evening.

---

[125] 2.469 vergees were equivalent to one English acre.
[126] This was possibly a mistake, as Mollet had named Jean Tupper as the farmer of the harbour dues the previous year (see 18.1.73).

Sat 12 Mar: [...] Sowed haws & holly berries at the turning & in the lower garden. Sowed annual flowers in the border beside the quicksets.

Sun 13 Mar: Mr Pierre Havilland came here in the morning & I accompanied him around the Castel, St Saviour, the Forest & St Andrew to canvass for votes for his brother Martin.[127] We had promises of 23. We returned here to dine & Mr Mourant joined us.

Tues 15 Mar: [...] Today the Court forbade anyone to shelter Danl Brouard or help him leave the Island on pain of a fine of 1000 *livres*.

Mon 21 Mar: I engaged Leonard Chan [Jehan] as a farm servant for 25 *écus* a year.

Weds 23 Mar: [...] My sister was delivered of a stillborn infant.

Sat 26 Mar: to town. Dined at my sister's. Had 3 cartloads of sand. Danl Brouard was re-arrested on Wednesday & has been remanded in prison until after Easter.

Sat 2 Apr: to town & to the States. The proposal made by the owners of the houses between the High Street & the harbour concerning the quay was agreed to. Dined at my sister's.

Sun 10 Apr: my Dear Mother left for Jersey with Charles Lerrier.

Mon 11 Apr: the carpenters came to make wheels for the large cart.

Sun 24 Apr: Mr Jean Guille, Mr Bob Marchant[128] & my sister dined with me.

Tues 3 May: bottled a barrel of cider which I bought from Mme de la Houguette. Half the bottles are for ourselves, a quarter for Mr Mourant & a quarter for Mr Jean Guille. Had 2 cartloads of sand. Weeded the wheat. Planted a few early Hotspur peas in the lower garden. Also sowed some Turnip Rooted Cabbage there.[129]

---

[127] Martin De Havilland (1746–1806) was standing for election as HM Prévôt.
[128] 'Bob Marchant' was Robert Porret Le Marchant (1755–1840), the son of Bailiff William Le Marchant and a future Bailiff himself.
[129] 'Turnip Rooted Cabbage' is written in English. This was an early term for swede.

Weds 11 May: sowed barley at la Senciere.

Thurs 12 May: had the small mare covered.

Sat 14 May: Danl Brouard was sentenced to 100 lashes & banished for 6 years for forging a note.

Tues 17 May: both mares were covered.

Sat 21 May: [...] Paid Captn Priaulx 8 guineas for [bringing over] 10 quarters of barley.

Sun 22 May: [...] My sister has been staying here since Thursday.

Tues 31 May: my Dear Mother arrived back from Jersey. Had 3 cartloads of stone. Weeded the wheat at le Ruquet.

Thurs 9 Jun: André Cohu & I inspected the roads.

Sun 12 Jun: I did not go out. I dismissed Leonard Chan [Jehan].

Weds 15 Jun: [...] Nicolas Brouard returned to work here as my farm servant.

Thurs 16 Jun: [...] Ph. Lerrier arrived from Jersey.[130]

Mon 20 Jun: [...] To town in the evening for the concert.

Tues 21 Jun: Doctor [Richard] Guille & Ph. Lerrier came to dinner.

Fri 24 Jun: to les Mielles in the morning to see the Castel & St Andrew's Regiments. Messrs Mourant, Ph. Lerrier, Martin de Havilland, Richard Guille, Abraham Mesurier & Doctor [William] Mesurier came to dinner.[131]

Weds 13 Jul: planted broccoli in the lower garden. The masons finished the new cowshed today.

---

[130] Philippe Lerrier (1755–1823) was Mollet's nephew, the eldest son of his Jersey-based sister.
[131] For Abraham Le Mesurier, see n. 63, above. His younger brother William was a surgeon in the employ of the East India Company.

Thurs 21 Jul: [...] Manon & Edouard Lerrier arrived from Jersey.[132]

Fri 22 Jul: Billy Chepmell arrived from Jersey.

Sun 24 Jul: Billy Chepmell & I went to St Peter's church in the morning & Castel church in the afternoon.

Tues 26 Jul: [...] Mr Lihou raised a *clameur de haro* against the masons who were working on his footpath.[133]

[*Charles Mollet turned thirty-two during the course of August 1774*]

Sun 7 Aug: the Mourant family, Mrs Condomine & her two children came to dinner.

Sat 13 Aug: to town. I borrowed 200 *livres* from Daniel [Le Cheminant].

Mon 15 Aug: Billy Chepmell left for Jersey. He arrived here 3 weeks ago last Friday.

Weds 17 Aug: Manon & I went to dine at Mr Jean Careye's (the elder).

Thurs 18 Aug: Mrs Pelley, her son & daughter, & her son-in-law Mr Falla came in the afternoon.[134] I planted some carnations I had from Mr Jean Careye under the walnut tree at the turning.

Mon 22 Aug: dined at Mr Andros's. Went fishing at Lihou Island.

Fri 2 Sep: my brother[-in-law] arrived from Jersey. Planted kale at le Marquet.

Weds 7 Sep: [...] My brother[-in-law], my sister & Edouard left for Jersey.

---

[132] 'Manon' was Mollet's eldest sister Marie. Edouard was her nine-year-old son.
[133] The *clameur de haro* was a judicial procedure for imposing an immediate injunction on the alleged perpetrator of wrongful interference with a person's possession of immoveable property.
[134] The Le Pelleys were neighbours of Mollet's. Over subsequent decades, Mollet had many dealings with Mrs Le Pelley's sons Jean (born 1753), Denis (1755), Nicolas (1757) and Thomas (1760). Her daughter Susanne (1752–96) was married to Daniel Falla (1751–92) of les Maisons au Comte in the Vale. For Mrs Le Pelley, see 15.11.71.

Sun 11 Sep: to church in the afternoon. Mr Godefroid preached. We notified parishioners that the tithe collection will begin tomorrow. I let la Daumaillerie to Pierre Le Lievre for 4 years at 48 *livres* per year.

Mon 26 Sep: we collected Nic. le Nourry's tithe & finished the tithe collection.

Mon 3 Oct: to Chief Pleas. *Rentes* were fixed at 11 *livres*, hens at 30 *sous* & capons at 45 *sous*.

Fri 7 Oct: dined at the Bailiff's with the Governor & three French gentlemen, &c. The young ladies of the Castel & their mothers held their afternoon gathering here.[135]

Sat 8 Oct: [...] James Moullin came here to make baskets.

Sun 9 Oct: [...] My sister & her children, their Uncle le Cocq & his son came to dinner.[136]

Tues 11 Oct: [...] Tom Andros & Josias Le Marchant came to dinner.[137] Bundled our bracken.

Mon 17 Oct: the Governor & Mrs Irving, Messrs Nico Dobrée, Gosselin, Matth. de Sausmarez, & Josias Le Marchant came to breakfast, after which we went out hunting. They all returned to dine here, except Messrs Gosselin & Dobrée.

Weds 2 Nov: Mr Nico Dobrée, Mr Gosselin & the Procureur[138] came to breakfast, after which we joined the company at Mr de St George's to hunt one of his deer. The deer ran for about 3 hours before he was taken. Had 2 cartloads of sand. J. Guignon & Danl Brouard have finished the greenhouse.

---

[135] Mollet later referred to this gathering as 'the Castel Club' or 'Castel Young Ladies' Club'. He recorded attending eighty-four sessions between 1774 and 1779.
[136] Mollet's sister's children were Patty, Mary, Nancy and Peter Mourant. They were aged between nine and four. See Appendix 2.
[137] Josias Le Marchant was the eldest son of the late Josias Le Marchant of la Haye du Puits. See n. 5, above.
[138] Hirzel Le Marchant (1752–93), the son of Bailiff William Le Marchant, was now HM Procureur. He had taken his oath of office on 17 May 1774.

Fri 4 Nov: to the theatre. Saw 'The London Merchant' & 'The Padlock'. The heifer calved.

Tues 8 Nov: [...] Received news of Aunt Bété's death.[139] She died yesterday evening.

Fri 11 Nov: [...] Rain all day. Nic. Bisson's house at les Maingis burned down yesterday evening.

Sat 12 Nov: to town. My Dear Mother left for Jersey today.

Weds 23 Nov: [...] went to the theatre, where I saw 'The Fop's Fortune' & 'The Author'.

Mon 28 Nov: [...] dined at Mr Jean Careye's (the Magistrate) & went to the theatre in the evening. Saw 'The Stratagem' & 'The Contrivances'.

Sat 3 Dec: to town. We lost our cause against Mr de St George & have appealed.[140]

Sun 4 Dec: [...] My brother[-in-law] arrived from Jersey.

Mon 5 Dec: Messrs Ch. Andros, Nico Dobrée, Jean Careye, Josué Gosselin, Pierre Havilland, Tom Andros, Billy Careye, & my brother[-in-law] came to dinner. In the evening I went to the theatre, where I saw 'Rule a Wife & Have a Wife' & 'The Citizen'.

Thurs 8 Dec: my brother[-in-law] came to dinner. Nico Guille, who arrived here on Monday, came to see me in the evening.

---

[139] 'Aunt Bété' was Mollet's mother's younger sister Elizabeth, born in 1716.
[140] This concerned a lane though the estate of St George by which farmers living to the south of the property reached their fields to the north. Jean Guille, sen. applied to the Royal Court for an order to prevent trespass on his land, including the lane through the estate. This was formally contested by the Castel parochial authorities, but the Court nevertheless granted the order. For more on this episode, see R. Hocart, 'Monsieur de St. George: Jean Guille (1712–78)', *Transactions of la Société Guernesiaise*, 26 (2010), pp. 681–2.

Weds 14 Dec: dined at Mr Pierre Havilland's amid much company. My brother[-in-law] & Nico Guille were there. To the theatre in the evening. Saw 'The Wonder: A Woman Keeps a Secret' & 'The Jubilee'.

Thurs 15 Dec: sowed wheat at la Grande Senciere. My brother[-in-law] left for Jersey.

Fri 16 Dec: went to fetch the large tun which Jean Collins has made for me. It holds 800 gallons & cost fifteen guineas.

Sat 17 Dec: to town. Nico Guille returned here with me & stayed overnight.

Sun 18 Dec: Josias Le Marchant & Mr Mourant came to dinner. We all went to la Houguette in the afternoon.

Weds 21 Dec: dined at the Governor's & went to the theatre. Saw 'Alonso' & 'The Jubilee'.

Thurs 22 Dec: Thos Brouard finished thatching the roof of the cowshed & cartshed.

Sun 25 Dec: Mr Mourant & my cousin James [Le Cheminant] came to dinner with their families.

Mon 26 Dec: dined at la Haye du Puis with Mr Andros & his family, Mr Samuel Bonamy, Mr & Mrs Havilland, & Mr & Mrs Martinault.

Weds 28 Dec: to the theatre. Saw 'The West Indian' & 'The Golden Pippin'.

Sat 31 Dec: to town. Dined at Mr Tom Guille's.[141]

---

[141] Thomas Guille (born in 1737) was a son of Jean Guille, sen., of St George.

Notes relating to 1774

During the course of 1774, Mollet gave work to thirty-eight individuals (aside from his live-in servants). About half of these were tradesmen, and the other half day labourers and piece-workers. Mollet's three regular day labourers were Charles Nicolle (291 days), Thomas Le Page (167 days), and Etienne Lihou (99 days). Mollet also used the services of Jean Cateline Nicolas Le Tocq, Henry Le Geyt, Hellier Le Pelley and others for piece-work, which included digging, weeding and threshing.

1775

Sun 1 Jan: to church in the morning.

Mon 2 Jan: to town in the morning. Afterwards, I dined with Mr Andros & his family in company with Mr Godefroid & his family, Mr & Mrs Havilland, & the Haye du Puis family.

Tues 3 Jan: dined at la Mare de Carteret with Messrs Vallat, Marret, George Le Fevre,[142] & other good company. Pressed the 4th layer.

Weds 4 Jan: Sr Nic. Le Beir was elected a Douzenier.

Fri 13 Jan: dined at the Greffier's amid good company. Went to the theatre in the evening & saw 'The Conscious Lovers' & 'The Irish Widow'.

Sun 15 Jan: to church in the afternoon, & then to la Haye du Puis for the Young Ladies' Club.

Fri 20 Jan: Messrs Nico Dobrée, Jean Carey, Pierre Havilland, Vallat, Marett, Bradby, Matth. de Sausmarez, Nico Guille & the Greffier came to dinner. Went to the theatre in the evening. Saw 'A Word to the Wise' & 'A Trip to Scotland'.

Weds 25 Jan: [...] To the theatre in the evening. Saw 'Cymon' & 'Catherine & Petruchio'.

Fri 27 Jan: to the theatre in the evening. Saw 'The Clandestine Marriage' & 'High Life Below Stairs'.

Tues 7 Feb: to town. We lost our appeal against Mr de St George in respect of his road.

---

[142] George Lefebvre, sen. (1722–1812) was the Seigneur of Blanchelande. Mollet was associated with the Lefebvre family for many years, but he always spelled their name 'Le Fevre'.

Mon 13 Feb: had two cartloads of seaweed. To the theatre in the evening. Saw 'The Fair Penitent'.

Sat 18 Feb: to town & to Court. Ten of the Magistrates left the Court on the Bailiff's refusal to seek their opinion on the subject of the Seigneurial Courts. Only Mr Fiott remained on the bench.[143]

Sun 26 Feb: to St Saviour's church in the morning. Dined at la Haye du Puis. Returned there after the sermon for the Young Ladies' Club.

Sun 5 Mar: to St Peter's church with Nico Guille & Josias [Le Marchant] in the morning. We returned here to dine with Messrs Vallat, Marret, Andros, Gosselin, Havilland, Nico Dobrée & Jean Carey.

Mon 13 Mar: dined at Mr George Le Fevre's amid good company.

Tues 21 Mar: I summoned the Douzeniers to a meeting at les Grands Moullins, but no one came.

Sat 25 Mar: to town. Lodged a complaint with the Court regarding Mr des Touillets the churchwarden.

Tues 28 Mar: went to approve the roadside boundaries of my cousin Pierre Le Cheminant's property.

Sat 1 Apr: to town. The Court has been made to resume its sittings by an Order in Council.

Mon 3 Apr: […] Yesterday night Nic. Rougier of the Forest stabbed Jean du Four (son of Nic.) at le Bourg & killed him.[144] This evening, I went to warn boat-owners in the parish not to give Rougier a passage out of the Island.

Weds 5 Apr: […] Nic. Rougier who killed Jean du Four on Sunday night was caught in St Martin.

---

[143] On this episode, see R. Hocart, *Peter de Havilland: Bailiff of Guernsey, A History of his Life, 1747–1821* (Guernsey, 1997), pp. 14–15.

[144] For more on this murder, see R.-M. Crossan, *Criminal Justice in Guernsey, 1680–1929* (Benderloch, 2021), p. 185.

Sat 8 Apr: to town. Dined at Mrs Carey's (*de la Brasserie*).[145]

Thurs 27 Apr: over the past 2 days, Charles [Nicolle] has been carting the 25 quarters of Sark barley needed for the parish.

Thurs 4 May: [...] The Douzaine examined & passed my accounts. We also set a tax for our needs & appointed Joseph Robert as our *messier*.[146]

Mon 8 May: [...] Pierre Gavet started here as a farm servant.[147]

Tues 9 May: accompanied the young ladies on an excursion to Plein Mont in the morning, after which we all breakfasted at Miss de la Mare's.[148]

Sat 13 May: to town. Had a number of Castel parishioners fined for keeping dogs in contravention of the Ordinance.

Fri 19 May: attended the Ladies' Club at Mr Godefroid's in the afternoon.

Sat 20 May: to town & to Court. We had [previously] initiated actions against 3 of the Douzeniers for missing the meeting of 27 March, as also against Mr Ozanne the churchwarden in order to overrule his opposition. Our causes did not however come on.

Weds 24 May: to town first thing, then Mr Jean Carey, his brother Tom & I went on foot to breakfast at Mrs Tourtel's.[149] After breakfast, we walked to Petit Beau, les Sommeilleuses & le Bourg. There the Procureur joined us, & we continued via St Andrew & St Saviour's church to la Grande Rue at St Saviour, where the 4 of us dined at Mrs Martel's in the company of Mr Marchant the Minister, Messrs Vallat, Nico Dobrée, Josué Gosselin & Pierre Havilland. In the evening, all of us except Mr Marchant & Tom Carey supped

---

[145] Mrs Carey was Caroline, *née* Guille, the widow of Jurat Laurent Carey. This branch of the Carey family were known as *de la Brasserie* on account of their ownership of a brewery (*brasserie*) in St Peter Port.
[146] *Messiers* were responsible for impounding stray animals.
[147] Pierre Gavet was twenty-three. Mollet maintained an association with Pierre until the latter's death in 1818. See Appendix 4.
[148] 'Miss de la Mare' was probably a daughter of Jurat Jean De La Mare of Les Padins in St Saviour (for whom, see 24.2.85).
[149] Mrs Tourtel ran a tavern in St Martin.

at Mr Vallat's. We left Mr Vallat at 10 o'clock, & I accompanied Mr Jean Carey & the Procureur as far as Bailiff's Cross.

Sat 27 May: to town. Dined at Mr Pierre de Havilland's. The Court ruled that Douzaine regulations should prevail in our cause against the Douzeniers. They also gave Mr Ozanne the churchwarden eight days to instruct an Advocate. Had 3 cartloads of sand.

Sun 28 May: [...] I repaid Daniel [Le Cheminant] the 200 *livres* he lent me on 13 August last.

Sat 3 Jun: dined at my sister's with Mr John Fergusson,[150] as also Mr & Mrs de Braham, Mr de Braham's nephew & Mr de Braham's brother-in-law.

Tues 6 Jun: Mr Fergusson & his party, Mr De Sausmarez, Mr Mourant & my sister came to dinner.

Weds 7 Jun: had an election for a Constable to replace Sr André Cohu. Mr des Touillets & all the Douzeniers voted for Sr Nic. le Beir. To town, where I went on board Mr Fergusson's vessel.

Sat 10 Jun: [...] Nico Guille was married the day before yesterday to Miss Carey Carey [*sic*].[151]

Thurs 15 Jun: light rain has fallen at intervals this past week. This is almost our first since 12 March.

Sat 17 Jun: to town. Dined at my sister's & spent the afternoon at the Greffier's. Sr Nic. Le Beir was sworn in as Constable to replace André Cohu, but the Court refused to let him call himself *Connétable d'Etat*, as he requested (a title which the Douzeniers who elected him had accorded him).[152]

---

[150] Lieutenant John McPherson Fergusson, RN (1731–1818), commander of HMS Cherokee. Fergusson later attained the rank of Admiral.
[151] Mollet's friend Nicolas Guille married Caroline Carey.
[152] *Connétable d'Etat* = States Constable. Such a move would presumably have given Le Beir a monopoly of the parish seat in the States, thereby excluding Mollet, who remained the other Constable.

Tues 20 Jun: rowed out to the roadstead to take my leave of Mr Fergusson & his party as they were about to set sail.

Thurs 22 Jun: [...] Mr Fergusson, who is in command of HMS Cherokee, left yesterday morning for Madeira, Carolina, &c.

Sat 1 Jul: to town. Nic. Rougier was sentenced to be hanged on 14 July for the murder of Jean du Four at le Bourg on 2 April.

Sat 8 Jul: to town. The Court lifted its ban on the export of cows (given that there will be scant fodder for livestock this coming winter).

Thurs 13 Jul: the summer cut of seaweed began this week. Mrs Carey *de la Brasserie* (Caroline Guille) died yesterday.[153]

Fri 14 Jul: Nicolas Rougier was hanged today on the beach below Hougue a la Perre (around the half-tide mark). Brought in the hay from the top of les Eturs.

Sat 15 Jul: to town. Started sea-bathing today. Cut the hay at the bottom of les Eturs.

Sun 30 Jul: [...] Repaid my cousin James [Le Cheminant] the 400 *livres* he lent me on 15 August 1773.

[*Charles Mollet turned thirty-three during the course of August 1775*]

Sun 6 Aug: to St Peter's church with the young ladies in the afternoon. After the service, we drank tea at Miss Andros's & took a turn around Torteval & the Forest.

Sat 26 Aug: [...] Tom Andros (son of James Andros) was sworn in as an Advocate.[154]

Thurs 31 Aug: tithe collection began today, but we have had strong winds & heavy rain.

---

[153] Mrs Caroline Carey *de la Brasserie* was about forty years old (see n. 145, above).
[154] This was Thomas Andros (1755–1831). He was to leave Guernsey in 1780 after killing a man in a duel.

Mon 11 Sep: today we had 20 men from the Castel parish quarrying stone for the fortifications at Vazon. Spent the afternoon at le Houmet.

Weds 13 Sep: had 12 Castel men & 6 carts working on the fortifications.

Thurs 28 Sep: the [tithe] farmers came here. We settled our accounts for the tithe collection & paid our instalments for the first quarter.

Sun 1 Oct: I sent for Doctor Sausmarez, having been unwell for a fortnight.

Tues 17 Oct: my Dear Mother returned from Jersey.

Weds 25 Oct: I have been in bed since 6 October. However, I have been almost pain-free since last Monday, when I began to be bathed.

Thurs 16 Nov: I went to town in Mr Nic. Dobrée's chaise. I have kept to my bed since 6 October, except for the last few days when I have been up for short spells.

Sun 26 Nov: left Guernsey with Pierre [Gavet] at 11 o'clock on board Captn Mourant.

Mon 27 Nov: Captn Mourant anchored about a league off Lymington, where I asked to be taken ashore. From there I took a post chaise to Southampton, where we arrived at half past seven.

Weds 29 Nov: I left at noon for Salisbury, where I arrived at 4 o'clock.

Thurs 30 Nov: left Salisbury in the morning. [...] Arrived at Bath in the evening & put up at Mrs Viel's on Abbey Green.[155]

Sat 2 Dec: wrote to my Dear Mother.

Tues 5 Dec: started to bathe. Did not go out.

Fri 8 Dec: began to drink the water at the Pump Room.

---

[155] Mrs Viel may have been the wife of the Guernsey-born cooper John Viel who opened a wine-shop in Bath in 1761 (T. Fawcett, *Bath Commercialis'd: Shops, Trades and Market at the 18th-Century Spa* (Bath, 2002), p. 128).

Tues 12 Dec: left for Bristol with the 2 Miss Clutterbucks. Put up at the Lamb in Broad Mead.

Weds 13 Dec: returned to Bath in the evening.

Weds 20 Dec: went for a walk in Prior Park.

Sat 23 Dec: bathed for the 8th time. Spent the afternoon at Mrs Chaldwhich's.

Mon 25 Dec: to the Moravian meeting with Mr Sleech in the morning.

Tues 26 Dec: […] to the theatre in the evening. Saw 'Edward & Eleonora' & 'Le Bon Ton'.

Thurs 28 Dec: left for Bristol. From there I went to Bedminster & to [Hot]wells, where I put up at the Ostrich on Durdam Down.

Fri 29 Dec: went to see Clifton & Cook's Folly. Dined at Bristol & then returned to Bath.

Sat 30 Dec: bathed for the 10th time.

Sun 31 Dec: went to the Quaker meeting in the morning & the Papist Chapel in the afternoon.

Notes relating to 1775

Mollet's notes for 1775 show that, in the course of the year, he gave work to seventeen individuals aside from his live-in servants. Of these, nine were tradesmen and eight day labourers. As in previous years, the bulk of labouring work went to just three men: Charles Nicolle (236 days), Thomas Le Page (120½), and Etienne Lihou (95½). Mollet also recorded piece-work done for him by Nicolas Le Tocq, Hellier Le Pelley and Henry Le Geyt (digging, weeding and threshing).

An inventory of Mollet's wine cellar taken on 20 May 1775, showed that it contained 185 bottles of wine, cider and 'shrub'. His wines included Port (48 bottles), French and Spanish red (31 bottles), Montagne (24 bottles), Madeira (9 bottles) and Frontignan (7 bottles).

1776

Mon 1 Jan: dined at Colonel Sabine's. Bathed for the 11th time.

Weds 3 Jan: Pierre [Gavet] was bathed. Mrs Viel, her sister & her son breakfasted with me.

Thurs 4 Jan: left Bath at 10 in the morning & arrived in Southampton at 8 in the evening.

Tues 9 Jan: Pierre & I arrived in Guernsey between 9 & 10 in the morning. I learned that my Aunt Françoise had died on 17 December & my Grandmother had died on 27 December.[156]

Sun 21 Jan: [...] Nicolas Brouard left our service. He started here as a farm servant on 15 June 1774.

Mon 22 Jan: it began snowing on the evening of the 13th & continued intermittently until Wednesday [17th]. There has been snow on the ground until today, when a thaw set in.

Mon 29 Jan: to town in the morning. My sister was delivered of a dead infant.

Fri 2 Feb: our measurements show that dug soil has lately been frozen to a depth of about 13 inches, & undug soil to a depth of about 9 inches.

Fri 16 Feb: Thos Lihou came to prune our pear trees. Messrs Vallat & Pradon came in the afternoon. Dunged the top of les Eturs & part of the bottom. Finished digging la Senciere for parsnips.

Mon 4 Mar: sowed larkspur & polyanthus by the upper gate.

Fri 8 Mar: my Uncle arrived from Jersey. Planted raspberries by the middle gate.

---

[156] Françoise was Mollet's mother's younger sister, born in 1711. The grandmother Mollet refers to was his mother's mother, Marie Le Vavasseur dit Durell, *née* Romeril, born in 1687.

Sun 10 Mar: embarked on board Captn Kerby (with Pierre), but the sailing was abandoned & I returned home in the evening. Hellier Marqui will sleep at my house during my absence.

Mon 11 Mar: left Guernsey at half past seven & arrived in Jersey at half past twelve.

Weds 13 Mar: dined at my Aunt's, where I am staying. At my request, Centenier Patriarche has barred my Uncle from taverns.

Tues 19 Mar: re-designed my Aunt's garden.

Weds 27 Mar: dined at the Vicomte's.[157] In the evening, we went to have ourselves electrified [*electrisé*] at Mr Jacques Poignant's.

Tues 2 Apr: left for Guernsey on board Tom Thacker at six in the morning with Pierre [Gavet] & Nancy Mourant.[158] Arrived at three in the afternoon.

Weds 10 Apr: […] Accompanied Mr Pierre Havilland to solicit votes from the Douzeniers of the Castel & St Saviour for his brother Martin in the election for Prévot. Mr Havilland dined here.

Sun 14 Apr: […] My Dear Mother left for Jersey with Tom Thacker at six in the morning.

Weds 24 Apr: spent the day at Lihou Island with Doctor Guille, Josias, the two Miss Marchants, Miss Guille, Miss Judith Ozanne & Miss de la Mare. We breakfasted at Miss de la Mare's & took tea there in the evening.

Weds 15 May: picked the first scarlet strawberries at le Marquet.

Fri 17 May: the mare gave birth to a colt. Transplanted cucumbers to the 2 trenches at le Marquet.

---

[157] This was Thomas Durell, who served as Jersey's Vicomte (a Court officer) between 1743 and 1785.
[158] Nancy was Charles Mollet's seven-year-old niece, whom he was presumably fetching back from a stay with her Jersey relatives.

Weds 22 May: Messrs Jean Carey, Josué Gosselin, Pierre Havilland & Tom Andros breakfasted here. The leases on le Ponchez fields were up for renewal this morning. I renewed my lease on le Courtil Robin for another 6 years at 56 *livres* per year. To town in the evening.

Mon 27 May: Whitsun. I did not go out & had no visitors.

Sat 1 Jun: to town. Dined at my sister's. An Order in Council was read out to the Court discharging the Magistrates Guille, de la Mare, Andros, Thos Dobrée, Nic Dobrée, de Beauvoir, Reserson, de Jersey, Tupper & Carey as per their request, & ordering the election of ten others to replace them.[159]

Sun 9 Jun: to church in the morning. Mr St Dalmas preached.[160] Dined at la Haye du Puis with the family, Messrs Andros, de Havilland & Bonamy.

Sat 15 Jun: [...] We had 250 mackerel for salting. The ten Jurats who were discharged a fortnight ago were re-elected by a large majority. I did not attend the election.

Mon 24 Jun: to l'Ancresse to see the 3 Regiments. An English gunner was killed.

Weds 26 Jun: accompanied the Douzaine to approve the roadside boundaries of Sr Jean de Jersey's land at les Pins. Messrs Nico Dobrée, Jean Carey, Ch. Andros, Pierre Havilland, Tom Andros, Josias Le Marchant & Mr Commissary Pipon took tea & supped with me. Mr Pipon stayed overnight.

Tues 2 Jul: dined in good company at la Mare de Carteret. Mr Guillaume Patriarche was there.

---

[159] On this episode, see R. Hocart, *Peter de Havilland: Bailiff of Guernsey, A History of his Life, 1747–1821* (Guernsey, 1997), pp. 18–19.
[160] François Emeric de Saint-Dalmas (1724–1803) was a former Roman Catholic priest from Piedmont who converted to Anglicanism and served as curate of St Peter Port between 1774 and 1789 and Rector of St Peter between 1789 and 1803.

Thurs 4 Jul: had a quarter-cask of French red wine from Mr Reserson. Cut about half the clover at le Brulin. Received the news that Mrs Fergusson died 8 days ago.[161]

Thurs 11 Jul: dined at Jean Carey's (the Magistrate). There were 17 of us. In the evening we went to the Castle.[162]

Sat 13 Jul: to town in the morning. Mr Mourant & my sister left for England yesterday.

Weds 17 Jul: Billy Chepmell arrived from Faro yesterday evening & came here in the morning.

Mon 22 Jul: to town in the morning. Billy Chepmell left for Jersey.

Sat 27 Jul: to town in the morning. The Bailiff had an Order in Council read out to the Court confirming the election of the ten Magistrates.

Sun 28 Jul: to St Peter's church with Miss Judith Ozanne in the afternoon.

[*Charles Mollet turned thirty-four during the course of August 1776*]

Sat 3 Aug: to town. Messrs Guille, de la Mare, Andros, Reserson, de Jersey & Tupper were re-sworn as Magistrates. Messrs Thos & Nico Dobrée, De Beauvoir & Carey refused to take the oath.

Tues 6 Aug: Miss Allez, Miss Andros, Mrs & Miss Isaacs & I went to Petit Beau & took tea at le Bourg.

Tues 27 Aug: bought a heifer from Jersey for 25 *écus*. Had two sacks of wet wheat from on board a vessel.

Mon 9 Sep: […] I dismissed Rachel Ingrouille.

---

[161] 'Mrs Fergusson' was Anne, *née* Lerrier, the sister of Mollet's brother-in-law Philippe Lerrier and the mother of Mollet's friend William Chepmell.
[162] Castle Cornet, where the British garrison was headquartered. The Castle was situated on an islet about half a mile off St Peter Port.

Tues 10 Sep: Pierre (Gavet) left us this morning. He had been here 16 months. Bought a 5-year-old grey horse from Matth. Tostevin for 8½ guineas & a pig from Ab. Collenette for 10 *livres*.

Weds 11 Sep: tithe collection began today. We had 2 cartloads of tithe.

Thurs 12 Sep: Pierre Gavet came back this morning. Had 2 cartloads of tithe.

Mon 16 Sep: Sr Jean Blondel from le Moullin du Milieu was found drowned in le Braye du Valle.

Weds 18 Sep: attended Sr Jean Blondel's funeral. Had a cartload of tithe. Doctor Sausmarez went to see Patty Mourant.[163]

Thurs 19 Sep: had a Douzaine meeting to raise a tax for the Hospital. Collected the rest of the tithe.

Tues 8 Oct: the Douzaine went to determine James Moullin's *vingtième*.[164] Afterwards, I accompanied them to les Moullins to examine Sr Nic. Le Beir's accounts. To town in the afternoon.

Thurs 17 Oct: [...] There was a Constable's election, which I did not attend. Sr Danl Moullin was chosen to replace Sr Nic. le Beir.

Thurs 24 Oct: to town in the morning. Mr Mourant & my sister returned yesterday from England, where they spent about 3 months. Patty has been ill for 6 weeks.

Tues 12 Nov: my sister & Patty left for Jersey.

Thurs 21 Nov: pressed the 4th layer. Started feeding parsnips to the two oxen. They have been eating turnips for about 2 months.

Mon 16 Dec: sent some pigeons & rabbits to my Dear Mother.

---

[163] Patty (Martha) was Mollet's eleven-year-old niece, whose parents were away in England.
[164] Male heirs to estates outside St Peter Port were entitled to take one-twentieth (*le vingtième*) of the estate in a single location before the rest was divided among the other heirs. The Douzaine was responsible for determining where this twentieth should lie.

Weds 25 Dec: dined at la Haye du Puis with Mr Andros & his family, Mr & Mrs Havilland & Mr Bonamy.

Tues 31 Dec: awoke to a frost. Snow on & off throughout the day. Planted kale in the new garden.

Notes relating to 1776

Mollet gave work to twenty-six individuals in 1776 (aside from his live-in servants). Some fifteen were tradesmen of various kinds, and the rest were day labourers. One of the day workers – Marie Batiste – was a woman, although Mollet did not note what work she performed. Most day labour around the farm was performed by just three men: Thomas Le Page (156 days), Etienne Lihou (131 days) and Hellier Marquis (75 days). Charles Nicolle, who had been Mollet's most regular labourer in previous years, worked only 22½ days for him in 1776.

1777

Weds 1 Jan: more snow.

Sat 11 Jan: the snow has all melted.

Sat 18 Jan: to town. I took Jean Blondel to Court on suspicion of having stolen 12½ guineas from Ch. Toraude. The Court released him after examining him. At the request of the Town Constables, we had a meeting with the other Constables on the subject of the disagreement between the Bailiff & the acting Prévôt.[165] Pressed the 9th layer.

Sat 25 Jan: [...] Today the Constables went to see the Bailiff about the affair between him & the Prévôt, but I did not go with them. He gave them very short shrift.

Mon 3 Feb: [...] In the evening, I went to see Mr Herman Boas, the famous conjuror.[166] He is very skilled at his profession.

Weds 12 Feb: my cousin Pierre died last night.[167]

Thurs 20 Feb: snow & strong wind until noon, then rain for the rest of the day. I had invited Messrs Vallat, Godefroid, Pradon, Martinault & Ch. Le Marchant to dinner, but none of them came.

Fri 21 Mar: [...] Charles le Cras put up the weather vane.

Sun 23 Mar: [...] My Dear Mother returned from Jersey last night. She had been there since 14 April last. To church in the afternoon.

---

[165] See R. Hocart, *Peter de Havilland: Bailiff of Guernsey, A History of his Life, 1747–1821* (Guernsey, 1997), p. 20.
[166] Herman Boaz (c.1736–1820), otherwise known as 'the Wizard of the North', was an Englishman named James (or Thomas) Bowes.
[167] Pierre Le Cheminant, born in 1718.

Sat 29 Mar: to town in the morning. The Order in Council ordering the election of four Magistrates to replace Messrs Thos & Nic. Dobrée, Richard de Beauvoir, & Jean Carey (son of Thos) was read out to the Court.

Thurs 3 Apr: inspected the roads. My sister called here briefly.

Mon 7 Apr: to town in the morning. Visited Mr Andros in the afternoon while my Dear Mother was at la Houguette. Bought a cow from old Jean Batiste for 26 *écus*.

Thurs 10 Apr: Mr Jean Carey came to dinner. We had a Douzaine meeting at les Moullins to discuss a *Billet d'Etat* regarding the election of 4 Magistrates next Wednesday.

Weds 16 Apr: an election was held for the 4 Magistrates. Mr Jean Carey will replace Mr Thos Dobrée; Mr Thos Dobrée of la Piette will replace Mr Richard de Beauvoir; Mr James Hubert will replace Mr Nic. Dobrée; & Mr Falla of la Maison Beaugy will replace Mr Jean Carey (son of Thos).

Sun 20 Apr: […] Billy Chepmell arrived from England yesterday & came here today.

Sun 4 May: I did not go out. My Dear Mother left to spend the week in town.

Sun 11 May: Billy Chepmell, Mr Bob Marchant & Mr Ph. Seward came to dinner.[168]

Tues 13 May: finished sowing barley at le Courtil Robin. There are 11 strips in all. We mixed the barley with clover seed in the six southern strips, with turnip seed in the 7th & 8th, with cabbage seed in the 9th, with kale seed in the 10th, & with turnip seed in the 11th.

Sat 24 May: to town & to Court. Our actions against Sr Pierre Martel, Sr Pierre Le Sauvage, Sr Massy de la Rue & Sr Henry Breton for [illegal] peat-digging commenced.

---

[168] Philip Seward, of Jersey origin, was a merchant in Southampton who acted as a forwarding agent for Channel Islanders.

Sat 31 May: to town & to Court. Sr Pierre Martel & the others were sentenced to pay costs for not obeying Sr Le Beir when he ordered them (as Constable) to stop digging peat.

Thurs 19 Jun: Mr Moullin & I expelled Wm Nicolle from his brother Thomas's house (at Thos Nicolle's request). Weeded the potatoes at la Senciere.

Tues 24 Jun: to l'Ancresse to watch the three Regiments. ……… Le Tissier, the brother of Jean Le Tissier the ropemaker, was seriously wounded.

Fri 27 Jun: attended the Club at les Touillets.

Fri 4 Jul: […] My Dear Mother has gone to town for a week.

Sat 5 Jul: to town in the morning. Wind & rain these past few days. Went to inspect the public houses at about eleven in the evening & found a great many people at Hellier Carré's, where they were having a party. I made them leave. I also found many people at Charles Batiste's.

Weds 9 Jul: to town in the morning. Billy Chepmell returned from England in Mr Marrett's vessel. Yesterday I was seized with a pain in my foot which we think might be gout.

Weds 23 Jul: to la Haye du Puis in the afternoon. Planted about 500 leeks by the upper gate. I have been indisposed for a fortnight.

Sun 27 Jul: to church in the afternoon. My sister, her family & Mr Chepmell came to dinner.

[*Charles Mollet turned thirty-five during the course of August 1777*]

Weds 13 Aug: collected the muskets for the Castel companies from Danl le Cheminant's, where they had been left.

Thurs 21 Aug: Ph. Lerrier, who arrived from Jersey with Billy Chepmell yesterday, breakfasted here.

Tues 2 Sep: the Procureur, the Comptroller (Tom Sausmarez),[169] Doctor Guille & Messrs Char. Dobrée, Josias le Marchant, John Sausmarez & Billy Chepmell came to dinner. Ph. Lerrier left for Jersey this morning.

Mon 8 Sep: Mr Chepmell & I dined at the Bailiff's, in company (among others) with a French gentleman by the name of Monsieur le Comte de St Etienne. Later, we supped at la Mare de Carteret, where we stayed very late amid good company.

Sun 14 Sep: to church in the morning. Danl Moullin & I went to inspect the public houses. Afterwards I went to la Haye du Puis, where I had been invited to dine with the family. We notified parishioners that the tithe collection will begin tomorrow.

Mon 15 Sep: had a cartload of tithe.

Fri 19 Sep: had one more cartload of tithe, which was all that remained to be collected.

Weds 1 Oct: at the request of Thomas Nicolle, Mr Moullin & I had the remainder of his brother William Nicolle's furniture removed from Thomas's house. Mr Moullin dined with me. Heavy rain.

Mon 6 Oct: to Chief Pleas. *Rentes* were set at 10 *livres*, hens at 30 *sous* & capons at 45 *sous*. Bundled the bracken.

Fri 10 Oct: [...] On Wednesday evening, the eldest son of Nic. Machon of Vauvers broke his arm at le Moulin du Roi & had to have it amputated. Yesterday afternoon Mr James Hocar's house was completely burnt down. His farm servant & his house servant perished in the flames.

Sun 26 Oct: [...] In the morning, Mr Moullin & I went to taste the cider at several public houses.

Mon 3 Nov: [...] Thomas Guilbert started here as a farm servant.

---

[169] HM Comptroller was a Law Officer with duties similar to those of HM Procureur, though lower in status. Thomas De Sausmarez (1756–1837) who had become Comptroller in June 1777, was to remain a frequent visitor to Mollet's for the rest of his life. For more on De Sausmarez and his family, see Appendix 3.

Sat 8 Nov: to town & to Court. I had actioned Mr [Thomas] Falla to oblige him to hand over the parish papers, but my cause did not come on.

Sat 15 Nov: […] The Court appointed commissioners to arbitrate in the cause between Mr Falla & myself.

Fri 5 Dec: to town in the morning. Winnowed. My Dear Mother is spending a week in town.

Mon 22 Dec: I conducted a search […] for the suet & beef which was stolen in town last Saturday.

Thurs 25 Dec: dined at la Haye du Puis with the Le Marchant family, Mr Andros, Mr & Mrs Havilland, Mr & Mrs Martinault, Mr Bonamy & the two Miss Ozannes. My Dear Mother dined at la Houguette.

Fri 26 Dec: […] I dismissed Thos Guilbert yesterday. He was here nearly two months.

Weds 31 Dec: snow fell all day. Some of the snow has melted, but the ground remains covered.

Notes relating to 1777

In 1777, Charles Mollet recorded giving work to seventeen individuals aside from his live-in employees. Seven of these were tradesmen, and the rest day labourers. The bulk of day labour was performed by Etienne Lihou (162½ days), Thomas Le Page (142 days) and Paul Ingrouille (100 days), but others such as Pierre Rabey and Jean Cateline put in more than 50 days each. Mollet also employed four men on piece-work.

1778

Thurs 1 Jan: the thaw continued all day, but there is still some snow on the ground.

Mon 19 Jan: to town & to Chief Pleas. The Castel Douzaine petitioned the Court for an Ordinance to prohibit the Constables of this parish from serving more than one year.

Mon 26 Jan: [...] Mr Mourant has agreed to let me have a 64th share in the four privateers he has an interest in: the Vulture (commander Captn Cabot, *armateurs* Messrs Danl Tupper & ....); the Hunter (commander Captn Tuck, *armateurs* Messrs Richard Guille & Jean Wood); the Swift (commander Captn Hellier Gosselin, *armateur* Mr Mourant); & the Hero (commander Captn Scott, *armateurs* Messrs Carteret & Lihou).

Tues 27 Jan: I put my remaining hats on board Captn Marrett to be sold in either Madeira or America.

Weds 28 Jan: [...] Mr Mourant is to let me have a 64th share in another privateer commanded by Captn Nicolas Mallet of Jersey.

Fri 27 Feb: [...] Bad weather in the afternoon – high winds with wet snow.

Fri 6 Mar: to town in the morning for my arbitration with Mr Falla. He claimed not to have any of the papers I wished to see.

Sat 14 Mar: to town & to Court. [...] I had had Mr Falla summonsed to hear the Court's judgment on the Commissioners' report, but he did not appear.

Sat 21 Mar: to town & to Court. I had a tooth drawn. My cause did not come on.

Thurs 2 Apr: on the orders of the Governor, Mr Moullin & I went to warn all boat-owners that they are forbidden to transport any foreigners out of the Island.[170]

Weds 8 Apr: [...] Fetched the muskets for returning to the 3 Castel companies in the evening.

Mon 13 Apr: Mr Moullin & I went to the Castle to fetch 3 casks of powder for the parish.

Sun 19 Apr: to church in the morning. Communion today. To town in the afternoon. Captn Scott has captured a prize loaded with 100 barrels of tobacco which is believed to be worth about £5000 stg.

Mon 4 May: [...] Captn Scott's prize has been brought in. She is carrying 160 barrels of tobacco.

Tues 5 May: [...] Captn Cabot has taken a prize – a French vessel carrying goods to America.

Fri 8 May: [...] Captn Tuck has brought in a prize, & a prize has also been brought in by a Jersey privateer.

Sat 9 May: [...] I have taken a 32nd share in a privateer of which Mr Mourant & Captn Kennet are the *armateurs*. This is the Tartar, which Captn Wm Le Mesurier will command. I also took a 16th share in another privateer of which Messrs Nico Dobrée & Waugh are the *armateurs*. I will cede one 64th to Mr Josias le Marchant & half of the rest to Mr Andros.

Sun 10 May: I lent my cousin James [Le Cheminant] 400 *livres*.

Weds 13 May: to town in the morning. To Mr de St George's funeral in the afternoon.[171]

---

[170] Britain was now at war with France, the latter having entered the War of American Independence on 17 March.
[171] Jean Guille, sen., Seigneur of St George, was sixty-six years old.

Thurs 14 May: the Douzaine met at Richard Moullin's this morning to inspect my accounts. They examined them, but refused to approve them. To town in the evening.

Sat 16 May: I had had Mr Falla summonsed to hear the Court's judgment on the Commissioners' report, but my cause did not come on.

Sat 23 May: to town & to Court. Mr Falla requested a postponement & a copy of the report.

Mon 1 Jun: [...] Yesterday a regiment of Highlanders arrived, of which My Lord Macleod is the colonel.[172] Half the regiment will stay here, & the other half will go to Jersey.

Weds 3 Jun: there was an election for a Magistrate today. Mr Jean Guille was elected to replace his father by a large majority.[173] The election was followed by a States meeting. At the request of the other Constables, Mr de Sausmarez & I purchased a quantity of iron pots, &c., as the country parishes' contribution towards the troops' supplies.

Thurs 18 Jun: weeded. Pierre [Gavet] took the cart to work on the fortifications at l'Ancresse.

Sat 20 Jun: to town. The Court sent Mr Falla & myself back to our Commissioners in order to draw up an inventory of papers in Mr Falla's possession. To Mr Vallat's in the afternoon.

Thurs 9 Jul: my Dear Mother returned from town, where she has spent nearly 9 weeks.

Fri 10 Jul: [...] My sister was delivered of a dead infant.[174]

Mon 20 Jul: we had our first rain after a long & severe drought which began on 13 May.

---

[172] This was the 73rd Regiment of Foot, raised in 1777 by Major-General John Mackenzie, Lord MacLeod.
[173] Jean Guille, jun. (1734–1820) was also the new Seigneur of St George.
[174] Mollet's sister Marthe Mourant was thirty-eight. She had four children living. This was her fifth and last stillbirth (as documented by Mollet).

[*Charles Mollet turned thirty-six during the course of August 1778*]

Sun 16 Aug: […] Received the news that the Tartar has taken le Grand Terrien.

Tues 1 Sep: tithe collection began today. Had 2 cartloads of tithe.

Sat 5 Sep: to town in the morning. Had a cartload of tithe. There is very little left to collect.

Mon 21 Sep: at my sister's in town all day. Attended a sale of goods from the Princess of Orange, a prize captured by Captn Gosselin (his first).

Mon 28 Sep: Rachel Le Beir started here as a house servant. Olimpe [Girard] declared she was leaving in the morning, but she returned here in the evening. To town afternoon & evening.

Sun 4 Oct: to church in the morning. Josias le Marchant dined with me. After dinner, we rode to Plein Mont, then through the Forest to Fermains, where we took tea.

Mon 5 Oct: […] The Court ordered that Constables who have been in office for more than a year should resign [and call an election].[175] Dined at Captn Solbé's with the Commissioners for the examination of prisoners. Bought two shares from Jonathan Emerson, a sailor on board the Tartar, Captn le Messurier.

Weds 7 Oct: at my sister's in town all day. There was a sale of water-damaged goods from the Cadette, a prize taken by Captn Gosselin which arrived here on Saturday.

Mon 12 Oct: in town all day at the Cadette sale. Dined at my sister's. Borrowed 400 *livres* from Danl le Cheminant.

---

[175] Mollet seems to have been under a misapprehension. The Ordinance of 5 October 1778 prescribed three years as the maximum term which a Constable could serve without calling an election.

Fri 16 Oct: to town. Dined at my sister's. Attended a sale of merchandise from a prize of Captn Scott's, where I bought about £20 stg worth of velvet & velveret.

Sun 18 Oct: to church in the morning. My Dear Mother returned from town, where she has spent the past month. She & I dined at la Haye du Puis with Mr Andros & his family, Mr Bonamy, Mr & Mrs James de Havilland, & Miss Judith Ozanne. Rachel le Beir has left our service. She was here 3 weeks.

Sun 25 Oct: to town in the morning & to church in the afternoon. A Danish vessel has run aground at Vazon. It was demasted several days ago but is not otherwise damaged.

Tues 10 Nov: to town in the afternoon. Captn Gosselin's prize, les Quatre Dames, keeled over in the harbour last night. In the morning, Mr Moullin & I went to le Houmet to warn 17 quarrymen that they were not to continue quarrying rock from below the half-tide mark on the beach.

Sat 14 Nov: to town in the morning. Actioned Mr King for not having provided a cart for l'Ancresse.

Thurs 19 Nov: [...] The soldiers of My Lord Macleod's Regiment have embarked in preparation for departure, & those of My Lord Seaforth's Regiment have come ashore to replace them.[176]

Sat 28 Nov: [...] We won our cause against Mr King. The Court decided that he would in the future be obliged to provide a cart. However, they refused to record their decision in the form of an act.

Sun 6 Dec: to church in the morning. Inspected the public houses.

Sun 13 Dec: I did not go out. My Dear Mother returned from town, where she has spent the last month.

---

[176] The latter was a regiment raised by Lieutenant-General Francis Humberston Mackenzie, 1st Baron Seaforth. It became the 78th Regiment of Foot (Ross-shire Buffs) in 1793.

Fri 25 Dec: my Dear Mother & I dined at la Haye du Puis with Mr Andros & his family, Mr & Mrs Martinault, Miss Judith Ozanne & Mr Samuel Bonamy.

Sat 26 Dec: [...] Inspected the public houses in the evening. Broke up a party at Thos Cohu's.

Thurs 31 Dec: removed the dung from under the livestock & started making a dungheap at les Eturs. To town in the morning. Strong winds in the afternoon.

Notes relating to 1778

In 1778, Charles Mollet gave work to twenty-four individuals aside from his live-in employees. One of them, Marthe Robert, was a woman. She worked two days for Mollet in June, but the work she performed is not noted. About half of the male workers were day labourers, and the rest tradesmen. Etienne Lihou was Charles Mollet's most regular day labourer in 1778 (155 days). William Nicolle was the next most regular (91 days), followed by Charles Nicolle (61 days). Five or six other labourers worked around 20 days each, usually at peak periods in the agricultural year. One or two men dug and/or weeded for piece-rates.

1779

Fri 1 Jan: my Dear Mother & I dined at Mr Andros's with the Andros family, Mr Godefroid, the young people from la Haye du Puis, Miss Judith Ozanne, & Mr James Andros.

Sat 2 Jan: [...] In the evening I inspected the public houses which were holding parties.

Thurs 7 Jan: [...] My sister came to dinner with Patty & Peter. Polly & Nancy have been staying here these past few weeks.[177]

Sun 10 Jan: [...] Billy Chepmell came to dinner. He was engaged to Miss Coutart last week.[178]

Weds 13 Jan: at the request of Thos Nicolle, Mr Moullin & I went to expel his brother William from his house. William however refused to leave & threatened to break the arms of the first person who dared touch his furniture. Seeing William seize his brother by the collar & threaten to strike him, we arrested William & took him to the guardhouse. There was a Constable's election (which I did not attend) to replace Mr Moullin. Mr Josias le Marchant was elected.

Fri 15 Jan: Produced Wm Nicolle in Court. He was discharged on his promise to behave better.

Weds 20 Jan: [...] the le Pelley brothers (Jean, Nicolas & Thomas) spent the evening with me.[179]

Sat 20 Feb: [...] An English boy was sentenced to 36 lashes for stealing from the harbour.

---

[177] Mollet's nephew Peter Mourant was aged eight at this time. His nieces Patty, Polly (Mary) and Nancy were thirteen, eleven and nine respectively.
[178] William Chepmell's fiancée was Elizabeth Effart Coutart (1761–1806), the daughter of Captain William Coutart, who was a brother of Advocate Pierre Coutart.
[179] For the Le Pelley brothers, see n. 134, above.

Mon 1 Mar: to town. Dined at my sister's. I engaged Pierre Capdion (a French prisoner-of-war) to work here, on payment of a £20 stg security to Mr Nico Dobrée.[180]

Weds 7 Apr: to town in the morning. I engaged the French prisoner Jean Level to work here on payment of a £20 stg security.

Sat 1 May: [...] went to Gerbourg, where I saw a French fleet of 53 vessels.

Sun 2 May: [...] In the evening, I went to town on hearing that the French fleet which I saw on Saturday had staged a sham attack on Jersey that very day. I was on the road until midnight, having been to la Houguette & to Mr Andros's, & having also accompanied Jean du Maresq on watch-duty.

Mon 3 May: Danl Moullin came here at three in the morning to tell us there was an alarm. Beacons were lit & bells were rung in almost all the parishes. I went to various places before breakfast, & even as far as Plein Mont, but it seems it was a false alarm, since there was no fleet to be seen. Later in the day, I went to town & to several other places. In returning from the Vale between two & three in the afternoon, I caught sight of a fleet to the north of us, in which I counted more than 60 vessels. The Governor gave the alarm signal at about four, & we remained under arms until seven, when it was confirmed that the fleet was an English one. This fleet, under Admiral Arbuthnot, had been on its way to New York when it received the message that the Islands were in danger, & came to our aid on the Admiral's own initiative (for which I hope he will receive the thanks which he deserves).[181] Our people showed themselves brave & alert. Some men from the local companies went as far as le Braie du Valle. I returned here after eight in the evening feeling somewhat tired. I was almost constantly in the saddle from three in the morning & changed horses several times. I think I must have ridden about 100 miles.

Tues 4 May: Josias [Le Marchant] & I went to give orders about the horses in the morning, & in the afternoon we rode to Plein Mont & Fermains. Eleven

---

[180] Mollet's friend Nicolas Dobrée (for whom see n. 38, above) was the British government agent responsible for prisoners-of-war held in Guernsey during the American War of Independence.

[181] The Admiral alluded to was Vice-Admiral Mariot Arbuthnot (1711–94), who was on his way to take up an appointment as commander-in-chief of the North American station.

English warships passed close to the Island in pursuit of Saturday's French fleet, which, people say, was on a mission to attack one or other of our Islands with a force of 1500 troops under the ~~Comte de St Luce~~ Prince of Nassau.

Weds 5 May: met the other Constables in town in the morning & bought 400 blankets from the Governor of Alderney & 400 planks from Mr Pierre de Carteret for the use of the soldiers who are camping out. The Governor ordered an embargo, of which we notified the Castel boat-owners.[182] We had all oars taken to Pierre le Cheminant's & to la Haye du Puis, & posted sentinels to guard them, as also to guard the boats belonging to the parish. The English fleet gave up their pursuit yesterday on account of the weather. There are at present 12 warships & frigates in the roads.

Sat 8 May: [...] The Governor lifted the embargo at noon. The frigates left for Jersey yesterday.

Weds 26 May: Attended Mr Pierre Hocart's funeral. His wife, the daughter of Master Jean Naftel the thatcher, gave birth to a son two days ago, & his brother James (whose house burned down on 9 October 1777) died recently in the Indies. The 83rd (Glasgow) Regiment arrived yesterday. Its soldiers will be distributed between the two Islands. The 5 companies of Seaforths will camp out at the Vale.

Thurs 10 Jun: Etienne Breton's house burned down.

Mon 14 Jun: had a Douzaine meeting at Danl le Cheminant's to raise a tax. We agreed that each of us would contribute 2 *sous* for every quarter of our taxable property to rebuild Etienne Breton's house.

Mon 28 Jun: to town in the morning. The Governor wishes to widen the roads from town to Vazon to allow cannon to pass.

Mon 5 Jul: [...] dined at Grayman's to mark the commissioning of the Resolution, Captn Gosselin.

Sat 17 Jul: to town in the morning. I went sea-bathing in the evening.

---

[182] An embargo was an official prohibition against going out to sea.

Weds 28 Jul: gave evidence to the Procureur against Charles Nicolle for having assisted six Frenchmen who came ashore at Albecq on Monday morning & allowed them to depart again.

Thurs 29 Jul: to town. Dined at my sister's. Mr Mourant has secured for me a 64th share in the privateer Arbuthnot, commanded by Denis le Pelley.

[*Charles Mollet turned thirty-seven during the course of August 1779*]

Sat 21 Aug: to town twice. The prisoners Capdion (here since 1 March) & Level (here since 7 April) have both left, the Governor having ordered all French prisoners to be sent to England.

Weds 25 Aug: [...] Tithe collection has begun. I collected tithe in the morning,

Sat 28 Aug: My sister, Patty & Mr Mourant had departed the island for England yesterday, but their vessel was obliged to return [temporarily] to port.

Fri 3 Sep: Mr Bob Marchant & I spent last night at Plein Mont, where we were on watch-duty for 24 hours, 16 of us gentlemen having agreed to do duty in pairs for 24 hours each. We were the last pair, the watch having begun 8 days ago. We had a tent, &c., & spent the time most agreeably.

Mon 6 Sep: had a further small amount of tithe from Sr Nic le Prevot, which makes a total of 11 cartloads from les Hougues. To town after dinner.

Sat 11 Sep: to town, where I dined with my Dear Mother. She is staying at my sister's house while they are absent from the Island.

Weds 15 Sep: [...] An express arrived informing us of the capture of two French West Indiamen by the Resolution, Captn Gosselin, who has taken them to Ireland.

Weds 22 Sep: to town in the morning. A fleet of warships has arrived. There are four ships mounting 74 cannon, & twelve ships with fewer cannon. Mr Elizée le Marchant of la Haye du Puis died last night at the age of 93 years & 4 months.

Tues 19 Oct: I have let les Monts de Vaux to Thos Lihou, father & son, for 10 years.

Sat 23 Oct: to town. Mr Mourant & my sister returned this morning from England.

Tues 26 Oct: [...] My Dear Mother returned here after spending about two months in town.

Thurs 4 Nov: to town in the morning. We were to have had a meeting of all the Constables to set a tax on innkeepers (for the cost of quartering the soldiers), but it was postponed until next Thursday.

Thurs 11 Nov: slept at my sister's last night, & spent the day there today. Had a Constables' meeting at the Court to set a tax on innkeepers. They will be taxed at the rate of 10 *sous* per week from 1 July.

Tues 16 Nov: [...] Yesterday the Marquise de Marbeuf, one of Captn Gosselin's prizes, ran aground at Fermains with 8 feet of water in her hold. Last night the Valentine, an English ship of 1100 tons belonging to the East India Company, sank near l'Isle des Marchands [Brecqhou] off Sark, where she had lain at anchor since yesterday, having lost her mast.

Sat 11 Dec: to town. A military sergeant came yesterday to report the theft of a pair of sheets. I made enquiries but could find no evidence to identify the culprit.

Tues 14 Dec: to town. Elizabeth le Geyt started here as a house servant.

Weds 15 Dec: rain all day. Olimpe [Girard] left us.

Sat 18 Dec: [...] Bought two shares in the Kite from Thos le Rai. Dined at my sister's.

Sat 25 Dec: dined alone with Pierre & Elizabeth [the live-in servants]. Denis Le Pelley spent the afternoon here & supped with me.

Weds 29 Dec: dined at Grayman's to mark the commissioning of the Rambler (formerly the Favourite), Captn Pyrvault. Spent the evening at Danl Moullin's with Jean le Pelley & Jean du Maresq.

Fri 31 Dec: to town, where I dined. Passed contracts with Mr Pierre de Havilland for the warehouses & garden at the top of la Profonde Rue, which I am buying for 22 quarters.

Notes relating to 1779

Charles Mollet gave work to only eleven individuals aside from his live-in servants in 1779. This was mainly because he had two French prisoners-of-war living and working at the farm for part of the year. Eight of Mollet's non-resident workers were day labourers, and just three were tradesmen (Mollet had had a significant amount of work done on his premises the previous year, and only sought basic services from tradesmen this year). Mollet's most regular labourers in 1779 were Etienne Lihou (154 days), William Nicolle (90½ days) and Guillaume Lihou (62 days). A handful of other labourers performed particular tasks for piece-rates.

1780

Sat 1 Jan: one of our hens was today sitting on a clutch of eggs in the cartshed. Another has been sitting on a clutch on the cowshed roof this past week.

Mon 3 Jan: dined at Doctor [Jean] Sausmarez's. Attended Billy Chepmell's wedding in the evening.

Thurs 6 Jan: Wm Ogilby & .... Henderson, two soldiers from Major Ramsay's company in the Glasgow Regiment, began working here.

Thurs 20 Jan: to town. Had a meeting of all the Constables to settle our expenses for quartering soldiers for the three months ending 1 January. More heavy rain.

Thurs 27 Jan: Pierre [Gavet] (& Ogilby on my Dear Mother's behalf) went to work on the bulwarks at Petit Beau.

Weds 9 Feb: […] Elizabeth Le Geyt left our service. She was here for about two months. My Dear Mother returned from town, where she had been staying since 19 December.

Mon 21 Feb: […] Supped at St George with the officers, Mr Josias le Marchant, his wife & his sister-in-law.[183]

Thurs 24 Feb: Pierre [Gavet] took the cart to work on the breastworks at Vazon.

Fri 3 Mar: I boarded David le Dain's vessel at seven in the morning & arrived in Jersey at two.

Sat 4 Mar: I am staying at my sister's. Paid several morning visits.

---

[183] Josias Le Marchant of la Haye du Puits had married Judith Ozanne (1756–1835) of la Houguette on 5 January 1780. Judith's older sister, Marie Ozanne (1753–1834), remained unmarried at this time, and was the sister-in-law Mollet referred to. See nn. 5, 96, 101, above.

Mon 13 Mar: tried to sell the house at auction, but without success.[184] Supped at Doctor Fergusson's.

Fri 24 Mar: boarded Jean Le Serson's vessel at seven & arrived in Guernsey at half past eleven.

Tues 18 Apr: Judith du Port started here as a house servant yesterday.

Mon 1 May: Mr Naftel, &c., came to install the Blowing Stove in the parlour.

Sun 14 May: my Dear Mother went to stay in town. Nico le Pelley dined with me. Heavy rain.

Weds 17 May: Elizabeth de Garis started here as a house servant. Weeded the onions at le Marquet.

Sat 3 Jun: to town & to Court. I engaged Edward Floyd (a Welshman) to work here as a farm servant.

Mon 5 Jun: [...] I gave 43 shillings & 6d to Captn Patourel to pay Mr Tarrant of Southampton for a saddle, &c. Weeded the turning.

Fri 9 Jun: [...] Mr Mourant, my sister & Polly left for England. I engaged Robert Ingilby, a Welshman, to work here as a farm servant. Jean Cateline spent the day cutting hay at les Eturs.

Sat 10 Jun: Colonel White's Regiment arrived here today (the 96th).[185] All the 96th are staying in Guernsey, along with half of the 78th (Lord Seaforth's) & half of the 83rd (Glasgow Regiment). This makes a total of between 1700 & 1800 men, not counting ...... companies of Invalids.

Sun 11 Jun: [...] Richard Moullin came to report that a number of militiamen from St Martin were threatening to assault their officers. Mr Ozanne & I went to investigate.[186] We had two men taken to the guardhouse: Sr Jaques Guille (for disrespect & disobedience to the Constables) & James Robert of

---

[184] This was presumably Mollet's uncle's house. See 2.7.71.
[185] This regiment (otherwise known as the British Musketeers) had only been raised in April 1780. It was commanded by General Richard Whyte.
[186] By this point Mollet's fellow Constable was Richard Ozanne of les Mourains.

les Rues (at the request of his Captain, Mr Thos Andros, son of James). Wm Thoume, son of ...... Thoume of les Blanches, & Jean le Page of les Mouillepieds refused to assist us, & Sr Thos le Retillé threatened to punch the Comptroller (who was giving me advice), calling him a bugger & telling him this was none of his business. Our two English farm servants left us (see 3rd & 9th June).

Mon 12 Jun: to Court. Jaques Guille & James Robert, whom we had sent to the guardhouse, were constituted prisoners under the custody of the Prevot. The Prevot was also instructed to arrest Wm Thoume & Jean le Page, who had denied us their assistance, & Sr Thos le Retillé & James Thoume who had behaved badly towards the Comptroller & other officers.

Tues 13 Jun: to town again. The Court released James Thoume & Jean le Page after they publicly apologised for their behaviour. They ordered the four other men to be remanded in the Castle until Saturday unless they deposited bail of 300 *livres* each, which all four men did.

Tues 4 Jul: my Dear Mother & Pierre [Gavet] left for Jersey on board Pierre Dorey.

Sat 8 Jul: to town & to Court. James Robert & Sr Thos le Retillé were fined 10 *écus* each (the fines are to go to the poor). They were also required to make a public apology & pay costs.

Sun 9 Jul: Pierre returned from Jersey.

Thurs 27 Jul: [...] to town in the morning. Had another 6 quarters of oats. Went for a bathe.

Fri 28 Jul: Mr Mourant & my sister returned from England.

Sun 30 Jul: there was a General Review at Vazon. The Governor & his grandson, Captns North & Rowley of the 96th Regiment; Lieutenant Gordon of the 78th; Major Munro; Doctors Sausmarez & Walters,[187] Messrs Obins, Tom Marchant & Danl Tupper came to dinner.[188]

[*Charles Mollet turned thirty-eight during the course of August 1780*]

Sat 19 Aug: [...] I passed contracts for Jean Batiste's house.[189]

Weds 23 Aug: I was woken in the early morning to deal with 5 sailors who had deserted from the frigate Medea. I apprehended them at le Mont de Val & handed them over to Mr de Havilland.

Tues 5 Sep: tithe collection began today. Had two cartloads from les Hougues & one from le Nanage.

Sun 10 Sep: heavy rain until 3 in the afternoon. The weather nevertheless stayed fine throughout the harvest, & there has been no rain at all for the best part of the tithe collection.

Thurs 14 Sep: [...] There have been 12 funerals in the parish since the beginning of this month.

Sat 16 Sep: [...] Visited several of the sick & distributed medicine from Dr Sausmarez.

Sun 17 Sep: visited several of the sick in the morning & evening. To church in the afternoon.

Thurs 21 Sep: [...] Doctor Sausmarez came in the afternoon, & we visited several of the sick.

Sat 23 Sep: [...] Danl Moullin, Jean du Maresq & I went to see James Lihou, who told us how he wishes to dispose of his money & belongings.[190]

---

[187] These two doctors were Dr Jean [De] Sau[s]marez (for whom see n. 35, above and n. 300, below) and Dr Robert Walters (1752–1833). Dr Walters was to serve as Inspector of Army Hospitals in Guernsey during the French Revolutionary and Napoleonic Wars.

[188] Daniel Tupper (1753–1808), a merchant, was the eldest of Jurat Elizée Tupper's sixteen children.

[189] Mollet later referred to this house (which was contiguous to his own property) as the 'upper' house.

[190] James Lihou was dying and had sought help to wind up his affairs.

Weds 4 Oct: [...] James Lihou was buried.

Thurs 12 Oct: Pierre [Gavet] left for Jersey this morning.

Fri 13 Oct: [...] Pierre returned alone from Jersey, my Dear Mother will spend the winter there.

Fri 20 Oct: [...] Pierre [Gavet] left my service.

Mon 23 Oct: Pierre returned full of remorse for his ill-conduct & asked me to take him back.

Tues 15 Nov: put up a new clock which I bought from London for 9 guineas.

Mon 21 Nov: [...] I divided the rest of James Lihou's money among his nieces & nephews according to his wishes. Marie Langlois started here as a house servant.

Fri 24 Nov: to town, where I dined. Bought two barrels of Bordeaux wine from one of the prizes captured by the Hero, one for £5 5s stg & the other for £4 12s.

Weds 29 Nov: to town, where I dined. Spent the evening at Danl Moullin's with the 3 Mr Pelleys.

Fri 1 Dec: [...] Pierre Girard reported a theft of some wood. I went to search for it among the soldiers at the Hospital & found some wood under a bed, which Pierre Girard recognised as belonging to him.[191] I arrested the two soldiers who slept in the bed with the intention of taking them to town. However, the officer on duty (Mr Waldron) would not allow me to take the soldiers away in the absence of the regiment's commanding officer.

Sat 2 Dec: I reported yesterday's incident to the Court, & the Crown Officers were deputed to ask the Governor to order that soldiers suspected of crimes should always be handed over to them.

---

[191] The country parishes had quartered the troops for whose billeting they were responsible in the local workhouse rather than in taverns or with private individuals, as in the past.

Thurs 7 Dec: […] Pierre caught a man by the name of Mactavy stealing my cress & confiscated his basket & gun. Yesterday he found 4 men making away with my turnips & confiscated their sack. This evening Mr Moullin & I seized nearly a bushel of potatoes from two men who had just stolen them from Sr Jean le Pelley.

Mon 11 Dec: to town where I gave evidence in a private session of the Court concerning several thefts & depredations recently committed in the parish.

Weds 13 Dec: I was awoken last night by neighbours who came to tell me that some soldiers were stealing my turnips. We were unable to catch any of them.

Thurs 14 Dec: […] attended Court in company with the persons called to give evidence as a result of my report to the Court last Monday. Each of us made our declaration as to the thefts, depredations & threats we have suffered. Several other people from town & elsewhere have made similar complaints.

Sat 16 Dec: to town & to Court. Mr Waugh gave me two piglets.[192]

Mon 18 Dec: to town & to Court, where (in private) I repeated the declaration I had made on Thursday. The Court showed me a letter passed to them by the Governor. It was written by Ensign Crooks to the Commander of the 96th Regiment. The letter took the form of a complaint about me, making a number of allegations which are false & which I positively denied.

Sat 23 Dec: to town, where I dined. Visited Hellier Nicolle's public house at 11 o'clock & found 6 or 7 persons there. Proceeded to Danl le Cheminant's at half past 11. Found it full of company.

Mon 25 Dec: I did not go out.

Sun 31 Dec: to church in the morning. To town in the afternoon. Thos Le Pelley supped with me.

---

[192] John Waugh was a Scottish military officer on the permanent staff of the garrison. He had married local woman Elizabeth Le Pelley in 1762.

Notes relating to 1780

In 1780, Charles Mollet gave work to sixteen men aside from his live-in employees, about ten of whom were day labourers. These ten labourers included six men with non-local names, most of whom were soldiers. Mollet's most regular workers in 1780 were Guillaume Lihou (153½ days) and Etienne Lihou (149½ days). Eleazar Ingrouille worked 35 days for Mollet in 1780.

1781

Mon 1 Jan: to town in the afternoon.

Sat 6 Jan: to town, where I dined. Word reached us between 2 & 3 in the afternoon that the French landed covertly in Jersey early this morning. They captured the town by surprise at about 6, & took the Governor prisoner at 7. The alarm was sounded here, & the Regiments remained on high alert all night.

Sun 7 Jan: the Castel Regiment was posted to Anneville. I made several patrols through the parish & 4 journeys into town, spending the rest of my time with the officers at Anneville. The alarm remained in force from yesterday evening until 10 o'clock this morning, when an express arrived from Jersey to inform us that our troops had recaptured the town & freed the Governor the previous evening with the loss of 50 men killed & 25 wounded. On the French side, there were several hundred killed, 50 wounded, & 500 taken prisoner. The rest escaped into the countryside. I went to town in the early afternoon in hopes of sailing for Jersey, but the ships had already departed.

Fri 12 Jan: I have been almost continuously in town since Sunday, sleeping there 3 or 4 nights with the intention of leaving for Jersey. The bad weather has however prevented my departure. We have every reason to be worried, having received no news all week.

Sat 13 Jan: today we received a letter from my brother[-in-law] giving us news of everyone. No one was hurt at his house, although nearly all his windows were broken & his doors were pierced by gunshot. Baron de Rullecourt, the French General, died at his brother's house.[193] I have sent Pierre [Gavet] to Jersey for more news of my Dear Mother & the rest of the family. He left at 10 this morning.

---

[193] Mollet's statement regarding Lerrier's brother's house is puzzling, as Philippe Lerrier's only brother appears to have died in infancy. It is possible that Mollet may have written *frère* for *fils*, since Lerrier's son, another Philippe Lerrier (1755–1823), was a doctor by profession, and Rullecourt is known to have been tended in his final moments by the doctor in whose house he died.

Tues 16 Jan: […] to town in the evening. Pierre arrived back from Jersey.

[*The second extant volume of Charles Mollet's diaries ended on 18 January 1781 without further significant entries. The next volume in the series (which covered the four years 1781–4) is missing. The third surviving volume began on 1 January 1785, by which time Charles Mollet had reached the age of forty-two. He remained unmarried, but was no longer a Castel parish Constable.*]

1785

Sat 1 Jan: dined at the Governor's.[194] There were 18 of us at table.

Tues 4 Jan: [...] Paul Perron, whom I dismissed on 26 December, returned, unable to find other work. I took him back.

Sat 15 Jan: to town. Passed contracts with Mr Pelley for the purchase of his two fields & meadow at les Tuzets. Sr André Cohu will continue to rent them from me for another 4 years.

Sun 16 Jan: [...] I dismissed Paul Perron, who returned here on 4 January.

Weds 26 Jan: Judith Brehaut left our service. She was here 4½ months. To the Forest in the afternoon. The heifer calved. Bon Dobrée & Polly Lerrier arrived from England yesterday.[195]

Thurs 27 Jan: to town. Dined at Candie with Henry Brock.[196]

Tues 15 Feb: [...] Pierre [Gavet], Charles [Le Geyt], Jean le Pelley (son of Hellier) & Eleazar [Ingrouille] went to dig for Jean Marqui.[197]

---

[194] This was Lieutenant-Colonel William Brown, who had been appointed Lieutenant-Governor of Guernsey in 1784. Brown (1739–93) was originally from Berwickshire in Scotland. Mollet had known him before his arrival in Guernsey and was a personal friend of his.
[195] Bonamy (Bon) Dobrée (1755–1821) was the eldest son of Pierre Dobrée of 'Beauregard' (see Appendix 3). Bonamy had married Mollet's niece Patty Mourant (1765–98) in 1783. Polly Lerrier (1757–1834) was one of Mollet's Jersey nieces, the daughter of his sister Marie and Philippe Lerrier.
[196] Henry Brock (1761–1812) was a merchant who had married Mollet's niece Mary Mourant (1767–1852) in 1784 (for more on the composition of the Brock family, who henceforth featured regularly in Mollet's journal, see Appendix 3).
[197] Eleazar Ingrouille (1766–1832) was a day labourer who had started working for Mollet in the early 1780s (see Appendix 4). This Eleazar should not be confused with an earlier labourer of the same name, who was probably a relative. The younger Eleazar was to become an important figure in Charles Mollet's life, remaining associated with him as a neighbour and a friend until Mollet died in 1819. Jean Marquis was a neighbour of Mollet's, whom he (or rather his men) sometimes helped with agricultural tasks in return for reciprocal help from him. Mollet maintained such relationships with many of his neighbours.

Weds 23 Feb: [...] Judith Perrin started here as a house servant.

Thurs 24 Feb: [...] Mr Pierre de Havilland has been elected a Magistrate to replace Mr [Jean] de la Mare.

Fri 25 Feb: to the Vale in the morning, where I chanced upon the two Messrs Brock.[198] I accompanied them to town & dined at my sister's. Drew off eleven barrels of the cider which we have at Thos Lihou's house.[199]

Weds 2 Mar: some of the snow which fell a week ago last Sunday still remains on the ground.

Fri 11 Mar: [...] I went shore-gathering with Pierre [Gavet] & Eleazar [Ingrouille] on the low tide at le Houmet, & we brought back some ormers.

Sun 13 Mar: [...] Yesterday, I discovered that someone had taken pot shots at two of my large rosebushes & broken them (they came from Bristol & cost me 15 shillings).

Sun 27 Mar: to church in the morning. Communion today. The Governor, Major [John] Waugh, Messrs [Isaac] Vallat, Dan Waugh, Nico Dobrée, Bon Dobrée, Harry Brock, Dr [Jean] Sausmarez & Captn James Sausmarez came to dinner.[200]

Mon 18 Apr: [...] a light shower of rain – our first rain since 5 February (10 weeks ago last Saturday), apart from a few drops on 24 February & some snow on 20 February (8 weeks ago yesterday). Between 20 September & 1 November last year, there was no rain at all, & the winter has in general been exceptionally dry. The usual winter streams did not appear, & some streams which flow all year dried up. This has made it very difficult for the millers & stunted the growth of grass.

---

[198] The 'Messrs Brock' were Henry Brock (husband of Mollet's niece Mary) and his brother William (1756–1831), who was later to marry Mary's sister Nancy Mourant (1769–1838). See Appendix 3.
[199] Mollet had bought Thomas Lihou's house in le Préel in February 1784.
[200] Captain James Saumarez (1757–1836) was a naval officer. He was later promoted to Admiral and subsequently became the 1st Baron de Saumarez. He was a son of the late Dr Matthew De Sausmarez, and brother to Dr Jean [De] Sau[s]marez (for both of whom, see n. 35, above and n. 300, below).

Sun 8 May: to church in the morning. My Dear Mother returned here after eight months in town (she has been there since 29 August).[201]

Sun 15 May: I did not go out. Patty & Polly Mourant came to dinner.[202] The Duke of Richmond, who has been here since Thursday, left this morning.

Fri 3 Jun: Mr Mourant, my sister, Polly, Nancy, Miss Roche, Mrs [Marie] Coutart & her daughters Janneton & Nancy, & Mr Dobrée the Minister came to dinner.[203]

Sat 4 Jun: the King's Birthday. I dined at the Governor's ([who lives] in the small house belonging to Mr Dobrée). There were 30 of us.

Sat 11 Jun: [...] Our older peahen hatched 5 chicks today (from 5 eggs). The other peahen has 2 four-week-old chicks.

Mon 13 Jun: [...] My sister Lerrier & young Nancy have arrived from Jersey.[204]

Thurs 23 Jun: the Revd Mr Dobrée, Mr Bullen,[205] Bon Dobrée, Patty, Harry Brock, Polly, Nancy & Polly Lerrier came to dinner. I went briefly to town in the morning.

Sat 9 Jul: went for a bathe in the evening.

---

[201] Mollet's mother was now aged seventy-six.
[202] Mollet's nieces were both married, but he continued (as per local practice) to identify them by their maiden name.
[203] Nicolas Dobrée (see n. 38, above) had been inducted as Rector of the Castel in 1784. The 'Miss Roche' Mollet referred to was Anne Roche (1743–1831), a lifelong spinster; Mrs Marie Coutart (1740–1808) was her sister, the wife of Advocate Pierre Coutart (see nn. 27, 34 and 39). Any future references to 'Miss Roche' will be to Anne.
[204] Mollet's sister Marie Lerrier was now forty-nine years old. Nancy (Anne), her youngest child, was seven.
[205] 'Mr Bullen' was a clergyman: Jacques Boul[l]en, born to Huguenot parents in London in 1756 and at this point serving as curate of the Vale and St Sampson. He was to marry Rachel Godefroy, daughter of the Reverend Jean Godefroy, in 1789, and later became Minister of Holy Trinity church in St Peter Port.

Sun 17 Jul: went to watch the Blue Regiment at Vazon in the morning.[206]

Thurs 28 Jul: weeded in several places. My sister Lerrier left for Jersey with her two daughters.

Fri 29 Jul: started demolishing Jean Batiste's small house.[207]

[*Charles Mollet turned forty-three during the course of August 1785*]

Mon 1 Aug: to town in the morning to see Mr Gibert the Minister.[208]

Tues 16 Aug: [...] My Dear Mother returned here. She had been in town since 20 July.

Mon 29 Aug: [...] This year I am collecting tithe from the district of les Hougues & ceding half to Mr Moullin.

Mon 5 Sep: [...] Strong winds & heavy rain in the evening. We have had no rain since 5 February (30 weeks ago last Saturday), save a little on 24 February, 18 April, 20 & 29 May. Everyone has had difficulty feeding their livestock & there has scarcely been any hay, nor barley, nor clover among the barley.

Sat 24 Sep: dined at Major Waugh's with Mr Barclay the Storekeeper.[209]

Tues 27 Sep: [...] Pierre went to fetch 1000 lb of old biscuit from the Stores which Major Waugh sold me for 6 shillings per 100 lb.

---

[206] The 'Blue' regiment was the Third or South militia regiment (comprising men from St Martin, St Andrew and the Forest), so called because they wore blue facings on their tunics. The three other infantry regiments were the First or Town Regiment (comprising men from St Peter Port and St Sampson, with buff facings on their tunics); the Second or North Regiment (Castel and the Vale, green facings); and the Fourth or West Regiment (St Saviour, St Peter and Torteval, black facings). Mollet often referred to these regiments by their colours.

[207] This was a ruin next to what Mollet called the 'upper' house (which he had bought from Jean Batiste in 1780).

[208] 'Mr Gibert' was the Reverend Etienne Gibert (1736–1817), a Huguenot refugee from the Cévennes. Gibert was based in London at this time, but was to serve as Rector of St Andrew between 1794 and 1815.

[209] 'Storekeeper' (which Mollet wrote in English) was the old name for what was later known as Commissary General (head of the department sourcing and supplying provisions, etc., to a body of troops).

Weds 28 Sep: [...] Destroyed two wasps' nests at this end of the furzebrake at le Brulin. This makes 27 nests we have destroyed so far this year.

Sun 2 Oct: [...] My Dear Mother returned to Candie in the evening. She had been here since 16 August, & before that, she was here between 8 May & 20 July.

Tues 11 Oct: [...] We have caught 3 weasels in the past 3 days.

Mon 17 Oct: started digging at the bottom of le Prey du Pommier in order to make a small pond there.

Weds 19 Oct: [...] Finished digging the pond at le Prey in the morning. It took about seven man-days. The pond is 20 feet square and 3 feet deep.

Sat 29 Oct: [...] went to see Patty who has been very ill at Candie for some time.

Sun 30 Oct: went to see Patty in the morning. She seems a little better than yesterday, but is still in great danger.

Tues 1 Nov: it has been raining lately. Patty gave birth at about eight in the evening to a boy who lived for half an hour. She is very weak.

Thurs 3 Nov: attended the sale of le Moullin du Milieu in the morning. It was being auctioned by young Harry Blondel's guardian. It went to Paul Ingrouille for 294 *livres* in *rente* & 585 *livres* in cash (memo: this bid was later withdrawn).[210] In the afternoon I went to see Patty, who is much better.

Tues 13 Dec: in the morning I went to ask Mr Nico Moullin of les Vallez (the Procureur des Pauvres) for assistance for Pierre le Lievre's family. To town for a short while after dinner. Strong winds & heavy rain.

Weds 14 Dec: [...] Yesterday I gave Pierre le Lievre's wife leave to remain at Thos Lihou's house for a few weeks, until she is able to find other lodgings.[211]

---

[210] The miller Paul Ingrouille (1741–1802) was the father of Mollet's young labourer Eleazar Ingrouille.
[211] The Le Lievres had previously lived at la Daumaillerie (see n. 124 and 11.9.74). It is possible that Pierre had abandoned his family.

Thurs 15 Dec: to Candie in the morning to pay Mr Mourant the outstanding balance on my account with the firm of Mourant & Chepmell.

Sat 17 Dec: to town. Assigned 3 quarters & 2 bushels of wheat *rente* to Mr Olivier of le Mont Durand, (which I owed him), in exchange for 10 bushels & 3 denerels which he owed me & 1 quarter of *rente* owed me by Sr Nic. Thoume. There was one surplus cabot which I sold to Mr Olivier to complete the bargain. I also assigned to Mr Ozanne of la Porte the 2 bushels owed me by Mr Falla, in exchange for the 2 bushels which I owed him.

Thurs 22 Dec: [...] Mr du Ponchez,[212] Mr Henry, Jack & Thos le Pelley supped & spent *la longue veille* with me.[213]

Sat 24 Dec: snow has been falling nearly all day & the ground is covered. I was invited to dine at the Governor's, but the snow prevented my going.

Sun 25 Dec: snow fell nearly all morning. It is 3 inches thick on the ground. I did not go out. Thos le Pelley came in the afternoon & stayed for supper.

Sat 31 Dec: snow fell last night & during the day. It is lying about 5 inches deep. Killed a snipe.

Notes relating to 1785

Aside from live-in servants, Charles Mollet gave work to fourteen individuals in 1785. Ten of these were day labourers. Four men shared the bulk of the work: Charles Le Geyt (142½ days), Eleazar Ingrouille (120 days), Thomas Collenette (114½ days) and Etienne Lihou (107½ days). Mollet also employed Thomas Le Tissier to dig and weed parsnips for a piece-rate of 11 *sous* per perch. He paid Le Tissier a total of 26 *livres* 19 *sous* for taking care of 49 perches.

---

[212] 'Mr du Ponchez' was Nicolas Moullin (1763–1811), the son of Nicolas Moullin, sen. and Marie, *née* Tourgis.
[213] *La longue veille* was islanders' chief Christmas celebration, marked by parties, culinary treats and mulled wine. Historians of insular customs state that it took place on the evening of 23 December, but this was clearly not always the case. For more detail, see E.F. Carey (ed.), *Guernsey Folk Lore from MSS by the Late Sir Edgar MacCulloch* (London, 1903), p. 33.

1786

Sun 1 Jan: [...] The temperature has been below freezing all day. I did not go out. Jack Pelley supped here & spent the evening with me.

Sun 15 Jan: Eleazar [Ingrouille] dined here. His father came here afterwards & I joined them at their house for a while in the evening. They are both reasonable men & think in similar ways – good people to whom I owe many a favour.

Mon 30 Jan: ploughed the western side of la Censiere for parsnips. Thos le Pelley, Sr Jean le Pelley, Jean le Pelley (son of Hellier), Jean Roussel & Hellier Nicolle, jun., helped us with their animals. Pierre [Gavet], Eleazar [Ingrouille], Thos Collenette & Charles [Le Geyt] also helped.[214]

Sat 4 Feb: [...] Prince William Henry arrived yesterday & left again this morning.[215]

Weds 8 Feb: [...] Pierre & Eleazar took up the flagstones in our stable & re-laid them in my warehouse at la Profonde Rue.[216]

Mon 27 Feb: heavy snow last night. There was about a foot on the ground by dawn, & it continued to fall till about ten o'clock, reaching a depth of 18 to 20 inches.

Mon 13 Mar: [...] some snow still remains on the ground. It began falling a fortnight ago last Saturday. The temperature has been below freezing every night & almost every day since 22 February.

---

[214] This was the first time Charles Mollet had used a plough to prepare his ground for parsnips.
[215] Prince William Henry was the future William IV, then a twenty-one-year-old naval officer.
[216] For Mollet's purchase of two warehouses at la Profonde Rue in St Peter Port, see 31.12.79.

Fri 31 Mar: [...] My Dear Mother returned from my sister's, where she has been since 2 October. We had no labourers here today – they were all digging peat.

Sat 1 Apr: [...] I accompanied the Governor to le Chateau des Maresq.[217]

Sun 2 Apr: Messrs Bon, Sam & Elizée Dobrée,[218] Billy & Harry Brock, Polly & Nancy Mourant, young John Roche & Stephen Mourant came to dinner.[219]

Sat 22 Apr: [...] dined at Mr Nic. Dobrée's, where I spent a very pleasant afternoon. There were eight of us, including Monsieur le Blanc from Sette. Mr MacDonald, the new Storekeeper, died yesterday. Bought a box of fine lemons from Billy Combs for 12 shillings.

Tues 16 May: [...] At nine in the evening, as I was upstairs getting ready for bed, my Dear Mother, who (as is her habit) was going up last, fell down the stairs, a distance of 4 or 5 steps. I went to her aid immediately & found that her left arm was broken above the wrist & she had bruising to the head & shoulder. I sent Pierre to town straight away, & in less than 2 hours he returned with my sister & Monsieur Brusault, who, after having set my Dear Mother's arm, left us around midnight. My sister remained here.

Fri 19 May: [...] Monsieur Brusault came. My Dear Mother is mending quietly.

Thurs 25 May: Mrs Pelley dined with us. My sister Mourant has been here since the 16th.

Sun 28 May: my sister Lerrier arrived from Jersey.

---

[217] Le Château des Marais was a dilapidated medieval fort on the east coast also known as Ivy Castle. Lieutenant-Governor William Brown had had a garden laid out there, and it was a favourite retreat of his in the spring and summer.

[218] These three Dobrées were all sons of Pierre Dobrée of 'Beauregard' (see Appendix 3). Samuel Dobrée (1759–1827) traded as a banking agent in London. Elizée (Elisha) Dobrée (1756–1844) kept a diary of which three volumes survive at Guernsey's Island Archives. He recorded this dinner at Mollet's (AQ 1572/04).

[219] Stephen Mourant was an older brother of Peter Mourant of Candie.

Mon 29 May: [...] Elizabeth Queripel of le Variouf started here as a house servant to replace Marie Nicolle.

Tues 30 May: to town in the morning. The Court came to inspect la Profonde Rue (below my warehouses), as also the road at Candie. They ordered that both roads be provided with footpaths. [...] My sister Mourant returned home in the evening. She had stayed with us for a fortnight. My Dear Mother continues to recover, but she remains in her room. My sister Lerrier has come to stay.

Mon 5 Jun: [...] Whitsun. Nancy Mourant married Billy Brock this morning at St Andrew's church.

Tues 6 Jun: [...] Prince William Henry, who was here about ..... months ago, arrived yesterday & dined with the Governor today. Pierre [Gavet] spent the day at the Governor's waiting at table.

Weds 7 Jun: to town in the morning. There was a *Chevauchée* today.[220] This is the first for 18 years (or rather 16 years, see 9 June 1770).

Thurs 8 Jun: [...] I dismissed Elizabeth Queripel, who has been working here since 29 May.

Weds 21 Jun: departed for Cherbourg at 9 in the morning in Captn Pierre le Lievre's vessel, which a group of us have hired for a few days. The group consists of Messrs Mourant, Bowden, Condomine, Ludlam, Bon Dobrée, Harry Brock, Nicolas & Jean Maingy (Nicolas Maingy's sons), Billy le Marchant (Jean le Marchant's son), Elizée Dobrée, Captn Gosselin & myself. Captn Danl Lauga also sailed with us, although he was originally going on the Liberty with Messrs Guerin, Jack Dobrée, & the brothers Billy & Danl Brock (these 4 gentlemen often kept company with us during our stay at Cherbourg & slept every night on our vessel). We arrived off Cherbourg at 7 in the evening, & went ashore at 9. Mr Nic. Maingy & I slept on land, having by chance & favour obtained beds in the same room for 6 *livres* each. On

---

[220] A *Chevauchée* was a ceremonial inspection of the king's highway under the auspices of the Court of the Fief of St Michel. It involved *inter alia* the procession around parts of the island of Court members with a large accompanying retinue. For more details, see E.F. Carey (ed.), *Guernsey Folk Lore from MSS by the Late Sir Edgar MacCulloch* (London, 1903), pp. 65–77.

subsequent nights, the price of a bed rose to between 12 & 24 *livres* on account of the demand occasioned by the King's visit to Cherbourg to inspect the government works.

Thurs 22 Jun: strolled around the town & examined the cones not yet put in place. One was finished, another was almost finished, & work was proceeding on a further two. Seven cones have already been positioned at sea as part of a defensive ring around the port. The King (Louis the 16th) arrived at eleven in the evening. A large number of notables had preceded him, including two of his Ministers (le Maréchal de Castres & le Maréchal de Ségur). Dined & slept on board ship.

Fri 23 Jun: this morning I witnessed the floating out to sea of the finished cone we saw yesterday. Borne up by a large number of empty barrels, it was manoeuvred into the position where it was to be sunk, close to one of the cones which was already in place, on which the king & his retinue were standing. We witnessed the piercing of the cone, which was accomplished with perfect success. Mr Pierre de Jersey of Smith Street dined with us on board ship, & I went ashore with him in the afternoon to visit le Fort du Homet. We saw the King very clearly while he was with le Duc de Harcourt.

Sat 24 Jun: the King went on board his naval flagship in the morning (le Patriote, 64 guns). The flagship then accompanied six frigates out to sea, which proceeded to stage a mock battle.

Sun 25 Jun: the King sailed almost as far as Querqueville in the morning, then made a wide circuit so as to pass alongside us. We saluted him in the English fashion. He looked at each of us attentively & instructed one of his retinue to enquire whether we were from Jersey or Guernsey. He was accompanied by 20 or 25 notables. The one who questioned us spoke in English. Billy Marchant answered him.

Mon 26 Jun: the King left by coach for le Havre de Grâce between 6 & 7 in the morning. We set sail at about the same time & arrived in Guernsey at 5 in the afternoon. We almost always ate on board during our sojourn, & I slept on board with the others every night save the first. We are all very pleased with our voyage, having spent the time very merrily & enjoyed each other's company. We had hired Captn le Lievre & his vessel for three days at a cost of ten guineas, & two guineas per day for any time in excess of that.

Weds 28 Jun: Nanon le Page started here as a house servant to replace Marie Nicolle.

Mon 3 Jul: [...] My sister Lerrier, who is planning to leave Guernsey shortly, went back to town.

Tues 4 Jul: [...] I escorted my Dear Mother to town, where she is to remain for a few weeks.

Sat 22 Jul: [...] The Governor introduced me to the Duke of Richmond, who arrived this morning.[221]

Mon 24 Jul: there was a General Review at l'Ancresse in honour of the Duke of Richmond, who attended with his Duchess & their companions. [...] I had the honour of conversing with the Duchess for half an hour.[222] She spoke to me very graciously, & afterwards I accompanied her to Vazon via les Grands Moullins (with three of her attendants). She expressed a strong desire to see my property, but, since she was to dine in town & it was already 3 o'clock when I left her at les Eturs crossroads, she did not have the time.

Tues 25 Jul: the Duke & Duchess had planned to leave for Jersey today, but this morning I received an urgent message from them requesting me to join them for dinner at the Governor's. [...] The Duke insisted that I sit next to him at table, & in the evening I accompanied the Duchess to the Rooms, only leaving when she left at eleven. I escorted her to the Governor's door but declined an invitation to stay for supper, preferring to return here. In the morning, I sent the Duchess some fruit, together with some yellow carnation plants & pompom roses. She returned a very gracious note of thanks, which the Governor believes was the only letter she wrote during her stay here.

Weds 26 Jul: [...] Spent the morning with the Duke & Duchess & their entourage until they embarked for Jersey at 11 o'clock. [...] The Duke &

---

[221] Charles Lennox, 3rd Duke of Richmond (1735–1806), then serving as Master-General of the Ordnance.
[222] Lady Mary Bruce (1740–1796).

Duchess thanked me again before they left, & the Duchess invited me (as she already did yesterday & the day before) to visit her in England.

Thurs 27 Jul: departed for Jersey at 9 in the morning on board Captn le Maitre with Messrs Nico Dobrée, sen., James & Billy Brock. Arrived at two in the afternoon.

Fri 28 Jul: [...] called on the Duchess of Richmond in the morning.

Mon 31 Jul: [...] attended a ball & supper given to the Duke & Duchess of Richmond by the inhabitants of Jersey. The Duchess took much notice of me, speaking to me at intervals & sometimes at length. She even left her seat to come & sit beside me for more than half an hour.

[*Charles Mollet turned forty-four during the course of August 1786*]

Thurs 3 Aug: [...] I went to see the Duchess for the last time & took my leave of her.

Fri 4 Aug: departed Jersey at 10 on board Ph. Mourant & arrived in Guernsey at six in the evening.

Mon 21 Aug: dined at the Governor's. It was a Turtle Feast.[223] There were 17 of us.

Weds 23 Aug: my servant Pierre Gavet, who has been with me since 8 May 1775, was this morning married to Marie Nicolle (daughter of Hellier), who was here from 25 Nov 1782 until 3 August this year. They will live in Jean Batiste's old house.[224] Both will continue working for me as the need arises.

Thurs 24 Aug: collected tithe all day. Had one cartload. Lifted potatoes at la Censiere.

Weds 30 Aug: [...] My Dear Mother returned from Candie, where she has been since 4 July.

---

[223] The consumption of turtles in a 'turtle feast' was a fashionable activity in the second half of the eighteenth century, largely as a result of the colonisation of the West Indies.
[224] The 'upper' house.

Fri 1 Sep: to town in the morning. The Governor accompanied me back here & we went to les Hougues to take Charles le Geyt (who was collecting tithe) his dinner. [...] We had very nearly another cartload of tithe, which will be our last this year.

Thurs 21 Sep: to town in the morning. Started gathering cider apples. Our gatherers were Hellier Nicolle, his two sisters, three of Marg. de la Rue's children & Marie Ingrouille.

Sat 23 Sep: Pierre [Gavet] & I went shore-gathering.

Thurs 5 Oct: the Governor, Sir Robt Stuart, Major Waugh, Billy, Harry & Jemmy Brock, Mary & Nancy came to dinner.[225] There was horse-racing at Vazon this morning, which we went to see.

Fri 6 Oct: Guillaume Lihou has been here every day since Thursday of last week re-hooping our casks & barrels. Today he finished re-hooping all that we have here.

Tues 17 Oct: dined at the Procureur's [Hirzel Le Marchant] in Smith Street. Mr de St George & his son were there, as also Messrs Andros, Pierre Havilland, Charles, Josias & Bob Marchant.

Fri 20 Oct: more horse-racing at Vazon, which I attended.

Weds 25 Oct: [...] Eleazar & I weeded le Brulin & le Prey.

Fri 27 Oct: escorted my Dear Mother back to town. She has been here since 30 August.

Sat 4 Nov: [...] We have had constant northerly winds since 11 October.

Thurs 9 Nov: dug the top of le Marquet in preparation for sowing acorns.

Fri 10 Nov: [...] I engaged Wm Allez (son of Thos Allez of la Hougue du Pommier) to work here as my farm servant for 30 *écus* per year. He will start on Monday.

---

[225] 'Jemmy Brock' was James Brock (1767–1805), the younger brother of William and Henry Brock.

Mon 13 Nov: [...] our first frost of the season.

Sat 18 Nov: to town in the morning. Jean Letocq & Nico Brouard came to replace the head of the tun. Mr Moullin & Thos le Pelley spent the evening here. A house burned down at Hougue a la Perre.

Mon 20 Nov: to town. Dined at Candie. Sowed acorns & beech mast at the turning.

Thurs 7 Dec: dined at Bon Dobrée's with my Dear Mother, my sister & her family & Messrs Elizée & Jack Dobrée.

Mon 11 Dec: Wm Allez has left. I dismissed him. He was here for 4 weeks.

Tues 12 Dec: dined at the Alderney Governor's with the Governor's son & Messrs Andros, Jean Guille & Pierre Havilland. Brought in our wheat (111 sheaves, including 60 of tithe wheat).

Fri 22 Dec: [...] Jack & Thos le Pelley spent *la longue veille* with me.

Mon 25 Dec: Mme de la Houguette dined with me. Icy conditions all day.

Sun 31 Dec: [...] Danl Moullin & Jean du Maresq supped & spent the evening with me.

Notes relating to 1786

Aside from his live-in servants, Charles Mollet gave work to eighteen individuals in 1786, of whom five were tradesmen and thirteen day labourers. Most of the day labour went to six men who worked between 72 and 146 days each. The rest worked just a handful of days. Mollet's regulars were Etienne Lihou (146 days), Charles Le Geyt (139 days), Eleazar Ingrouille (111 days), Pierre Gavet (102½ days), Thomas Collenette (96½ days), and William Nicolle (72½ days).

1787

Mon 1 Jan: sold three of the old sow's piglets […] Eleazar [Ingrouille] & Pierre Roussel dined here.

Thurs 11 Jan: Judith Perrin left us. She has been here for two years less six weeks.

Fri 19 Jan: […] Sr Jean de Jersey of les Pins was buried today. He was elected a Douzenier when my Dear Father resigned from the Douzaine.

Thurs 25 Jan: dined at la Haye du Puis. Mr & Mrs Bob Marchant were there.[226]

Sun 28 Jan: […] In the evening, we surprised an intruder (probably a thief) in the cartshed. He escaped by climbing into the loft & jumping from there on to the passage.

Sun 4 Feb: […] the eldest son of Mr des Touillets (Tom) came unexpectedly to visit me,[227] which surprised me somewhat, given that I had never made his acquaintance. In two days' time he is to leave for the West Indies. He supped here with me & Jack Pelley, who came in the evening.

Mon 12 Feb: dug the lower garden. Young Ab. Collenette (son of Abraham Collenette, jun., & Madeleine le Page) came to live here as my farm servant.

Fri 23 Feb: […] Received two notices informing me of Mr des Touillets' intention to have my goods distrained. I sent him the 3 quarters of wheat *rente* I owed him on Thos Lihou's house.

Tues 27 Feb: […] Marie Collenette (daughter of Pierre Collenette, son of Ab.) started here as a house servant.

---

[226] Mollet's friend Robert Le Marchant (a future Bailiff) had married Marie Ozanne of la Houguette in 1782. See nn. 128 and 183, above.

[227] Thomas De Jersey (c.1770–1816) was the son of Mollet's neighbour Jurat Pierre De Jersey (for whom, see n. 104, above). See also 31.10.16.

Tues 6 Mar: [...] Pierre Gavet's wife Marie gave birth to a daughter, their first child.[228]

Thurs 8 Mar: [...] My niece Nancy Mourant, wife of Mr Billy Brock, gave birth to a daughter yesterday, their first child.[229]

Sat 10 Mar: [...] A white dog belonging to Mr des Touillets killed eight of my month-old ducklings.

Tues 10 Apr: Fair day. Bon Dobrée & Patty, Mrs Bainbrigge & her sister,[230] Betsy & Nancy Coutart all arrived back from England.

Weds 18 Apr: my Dear Mother returned from Candie. She has been there since 27 October.

Sat 21 Apr: Patty has been coming every day to see my Dear Mother. Polly & Nancy came yesterday.

Sun 22 Apr: to church in the morning. Mme de la Houguette & Judith le Cheminant came in the afternoon. [...] Nico Martel, who works for Mr des Touillets, came to speak to me about working here.

Weds 2 May: Nico Martel (son of the late Nicolas Martel of les Niots) started working here as a farm servant. He left the employ of Mr des Touillets this morning.

Thurs 3 May: [...] I paid a visit of reconciliation to les Touillets.

Mon 7 May: [...] Mr des Touillets & his wife came to call on my Dear Mother this morning.

Weds 9 May: my Dear Mother fell in the courtyard yesterday afternoon & hurt her thigh. She was unable to walk, so she had to be carried up to bed last night & carried downstairs in the morning. I sent word to my sister yesterday

---

[228] The child was named Marie, after her mother.
[229] The child was named Martha, after her grandmother.
[230] Bonamy Dobrée's sister Rachel (1764–1842) had married Philip Bainbrigge (an officer of the garrison) in 1781. The other sister mentioned was perhaps their youngest sibling, Elizabeth Dobrée, born in 1770.

evening, & she came here to sleep. Dr [Jean] Sausmarez also came to see my Dear Mother. Mme de la Houguette, Mr Mourant, Bon Dobrée & Patty came to see her in the afternoon. My sister returned to town this evening.

Fri 18 May: [...] Patty gave birth to a son. This is her 3rd child (her 2nd child died).[231]

Sat 19 May: [...] Patty's infant died yesterday evening.

Sun 27 May: [...] Polly Marchant of la Haye du Puis (the wife of the Procureur Hirzel le Marchant) was buried today.[232]

Weds 6 Jun: I went to town in the morning, then joined the Governor at le Chateau des Maresq.

Tues 12 Jun: my brother[-in-law] & Manon arrived from Jersey this morning. [...] Manon will stay here. Weeded the parsnips in the morning. Weeded the strawberries at le Marquet in the afternoon.

Fri 13 Jul: the Governor, General Sir William Green,[233] Colonels Dawber, Morse & Durnford, Captn Evelegh, Major Waugh, Mr Johnston & Mr Test stopped here for refreshments in the morning.

Mon 18 Jun: [...] Yesterday Jean Ozanne's eldest son Jean was drowned at la Crabiére, where he had gone bathing with his brother.

Tues 24 Jul: [...] Manon left us yesterday to spend a few days in town before she returns to Jersey.

Sat 28 Jul: [...] My sister Lerrier [...] will leave for Jersey tomorrow.

[*Charles Mollet turned forty-five during the course of August 1787*]

Sat 4 Aug: to town. Dined alone with the Governor.

---

[231] The child was baptised Bonamy. Patty's first child, Peter, was born in 1784, and her second child, Henry, in 1785.
[232] Marie Le Marchant (sister of Josias Le Marchant) was thirty years old.
[233] This was Major-General Sir William Green, 1st Baronet of Marass, an expert in military fortifications who had been appointed Chief Engineer of Britain in 1786.

Weds 15 Aug: […] I breakfasted with Patty, then accompanied the Governor to the Chateau [des Marais], where I dined & spent the afternoon alone with him.

Sun 19 Aug: […] To les Terres to hear Mr [John] Wesley the Methodist preach in the afternoon.

Sat 1 Sep: […] to town in the evening to hear Mr Wesley the Methodist preach at les Terres.

Tues 4 Sep: […] Eleazar [Ingrouille] & I collected tithe all day. Pierre [Gavet] accompanied us in the morning. Billy Brock, Nancy & Mary dined with me in Marie de Lerée's furzebrake, after which they took tea with my Dear Mother.

Sat 8 Sep: […] we had about 12 cartloads of tithe this year. […] August, the harvest & tithe collection all passed without rain, so that little grain was spoilt, &, thank God, the harvest was abundant.

Sat 29 Sep: […] Pierre (Gavet) has moved out of the upper house, where he & Marie have lived since their marriage on 23 August 1786. They have moved to Danl le Cheminant's house at les Moullins.

Sun 30 Sep: Pierre came to see me in the morning. I paid him all that I owed him. He left me without any expression of gratitude, only 'Thank you & Goodbye'. He did not even go in to see my Dear Mother. After I paid him, we saw nothing more of either him or Marie for the rest of the day. In the evening, Pierre returned to hand the key to Nanon in the wash-house. He refused her invitation to come into the house to speak to me. He started here as my farm servant on 8 May 1775. I would have liked him to stay on, as I am much attached to him & appreciate his hard work & good qualities. However, his proud temperament makes him impatient of dependence. I feel he has nothing to complain of as regards my treatment of him, & I hope he will become aware of the debt which he owes me & realise that I have rewarded him well for his services. He has lived in the upper house since his marriage on 23 August 1786, & has had gratuitous use of half the garden there for two years. His wife, Marie Nicolle, began living here as a house servant on 25 November 1782. We always found her a good servant. I will miss them both very much & I will find it hard to do without their assistance in my household. Nevertheless, I cannot descend to begging, after having already asked them several times to stay. Neither am I wealthy enough to offer them more perquisites than they already enjoyed here.

Sat 6 Oct: [...] to le Chateau des Maresq with the Governor. We spoke seriously about my intention of going to Alderney. He is against it & hopes he might be in a position to do something for me.

Fri 12 Oct: dined at Mr Pierre le Mesurier's,[234] & embarked with him for Alderney at seven in the evening. I spent the next few days pleasantly in Alderney (from the 12th till the 26th). I lodged at the Governor's & passed the time without boredom.

Mon 29 Oct: [...] went to the theatre with Eleazar [Ingrouille] & Nico [Martel] to see a French troupe perform 'Le Pere de Famille' & 'Les Trois Freres Rivaux'.

Sat 3 Nov: to town. Dined at the Governor's.

Weds 7 Nov: [...] To the theatre in the evening. Saw 'Le Méchant' & 'L'Amant Auteur et Valet'.

Weds 14 Nov: [...] To Candie in the afternoon, where Mr [Thomas] Marett came to speak to me.[235]

Sat 17 Nov: [...] To the theatre in the evening. Saw 'Le Joueur' & 'L'Avocat Patelin'.

Sun 18 Nov: [...] Wm Mahy the Methodist came here in the morning. I engaged him in debate for an hour or so.

Thurs 22 Nov: escorted my Dear Mother back to Candie [...]. She has been here since 18 April.

---

[234] For Peter (Pierre) Le Mesurier, see n. 24, above.
[235] Thomas Marett became Mollet's business partner in Alderney. He had been born in St Peter Port in 1747. His father was another Thomas Marett and his mother was Elizabeth Day.

Fri 23 Nov: to town in the morning. Mr Marrett & I signed our articles of association.

Sat 24 Nov: [...] To the theatre in the evening. I saw 'La Métromanie' & 'Le Médecin Malgré Lui'.

Sat 1 Dec: made an agreement with Pierre Gavet & Eleazar [Ingrouille] [by which] I will let the house & gardens to them for six years at £50 stg per year, & le Brulin at 10 quarters per year. I have reserved the option to take everything back after four years on the provision of 3 months' notice.

Thurs 6 Dec: [...] signed three agreements – the first to let the house, gardens & Brulin to Pierre & Eleazar for 800 *livres*; the second to let the two fields & meadow at les Tuzets to James Torode for 16 quarters; & the third to let la Censiere to Jean Roussel for 9 quarters.

Sat 8 Dec: [...] Pierre Falla of les Capelles (a Methodist) was imprisoned in the Castle for refusing to give evidence on oath, having been called as a witness in Pierre Arrivé's action against Mr James Falla.

Mon 10 Dec: [...] Made an agreement to let le Ruquet to Etienne [Lihou] for 6 bushels, & to let les Eturs to Jean Moullin for 12 quarters & 2 bushels.

[*Mollet sold his livestock, some farming equipment and some cereals at auction on 13 December.*]

Tues 18 Dec: sent some empty bottles to town, where I will have them filled with wine to take with me. Packed the earthenware & various other things in chests & hampers.

Fri 21 Dec: [...] Fine weather. Pierre & Eleazar spent *la longue veille* with me.

Weds 26 Dec: yesterday I dined & supped at the Governor's. There were 14 of us.

Fri 28 Dec: [...] I have let the house at le Prais [Préel] to Nic. Mauger, jun., for 6 years.[236]

---

[236] This was the house in le Préel which Mollet had bought from Thomas Lihou in 1784.

Mon 31 Dec: to town. I signed an agreement to rent Mouriaux House from the Alderney Governor for six years at £30 stg a year. I also signed an agreement (in the company's name) to rent his two vaults at Braye for six years at £40 stg a year.[237] Pierre [Gavet] & Nico [Martel] took a cartload of boxes & beds to town. We put part of the load on board the Governor's cutter, & the rest on board Captn [Stephen] Bedbrook.

Notes relating to 1787

Charles Mollet gave work to twenty individuals aside from his live-in employees in 1787. About half were tradesmen and the other half were day labourers. Most of the day labour went to three men: Pierre Gavet (172½ days), Etienne Lihou (154½ days), and Eleazar Ingrouille (148 days). After Pierre Gavet moved to a house in the King's Mills at the end of September, he stopped working for Mollet. On 3 December, however, he started working for him again (perhaps because of his intention to continue working the farm in partnership with Eleazar Ingrouille while Mollet was in Alderney). Mollet's live-in farm servants in 1787 were Abraham Collenette and Nicolas Martel.

---

[237] In referring to the 'Alderney Governor', Mollet rarely distinguished between Jean Le Mesurier, who was Governor from 1744 until his death aged seventy-six in 1793, and his son Peter, who succeeded him as Governor in 1793, but filled the post of Lieutenant-Governor from 1773. The cutter Mollet mentioned belonged to Peter; Mouriaux House was built and owned by Peter; and the vaults at Braye were the property of Peter as well.

1788

Tues 1 Jan: I joined Mr Pierre le Mesurier on board his cutter at nine & we arrived in Alderney at half past eleven. We had a good passage. I have brought with me as my manservant Nico Martel & as my house servant Nanon le Page. Abraham Collenette also accompanies us, but he will stay only a few weeks. Pierre [Gavet] will arrive soon with the rest of my belongings & spend a few days here. I have entered into a commercial partnership with Mr Marrett for six years; I have let out my property for six years; & I have agreed to rent les Mouriaux House for six years. I intend to make Alderney my general place of residence during this period, unless the affection I have for my Dear Mother (& she for me) should check my design, or God should cause me to alter my plan for some other reason.

Fri 4 Jan: began to settle ourselves at Mouriaux House. Nanon & the boys are eating there, but I am still eating & sleeping at Mr Mesurier's, who is alone here with his son. Mrs Mesurier & the three girls are spending the winter in Guernsey.[238]

Mon 7 Jan: Pierre [Gavet] brought me six pullets & a couple of hens, some flowers in pots, & several other things, all of which we unloaded today.

Tues 8 Jan: Mr Ahier was married this morning to Miss ……… Lorenni, daughter of Mr Lorenni.[239] Mr Mesurier, Mr Marett & I joined the newly-weds in the evening for tea & mulled wine. There was much company (perhaps 100 persons), who all seemed greatly to enjoy themselves.

---

[238] Peter Le Mesurier was married to his first cousin Mary Le Mesurier (1757–1800). Their children at this time were John (aged six) and his younger sisters Mary, Harriet and Amelia. Peter's father, Jean Le Mesurier (the Governor), had been a widower since 1763.

[239] James Ahier had married Rachel Lorani. Both the Ahier and Lorani families had moved to Alderney from Guernsey to engage in trade. The groom was the son of James Ahier of St Peter Port. The bride was the daughter of Joseph Lorani (a second-generation Italian born in Guernsey in 1734) and Elizabeth, *née* Allez (sister of Jeanne Allez who had married the Reverend Isaac Vallat – see n. 113). The Loranis had several other Alderney-based children, including a twenty-eight-year-old son also named Joseph who was married to Marie Hocart. Mollet frequently alludes to social engagements with the Loranis in his Alderney diary entries, but it is not always clear which generation was involved.

Fri 11 Jan: [...] Pierre left for Guernsey this morning on board Tom Robert.

Thurs 17 Jan: to Burhou with Messrs Mesurier, Olivier & Williams.[240] Fine weather.

Fri 18 Jan: Mr Marrett & his family arrived from Guernsey on board Tom Robert. They were entering the harbour when their sloop struck a rock & sank in shallow water. The 12 persons on board were rescued within 10 or 12 minutes, but they had for a while been in serious danger. They all came here in the evening, except Mr Marett's sister who remains unwell at Braye. The sloop was unloaded in the evening, & their furniture, almost all of which was wet, was put on the quay. I myself stayed at Braye until ten. I had two hens, two ducklings & ten chicks on board the sloop.

Sat 26 Jan: we took possession of the two stores we are renting at Braye today, although our lease nominally began on 1 January. The delay in taking possession was due to the fact that Mr Mesurier continued the business on his own account until Mr Marrett was present in Alderney.

Tues 29 Jan: made our first sales today: 183½ gallons of liqueurs, gin & brandy, & 44 four-gallon kegs.

Weds 30 Jan: Mr Mesurier took tea here in the evening. Opened our accounts ledger.

Thurs 31 Jan: Mr Tom Williams took tea with me.

Fri 1 Feb: made a reasonable number of sales.

---

[240] Thomas Williams was Alderney's Greffier between 1773 and 1819. He also held the office of Procureur for part of that time. Williams was the son of the late Reverend Thomas Williams, Rector of St Sampson and Vicar of the Vale 1730–43, and Rector of St Saviour 1743–63. He was married to a Jerseywoman named Rachel De La Taste with whom he had two sons, Thomas, born in Guernsey in 1769 and Frederick, born in Jersey in 1775. Frederick Williams succeeded his father as Greffier in 1819 and held the post until 1851. During Mollet's sojourn in Alderney, the diarist had frequent dealings with both Thomas Williams the Greffier and Thomas Williams, his twenty-year-old son. In Mollet's diary entries, it is not always possible to tell whether he is referring to Thomas the son or Thomas the father.

Sun 3 Feb: [...] Dined at the Governor's with Sr Philippe & Mr & Mrs Solier.[241]

Fri 8 Feb: [...] I dismissed Abraham [Collenette]. He has worked for me since 12 February 1787.

Weds 13 Feb: [...] Yesterday evening we saw a beacon lit at le Casquet & today a signal has appeared announcing the death of the lighthouse keeper.

Thurs 14 Feb: [...] The cutter (which was unable to reach le Casquet yesterday) crossed to the lighthouse this afternoon & confirmed that the keeper had died. His wife & daughter will stay there with Cooper, Dady & Fadu.

Fri 15 Feb: [...] Tom Williams has taken tea & supped with me every day since the 8th.

Sun 17 Feb: to church both morning & afternoon. Tom Williams dined with me.

Tues 19 Feb: made more sales today than on any day so far.[242]

Sat 23 Feb: Messrs Serane, Lerfeu, Jack Hocart & Colomez came to dinner.[243]

Tues 4 Mar: [...] Mr Marrett & I were going to appoint arbitrators, but he changed his mind, so each of us will continue to abide by his own interpretation of article 9 (concerning repairs).

Weds 5 Mar: Tom Williams & I went to le Casquet in Mr Le M.'s cutter. Nico accompanied us. Our purpose was to bring over the new keeper (Michel Mesné), & return Mr Cooper to Alderney.

Thurs 13 Mar: Eleazar [Ingrouille] arrived this morning on board Captn Bedbrook.

---

[241] Pierre Solier (1725–1808) was a Huguenot refugee from Languedoc who served as Anglican Minister of Alderney between 1763 and 1808.
[242] This is the last time during his Alderney sojourn that Charles Mollet mentions sales.
[243] Frenchman Jean Colomez was Alderney's resident surgeon.

Mon 17 Mar: Eleazar helped Nico [Martel] dig the garden in the morning.

Sun 23 Mar: Easter Sunday. To church in the afternoon, after which I remained entirely alone until Eleazar returned at nine in the evening.

Mon 24 Mar: [Easter Monday] spent all afternoon & evening alone. Eleazar came back very late. Nanon slept out, not having returned by midnight.

Tues 25 Mar: Eleazar neither breakfasted, dined nor supped here. He only returned at 8 in the evening after I sent someone to call him (the third time I have had to do this). However, he went out again shortly afterwards, & I was obliged to go & fetch them all from a party at half past twelve.

Sun 30 Mar: to prayers in the morning & to church in the afternoon. I left after the 2nd psalm to fetch Eleazar & Nico from the Fort.[244]

Mon 31 Mar: [...] I wrote to Messrs B. Dobrée & Co., enclosing the letter Mr Mourant had written for me to Messrs Arfvidson ordering planks & iron for the business I am setting up with Jean Carré.

Sat 5 Apr: sowed peas, carrots, onions, leeks & flowers in the garden.

Sun 6 Apr: left Alderney with Eleazar on board Captn Bedbrook at half past seven. Arrived in Guernsey at noon. Dined at Candie. Saw the Governor in the afternoon. Returned to the Castel to sleep.[245]

Tues 15 Apr: [...] Made an agreement with Jean Carré to form a company to sell planks & iron. It will be two-thirds mine & one-third his. I will order the merchandise & he will sell it.

Fri 18 Apr: [...] Left Guernsey on the Alderney Governor's cutter at half past one (with all his family). Arrived in Alderney at half past four.

Tues 22 Apr: worked in the garden. Tidied up the flowers in pots, planted my geraniums, &c.

---

[244] This was probably what is now known as Essex Castle. It may have accommodated some sort of tavern within its walls.
[245] Mollet had reserved a small attic bedroom at the farm for himself.

Sat 26 Apr: [...] Made a second sowing of beans in the field adjacent to the road. Sowed two rows of green peas on either side of the garden path.

Mon 28 Apr: fine, warm weather. Last week's winds have died down. Saw swallows for the first time today. The cuckoos had already been here 3 or 4 days when I returned from Guernsey.

Weds 30 Apr: visited Mr Havilland Le M. in the morning. He & his wife, the Governor, & Mr & Mrs le Mesurier took tea with me in the afternoon.[246]

Thurs 1 May: dined at the Governor's. To Braye in the morning & afternoon.

Mon 5 May: [...] Nanon [Le Page] has confessed to Monsieur Colomez that she is three months pregnant for Nico [Martel]. [...] Nico denies responsibility, but nevertheless acknowledged to Mr Williams & myself that he had slept with Nanon.

Weds 14 May: left on board Captn Bedbrook at two in the afternoon & arrived in Guernsey at six.

Sat 17 May: [...] Yesterday I engaged Marie Batiste & today I engaged Nanon Heaume to be my house servants in Alderney. I also engaged Nico le Page (son of Nicolas of les Mielles) as my manservant.

Sun 18 May: set sail for Alderney at three [in the morning]. Did not arrive until seven in the evening.

Tues 20 May: I dismissed Nico (Martel). He returned to Guernsey with Captn Bedbrook.

Thurs 22 May: went to hear Gueuzed, the Methodist preacher, in the evening.

Tues 27 May: my new servants Nico le Page, Marie Batiste & Nanon Heaume arrived on board Captn Robin this morning. Received letters from Mr Mourant, Pierre & Eleazar. Mr Mourant sent me some artichokes, broad beans, &c. Pierre sent me some peas & a piglet.

---

[246] Havilland Le Mesurier (1758–1806), a serving military officer, was a son of Governor Jean Le Mesurier and a brother of Lieutenant-Governor Peter Le Mesurier. He was married to Elizabeth, *née* Dobrée (1763–1804), a daughter of Isaac Dobrée.

Fri 30 May: the Governor, Mrs Le M., her children, & Tom Williams came to dinner.

Tues 3 Jun: Mr Williams dined with me.

Weds 4 Jun: I have been picking strawberries every day since Friday.

Tues 17 Jun: Nanon (Le Page) returned to Guernsey on board Bedbrook.

Weds 18 Jun: [Captn] Feugere arrived from Guernsey last night with a letter from Mr Mourant informing me that my Dear Mother had had an accident on Saturday. Feugere also brought me letters from Pierre & Eleazar, eight ducks, a pot of butter, some strawberries & some gooseberries.

Thurs 19 Jun: left for Guernsey at ten on board Captn Sanford. […] Found my Dear Mother obliged to keep to her room & spend most of her time in bed. She is nevertheless in good spirits, thank God. It was the same sort of accident as she had on 9 May last. Slept at the Castel.

Sun 22 Jun: left on board Captn Bedbrook at six […] Arrived in Alderney at eleven.

Tues 1 Jul: Mr Williams dined with me. Captn Le Cheminant arrived from St Croix in the West Indies.

Sat 5 Jul: Mrs Le Mesurier's little girl (Amélie) died at midday at the age of one year.

Sun 6 Jul: […] In the evening, I accompanied Mr Le Mesurier to see his little girl buried.

Mon 14 Jul: Mr Williams dined & supped with me. Tom Barbenson joined us for supper.

Fri 18 Jul: Mr & Mrs Marrett returned from England last night. They left on 24 May.

Tues 29 Jul: Mr & Mrs Le Mesurier came to dinner. The Governor, who is unwell, could not come, but we all later went to take tea with him at his home.

Thurs 31 Jul: […] Nanon Le Page (who left on 17 June) returned to my service. While in Guernsey, she stayed with Pierre & Eleazar.

[*Charles Mollet turned forty-six during the course of August 1788*]

Sun 3 Aug: […] Marie Batiste, who came here with Nico [Le Page] & Nanon Heaume on 27 May, returned to Guernsey.

Mon 4 Aug: the Trinity House yacht arrived this morning with several gentlemen on board. Mr Le Mesurier accompanied them to le Casquet.

Fri 8 Aug: […] Transplanted my 2nd sowing of chicory. Made another sowing (the 4th) today.

Mon 18 Aug: sowed some turnips in the field.

Mon 25 Aug: the Alderney farmers began carting their grain. Rain on & off all day.

Thurs 28 Aug: Messrs Marrett & Williams dined with me. To Braye in the morning. Watched the farmers carting their grain in the afternoon. Sowed lettuce & chicory among the currant bushes.

Tues 2 Sep: […] Captn Feugere arrived from Guernsey. I received a letter from Pierre, some plums, a bottle of rose water & some tulip bulbs.

Weds 10 Sep: […] Mr Tom Gosselin (the naval lieutenant) entered the harbour for shelter on his way from Guernsey to England.[247] I took him to the Governor's for tea & accompanied him back to Braye in the evening.

Fri 12 Sep: […] In the evening, two Dutch galliots arrived. Mr Berghaus's galliot was carrying 10 casks of gin for us & Mr Roche's was carrying 35 casks of gin for us.

---

[247] This was Thomas Le Marchant Gosselin (1765–1857), the son of the Greffier Joshua Gosselin. He was promoted to the rank of Rear-Admiral in 1814.

Tues 16 Sep: [...] Captn Feugere arrived from Southampton with 5 dozen flower pots & six large earthenware seed pans for me.

Weds 17 Sep: [...] received a letter from Eleazar informing me of his engagement to Elizabeth Robert.[248]

Mon 22 Sep: [...] Took tea at Mr Cocq's. Mr Williams dined here.

Thurs 25 Sep: spent the morning & afternoon at Braye. Bought 100 English cabbages for planting. Mr Williams breakfasted & dined with me.

Sun 28 Sep: at home all day. Mr Williams dined with me.

Tues 30 Sep: spent the morning at Braye. Mr Williams dined with me. I took tea at the Governor's in the afternoon.

Thurs 2 Oct: Mr Williams breakfasted & dined here.

Mon 6 Oct: Chief Pleas. Dined with the Governor at Sr Jean Olivier's by invitation of the Judge.[249]

Tues 7 Oct: Mr Williams breakfasted, dined & took tea here.

Thurs 9 Oct: Mr Williams dined & took tea here. Strong easterly & north-easterly winds since Tuesday evening, but no rain. Captn Cohu attempted to enter the harbour on his return from England yesterday, but was unable to do so & pressed on towards Guernsey – not without danger, however.

Weds 15 Oct: at five o'clock this morning, Mr Williams & I went on board les Maillotins [...] We arrived at Plainville at half past nine & breakfasted with the Curé of Omonville, who received us with all possible affability, even though we had no introduction & were strangers to him. We then walked to Cherbourg, where we arrived reasonably early & supped & slept at Mme Hamel's.

---

[248] Eleazar Ingrouille was by this time twenty-two. His fiancée Elizabeth Robert was twenty-seven.
[249] Jean Gauvain (1724–93), who presided over the Alderney Court.

[*Charles Mollet and Thomas Williams were in France until 20 October, visiting several people in Cherbourg and Caen. Ten days after his return to Alderney, Mollet left for England on his own. He stayed there between 31 October and 15 November, calling on various people in Hampshire, Dorset and Devon, ostensibly to collect payments for goods he had sold them.*]

Fri 31 Oct: went ashore at Weymouth at nine. [...] Saw Mr Martin. Left for Dorchester in the mail cart at ten (8 miles). Dined at the King's Head (Mrs Bryer). Left for Blandford in the Exeter stage at two. Put up at Blandford.

Sat 1 Nov: [...] Took another chaise as far as Ringwood, where I put up.

Sun 2 Nov: visited Mr Warne last night & returned there in the morning. Brought him to the Crown for dinner, having called on Mr Tunks in his company. Mr Early came to see me in the afternoon. Left in a chaise for Southampton at six in the evening.

Tues 4 Nov: [...] Mr Warne came to see me in the afternoon. Yesterday Mr Warne gave Mr Tunks £100 stg, which Mr Tunks remitted to Captn Priaulx. Wrote to Mr Marrett.

Thurs 6 Nov: left Southampton at nine in the morning in the Bath coach. Arrived at Salisbury at noon. Stopped off at the Black Horse (Mr Webb), where I dined & took tea. Left again for Exeter at six. I was the only passenger in the coach.

Fri 7 Nov: spent all night alone in the coach, passing through Blandford, Dorchester, Bridport & Axminster, where we stopped at nine in the morning for breakfast. Continued towards Honiton after breakfast & arrived in Exeter at half past four.

Sat 8 Nov: left Exeter at eight in the morning, having hired two horses & a guide. [...] Arrived in Dowlish [Dawlish] at ten & breakfasted at the New Inn (Wm Hoare). Saw Mr Potter.

[*Mollet continues the entry in English*]

Gone to Newton Bushel where arriv'd at one oclock & seen Mr Syms & Mr Richardson. Arriv'd at Paynton between 3 & 4. Din'd at the Crown & Anchor

(Mr Guddridge), then through Guddington, &c., to Brixham, where arriv'd at dark. Put [up] at the London Inn (Mr Underhay). Saw Mr Rackstraw & Wm Efford.

[*reverts to French*]

Sun 9 Nov: wrote to Mr Williams. Left Brixham at eleven. Arrived at Newton Bushel at one. Baited at the London Hotel (Mr Cawse). […] Arrived at Exeter at four.

Mon 10 Nov: supped & slept at the London hotel. Left in a chaise at 8 in the morning. Arrived at Woodbury at 10. Breakfasted at Mrs Lempriere's. Crossed the common to Sidmouth & thence to Bere. Stopped at Mr Pottam's, where I saw Nic. Olivier & received ……. from John Lane & Wm Woodgate. Went on to Seaton, where I visited Mr Trott (the last house in the village) & saw Geo. Tozer. Arrived at Lyme at 7 in the evening, where I put up at the Three Bells.

Tues 11 Nov: supped, slept & breakfasted at the Three Bells (Mr Scrivens) in the company of Mr Knight, a retired lawyer from Sidmouth. Left Lyme in a chaise for Weymouth at nine. Arrived there at four.

Thurs 13 Nov: left Weymouth by chaise at eight. Passed through Preston, Osmington, Helwarden & West Lulworth to East Lulworth, where I stopped at the Red Lion near the castle & saw Mr Green, Geo. Lukis, Mr Woolfreys (wounded),[250] Mr Napper Roper, Saml Pope & Mr Whitfield (a new acquaintance). From thence I went to Wareham, where I changed chaise & continued to Ringwood.

Fri 14 Nov: Mr Warne dined & spent the afternoon with me. Called on Mr Tunks & Mr Cobb. Left in the mail coach at six in the evening & reached Southampton at half past eight.

Sat 15 Nov: spent the night at Mr Knight's. Wrote to Mr St Croix & Captn Bradby. Went on board Pierre Le Lievre, jun., & Nico Enouf at two in the afternoon.

---

[250] The word 'wounded', without further explanation, is in English.

Sun 16 Nov: arrived in Guernsey at nine in the morning. Dined at Candie, where I found my Dear Mother in better health than I expected.

Mon 17 Nov: slept, dined & supped at Candie. Breakfasted at the Governor's.

Tues 18 Nov: went on board the cutter at six. Arrived in Alderney at two in the afternoon.

Sat 22 Nov: Mr & Mrs Le M. & their children took tea here.

Tues 25 Nov: took tea at Mr Le M.'s yesterday & today. Mr Williams dined with me.

Weds 3 Dec: Captn Cheminant left for Sette & Captn Andrews arrived from Sette. Messrs Williams, Nico Barbenson & Cohu took tea & supped with me.

Fri 5 Dec: Sr Nico du Four the tailor & Mr Williams dined with me.

Weds 10 Dec: Nico le Page of les Mielles (who came here as my servant on 27 May) left my service & returned to Guernsey on board Bedbrook.

Sat 20 Dec: Mr Le Mesurier's cutter arrived from Guernsey last night, bringing me a letter from Mr Mourant & £100 stg in *six-livre* coins. Wm Lihou the tailor has been working for me.

Sun 21 Dec: Wm Lihou was intending to return to Guernsey with Mr Ahier's masons, but they were prevented from leaving by the strong winds. Captn Feugere arrived with letters from Pierre & Eleazar. He also brought with him Hellier le Pelley (Judith Lihou's son) who has come for a trial period as my manservant.

Tues 23 Dec: I did not go to bed last night, intending to leave for Guernsey at four in the morning with Jean Dolbel of Jersey. However, his vessel was unable to leave, & I lost heart.

Thurs 25 Dec: Messrs Vivian, Hardy & Williams breakfasted with me. Mrs Gosselin, Mr & Mrs Williams & their son came to dinner.

Mon 29 Dec: embarked on board Captn Bedbrook at ten in the morning & arrived in Guernsey at one in the afternoon. My very good friend Governor Brown met me off the boat & took me back to his house, insisting that I should stay with him during my sojourn in Guernsey. Thus I returned to his house after seeing my Dear Mother, whom I found in good health.

Weds 31 Dec: wrote to Messrs Marrett & Williams. The Procureur supped with us.

1789

Thurs 1 Jan: the Governor had company to dinner. I stayed at his house all day, except for a few hours in the morning, when I went to see the Bailiff & the Alderney Governor.

Sun 4 Jan: to Castel church in the morning. Dined at la Haye du Puis, then went to my home in the Castel. Visited Mrs le Pelley in the evening. Eleazar came to fetch me, & I slept at the Castel. It is excessively cold.

Tues 6 Jan: dined at Mr Robert Le Marchant's. Saw Jean Carré at Mr Mourant's counting-house in the evening.

Weds 7 Jan: dined & supped alone with the Governor.

Fri 9 Jan: there is about a foot of snow on the ground & drifts 4 or 5 feet deep. Went to the Castel & visited Mr Andros on horseback in the afternoon. Slept at my home.

Mon 12 Jan: returned to the Governor's.

Tues 13 Jan: awoke to a southerly wind & a general thaw which set in overnight. The Greffier breakfasted with us, & I accompanied him to see the damage the sea has wrought at Glategny.

Fri 16 Jan: bought 6 puncheons of rum from Mr Mourant.

Sun 18 Jan: to church with the Governor in the morning. Dined at Candie.

Tues 20 Jan: Pierre, Eleazar & Nico le Pelley brought some grain, flour & apples to the harbour from the Castel, & we loaded them on board Nico le Rai.

Fri 23 Jan: to the Castel in the afternoon. Snow remains on the ground here & there.

Sun 25 Jan: dined at Candie. Yesterday evening a French vessel of 300 tons was lost off the Vale; 23 men were drowned & 2 rescued.

Tues 27 Jan: left Guernsey at ten in the morning [...] Arrived in the Alderney roads at four in the afternoon & remained there until the vessel was able to enter the harbour at six.

Mon 2 Feb: the Judge of Alderney [Jean Gauvain], Messrs Simon Gauvain, Ph. Pezet, Thos Le Cocq, Jean Olivier, Jean Simon, Sr Thos Simon (Comptroller), André Gaudion (Sergeant), Jean le Beir & Sr Pierre le Cocq the chimney sweep (Constables), Srs Nico Guille Olivier & Collin Olivier (last year's Constables) came to dinner. The four last-mentioned gentlemen stayed to supper. I had also invited Mr Williams, sen. (Greffier & Procureur), but he declined.

Fri 13 Feb: [...] Wrote to Mr Mourant, Pierre & Eleazar. Sent my watch to be repaired. Bedbrook arrived & brought us 4 pipes of brandy & 2 puncheons of rum from Mr Mourant. He also brought letters from Nico le Pelley, Bon Dobrée & several of my correspondents in England.

Sat 14 Feb: Captn Peter Lambton (of Newcastle) arrived from Guernsey on the brig Rose of London, bringing us 50 casks of Sette brandy consigned to us by Messrs Burnet.

Sun 22 Feb: I did not go out today, having had a cough for a week.

Tues 24 Feb: briefly to Braye in the afternoon.

Weds 25 Feb: Mr Williams & Mr Carteret (Tom) took tea & supped with me.

Fri 27 Feb: planted peas & sowed lettuces in the field (along the wall to the west of the gate).

Mon 2 Mar: Jean Gaudion came with his horses to help us collect seaweed.

Sat 14 Mar: [...] I received the news that Nancy Mourant gave birth to twin boys on 5 March.[251] In the afternoon, I went to Braye, where I had not been since 24 February, having stayed mainly in the house on account of my illness.

---

[251] The newborn twins were William and Henry Brock, who lived until 1869 and 1812 respectively (see Appendix 2).

Thurs 19 Mar: paid a few visits in the afternoon. Planted green peas against the two western walls & more early Frame Peas against the wall to the east of the gate.

Thurs 26 Mar: spent the morning at Braye. Planted the artichokes.

Tues 31 Mar: there were celebrations to mark the King's recovery today. The militia was under arms & the town was illuminated in the evening. Having failed to put candles at our windows, we had 5 window-panes smashed.

Tues 7 Apr: I had an exceptionally clear view of Guernsey today. I could easily distinguish the small parlour of Mr Mourant's house, & (I think) two ploughs, one below the Castel church & the other near la Petite Hyvreuse.[252] Yesterday evening I saw people & livestock on the French coast.

Weds 8 Apr: sowed green curled broccoli, lettuce, larkspur, &c., in the north-western bed. Monsieur Colomez & Mr Williams took tea & supped with me.

Thurs 16 Apr: Nico le Rai, whom we chartered to go to Jersey, returned with 45 casks of brandy purchased from the Messrs Hemery. Captn Feugere & three other vessels also arrived.

Fri 17 Apr: Mr Le Messurier came to tell me that 'he was here as a friend to inform me most civilly that, because of what happened during last week's illuminations, he would be unable publicly to receive me as he had in the past. As a private individual, he was ready to render me any service he could, but as Governor, he could not receive my visits nor acknowledge me in any way.'[253]

Sun 19 Apr: I did not leave the house.

Mon 20 Apr: [...] Embarked on board Captn Nico Le Rai at four in the afternoon.

[Mollet begins writing in English]

---

[252] The entry for 16.5.89 reveals that Mollet owned two spyglasses.
[253] It seems likely that 'Mr Le Messurier' was Peter Le Mesurier, the Lieutenant-Governor, who had just returned to Alderney after an absence of a few days in Guernsey.

Tues 21 Apr: enter'd the Needles at six. Arriv'd at Southton a[t] ½ past one. Deliver'd Mr Hilgrove the 100 guineas & letter from Mr Ahier. Sup'd at Mr King, the King's Arms, with Captn Le Rai & passengers. Wrote to Mr Williams & Mr Mourant. Sleep at Mr Knight's.

Weds 22 Apr: [...] Gone in a post chaise to Ringwood where din'd. Seen Mr Tunks & Messrs Warne & Early.

Thurs 23 Apr: [...] gone thro' East Lulworth to West Lulworth, where slept at the Red Lyon.

Fri 24 Apr: gone by Upton Mills to Osmington & to Weymouth, where din'd at Mr Spicer's. Gone in the afternoon to Checkrel & Langton. Sup'd at Mr Martin's.

Tues 28 Apr: [...] Set out at six evening alone in the mail coach for Southton. Sleep at Mr Knight's.

Mon 4 May: gone in the mail coach to Ringwood. Stay at the White Lion, where found Captn Hall.

Thurs 7 May: left Ringwood alone on horseback (Mr Collins the taylor's horse). Gone thro' Langham, Lichiot, quite straight thro' Wareham over the bridge, & on to Corfe Castel about 4 miles further. Din'd at the Greyhound (I think a better house than the Ship). Seen the ruins of the Castel, then gone over the hills to East Lulworth, then down to Arish Mills where Naper Roper lives, & on to West Lulworth where stay the night.

Sun 10 May: left Weymouth & gone alone thro' Broadway, Upway, Winterborn & Martins Town, then thro' Bridport &c. to Lyme, where din'd at the George opposite the church. In the road to Seaton met 3 Italian sailors. Stay the night at Mr James Trott at Seaton.

Mon 11 May: gone to Beer. Rode in the afternoon to see the cliff that fell last year. Stay at Mr Potter's, the New Inn. Wrote to Mr Williams two letters from Seaton & Beer.

Thurs 14 May: rode to Mr Early's & Christchurch in the morning. Mr Nicholas Barbenson arriv'd from Alderney. Gone at six o clock in the mail coach to Southton.

Sat 16 May: Mr Chepmell arriv'd from Guernsey, going for London. Wrote by him & sent my two spying glasses & 60 guineas to Mr St Croix. Mr Roche arriv'd from London. Jean Carré arriv'd from London. Last night he has sup'd & been mostly with me all day. Wrote to Mr Mourant, Nicolas Brouard & Mr Williams.

Mon 18 May: Captn Fergusson arrived from Jersey & I spent the morning with him. In the afternoon, I walked around the town with Jean Carré.

Weds 20 May: Captn Fergusson left for London this morning. I went on board Nico Le Rai at eleven.

Thurs 21 May: arrived in Alderney at one in the afternoon.

Tues 26 May: spent the morning working in my garden. To Braye in the afternoon.

Thurs 28 May: Mr Williams took tea with me.

Sat 30 May: […] Spent the morning & afternoon at Braye. Called on the [Lieutenant-]Governor & Mrs Le Mesurier before dinner to pay the rent for our stores.

Mon 1 Jun: Mr Ludlam[254] & Mr Cohu (Abraham) came here in the evening & stayed until two, when we embarked on board Laurent Flere. At ten the next morning, we were put ashore in Herm. We dined there & left for Guernsey at two. We arrived in Guernsey at six. I found my Dear Mother & the rest of the family in good health.

Tues 2 Jun: wrote to Mr Williams.

Sun 7 Jun: to Castel church in the morning. Dined & spent the afternoon at my house.

---

[254] Peter Ludlam (c.1755–c.1807) was a Guernsey merchant. He was married to Rachel Le Mesurier, the niece of the Alderney Governor.

Tues 9 Jun: signed the charterparty (dated yesterday) with Captn Hellier Mahy who is to go to Gottenbourg for us.

Weds 10 Jun: breakfasted at Roquaine alone with the Governor, after which we dined & spent the afternoon at my house in the Castel. We had set out on horseback at seven in the morning & we returned to town at eight in the evening.

Mon 15 Jun: dined alone with the Governor. To le Chateau des Maresq in the evening.

Weds 17 Jun: prepared for my departure tomorrow.

Thurs 18 Jun: Thomas Pelley & I went on board Nico le Rai at eleven in the morning & were put ashore at les Trois Vaux at eight in the evening.

Mon 22 Jun: picked the first strawberries. Mr Williams supped with us.[255]

Sat 27 Jun: Mr Williams dined with us. We went walking at Gifouagne in the afternoon.

Sun 28 Jun: to church in the morning. Mr & Mrs Loranni, Mrs Mollet, Mr & Mrs Ahier, & Mrs Williams took tea here in the afternoon.

Thurs 9 Jul: Laurens Flere left in the morning. Mr Pelley missed the boat.

Fri 17 Jul: […] Mr Williams came to dinner & returned to sup with Ned Cocq, Mr Pelley & myself. We passed the time merrily until three in the morning, when we sent Mr Pelley off to Guernsey on board Nico le Rai.

Weds 22 Jul: […] We had news of a mutiny at Cherbourg last night.

Sat 25 Jul: Mr Duppa (an English painter)[256] & Mr Williams took tea with me.

---

[255] Mollet's Guernsey neighbour, Thomas Le Pelley (see n. 134, above), was staying with the diarist for a few days.
[256] 'Mr Duppa' is likely to have been Richard Duppa (1768–1831), a Romantic painter and author.

Tues 28 Jul: Peter Mourant arrived from Guernsey on board Captn Feugere.[257] Received letters from Mr Mourant & Eleazar.

[*Charles Mollet turned forty-seven during the course of August 1789*]

Sat 1 Aug: Peter dined at the Governor's.

Sun 2 Aug: [...] Bedbrook arrived from Guernsey. I received letters from Mr Mourant & Bon Dobrée, informing me that Captn Mahy has arrived from Gottenburg with our cargo of timber & iron.

Tues 4 Aug: embarked on board Captn Bedbrook at half past 7. Arrived in Guernsey at half past 1. Dined at Candie. To the Castel in the afternoon. Returned to Candie, where I will sleep.

Fri 7 Aug: [...] I engaged Abraham Machon as my manservant for 30 *écus* a year.[258]

Sun 9 Aug: [...] Received a letter from Mr Williams & the [news]paper from the 4th. To the Castel before dinner. Dined at the Governor's with Mr Tom Dobrée & le Marquis de Robien.[259]

Weds 12 Aug: set sail at six this morning on board Laurens Flere (Abraham has slept at Candie these past two nights). We were put ashore at les Trois Vaux at three in the afternoon.

Tues 18 Aug: Nanon Heaume left for Guernsey on board Laurens Flere. Wrote to Mr Mourant & Eleazar. Hellier le Pelley left my service. He has been with me since 21 December last.

Fri 21 Aug: Peter & I did not go to bed.[260] We left at two on board les Maillotins (Jean Pequeur) with Captn Lauga, Messrs Lambert & De Fougere.

---

[257] Mollet's nephew Peter Mourant was by this time nineteen years old.
[258] Abraham Machon (1770–1835) was to remain an employee of Charles Mollet's (with one or two short gaps) until the end of Mollet's life (see Appendix 4).
[259] This was Paul-Christophe de Robien (1731–99) of le Fœil in Brittany, an early *émigré* from the French Revolution.
[260] Mollet's nephew Peter Mourant had been in Alderney since 28 July.

We arrived at Cherbourg at ten in the morning, where we are staying with Madame Hamel. Supped at Monsieur Du Long Prey's.

Sun 23 Aug: accompanied Monsieur Du Long Prey to le Calvaire in the morning, where the militia was assembled [in Cherbourg]. We then followed the first militia company as far as the Basin, where about 4000 soldiers & militiamen were gathered in order to take the Oath of Fidelity to the Nation & the King, &c. The Oath was followed by a Mass & the singing of the Te Deum (inside a tent). We then dined at Monsieur De Fougere's, who took us out into the roadstead in the afternoon. We rowed the whole length of the breakwater & climbed up on one of the cones. To the theatre in the evening.

Mon 24 Aug: called on Monsieur de la Ville Eon in the morning & visited the gardens of Messrs Grandcamp & Beuxville. Took refreshments at Madame Haudri's in the afternoon.

Weds 26 Aug: [...] spent the night at sea & arrived off Mannez at ten in the morning. Messrs Marrett & Williams came out to fetch us in a rowing boat. Our baggage was brought ashore in the evening.

Sat 5 Sep: left on board Captn Bedbrook at 10 with Peter Mourant, Mr le Marchant & Mr Maingy. We were put ashore in Sark at six in the evening, where we saw Mr Le Pelley & Nic. Brouard. Supped in Sark & left for Guernsey at ten, arriving at one in the morning.

Sun 6 Sep: walked directly to the Castel (with a brief detour to Candie). Arrived at my house at three in the morning. Breakfasted there. Returned to Candie for dinner. Attended the Methodist meeting in the evening, then went to the Governor's.

Weds 9 Sep: dined at my house in the Castel with my sister & brother[-in-law] Lerrier, Mr Mourant, my sister, Patty, Nancy, Billy Brock & Bon Dobrée.

Sat 12 Sep: to the Chateau des Maresq in the morning.

Mon 14 Sep: I wrote to Mr Saml Dobrée & sent him £150 stg in notes.[261]

---

[261] For Samuel Dobrée, see n. 218, above.

Tues 15 Sep: went on board Captn Feugere at 9 in the morning & arrived in Alderney at two.

Weds 23 Sep: I had words with Mr [Pierre] Le Mesurier at Braye this morning. In consequence of this, Mr Williams took him a note this evening & brought back his response.

Thurs 24 Sep: Mr Williams refused to take my second note to Mr Le M., so I asked Mr Marrett to take it instead. However, Mr Marrett returned the note to me in the afternoon, saying he was not in a position to involve himself in this matter. At 4 o'clock I received a further note from Mr Le M. appointing six as the time for our engagement. He arrived at the prescribed time with Sr Jean Olivier. As I was unable to find anyone to act as my second (Messrs Williams & Marrett having refused), I offered to ask Sr J. Olivier to arbitrate between us. However, Mr Le M. declined to do this & went off.

Fri 25 Sep: Mr Le M. left for Guernsey on board Bedbrook this morning.

Sun 27 Sep: […] Captn Bedbrook brought Mr Le M. back from Guernsey. The Procureur travelled with him & paid me a visit in the afternoon.[262]

Sun 4 Oct: I left on board Captn Flere at six & arrived in Guernsey at noon.

Weds 7 Oct: Mr [Philip] Fergusson,[263] Eleazar & I slept at Mrs Wood's in the High Street. We embarked on board Captn Flere at half past five & reached Alderney in less than three hours. […] At 4 o'clock, Mr Le M. & I met at the appointed place, bringing our seconds with us. We both fired two shots, but without effect.

Thurs 15 Oct: Ph. Fergusson & Eleazar left for Guernsey on board Captn Le Cheminant.

Mon 19 Oct: […] Stormy weather since noon. Several boats went out to fish in the morning. Those of Jean Mesni & Henry De La Marche (among others) are not yet back. People are anxious for them.

---

[262] Hirzel Le Marchant (for whom, see n. 138, above) still occupied the office of HM Procureur. He was to act as Le Mesurier's second in the anticipated duel with Mollet.

[263] Philip Fergusson had agreed to act as Mollet's second. Born in 1766, he was the son of Dr William Fergusson and the late Anne, *née* Lerrier (the sister of Mollet's Jersey brother-in-law).

Sun 25 Oct: [...] Henry De La Marche & the others arrived back today. The wind had pushed them as far as the Isle of Wight.

Mon 16 Nov: Spent the morning at Braye. Spoke to Mr M[arett] & wrote to Mr Le M[esurier].

Weds 18 Nov: [...] Nanon Heaume, who left on 18 August, returned here.

Thurs 19 Nov: Mr & Mrs Le Mesurier & family left for Guernsey. I sent my letters. Thos Le Geyt arrived from Jersey & brought us 8 casks of brandy.

Weds 25 Nov: embarked on board Captn Feugere at noon & arrived in Guernsey at six.

Thurs 26 Nov: to the Castel in the morning. I am staying at Candie.

Weds 2 Dec: to the Castel again in the morning, then embarked on board Captn Feugere with Messrs Jack Le Pelley & Jean Carré. Set sail at noon & arrived in Alderney at six.

Sat 5 Dec: wrote to Mr Mourant, Bon Dobrée & Pierre [Gavet]. Sent two chests full of books & two sacks of potatoes to Guernsey.

Sun 13 Dec: to church in the morning. Pierre [Gavet] arrived at noon on board Captn Feugere.

Tues 15 Dec: I put up a notice announcing that there would be an auction today. I sold my 3 mahogany tables, some earthenware, some wine & some other things.

Thurs 17 Dec: stormy weather these past two days. Today, we packed up the furniture, &c.

Sun 20 Dec: we loaded 3 beds, a mattress & various other things on board Captn Feugere in the morning. Mr Pelley, Nanon Heaume & Pierre left with Captn Feugere at eleven.

Fri 25 Dec: stayed at home.

Weds 30 Dec: to Braye in the morning. Paid farewell visits to my friends. Messrs Ahier & Williams took tea with me. Gave the money (£ ......) & the keys of the chest to Mr Williams.

Thurs 31 Dec: [...] took the rest of my furniture & effects to the harbour & loaded them on board Captn Sturges' cutter. We were very busy all day.

Notes relating to 1788 and 1789

For the fifth and sixth surviving volumes of his journal (covering the years 1808–12 and 1815–18), Charles Mollet used old account books from his Alderney days which had only been partially filled. The fifth volume begins with several pages of old stock-lists and invoices. Many of these are pasted over with pictures cut out from Victorian children's literature, but such of the stock-lists and invoices as are visible between or on either side of the Victorian pastings shed light on Charles Mollet's activities while in Alderney. At the very beginning of the volume is part of a list of goods left in the stores belonging to Peter Le Mesurier (Lieutenant-Governor of Alderney) when Charles Mollet and Thomas Marett took out a lease on them in January 1788 (the pair styled themselves 'Messrs Charles Mollet & Co.' even though they were a partnership). The goods Peter Le Mesurier left in his stores at Braye became part of Mollet & Co.'s stock-in-trade, and the partners paid Le Mesurier for them. The first page of the list recorded the presence in the stores of 244½ gallons of brandy, 712 gallons of cognac, and 1,238 gallons of rum. Collectively, these were worth £235 13s 6d stg. The whole list occupied three pages in total, but only the first page is visible. Further on, there is an intact list of the stock remaining in the stores on 31 December 1788, after Mollet & Co.'s first year of trading. It included 4,304 gallons of brandy, 1,050 gallons of rum, 844 gallons of gin, 1,180 gallons of cognac, 7,418 gallons of liqueurs, 6 hogsheads of red and white wine, and some chocolate. Collectively, the stock was worth £929 11s 11d stg. The invoices in this volume all relate to purchases and provide evidence of the purchase and importation of wines and spirits from or through Valencia, Rotterdam, Ostend, the West Indies, Montpellier, Toulon, Lorient, Roscoff, and Guernsey. The wines and spirits arrived in large containers such as puncheons, pipes and hogsheads. Mollet & Co. (who also imported materials for cooperage) had them decanted into smaller containers on arrival in Alderney.

The first thirteen pages of Mollet's sixth surviving volume (1815–18) contains copies of bills of exchange issued when Mollet was in Alderney. The bills, issued as payment for goods purchased by the partnership's clients, were drawn on various English banks, most of them small concerns in the south-west of England. The outfits which figured most frequently were the Sherborne and Dorsetshire Bank; the Yeovil Bank; Chichester Old Bank; the Bath & Wells Bank; the Sussex & Chichester Bank; the City Bank of Exeter; and the Devonshire Bank. The sums in respect of which the bills were issued were usually in the hundreds of pounds. The largest was £477 15s 9d (on 22 January 1789). Prominent among customers paying these large sums were Peter Warne, John Early and Stephen Tunks. The first two, at least, were well-known smugglers from the Ringwood area of Hampshire.

1790

Fri 1 Jan: used the cart to take my furniture, &c., to Braye until two in the morning, then spent the rest of the night carrying the remainder of it by hand. [...] Nanon [Le Page], Abraham [Machon] & I went on board Mr Sturges' cutter (Captn Scavel) about seven in the morning, but the sea was so rough that we were unable to leave the harbour. We disembarked, & I spent the day at Captn Sanford's, dining & taking tea there. At five in the evening, we re-embarked & departed.

Sat 2 Jan: reached Guernsey at three in the morning. After calling at Candie, Abraham & I went to the Castel, where we breakfasted. Pierre & Eleazar accompanied us back to town with the cart, & we unloaded part of my furniture. I am sleeping at Candie.

Sat 16 Jan: [...] I dismissed Nanon Le Page & paid her up to the 28th of this month. She has worked for me since 28 June 1786.

Sun 24 Jan: [...] Paid Abraham Machon 39 *livres* & 11 *sous* for his 5 months & 5 days' service with me (10 August 1789 to 17 January 1790), at 30 *écus* per year.

Mon 8 Feb: to the Castel in the morning. Marie [Gavet] gave birth.

Weds 10 Feb: [...] Embarked on board Captn Le Ray at eleven in the morning. Spent the night at sea & arrived in Alderney at nine in the morning.

Sat 13 Feb: dined at Captn Sanford's. Took tea at Mrs Williams's. Attended the Club with her son. He handed me 200 guineas to give to Mr St Croix & 10 guineas to cover my expenses in England.

Sun 14 Feb: embarked on board Captn Le Ray at nine in the morning. Spent the night at sea & arrived in Guernsey at six the next morning.

Mon 15 Feb: Patty [Dobrée] gave birth to a daughter last night.[264]

---

[264] The infant was Elizabeth Dobrée, who lived until 1876.

Tues 16 Feb: to the Castel in the afternoon. Took Guillaume Lihou's horse out of the half of the furzebrake which belongs to me, rode him almost as far as la Vaudinerie, then handed him to Eleazar with instructions to take him to Gerbourg.

[*The diary now breaks off. It resumes on Wednesday 28 April. More than ten weeks are missing. No pages are torn out.*]

Weds 28 Apr: arrived from England on board Captn du Feu at 4 o'clock in the morning. Found my Dear Mother, Mr Mourant & the rest of the family in good health. To the Castel in the afternoon. I had departed for England on 17 February.

Sat 8 May: Mr Marrett & I signed articles dissolving our joint enterprise with immediate effect. I wrote to Mr Williams & to Mr Saml Dobrée, to whom I remitted £75 1s 6d.

Mon 17 May: left on board Captn Bedbrook at six in the morning & arrived in Alderney at ten.

Tues 18 May: […] I have come here to meet Mr Marrett to share out our remaining stock.

Thurs 20 May: […] Shared out the bottled wine, sugar & chocolate. Shared out the materials & appurtenances from our counting-house which we wished to keep & sold the rest.

Fri 21 May: shared out the distilled liqueurs, &c.

Tues 25 May: spent the night at sea & arrived in Guernsey at ten in the morning.

Weds 2 Jun: the Governor has appointed me one of his aides-de-camp. I entered his service this morning. I delivered orders to the forts & went to Roquaine in the afternoon.

Sun 6 Jun: I accompanied the Governor to breakfast at Major Parkes', where we found Colonel de Peister.[265] Afterwards, all four of us rode through St Martin & the Forest to Roquaine, where the Governor inspected the fort (as also the fort near Lerée).

Fri 25 Jun: left at noon with Captn Feugere & arrived in Alderney at four in the afternoon.

Sun 27 Jun: [...] Went to hear Mr Brackenbury preach in the morning.[266]

Tues 29 Jun: the brig Friendship, Captn Sylvers, arrived from Guernsey carrying 40 casks of Valence brandy for us.

Sat 3 Jul: finished unloading the rum & brandy. For my share, I have 13 pipes of Sette brandy (which I have stored in Captn Lauga's cellar); 25 pipes & 4 barrels of Valence brandy (in Mr Jean Robillard's store); 7 puncheons of rum; & 22 casks of gin. Received £52 10s from Mr Jean Robillard on account.

Mon 5 Jul: arrived in Guernsey at nine in the morning.

Fri 16 Jul: spent the day at the Castel. Nanon Le Page & Nanon Heaume cleaned & scrubbed the house. The two le Marchant ladies, Patty, Miss Carterette le Marchant, Mr Cuthbert, Captn & Mrs Melville took tea with me.[267] Bon Dobrée returned from England.

Thurs 22 Jul: Mr Mourant won his *vue de justice* against Mr Jean Le Mesurier in New Street.[268] Tom Williams arrived from Alderney & accompanied me to the Castel, where we took tea.

Thurs 29 Jul: our ship from Gottenburg struck the Castle rock while making for port this morning. She remained there all day & was brought into harbour in the evening.

---

[265] Lieutenant-Colonel Arent Schuyler De Peyster (1736–1822), an American-born British colonial military officer of French Protestant descent.
[266] Robert Carr Brackenbury (1752–1818), a Methodist preacher from Lincolnshire.
[267] Captain Philip Melvill of Dunbar (1762–1811) had married Bonamy Dobrée's youngest sister Elizabeth (1770–1845) in 1788.
[268] For *vue de justice*, see n. 46, above.

Sat 31 Jul: began unloading our timber yesterday & today.

[*Charles Mollet turned forty-eight during the course of August 1790*]

Sun 1 Aug: attended the English sermon in the morning. To the Castel after dinner. Tom Williams left for Jersey this morning.

Weds 11 Aug: the Governor & his son,[269] Major Waugh, Peter Dobrée,[270] Mr Mourant, my sister & Peter [Mourant] dined with me at the Castel.

Sat 4 Sep: […] News reached us of Mr Paul le Mesurier's bankruptcy.[271]

Thurs 9 Sep: Peter Mourant & I left Guernsey on board Captn Feugere at three in the afternoon & arrived in Alderney at half past six. Put up at Mrs Taylor's.

Sat 11 Sep: [Peter & I] left Alderney at seven & arrived at Cherbourg at half past nine (we chartered Captn Feugere to convey us there for two guineas).

Mon 13 Sep: young Flosseil (Mons. Du Chevreuil's son) breakfasted with us & took us on horseback to see Monsieur De Querqueville.[272] From thence we went to dine at the Curé d'Omonville's.

Sat 18 Sep: […] Left Cherbourg in a two-horse chaise at noon.

Mon 20 Sep: […] arrived in Caen at half past six. Put up at l'Hotel d'Espagne in la Rue St Jean.

---

[269] Although Lieutenant-Governor William Brown was not married, he fathered (and acknowledged) several children, some of whom were born in Guernsey. See n. 297, below.

[270] Peter Dobrée (1760–1843) was a younger brother of Bonamy Dobrée. Mollet also had a nephew named Peter Dobrée (1784–1870, the son of Patty and Bonamy), but he was he was only a boy of five at this time.

[271] Paul Le Mesurier (1755–1805) was a son of the Alderney Governor Jean Le Mesurier and the younger brother of Pierre Le Mesurier, with whom Mollet had a duel. Based in London, he was a Director of the East India Company and MP for Southwark.

[272] This was Jean-René-Marie De Leuvre de Qu[i]erqueville, whom Mollet was later to encounter as an *émigré* in Guernsey.

Tues 21 Sep: [...] Called on Mme Lamy & Messrs L'Honoré, Saml Paisant, Gautier, St Jore, Matthey & Lamy des Vallez. Supped at Monsieur Des Vallez's.[273]

Fri 1 Oct: [...] Supped at Mons. Des Vallez's (where Peter is now sleeping, having begun his residence in France).

Thurs 14 Oct: left Caen [for Coutances] in a chaise with Dom Costin.[274]

Sun 17 Oct: [...] visited the church with Dom Costin, with whom I dined *en famille*. In the afternoon, I went out on the leads at the top of the Cathedral tower, which I believe is about 250 feet high. On the landward side, one can see the countryside for about 7 leagues around. On the seaward side, one can see Granville, Chausey & Jersey. There are two parishes in Coutances apart from the one attached to the Cathedral. There are also two monasteries (Jacobins & Capucins) & two nunneries.

[*Mollet leaves Coutances on his own to visit le Mont Saint-Michel*]

Weds 20 Oct: the church at le Mont St Michel is, I believe, 350 to 400 feet above the sands. The tide goes out a distance of 5 leagues. It then rises vertically through 50 feet, submerging the walls of the mount in at least 15 or 20 feet of water (though I was told 30).

Thurs 21 Oct: [...] Passed through Pontorson & Antrain. Stopped at Fougeres, where I slept at l'Ecu.

Fri 22 Oct: returned to Antrain, where I was arrested for not having a passport. I was detained at the post office (Mons. Reval).

Sat 23 Oct: spent a rather dismal day.

Sun 24 Oct: [...] a letter from Mr Sebire to the Mayor of Antrain ... procured my release in the evening. I travelled on to Dol, where I slept at l'Image Notre Dame (Mme Landais).

---

[273] 'Monsieur Des Vallez' was probably Michel-Louis Lamy des Vallées (1728–1800), a prominent Protestant merchant and local politician.
[274] Dom Jérôme-Jean Costin (1759–1825), was a French ecclesiastic and teacher at the Catholic seminary in Coutances.

Mon 25 Oct: arrived at St Malo at ten in the morning. Was again arrested & confined to my lodgings (Mons. Hardy, Rue des Juifs). Mr Sebire wrote another letter (from his country house) & I was liberated at four in the afternoon. I went briefly to see le Couvent des Recollets in St Servan, then embarked on board the Jersey quarantine boat, which set sail at eleven at night.

Tues 26 Oct: arrived in Jersey at eight in the morning. Went to my sister's.

Thurs 28 Oct: embarked on board Captn Bisson at eight & arrived in Guernsey at noon. Mr Mourant has been ill with the gout, but is beginning to recover. [...] Mr Williams travelled from Jersey with me.

Sat 30 Oct: Mr Williams dined at Candie & spent the afternoon with us.

Thurs 11 Nov: wrote to my sister & Mr Williams.

Sat 20 Nov: wrote to Monsieur St Jore & Peter. Sent them two sacks of potatoes, a dozen bottles of rum & a dozen bottles of gin.

Thurs 9 Dec: bought 4 gallons of shrub from Captn Betts & a gallon of old Jamaica rum from Mr Duniere. Pierre & Eleazar took them to the Castel for me.

Tues 14 Dec: Etienne [Lihou] took some of my plants from le Jardin des Plantes to the Castel for me.

Tues 21 Dec: to the Castel, where I have dined these past two days. Planted the shrubs from Caen.

Fri 24 Dec: dined at the Governor's with Mr & Mrs Waugh, the Procureur & his wife, Dr & Mrs Sausmarez, Mr Johnston, Mr Nic. Dobrée, Mrs Fisher & Mrs Piercy.[275]

Sat 25 Dec: dined here [Candie] with the family (although I had been invited to Mr Nic. Dobrée's).

---

[275] Mrs Fischer and Mrs Piercy were daughters of Nicolas Dobrée of 'Bellevue' (see Appendix 3). Susanna (1759–1843) was married to John Siegfried Fischer, and Mary (1762–1808) was married to William Piercy.

Fri 31 Dec: [Captn] Mourant left for Exeter taking with him my carnations & rosebushes for Mr Heathfield, Mr Scrivener & Lord Courtenay.[276] Received some oak saplings from Mount Edgcumbe.[277]

Notes relating to 1790

Most of the notes relating to 1790 concern leases and rentals. Mollet recorded that he had been renting his vault at la Profonde Rue to the Bailiff (William Le Marchant) since September 1789 at six guineas p.a., as also the storeroom above the vault to the Receiver General (John Harris) since February 1789 at £5 stg p.a., and the stable belonging to his warehouses and about a third of the land there to Thomas Naftel since May 1790 at £5 stg p.a. He himself had been renting the bedroom above the wash-house at his home in the Castel from Pierre Gavet and Eleazar Ingrouille for 10 *livres* per year since 24 June 1790.

Mollet also recorded that he had paid the Le Pelley brothers 17 *livres* 10 *sous* for ploughing 4 vergees at le Mont d'Aval for him 3 times, and sowing barley there on 11 May 1790.

---

[276] Mollet probably became acquainted with these people during the visit he made to England between 17 February and 28 April 1790 (but did not record). 'Mr Heathfield' is likely to have been Anthony Heathfield of Lympestone in Devon, who was married to the Guernseywoman Judith Hubert. 'Mr Scrivener' has not been traced. 'Lord Courtenay' was probably William, 3rd Viscount Courtenay of Powderham (1768–1835), better known today for his involvement in a homosexual scandal (see G. Griffin, *Who's Who in Gay and Lesbian Writing* (New York, 2002), p. 17).
[277] Mount Edgcumbe was the seat of the naval officer and politician George Edgcumbe, 1st Earl of Mount Edgecumbe (1720–95).

1791

Sat 1 Jan: Monsieur Paisant (the younger) gave me a letter from Peter [Mourant] dated 25 December.

Weds 12 Jan: I dined at Major [John] Waugh's on 30 December, after which we began taking a census of houses & people in the town parish. We started at his house, proceeded to the far end of Glategny, then continued through le Bouet, la Ramée & la Couture, finishing for the day at St Jaques. Today I dined at Major Waugh's again & we continued our census. Starting from his house, we proceeded along Glategny in the other direction & went as far as le Grand Carrefour.

Mon 31 Jan: spent the morning at Mr Carré's. We settled our accounts.

Tues 1 Feb: spent all day at the Castel, where I dined. Planted the evergreen oaks & Mossy Cup oaks from Mount Edgcumbe at le Neuf Courtil & the turning, as also half of the anemones from Caen.

Fri 11 Feb: Mr Waugh & I continued our census, completing both sides of the High Street.

Thurs 24 Feb: spent the day at the Castel. Sowed 1500 acorns (from Barcelona) in the upper garden.

Weds 16 Mar: Mr Marrett has been here since Sunday but has left again without seeing me (except for a brief encounter – by chance – this morning). Took tea with Mrs Andros.

Thurs 31 Mar: Mr Waugh & I continued our census. Today we devoted our attention to Smith Street (as far as the College), the environs of the church & Cornet Street.

Fri 1 Apr: attended a meeting at Mr Nico Dobrée's regarding the accounts of the privateer Duchess of Kingston, which we approved & signed off.

Sat 9 Apr: dined at the Governor's with le Comte du Parc, le Comte de Kernel & le Chevalier de Médic.[278]

Sun 10 Apr: to the Castel. Jack & Tom Le Pelley dined with me. Sent letters to Tom Williams & Mr St Croix by Jack Condomine.[279]

Mon 11 Apr: to the Castel in the morning. Paid Mr Josias le Marchant the balance of £5 1s stg owed him on the privateer Duchess of Kingston, of which Mr Nic. Dobrée was the *armateur*.

Fri 15 Apr: took tea at Mr Andros's. Gave him the £7 10s he is owed from the Duchess of Kingston.

Mon 25 Apr: Easter Monday. Breakfasted with the Governor. Dined at the Castel. Paid a visit to Mrs le Pelley. Called at la Haye du Puis & St George.

Weds 4 May: Mr Boruwlaski, the famous Polish dwarf,[280] arrived here with a letter of recommendation addressed to me from the younger Monsieur Du Long Prey. To the Castel after dinner.

Sun 15 May: went to the Castel but did not dine there. Called briefly at St George in the evening. Mr Boruwlaski was there.

Mon 23 May: Thos Lenfesté & his two apprentices (Jean Allez & Jean Sarchet) started work on the lower of my two warehouses, which I intend to convert into two dwelling houses.

---

[278] These were probably all *émigrés* from the French Revolution. From this point onwards, Mollet frequently mentions *émigrés*. An effort has been made to identify them using lists preserved at the National Archives (HO 98/25 and HO 98/28); online resources; and the following reference works: H. Forneron, *Histoire Générale des Emigrés pendant la Révolution Française*, 2 vols (Paris, 1884); C. Hettier, *Relations de la Normandie et de la Bretagne avec les Iles de la Manche pendant l'Emigration* (Caen, 1885); R. de l'Estourbeillon, *Les Familles Françaises à Jersey pendant la Révolution* (Nantes, 1886); J. Vidalenc, *Les Emigrés Français, 1789–1825* (Caen, 1963); D.A. Bellenger, *The French Exiled Clergy in the British Isles after 1789* (Bath, 1986). All *émigrés* mentioned in Mollet's journal are listed in Appendix 7.

[279] 'Jack Condomine' was John Condamine (1763–1821), the son of HM Sergeant Jean-Jacques Condamine and Marie, *née* Néel (for whom see n. 116, above). John Condamine became HM Comptroller in 1797.

[280] Jósef Boruwlaski (1739–1837) was an accomplished violinist and guitarist who gave concerts throughout Europe.

Fri 27 May: attended Mr Boruwlaski's concert in the evening.

Sat 28 May: Patty gave birth to a daughter this morning.

Mon 30 May: accompanied Messrs Boruwlaski & Des Travaux around the Vale & St Sampson (Mr Des Travaux on horseback & Mr Boruwlaski & I in a chaise).

Mon 6 Jun: accompanied Mr Boruwlaski to see the Bailiff & the Governor. Following this, we went to Candie, & thence (in a chaise) to the Citadel. After dinner, I showed Messrs Boruwlaski & Des Travaux the Castel Hospital, & we later took tea at Pierre & Eleazar's. At the end of the day, we joined the Governor at le Chateau des Maresq, traversing the town in our chaise on the way.

Fri 17 Jun: Messrs Boruwlaski & des Travaux left for Southampton on board Captn Bienvenu.

Fri 24 Jun: feast of St John the Baptist. Breakfasted at Pierre's with the Governor & Mr Davyson, following which we went to see the Blue Regiment at Vazon & the Green Regiment at les Mielles. I was invited by the officers of the General Meeting to dine with the Governor at Sebire's.

Mon 27 Jun: having learned yesterday that Mr Marrett has been here since Friday, I wrote to request that he answer the letters I sent him on 3 January & 12 February, or otherwise meet me in person (as he had been unable to do on 16 March). Not long after sending my letter, I chanced to see him in Mr Dobrée's counting-house. He told me that he was on the point of departure, thus denying me the opportunity to come to an arrangement with him. (He told me by the bye that he had received the proceeds from selling the iron chest, as also some money from Mr Thos Rose – a circumstance of which he never informed me.) Mr Marrett also insisted that it was incumbent upon me (rather than him) to make proposals as to how to apportion or collect our debts, as it was I who had taken the initiative to write to him, & not the other way round. When I took issue with this, he responded that he would send me a copy of my letter as soon as possible in order to prove his case. In the meantime, Mr Dobrée has undertaken to find out from Captn Pierre Maingy how much the services of an English debt-collector might cost per day.

[Charles Mollet turned forty-nine during the course of August 1791]

Weds 10 Aug: Mr, Mrs & Miss Gibert,[281] Mons. & Mme Dargy, Mr Combs, Miss Bouquet & Mr Jean Le Mesurier (son of the Le Mesuriers of la Mare) dined with me at the Castel.

Fri 12 Aug: my sister fell in the garden & hurt her hip. She is confined to bed.[282]

Mon 15 Aug: my sister remains in bed. She is in considerable pain & has been unable to move since she was carried to her bed at 10 o'clock on Friday morning. I took tea with Mr Gibert.

Weds 24 Aug: to the Castel. Made a nursery for carnation cuttings in the gooseberry bed. Planted chicory among the pines. Sowed lettuce seed in various places.

Sat 27 Aug: Jean Carré & I signed our articles of separation (dated the 25th).

Mon 5 Sep: the roofers & masons have begun working on my [ware]houses again, having left off for a fortnight because of the harvest. To the Castel in the late afternoon.

Mon 12 Sep: went riding with le Marquis de Grego in the afternoon.[283]

Weds 14 Sep: to the Castel in the afternoon to speak to Pierre & Eleazar about their lease.

Sat 17 Sep: dined at the Governor's with Mr Thomson, Mr Nic. Dobrée & his sons.

---

[281] The Gibert family consisted of Rev. Etienne Gibert, his second wife Elizabeth, *née* Berry (1739–1815), and their thirteen-year-old daughter Cécile. Mollet had already met Gibert in 1785 (see n. 208, above). The couple were to move permanently to Guernsey in 1794, when Gibert became Rector of St Andrew.
[282] Mollet's sister Marthe Mourant was now aged fifty-one.
[283] This was Charles-François du Bot du Grégo, Marquis de la Roche (1741–1812). Grégo was a Royalist *émigré*.

Mon 19 Sep: [...] Captn le Ruais left for Holland yesterday with 18 French gentlemen on board.

Fri 23 Sep: Mr Harrington of St Malo arrived in his ship *en route* to l'Isle de France.[284]

Sat 24 Sep: gave Mr Harrington a letter for Tom Williams in Madras.

Tues 27 Sep: to the Castel in the morning. Danl Brouard has built a pigsty at the upper house, where he is to live. Started cutting the bracken in the furzebrake at la Piece.

Weds 28 Sep: to the Castel where six French gentlemen (aristocrats) took tea with me.

Tues 4 Oct: took tea at the Governor's with le Comte de la Marche.[285]

Fri 7 Oct: attended the funeral of Mme de la Houguette. She died at la Haye du Puis, where she had lived for several years.[286]

Mon 10 Oct: my sister Lerrier & her daughter Nancy arrived from Jersey this morning.

Mon 17 Oct: Monsieur De Beau Draps has come here to look into Mons. Turgot's affairs.[287]

Sun 23 Oct: breakfasted at the Castel. Eleazar [Ingrouille] & his wife are now living in the house by themselves. Pierre [Gavet] comes there to work during the day, but he & his family have been living at le Vauxbellez since last Monday.

---

[284] A contemporary name for the French colony of Mauritius.
[285] This was Louis-François-Joseph de Bourbon (1734–1814), an *émigré* and scion of the cadet branch of the French house of Bourbon who carried the courtesy title 'Comte de la Marche'.
[286] 'Mme de la Houguette' was the widowed Judith Ozanne (see n. 102, above). She was aged sixty-eight. Her daughter (also Judith) had married Josias Le Marchant of la Haye du Puits in 1780 (see n. 183).
[287] Monsieur Turgot, whom it has not been possible to identify, may have been an *émigré*. Monsieur De Beau Draps is likely to have been Thomas-François de Beaudrap, Seigneur de Biville, a Royalist sympathiser whose emigration has been documented.

Weds 2 Nov: heavy rain & hail. Sark was covered with snow.

Sat 5 Nov: the builders have finished their work at la Profonde Rue. It only remains to complete the backyards & appurtenances.

Thurs 24 Nov: paid Mr Robert Le Marchant, agent of Phoenix Insurance, to insure my two houses at la Profonde Rue to the value of £500 stg for 7 years. I also insured my house at the Castel for £300.

Sat 26 Nov: I passed contracts with Etienne le Noury & his wife (Judith Ozanne) for the sale of my house & garden at le Prais [Préel]. Purchase price 7 quarters of wheat, entry date Michaelmas. The house is currently let to Nic. Mauger. I bought it from Thos Lihou on 13 January 1784.

Mon 5 Dec: to the Castel. Etienne & Edouard took 17½ dozen bottles of Roussillon red wine there in Mr Mourant's cart. This is half of a barrel which I bottled a fortnight ago. Etienne & Edouard returned to town with 3 hampers containing six dozen bottles of my best Frontignac to send to Jersey with my sister Lerrier.

Sun 11 Dec: my sister Lerrier & her daughter Nancy left for Jersey.

Thurs 15 Dec: [...] I engaged Jean le Page (son of Nicolas le Page the blacksmith) as my farm servant for 30 *écus* a year. He will start tomorrow.

Fri 16 Dec: [...] My farm servant Jean le Page & Jean le Page from Candie took a cartload of beds, &c., to the Castel.

Mon 19 Dec: Nanon Heaume, who was with me for 1½ years in Alderney & left my service on 20 December 1789, began working for me again today.

Weds 21 Dec: Mr Naftel's apprentice came to clean the clock & re-hang it.

Thurs 22 Dec: Pierre [Gavet], who has been living at le Vaux Bellez since 17 October & has already taken most of his furniture there, removed a few remaining items from my house.

Sat 24 Dec: [...] Eleazar [Ingrouille] & his wife left my house this evening. Jean [Le Page], Nanon [Heaume] & I are now here by ourselves.

Sun 25 Dec: Judith Ingrouille was here today, but she left in the evening.[288] Jean Carré took tea with me.

Sat 31 Dec: […] Called at la Haye du Puis & Mrs le Pelley's in the evening. I have now been back here for a week.

---

[288] Judith Ingrouille (1778–1838) was Eleazar Ingrouille's sister.

1792

Sun 1 Jan: Eleazar, his wife & his sister dined with us. I slept the night at Candie. My Dear Mother stayed in bed today, feeling weaker than usual.

Weds 18 Jan: [...] Fine weather. My Dear Mother has not left her bedroom for over a fortnight.

Sun 5 Feb: left Candie at three in the morning. Returned there to sleep in the evening. My Dear Mother is very weak but still perfectly lucid. Her sufferings are slight, thank God.

Weds 8 Feb: [...] My Dear Mother is still conscious but very weak. She scarcely eats or drinks.

Sat 18 Feb: at Candie all day. Hard frosts & snow these past few days.

Sun 19 Feb: my Dear Mother died at nine o'clock this morning.[289] She had not left her bedroom since 6 January, nor her bed since 3 February. She has been almost constantly unconscious these past 3 or 4 days, as if she were asleep. She has lived entirely at Candie since 22 November 1787, shortly before I left for Alderney. Her tenderness & affection for me were such that my loss is inexpressible. My Dear Mother has been unable to walk without help since June 1788 when she injured herself in a fall. Since then, Marie le Rai has been in constant attendance on her. My Dear Father died on 20 May 1770.

Fri 24 Feb: my Dear Mother was buried at the Cimetiere des Freres at four this afternoon, as was her wish. The pall-bearers were Captn Coutart & his brother Advocate Coutart, Mr Nico Dobrée, Mr Jean la Serre, Mr Geo. le Fevre & Mr Pierre Dobrée (the Cardinal).[290]

---

[289] Mollet's mother, Marie, *née* Le Vavasseur dit Durell, was eighty-three years old.
[290] For the first five of these pall-bearers, see nn. 27, 38, 115, 142 and 178. The sixth and last was Pierre Dobrée of 'Beauregard' (1722–1808), a wealthy merchant nicknamed 'the Cardinal'.

Sat 25 Feb: I returned to my house in the evening. Ah, how sad I am when I think of my loss. I believe I would find my life unbearable, were it not for the affectionate friendship shown me by my brothers[-in-law] & my sister & her family.

Tues 28 Feb: planted ..... dozen seed parsnips in the new garden. Started planting my French quicksets at le Marquet. Tidied up the pear trees in the lower garden. Pruned the vines around the upper gate. Danl Brouard repaired the roof ridge at the upper house.

Mon 5 Mar: to town. Dined at Candie. Settled my accounts with Mr Carré up to 13 February. Drew £20 stg on Mr St Croix in Mr Carré's favour. […] Messrs Jean Guille & Josias le Marchant paid me brief visits in the evening.

Fri 9 Mar: wet snow fell overnight & for part of the morning. Frost in the evening.

Sat 17 Mar: […] Mr Mourant sent his big dog, Keeper, to live with me at the Castel.

Weds 21 Mar: Jean le Page has left my service & gone to work at le Ponchez. He had been with me since 16 December. Mr Moullin called here briefly in the evening.

Thurs 22 Mar: […] Abraham Machon came in the evening. I engaged him as my farm servant for 100 francs a year. He left Mr Moullin (for whom he has worked since leaving my service two years & two months ago) this morning.

Sat 31 Mar: breakfasted & dined at Candie. My brother[-in-law] left for Jersey on Monday. He had been in Guernsey since 13 January.

Sat 7 Apr: breakfasted, dined & took tea at Candie. My nieces Polly & Jenny Lerrier arrived from Jersey.[291] The Governor has been ill for a week. I last saw him on Wednesday.

Tues 10 Apr: […] bought a 2-year-old heifer from Henry de Garis (jun.) of Baubigny for 52 *livres*.

---

[291] Polly Lerrier was thirty-five. Her sister Jenny (Jane) was seventeen.

Sat 14 Apr: breakfasted at Candie. Dined at the Governor's. He is beginning to recover.

Thurs 19 Apr: planted some of our own early potatoes at le Neuf Courtil (adjacent to the garden). [...] Our cow calved. The horse & heifer have been in the furzebrake at la Piece since Saturday.

Sun 22 Apr: [...] Peter Mourant arrived from France yesterday evening. He has been away since 9 September 1790, when I accompanied him to Cherbourg.

Thurs 26 Apr: la Comtesse de Liscoet,[292] la Comtesse de Coatlis,[293] Tom Dobrée (Nico's son), Nico le Fevre,[294] Polly Lerrier, Peter Mourant, the Greffier & his daughter Sally came to breakfast.[295]

Mon 30 Apr: [...] I spent all day in town, where I had 18 workmen working for me – carpenters, plasterers, two locksmiths & the masons (who have started work on the two backyards).

Thurs 3 May: [...] Planted blue potatoes in the trench in the driveway. Also planted blue potatoes in the garden at le Prey, along with semi-dwarf peas.

Sun 6 May: [...] We have lately had persistent cold, dry northerly or northeasterly winds.

Thurs 10 May: [...] Pierre Gavet came to fetch the brushwood, peat, &c., which he had been keeping here. He came three times with two carts, but he did not speak to me, nor even acknowledge me.

Thurs 31 May: weeded the strawberries at le Carré. Planted about 60 cabbages adjacent to the earthbank at the bottom of le Neuf Courtil. Jean le Pelley started clearing the lower part of the Plantation. I am paying him 21 *sous* per perch, & a pint of cider each day.

---

[292] Catherine-Vincente Barbier de Lescoët, an *émigrée*.
[293] Marie-Jeanne-Aimée Poulpiquet de Coatlez, an *émigrée*.
[294] Nicolas Lefebvre (1768–1851) was a son of George Lefebvre, Seigneur of Blanchelande. He was to become HM Prévôt in 1806.
[295] Joshua Gosselin remained the Greffier (see n. 2, above). His daughter Sally was Sarah Anne Gosselin (1776–1801).

Weds 6 Jun: Eleazar [Ingrouille], Ab. [Machon] & I went shore-gathering at le Houmet.

Tues 12 Jun: Mr Wm Brock, Nancy & their children came to breakfast. Nancy & the 4 children stayed all day.

Mon 18 Jun: to town, where I dined. Jane Lerrier left for Jersey, but her sister Polly will remain at Candie for a while. They have been in Guernsey since 7 April.

Tues 19 Jun: [...] Elizabeth Le Lievre (daughter of Pierre) started working here as a house servant. I also have Nanon Heaume, who has been here since 19 December last.

Weds 27 Jun: [...] Richard Rabey (youngest son of the late Nicolas Rabey of les Moullins) started here as a farm servant. I also have Ab. Machon, who has been with me since 23 March.

Sat 14 Jul: [...] I bought a 3-year-old black French mare from Nicolas Allez (son of Thomas) of la Hougue du Pommier for £9 stg. Fine warm weather.

Mon 16 Jul: very warm these past two days. Thunder today – particularly loud in the afternoon, when there was a heavy downpour.

[*Charles Mollet turned fifty during the course of August 1792*]

Weds 8 Aug: Mr Guillaume Guille, the eldest son of Mr de St George, died this morning.[296]

Thurs 23 Aug: Ab. went to help Eleazar harvest his wheat.

Sat 8 Sep: Richard Rabey, who started here a farm servant on 27 June, left my service. I still have Ab. Machon, who has been here since 23 March. Spent all

---

[296] William (Guillaume) Guille was born in 1766. He had married Rachel Andros in 1787, and they had three young children. See Appendix 3.

day in town. Dined at the Governor's. His third son (the second to be born in Guernsey) was baptised Richard.[297]

Tues 11 Sep: Pierre Langlais came to dock the tail of the mare I bought on 14 July.

Weds 26 Sep: Mr Condomine, Mr Bowden[298] & the two Messrs le Moine came to dinner. The last two gentlemen are priests from Caen, one is the Curé of St Agnan & the other the Curé of Hubert Folie.

Mon 1 Oct: [...] Heavy rain in the morning. Peter [Mourant], Henry Brock & Mary arrived from England this evening. They have been away since 8 & 20 June.

Thurs 11 Oct: [...] Departed from Guernsey on board Captn Agnew at four o'clock.

Fri 12 Oct: arrived at Southampton at four in the afternoon. Put up at Mrs Richards' in West Gate Street. I have brought my mare with me.

[*There is now a gap in entries lasting more than ten weeks. The journal resumes on Charles Mollet's return to Guernsey.*]

Mon 24 Dec: arrived with Stephen Mourant on board Captn Agnew at eight in the morning. Dined at Candie & went to the Castel in the evening. On 12 December I broke my right collar-bone near Alton. This confined me to quarters in Southampton until I was able to take ship. I stayed at Mrs Knight's. Dr Sausmarez bound up my shoulder as soon as I arrived at Candie. It is not yet healed, but I hope it will soon mend. I sent Etienne to fetch Abraham [Machon], who came in the afternoon to bring home my mare & my luggage. I returned to the Castel to sleep in the evening.

Tues 25 Dec: to Candie for dinner. Stayed there overnight.

---

[297] Lieutenant-Governor William Brown's two Guernsey-born sons were George and Richard Skinner, baptised at St Andrew's church on 18 June 1786 and 2 September 1792 respectively. Their mother was Brown's servant Mary Skinner.

[298] John Bowden (1750–95) was a merchant, the son of John Bowden, sen. and Catherine Carey. He was married to John Condamine's sister Marie.

Mon 31 Dec: slaughtered our two pigs, which together weighed about 300 lb. Bought another pig from Pierre le Cheminant, which weighed 202 lb (I paid him 5 *sous* per lb). In addition to this, I had an old side of pork from James Toraude on Saturday, which weighed 157 lb. This makes a total of 659 lb of pork in all.

Notes relating to 1792

Charles Mollet gave work to twenty men aside from his live-in servants in 1792. Most of these were tradesmen working on the conversion of one of his warehouses at la Profonde Rue into two dwelling houses. Etienne Lihou and Eleazar Ingrouille performed most of the day labour around Mollet's farm, but they worked fewer days than they did in the past, as Mollet had two live-in farm servants for part of the year. Eleazar worked a total of 68 days, and Etienne 47 days. Neither worked during the ten weeks between October and December when Mollet was in England. Pierre Gavet did not work for Mollet at all in 1792.

1793

Tues 1 Jan: slept at Candie. Breakfasted at the Governor's. The heifer calved.

Thurs 10 Jan: [...] Hung up the pork. Planted kale & cabbages in le Neuf Courtil garden.

Sat 26 Jan: wrote to Mme Haudry & sent her 2 lb of chocolate by Captn Launay. Colonel Dundas (commander of this island)[299] arrived in Guernsey with Captn Tom Saumarez, who is Brigade Major.[300]

Mon 4 Feb: Etienne D'Ancel, a Frenchman from the parish of Magneville a few leagues from Cherbourg & not far from Valognes, came to live here as my farm servant today. Wash day.

Sun 17 Feb: Captn Bazin & l'Abbé Dancel (Etienne's father) dined here.[301]

Mon 18 Feb: [...] The 54th [West Norfolk] Regiment arrived here yesterday & disembarked today.

Mon 25 Feb: Abraham [Machon] worked on the construction of bulwarks in the Vale.

---

[299] Colonel Thomas Dundas (1750–94) served for a few months as commander of the garrison and militia under Lieutenant-Governor William Brown. He was appointed owing to escalating tensions with France. Britain had expelled the French ambassador in London after the execution of Louis XVI on 21 January 1793, and on 1 February France responded by declaring war on Great Britain.
[300] 'Captn Tom Saumarez' was Thomas Saumarez (1760–1845), the brother of Admiral Sir James Saumarez and Dr Jean [De] Sau[s]marez (for whom see Appendix 3 and nn. 35 and 200, above). He had joined the British army in 1776 and fought in the American War of Independence. In 1787, he had married Harriet Brock (1763–1858), the younger sister of William and Henry Brock, Mollet's nephews by marriage. Thomas Saumarez had recently been appointed Inspector of the Guernsey Militia. It is thought that he and his brother James had changed their surname from De Sausmarez to Saumarez to make it appear less French and hence more acceptable to the British forces in which they served. This was often extended by analogy to other members of the family.
[301] L'Abbé Dancel was an *émigré* French priest, most likely Jean-Charles Dancel (1762–1836), former Curé of Valognes. (It is somewhat surprising that a supposedly celibate Roman Catholic priest should have had a son, but not unprecedented.)

Tues 26 Feb: we had no day labourers here today – they are all working on the fortifications.

Sat 9 Mar: [...] The Southampton fleet arrived here for the first time since the start of this war.

Mon 18 Mar: to town, where I dined. Received news of an alarm of a French attack raised in Alderney.

Fri 22 Mar: [...] Breakfasted & took tea at Dr Saumarez's. He has rented the upper of my two [new] houses at la Profonde Rue to make a naval hospital there. He will take possession immediately. I have let the lower house to Mr Mitchell (the Sergeant-Major's son), who will move in on 25 March.

Mon 25 Mar: [...] On Saturday I took delivery of a one-eyed horse which Mr Brock has given me.

Mon 1 Apr: there was to have been a General Review at Vazon & I was expecting the Governor for breakfast. Everything was called off on account of the rain which persisted all morning.

Tues 16 Apr: the two Messrs d'Urville dined here today.[302]

Sun 21 Apr: [...] Heard my first cuckoo today. I began hearing wrynecks last week.

Weds 24 Apr: [...] There was an alarm in Jersey last night when a French fleet passed between Jersey & French coast. We saw lights from Jersey beacons all night, which made us fear the worst until a message arrived this evening informing us of the cause.

Fri 3 May: the Governor called here on his way to dine at Mesquesne's.

Sun 5 May: [...] Started seeing swallows & turtle-doves last week.

---

[302] These were French *émigrés*. Their precise identity has not been traced, but they were probably members of the Dumont d'Urville family, minor nobility from Urville, south of Caen.

Tues 7 May: sowed broccoli & leeks at le Neuf Courtil. Weeded the carnations at la Daumaillerie. Mr Serane, Mr Tom Le Marchant, the two Messrs d'Urville & Monsieur De Verson took tea here.[303]

Sat 11 May: I did not go out. Rain overnight. Ab. & I collected about 2000 slugs in the morning. We have been feeding slugs to the ducks since Wednesday.

Fri 17 May: Mr Mourant & Peter called here in the morning. My dear friend the Lieutenant-Governor Wm Brown died at 10 o'clock this morning. He was taken ill only two hours before his death. He arrived in Guernsey on 21 March 1785.[304] I went to see him on 24 March, & he visited me here on 1 April. I first met him in 1764 or 1765, when he was a Captn of Invalids in Jersey. We have been firm friends ever since. I was expecting him to call here around noon today, & I had invited him to breakfast next Monday with his aides-de-camp & Major Waugh. On Sunday, I was intending to spend the morning alone with him. I also received the news that my Uncle Jean died on Wednesday evening.[305]

Sun 19 May: I did not go out. My Uncle Jean Durell is to be buried today. He died at my sister Lerrier's where he had lived for several years.

Mon 20 May: [...] I attended the Governor's funeral. It was a military ceremony. I found it very sad.

Sun 26 May: [...] News reached us yesterday that Colonel Dundas has been appointed Lt Governor.

Thurs 30 May: Lisabo le Lievre (daughter of Pierre) who has worked for me since 19 June last, left my service today. Lisabo le Rai started here in her place.[306] Nanon Heaume is still with me.

---

[303] 'Monsieur de Verson', an *émigré*, was almost certainly Jean-François Bourdon (born in 1744), Seigneur of Verson, a few miles to the west of Caen.
[304] Mollet wrote '1785' in error. William Brown arrived in Guernsey on 21 March 1784.
[305] Jean Le Vavasseur dit Durell, Mollet's maternal uncle, born in 1720. For more on Mollet's uncle, see 2.7.71.
[306] 'Lisabo le Rai' was Elizabeth Le Ray (1775–1850), who was to remain with Mollet for the rest of his life. See Appendix 4.

Tues 4 Jun: in town. Attended Colonel Dundas's levée in the morning & his ball in the evening.

Fri 7 Jun: Mr Serane, Mr Tom Le Marchant, Monsieur De Verson, the two Messrs d'Urville, Monsieur De St Romain, Mr Boulen & Mr Mourant the Minister came to dinner.[307]

Weds 12 Jun: to town in the morning for the auction of the late Governor's furniture. Mr & Mrs Boulen, the two Messrs d'Urville, Messrs De Verson, De St Romain & De Trevoux took tea with me.[308] Etienne Dancel cut the hay at le Brulin. Yesterday Mr du Ponchez paid me 15 guineas for the mare I bought for £9 stg from Nic. Allez on 14 July last. Between 11 October & 24 December, I took her to England, where I rode between 10 & 11 hundred miles on her.

Mon 17 Jun: the two Messrs d'Urville, the two Messrs Grou, Messrs Dancel, Chapel & Bourget came to dinner.[309] Picked 6 or 7 lb of strawberries.

Sun 23 Jun: Polly Lerrier left for Jersey. She has been at Candie since 7 April 1792.

Sat 29 Jun: dined at Colonel Dundas's for the 1st time (he is living at Mr Nic. le Mesurier's house, which once belonged to Mr Nic. Dobrée & where Governor Irving used to stay). There were 14 of us.

Thurs 4 Jul: the two Messrs d'Urville, Messrs Jack Marchant, Nico le Fevre, De Verson, de St Romain, Vardonne, de St Fraquaire, de la Valinerie (father &

---

[307] 'Mr Mourant the Minister' was the Jerseyman Edward Mourant (1768–1836), who was to become Rector of the Forest and Torteval in 1797. He does not appear to have been related to Mollet's brother-in-law Peter Mourant. 'Monsieur De St Romain' was probably the *émigré* Bertrand Faure (1758–95), Seigneur of Saint-Romain-de-Colbosc in Normandy.
[308] 'Monsieur De Trevoux' was Joseph-Jean-Baptiste du Trévou, a Royalist *émigré* executed in Vannes in 1795 (see 3.8.95).
[309] All of Mollet's dinner guests save the d'Urvilles were *émigré* priests. The two Messrs Grou (Groult) were an uncle and nephew. The elder was Curé of Néhou in Lower Normandy. Mons. Bourget was l'Abbé Pierre Bourget, Curé of Noyal-sur-Vilaine in Brittany. The identity of Mons. Chapel has not been traced.

son) & le Tellier (de la Valinerie's nephew)[310] breakfasted with me & stayed here until two.

Sat 6 Jul: [...] Mr & Mrs Nat. le Cocq paid me a brief visit during the evening.[311]

Weds 10 Jul: [...] Elizabeth le Lievre (who left us on 30 May), James Letocq & one of Mesquesne's sons (all of them servants of Mr Ozanne of la Porte) drowned while out in Mr Ozanne's boat.

Fri 19 Jul: rain in the morning. Between the 7th & 17th July the heat was extreme. Last Tuesday my thermometer showed 17 degrees at 9 o'clock in the evening, & I learned that Dr Walters' English thermometer showed 82 degrees on the same day, a temperature similar to Madras in India.

[*Charles Mollet turned fifty-one during the course of August 1793*]

Sat 17 Aug: [...] I attended the funeral of the Procureur (Hirzel le Marchant, eldest son of the Bailiff & brother of Mr Bob).[312] His first wife was Polly le Marchant of la Haye du Puis who died childless in 1787. He then married Major Waugh's daughter who is also childless. Gales all day. Very stormy.

Mon 19 Aug: Mrs Jean Carey & Miss Mary Carey,[313] Patty, Henry Brock, Mary, Mrs Saumarez (the Doctor's wife) & Mrs Saumarez (the Major's wife) came to dinner.[314]

Weds 21 Aug: [...] I gave away 300 cucumbers (in two lots) to the Grenadiers of the 27th Regiment who are at the Houmet.

---

[310] Most of the five last-named *émigrés* have defeated attempts at identification. However, Monsieur Le Tellier may have been the priest Louis-Sébastien Le Tellier, who died in Jersey in 1794.
[311] Nathaniel Le Cocq (1750–1800) and his wife Carterette, *née* Guille (1760–1807), daughter of Mollet's neighbour Jean Guille of St George (see Appendix 3).
[312] Hirzel Le Marchant was forty-one years old.
[313] 'Mrs Jean Carey' was Mary, *née* Brock (1752–1800), the wife of Jean Carey of 'Choisi' (see n. 87, above). 'Miss Mary Carey' (1779–1864) was their daughter.
[314] For 'Mrs Saumarez (the Major's wife)', see n. 300, above. 'Mrs Saumarez (the Doctor's wife)' was Judith, *née* Brock (1758–1816). With the addition of 'Mrs Jean Carey', these women formed a trio of sisters. Their brothers were Henry and William Brock, Mollet's nephews by marriage (see Appendix 3).

Thurs 12 Sep: Lady Eleanor Dundas (the Governor's wife), Mesdames Saumarez (wives of the Doctor & the Major), Henry Brock, Patty & Mary breakfasted with me. Major Saumarez came here later. He & I took Lady Eleanor to Plein Mont & thence to dine with Captn McCrea at Roquaine.[315] The Governor had originally accompanied his wife to my house, but he was obliged to leave before we sat down to breakfast because a fleet had arrived with the 78th Regiment of Highlanders & was waiting to embark the 27th & 54th Regiments currently in garrison here, before proceeding to fetch the two regiments in Jersey.

Fri 27 Sep: my servant Nanon Heaume left this morning without even speaking to me. This was because she found the door locked against her when she returned from a party at three in the morning.

Sun 6 Oct: left at seven in the morning for Alderney, where I arrived at three on board Captn Taylor. I am paying Captn Taylor 5 guineas to take me to Brixham.

[*At this point, Mollet's diary breaks off abruptly, resuming a month later.*]

Thurs 7 Nov: returned from England at seven this morning on board Captn Etienne Martin. (I arrived at Torbay 4 weeks ago yesterday, having left on the Sunday morning & spent the first night in Alderney.) Had my clothes unloaded first thing. To the Castel to sleep in the evening. Jean Anquetil, the servant of Monsieur de Querqueville de l'Oeuvre, has been living at my house since he arrived from Southampton about a month ago.

Sat 9 Nov: paid my respects to Col. Craig, the new Governor & Commander of forces. He was sworn in today.[316] General Dundas left nearly 3 weeks ago. The former Comptroller (Mr Tom De Sausmarez) was sworn in as the new Procureur last week.[317] Mr Metivier was sworn in as Comptroller.[318]

---

[315] Captain Robert McCrea (1745–1835) had married a local bride (Jeanne Coutart, daughter of Advocate Pierre Coutart) in 1786 and was settled in Guernsey.
[316] This was Colonel James Henry Craig (1748–1812), who only served as Lieutenant-Governor for a few months.
[317] For HM Procureur Thomas De Sausmarez, see n. 169, above.
[318] The new Comptroller was Jean Carey Metivier (1757–96), husband of Esther, *née* Guille (1762–1839), the daughter of Jean Guille of St George (see Appendix 3).

Mon 11 Nov: planted the flowers which Mr Curtis of the Botanic Gardens gave me.[319]

Weds 4 Dec: I have been ill in bed for several weeks. Yesterday, I began to feel somewhat better.

Mon 23 Dec: my illness grew worse after 4 December. I have now begun to recover, but I lack appetite & I am so weak that I can scarcely rise from my bed. A week ago last Sunday, I spent the day downstairs, on a couch. This however tired me so much that I have not left my bedroom since. I have had frequent visits from my sister & her family throughout my illness, as also other friends.

Tues 31 Dec: I have spent the last two days alone.

Notes relating to 1793

Charles Mollet gave work to nine men at his Castel property in 1793 (aside from his live-in servants). Most of them were day labourers. The total number of man-days worked was much lower than in the past – only 339¼ days. Etienne Lihou (81½ days year-round) and Eleazar Ingrouille (78½ days year-round) were the men most frequently employed by Mollet. One reason for this year's lack of day labourers was that Mollet had two live-in farm servants (Abraham Machon and Etienne Dancel) for much of the year, as also that he had not grown cereals on a significant scale since his return from Alderney. His best cereal-growing fields, such as le Courtil Robin, were still in the hands of lessees.

---

[319] 'Mr Curtis' is likely to have been William Curtis (1746–99), who opened the semi-public 'London Botanic Garden' in 1779.

1794

Weds 1 Jan: I spent the day alone.

Thurs 2 Jan: Mr Josias le Marchant & the two Messrs D'Urville (who arrived from Jersey yesterday with Monsieur De Percy) paid me a brief visit in the afternoon.[320]

Mon 6 Jan: wash day. Jeanne Le Rai (daughter of old Danl Le Rai of la Terre Norgio) started here as a house servant. Elizabeth le Rai of les Clos au Compte has been with me since 30 May 1793, Abraham Machon since 23 March 1792, Etienne D'Ancel since 4 February 1793, & Jean Anquetil since last October.

Weds 15 Jan: Mary, Nancy & Patty Brock dined with me. We had word from Jersey that Jane Lerrier has married her Mr Griller at last.[321]

Sat 1 Feb: I have lately been tidying up the flower pots & transplanting a few geraniums.

Sat 8 Feb: the weather continues very damp. Danl Brouard of St Andrew & his wife have been living in the large kitchen of the upper house since Michaelmas, but I gave them permission to break their lease. His wife arranged for the key to be handed back to me last Thursday.

Fri 14 Feb: the spring cut of seaweed began today. Four of my servants (Abraham, Etienne, Jean & Janneton [Le Ray]) went to cut seaweed.

Tues 25 Feb: planted gooseberries & currants between the apple trees in the stackyard. Sowed broad beans in the upper garden. Jack Pelley dined & took tea with me. We settled accounts for our *rentes*.

---

[320] 'Monsieur De Percy' may have been the *émigré* René-Charles de Percy, Seigneur de Tonneville (1748–95).
[321] Jane Lerrier had married James Grellier in St Helier on 13 January.

Thurs 6 Mar: sowed semi-dwarf peas. Planted potatoes (using the plough) in the short strip at les Tuzets. Also sowed parsnips & planted potatoes in a strip at the bottom edge.

Mon 17 Mar: sold Mr Hayman a male elm measuring 33½ feet from the earthbank between the lower garden & furzebrake garden (for 2 shillings per foot), as also an ash of the same length from the bank beneath the cowsheds, & an ash measuring 15 feet from the bank between le Neuf Courtil & the top of the lower garden. Messrs Brock & Carey took tea with me & stayed here until eight.

Fri 28 Mar: to Candie for dinner with the intention of staying there until Sunday.

Tues 1 Apr: [...] Mrs Saumarez, the Procureur's wife, died this morning. She leaves 4 children. She was the daughter of the late Isac Dobrée.[322]

Weds 2 Apr: [...] Until last week, I had not been to town since 18 November last.

Thurs 3 Apr: [...] the two Messrs Durville took coffee here. [They] have lately arrived from Jersey & Alderney, whence they crossed twice to France to gather news. Rain nearly all day.

Mon 7 Apr: rain all day. Elizabeth Roussel (sister of Jean of les Rousseaux & widow of Nic. Collenette) started working here as a house servant. Elizabeth Le Rai is still here.[323]

Thurs 17 Apr: [...] Mr Robt Le Marchant, HM Receiver, farmed out the King's tithes today. I did not go. Mr Andros had those of the Castel.[324] Lopped the elms at the turning.

Mon 21 Apr: Easter Monday. Saw my first swallows today. Started hearing cuckoos last Thursday.

---

[322] Martha De Sausmarez, *née* Dobrée, was thirty-seven years old and had been married to HM Procureur Thomas De Sausmarez since 1780.
[323] Jeanne Le Ray, who started as a servant on 6 January, must have left, although Mollet did not record her departure.
[324] 'Mr Andros' was Mollet's godfather, Jurat Charles Andros of les Piques (1721–1805).

Sun 27 Apr: [...] Unseasonably warm weather several days last week.

Weds 14 May: Elizabeth Roussel, who has worked here as a servant since 7 April, left my service.

Thurs 22 May: the two Messrs Groult, the two Messrs le Moine, l'Abbé Dancel & Mons. Sauvegrain came to dinner.[325] The two Messrs Durville, Mons. De Percy & Mons. De St Romain joined us later.

Weds 28 May: dug the border adjacent to the drive in the stackyard. Received our first draff for feeding the pigs & ducks.[326] Took tea at la Haye du Puis.

Sun 1 Jun: to church in the morning. To St Andrew's Rectory after dinner, & thence to town to see Mr & Mrs Gibert who arrived from England this morning.

Sun 8 Jun: [...] Early this morning 5 French frigates gave chase to 3 English frigates (of superior strength) to the north of the Island. Towards noon, two of the English vessels made a dash to escape via les Hannois, & Sir James Saumarez in the Crescent narrowly avoided capture by sailing close to the rocks north of le Houmet, where he was fired on by 4 of the French vessels. Happily, he sustained no damage (owing to the French sailors' lack of skill). The 3 English vessels reached the safety of the roadstead in the afternoon.

Mon 9 Jun: Whitsun. I visited Mr Gibert at St Andrew in the morning.

Thurs 19 Jun: the Messrs Groult, the Messrs le Moine, l'Abbé Dancel, Mons. Sauvegrain, & the two brothers Jalobert (merchants who have recently taken refuge here from St Malo) came to dinner.[327]

Mon 30 Jun: to town in the morning. Dined at Sr Pierre le Lacheur's in St Andrew with some clergymen, Douzeniers & other parochial officers of St Andrew (by invitation of Mr Gibert).

---

[325] Monsieur Sauvegrain was Curé of Secqueville-en-Bessin in Normandy.
[326] Draff is spent brewer's grain.
[327] These two brothers were Denis Jallobert de Monville (1758–1819) and Dominique Jallobert de Monville (1767–1837).

Sun 6 Jul: departed for Alderney on board Captn Childs at nine in the morning & arrived there at three. Took tea at Captn Sanford's & then went to Major [John] Waugh's where I will stay.[328]

Weds 9 Jul: left Alderney at 7 in the evening on board Captn Feugere & arrived in Guernsey at midnight. Returned to the Castel to sleep.

Fri 18 Jul: ploughed our turnip ground for the third time. Rain in the evening – the first since 7 June.

Fri 25 Jul: Mr Mourant, my sister, Mrs Coutart, Miss Roche, Mr Gibert, Mr Boullen & Mr Bowden of Rotterdam came to dinner. Mrs & Miss Gibert joined us in the afternoon.

Sun 27 Jul: to church in the morning. The Revd Mr Mourant, the two Messrs le Moine, Monsieur Grou (sen.), Messrs Sauve Grain, D'Ancel & de la Foidre came to dinner.[329] Light rain in the evening.

Mon 28 Jul: sold an elm from the top of the path by the well to Mr Alex[ander] T[h]om. It is 46 feet long & 8½ inches in diameter. Sold Marie Toraude of Lerée a barrel of cider for 14 *livres*.

[*Charles Mollet turned fifty-two during the course of August 1794*]

Tues 5 Aug: […] Put a hen with 11 eight-week-old chicks & a hen with 6 six-week-old chicks on the old oat ground at les Grands Tuzets. We had 352 sheaves of oats in all. We also had 151 sheaves of wheat from le Courtil Robin. Light rain all day.

---

[328] The purpose of Mollet's journey to Alderney on this occasion was to buy a cow (see 1.10.94).

[329] There were two Messrs de la Foidre. They were the Curés of the Norman parishes of Moisville and Boissy-Lamberville respectively.

Fri 22 Aug: Mrs Coutart, Miss Roche, Mrs Condomine, Mrs Bowden & her daughter Nancy,[330] my sister, Mary, Nancy & Patty Brock came to dinner.[331] [...] Etienne took the small cart to help Mr Gibert transport his furniture.

Fri 12 Sep: [...] A dog belonging to the widow of Wm Nicolle of la Mare killed the peahen which was in the Plantation with her chicks. I caught the dog on the spot & had it killed.

Sun 14 Sep: the Marquis & Vicomte de Ste Suzanne (uncle & nephew),[332] the two Messrs Durville, Messrs De Verson, De Percy & De Barneville breakfasted here & stayed until nearly two o'clock.

Fri 19 Sep: [...] Drew lots for the pews in the new chapel which has been built on the Bailiff's land, & where the Revd Mr Mourant is to be chaplain.[333] I drew a lot for 13th choice & chose pew no. 14. This is a first-class pew & seats four. It will cost me £16 stg a year, plus 20s annually towards the chaplain's stipend (5s per seat). When all the places are taken, the chaplain will receive £70 stg a year.

Thurs 25 Sep: [...] Marie le Cheminant, daughter of my cousin James, died quite suddenly this afternoon. She was their only child.[334]

Weds 1 Oct: fine weather these past few days. I received a cow from Alderney which I bought for 6½ guineas from Richard Herivel. She is nearly 4 years old & expecting her 3rd calf.

---

[330] For Mrs Marie Coutart and Miss Anne Roche, see n. 203, above. Mrs Condamine is likely to have been Marie Coutart's daughter Elizabeth (1761–1804), who had married John Condamine (see n. 279) in 1788. Mrs Bowden was probably John's sister Mary, *née* Condamine (1761–1828), who had married John Bowden (n. 298) in 1780, although their daughters were named Mary and Catherine, not Nancy (but this may simply have been a slip on Mollet's part).

[331] Patty Brock was Mollet's great-niece, the seven-year-old daughter of his niece Nancy.

[332] The Marquis and Vicomte de Sainte-Suzanne were Adolphe-Charles de Mauconvenant (1743–1829) and Bonaventure-Corentin de Mauconvenant (1767–95). Monsieur de Barneville has not been traced.

[333] This chapel, opposite the Royal Court building, was later known as Bethel chapel.

[334] Marie was twenty-six years old and had married James Collenette the previous year.

Sat 18 Oct: [...] Jean Anquetil, who has worked here for a year, left my service today to work for Mr Frere. To Candie in the evening with the intention of staying overnight.

Sat 25 Oct: Miss Gibert died yesterday evening.[335] I called on Mr Gibert in the morning.

Fri 31 Oct: [...] Attended Miss Gibert's funeral. I was one of the mourners.

Tues 11 Nov: Messrs Gibert, De Verson, de St Romain & De Carné dined with me.[336]

Sun 23 Nov: I learned in the morning that my sister suffered a paralytic stroke yesterday so I went immediately to Candie & only returned here at 11 at night. [...] My sister is in a dangerous condition, but perfectly conscious. I truly wish that my own hour had come & that God would take me instead.

Mon 24 Nov: to town in the morning. My sister is slightly better. Slept at Candie.

Tues 25 Nov: my sister continues to improve. Finished gathering cider apples.

Thurs 27 Nov: [...] Took tea at Mr Gibert's. Stayed with him until eight o'clock. He is alone, as Mrs Gibert left for England last Saturday.

Tues 2 Dec: to town in the morning. The States held a vote regarding Lieutenant-Governor General Small's request for £500 stg to build a General Hospital for the troops.[337]

Mon 8 Dec: [...] Peter Mourant arrived from England yesterday. He has been on a visit to Holland.

---

[335] Cécile Gibert was only sixteen. She was the youngest of Etienne Gibert's six children, all of whom had died young.
[336] 'Monsieur de Carné' may have been the Royalist *émigré* Gilles de Carné-Trécesson (c.1759–95).
[337] Major-General John Small (1726–1796) served as Lieutenant-Governor between 1793 and 1796. Although Mollet had maintained friendly relations with the previous four Governors, he had no contact whatever with John Small.

Mon 15 Dec: started feeding limpets to our 9-week-old ducklings.

Thurs 25 Dec: my cousin James & [his wife] Judith dined with us. Snow overnight & on & off through the day.

Fri 26 Dec: the ground remains covered. Collected limpets for the ducks.

Mon 29 Dec: the Procureur, Messrs Gibert, Harry Brock & Tom Carey came to dinner.[338]

Weds 31 Dec: to town in the morning. Returned to the Castel at noon. Went back to town after dinner & stayed there until nine, when I returned to the Castel alone. Very fine weather.

Notes relating to 1794

Live-in servants aside, Charles Mollet gave work to thirteen men at his Castel property in 1794. Most were day labourers, but the number of man-days worked was low (244½), owing to the fact that Mollet had three live-in farm servants for most of the year (Abraham Machon, Etienne Dancel and Jean Anquetil). Day labourer Etienne Lihou worked the largest number of days (107), followed by Jacques Ozanne (53). Eleazar Ingrouille worked only 38 days for Charles Mollet this year. During the course of 1794, Mollet recommenced growing cereals in significant quantities. At the end of August, when the harvest had been brought in, he noted that he had a total of 482 sheaves of wheat, 485 sheaves of barley and 323 sheaves of oats.

---

[338] Thomas Carey (1772–1849) was the son of Charles Mollet's friend Jean Carey (of 'Choisi'). He was ordained on 31 May 1795, after which he became curate of the Castel, and, in 1798, Rector of St Saviour.

1795

Thurs 1 Jan: awoke to a frost which lingered all day. Messrs De Verson, De St Romain & De Carné took coffee with me. Bought 4 two-month-old goslings from Nicolas Des Perques.

Weds 7 Jan: […] Mr & Mrs Josias le Marchant & their two eldest daughters took tea & supped with me.[339]

Thurs 15 Jan: snow in the morning & on & off all day. There are about 2 inches on the ground. The temperature has been below freezing since Saturday evening.

Mon 19 Jan: Thos Mauger, who has been living at the upper house for 3 or 4 years, died suddenly this morning. He came from le Huré in St Andrew & leaves a widow (the daughter of Olivier Robert & Marie Pipet), & two small children (a boy & a girl). They are very poor.

Tues 20 Jan: more snow overnight & this morning. Peter Mourant & the two Brock boys (young Wm & Hy) dined here.[340]

Thurs 22 Jan: […] We have had freezing weather since the 10th & snow on the ground since the 15th.

Thurs 29 Jan: […] Supped at the Castel Rectory with the Revd Mr [Edward] Mourant. He took up residence there today, Mr Dobrée having now been in England for fully ten months.[341]

Tues 3 Feb: […] Replanted last year's tulip bulbs & the hyacinth bulbs which I received from Holland. There are still pockets of snow, some of them two feet deep. They have been there since 15 January.

---

[339] The Le Marchants' eldest daughters were Harriet (1781–1817) and Caroline (1782–1861). Mollet always referred to the former as Henriette.
[340] William and Henry were five-year-old twins (see n. 251, above).
[341] The Reverend Nicolas Peter Dobrée (see n. 38) was Rector of Furtho in Northamptonshire and Wigginton in Oxfordshire, as well as of the Castel. He had gone to reside in one of his English parishes. See 14.10.98.

Fri 6 Feb: to town in the morning. Returned via the Rectory, where I paid the Revd Mr Mourant a brief visit.

Fri 20 Feb: [...] Someone has been stealing potatoes from la Daumaillerie.

Sat 21 Feb: the elder Monsieur Durville, Monsieur de Belfonds & Monsieur de la Roque (all three of them Normans) & Monsieur De Chateau Briant, who comes from near St Malo, dined with me.[342]

Weds 25 Feb: [...] we caught 2 soldiers (stationed at le Houmet) stealing potatoes from la Daumaillerie. They had already taken potatoes 4 or 5 times last week. I handed them over to Sr Danl Dorey, the Constable, who, with Abraham & Etienne's assistance, took the men to the guardhouse in town.

Thurs 26 Feb: attended Court in the morning with Ab., Etienne & Constable Dorey thinking that the soldiers would be tried. We discovered that they had been allowed to escape from the guardhouse.

Weds 25 Mar: Mr Mourant, my sister, Peter, Polly Lerrier, Bon & Patty Dobrée & their children (Peter & Patty) came to dinner. Fine weather these past few days. A fairly hard frost last night.

Fri 10 Apr: to town in the morning to see my sister who is ill. Dined alone with the Procureur in his garden. I entertained Mons. De Verson & Mons. Lanjallais to coffee at Mrs Gullick's. Mons. Lanjallais is a prisoner-of-war from Caen who is about to return to France.

Sat 11 Apr: to town in the morning. Messrs Collings, Bowden, Nico le Fevre, Peter Mourant, Harry Dobrée & Savary Brock came to dinner.[343] Heard my first cuckoo of the year.

---

[342] The last of Mollet's dinner guests was probably Armand de Chateaubriand (1768–1809), a cousin of the Romantic author François-René de Chateaubriand. Armand is known to have been in Jersey at this period (his cousin the writer, also an *émigré*, was in England).

[343] John Savery Brock (1772–1844) was a brother of Major-General Sir Isaac Brock and future Bailiff Daniel De Lisle Brock. Harry Dobrée (1771–1851) was a son of Nicolas Dobrée of 'Bellevue' and half-brother of the Castel Rector. Both were to become frequent visitors of Mollet's in the last decade of his life.

Sun 19 Apr: breakfasted at Candie. Attended the Revd Mr Mourant's chapel. Returned to the Castel for dinner. The Revd Mr Mourant took tea & supped with me.

Mon 20 Apr: [...] Today the Messrs [William and Henry] Brock took up residence at les Touillets, which they are renting for two years, having sold their house at les Croutes to the Government. Mr des Touillets has gone to England to join his family who have been there for a year.

Tues 21 Apr: [...] Nancy's 4 eldest children spent the day with me. Nancy herself took tea here, & Mr Brock came to fetch them all later.

Weds 22 Apr: [...] Saw my first swallows.

Sat 16 May: loaded a keg of cider on board Etienne Martin to send to Monsieur De Querqueville de l'Oeuvre in Southampton, as also one keg & one cask to send to Messrs de Pirey, de Beaudraps & de Menildot in Romsey.[344] Took tea with my sister's family at les Touillets.

Sun 17 May: [...] Dined with Mr Nic. Dobrée at la Mare de Carteret, where we were joined by Messrs Carey, de Havilland & George le Fevre, jun.[345]

Weds 20 May: the Procureur (Thomas de Saumarez) & I left for Jersey on the Liberty at eight in the morning (with Messrs Savary Brock & Nico Le Fevre at the helm). We arrived in Jersey at four. Paid visits to various people in the evening. I am sleeping at my sister's.

Tues 26 May: to Gorey in the morning to see le Prince de Bouillon[346] & Mme de la Garde.[347]

---

[344] These are all *émigrés*. The last was probably Jacques-Louis-Gabriel du Mesnildot (1760–1821), a Royalist army officer from Valognes in Normandy.

[345] George Lefebvre, jun. (1765–1854) was the eldest son of George Lefebvre, sen. (Seigneur of Blanchelande). He had replaced Joshua Gosselin as HM Greffier in 1792.

[346] This was the Jerseyman Philippe D'Auvergne (1754–1816), a British naval officer with responsibility for French *émigrés* in the Channel Islands. He had been adopted by the Duke of Bouillon in what is now Luxembourg, and had assumed the title 'Prince de Bouillon'.

[347] Anne de Blégier Pierre Grosse, second wife of Louis-François-Antoine-Maurice de Payen de l'Hôtel, Baron de la Garde, a leading Royalist army officer.

Thurs 28 May: boarded the Liberty at eight in the same company as on the outward journey, with the addition of Mr Dick Budd. Arrived in Guernsey at four.

Mon 1 Jun: [...] Thos Carré from near les Cauvins was bayonetted to death between 8 & 9 yesterday evening at le Carrefour des Trois Vues. The murderers have not yet been found.[348]

Sun 7 Jun: the Procureur, Mr Pierre De Havilland, Mons. De Verson, le Marquis de Blangy, le Chevalier de Blangy (brothers) & le Comte de Blangy (their cousin)[349] came to dinner.

Sat 13 Jun: the Revd Mr Mourant took tea with me.

Thurs 18 Jun: [...] Mr Crespin, the Dean, was buried today.[350]

Sat 27 Jun: [...] A soldier was sentenced to hanging for robbing Mr Josué Priaulx on the public highway, but was recommended for a royal reprieve. A fortnight ago another soldier received the same sentence for robbing Mr Jean de Havilland.[351] Mary, Nancy & the children took tea here.

Mon 6 Jul: worked the hay. To town in the morning. My left hip has suddenly become very painful.

Fri 10 Jul: [...] I have been in bed since midday on Wednesday suffering badly from rheumatism. Dr Saumarez has been to see me, as also the Messrs Brock, Mary, Nancy & the Revd Mr Mourant.

---

[348] A few days later, James McGuire of the 102nd Regiment was brought before the Royal Court by the St Peter Port Constables on suspicion of Carré's murder. The Court however dismissed the case for lack of proof. Carré's murder was never punished (12.6.95, Livres en Crime, Greffe).
[349] The brothers were *émigrés* Pierre-Henri de Viconte de Blangy (1756–1823) and Auguste-Pierre de Viconte de Blangy (1766–1827). Their cousin was either Constantin de Viconte de Blangy (1722–1800) or his son Bon-Henri de Viconte de Blangy (1775–1827).
[350] Elie Crespin (1735–95), Dean since 1765.
[351] Private John Mullins of the 102nd Regiment of was sentenced to hang for the violent highway robbery of Jean De Havilland on 13 June. Private Allan Ramsay of the same regiment was sentenced to hang for a similar crime against Josué Priaulx on 27 June. Both soldiers were pardoned early the following year on condition of perpetual military service (13.6.95, 27.6.95, 13.1.96, Livres en Crime, Greffe).

Mon 13 Jul: […] The two Mr & Mrs Brocks took tea here. Mrs Le Marchant called here later. I felt rather better & took tea downstairs with my visitors.

Sun 19 Jul: […] The French *émigrés* who were based in Guernsey embarked on board ship yesterday & left the island today.

[*Charles Mollet turned fifty-three during the course of August 1795*]

Mon 3 Aug: […] News reached us that the *émigré* gentlemen who landed on the Quiberon peninsula under the protection of the English Navy were defeated in battle on 20–21 July & almost all killed. There were in all 10 to 12 thousand men, including some Bretons who joined the *émigrés* in France. I fear that Messrs de Percy, de Trevoux & de Carné may have perished in this action.

Sat 15 Aug: started pulling up the peas at les Tuzets. The Revd Mr Mourant took tea with me.

Sun 16 Aug: to church in the afternoon. The Revd Mr Mourant took tea here. Later, we went to les Eturs to watch the passers-by.

Sun 30 Aug: […] The Revd Mr Mourant took tea with me. Later, we went to les Eturs to watch the passers-by, as has been our custom these past two Sundays.

Mon 31 Aug: […] Ab. Machon left my service. He has been living here since 22 March 1792. He also lived with me in Alderney for the last five or six months I spent there in 1789.

Sun 6 Sep: Rachel Girard (daughter of Jean Girard of les Ruettes), who has worked here as a house servant since 27 May, left my service. Ab., who left me on Monday, spent the day here.

Mon 7 Sep: Sam le Page started living here as my farm servant.

Mon 14 Sep: […] Abraham worked here & will stay here to sleep.

Sat 19 Sep: finished lifting the early potatoes. I did not go out. The Revd Mr Mourant took tea with me.

Sun 27 Sep: to town. Breakfasted at Candie. Attended the English sermon, which Tom Carey preached. […] Visited the Revd Mr Mourant who is unwell. Abraham stayed with him overnight.

Tues 29 Sep: […] Took tea at the Rectory with the Revd Mr Mourant. Tidied up the strawberries in the furzebrake garden.

Fri 16 Oct: Etienne [Lihou] took the cart to help carry the Messrs Brocks' furniture to town. They are leaving les Touillets for the winter today.

Tues 20 Oct: […] Bought a colony of bees from Pierre le Tissier (son of Thomas) for 18 shillings.

Thurs 22 Oct: […] The two Messrs le Moine, the Revd Mr Mourant, & the two priests who are living at the Rectory (Mons. Paris & Mons. Morvan) came to dinner.[352]

Fri 23 Oct: Charles le Cras & his son repaired our pigsties (at la Daumaillerie, by the middle gate, & by the lower gate). They also mended a breach in the earthbank at le Neuf Courtil.

Fri 6 Nov: […] Mr Pierre de Jersey gave me his old mare. I am to keep her, & if she has a foal, he may elect to buy the foal for £25 stg when it reaches the age of two years.

Sat 21 Nov: […] The Bailiff was fined 500 francs for having partly crossed out an Act entered in the Court Register a few weeks ago & added some words to it. The Act related to an action against him by Mr Pierre De Havilland.[353]

Tues 24 Nov: heavy rain in the morning. Visited Mr Gibert, who is about to leave for England.

---

[352] 'Mons. Paris' may have been René-Jean Paris, assistant priest of the parish of Janzé (diocese of Rennes), who is known to have been in Jersey in the 1790s. The identity of 'Mons. Morvan' has not been traced.

[353] Bailiff William Le Marchant was engaged in a long-running feud with Pierre De Havilland (who later also became Bailiff). For more on this episode, see R. Hocart, *Peter de Havilland: Bailiff of Guernsey, A History of his Life, 1747–1821* (Guernsey, 1997), pp. 46–8.

Sat 28 Nov: to town. Dined with the Revd Mr Mourant, who is living there for a few weeks. He received news of his mother's death this week. Took tea & supped at Candie. The Court witnessed a scene even worse than last Saturday's, the Bailiff having brandished an unsheathed knife during a sitting. He was sentenced to a 60 *sol* fine & an arrest order in relation to Mr de Havilland's cause. The two Sergeants (du Port & Barbet) were fined 50 *livres* for failing to appear in Court when required to last Saturday.[354]

Sat 5 Dec: [...] The Court did not sit, as the Bailiff has confiscated the key to the courthouse & pasted a notice on the door announcing that all civil & criminal causes are postponed until after Christmas.

Fri 11 Dec: [...] Monsieur De Verson, le Chevalier Durville, Monsieur de la Cour & l'Abbé d'Ivetot (the last three of whom arrived yesterday) took tea with me.[355]

Sat 12 Dec: [...] The Bailiff was tried in his absence & sentenced to pay Mr Pierre De Havilland 1000 *livres* in damages, together with a fine of 10 francs to the Crown & costs. He was not however sentenced to atone for his injury to Mr De H.'s honour,[356] which came as a surprise to the public & suggested a bias among the Magistrates in favour of the Bailiff. But this is not the first example the Court has given [*several words scrubbed out*] of its lack [*more words scrubbed out*].

Fri 18 Dec: [...] Mons. De Verson & Mons. De Gonidec took coffee here.[357]

Sun 20 Dec: [...] Eleazar [Ingrouille] & his wife came in the afternoon & stayed for the evening.[358] [The Revd] Mr Mourant took tea here.

---

[354] See Hocart, *Peter de Havilland*, pp. 49–50.
[355] 'L'Abbé d'Ivetot' was probably Félix-Barnabé Yvetot (1764–1809), the former parish priest of Saint-Eny in Coutances, who later died in exile in Jersey.
[356] To make a formal apology to De Havilland at the Bar of the Court (a common sentence in such cases).
[357] Two members of the Le Gonidec family (minor Breton nobility) are known to have been in the Channel Islands at this time: brothers Armand-Mériadec Le Gonidec de Traissan (1752–1814) and Balthazar-Hyacinthe Le Gonidec de Traissan (1754–1817).
[358] For Eleazar Ingrouille's wife, see n. 248, above.

Fri 25 Dec: my cousin James [Le Cheminant] & his wife dined here. Fair weather, but damp.

Thurs 31 Dec: [...] Dug the top of the stackyard in preparation for planting raspberries.

Notes relating to 1795

Aside from his live-in servants, Charles Mollet gave work to fifteen men at his Castel property in 1795. About ten of them were day labourers, and the others tradesmen. Reflecting the fact that Mollet had three live-in farm servants for most of the year, the number of man-days worked by outsiders was comparatively low – 443½ in total. Most of the day labour was performed by four men: Etienne Lihou (103 days), Jacques Ozanne (84 days), Pierre Machon, brother of Mollet's farm servant Abraham (77½ days) and Samuel Le Page (68 days).

1796

Fri 1 Jan: fine weather. Filled two barrels with cider from the first layer. The cows are at les Eturs.

Mon 11 Jan: to town first thing, where I set off with Mr Metivier (the Comptroller) to gather subscriptions in aid of the *émigré* gentlemen. We started at Mr Nicolas Dobrée's house, proceeding down la Rue des Forges to le Grand Carrefour, after which we continued along la Plaiderie & returned through the High Street as far as Berthelot Street. We avoided calling upon ladies, & many gentlemen were not at home, but we nevertheless had pledges amounting to between £80 & £90 stg.

Weds 13 Jan: breakfasted at the Procureur's then continued collecting subscriptions with Mr Pierre de Jersey. The amount pledged has risen to £120 stg.

Sat 16 Jan: continued collecting subscriptions with Mr Harry Dobrée. We now have pledges worth £217, & I hope we will be able to raise the final total to £225.

Mon 18 Jan: […] Chief Pleas were to have been held today, but the Bailiff refused to allow Mr Pierre De Havilland to sit on the Magistrates' bench & even forbade his name to be called, so the Court broke up & there was a cessation of justice.

Mon 1 Feb: […] Fetched a barrel of Spanish red wine which the Revd Mr Mourant & I have jointly bought from Bon Dobrée.

Thurs 4 Feb: to town for a meeting of subscribers in aid of the *émigrés*. I was appointed to the Distribution Committee along with Sir Thos Saumarez & Messrs Pierre de Jersey, Matth. De Sausmarez, Josué Gosselin & Jack Condomine.

Sat 6 Feb: the Distribution Committee held its first meeting & distributed £10 stg (20s to each chosen recipient). We also resolved to have 100 shirts made.

Fri 26 Feb: [...] attended the funeral of Mr [Thomas] Marrett (my Alderney associate) who fell ill a fortnight ago.[359] He leaves a wife & eight children. The eldest daughter is married.

Fri 4 Mar: [...] I visited Mr Gibert in the afternoon. He arrived from England last Monday.

Sun 6 Mar: the Revd Mr Mourant & the younger Monsieur de la Houssaye (who lives at the Revd Mourant's with his father) took tea here.[360]

Mon 7 Mar: to town. The Christmas Chief Pleas were to have been held today pursuant to a Royal Order re-establishing the Court, but they did not take place owing to the dispute between the Bailiff & the Magistrates.

Sun 13 Mar: breakfasted at Mr Jean Carey's with the Procureur & Mr Pierre Havilland, then accompanied them to the French sermon preached by l'Abbé Coulon.[361]

Sun 20 Mar: breakfasted with the Procureur & accompanied him to l'Abbé Coulon's sermon.

Mon 21 Mar: [...] The Lieutenant-Governor (Major-General Small) was buried today. I never made his acquaintance.

Fri 25 Mar: Good Friday. Breakfasted at the Procureur's with Mr Jaques Hemeri. All three of us attended l'Abbé Coulon's sermon.

Sun 3 Apr: breakfasted at Mr Pierre Havilland's with the Procureur. Attended l'Abbé Coulon's sermon, after which we went to the Town Church to hear Mr Nico Carey deliver his funeral oration for Governor Small.[362]

---

[359] Thomas Marett was forty-nine years old.

[360] The Messrs de la Houssaye are likely to have been the Breton nobleman Jean-Baptiste Le Vicomte de la Houssaye (1732–1810) and his younger son Renaud (born in 1779).

[361] Claude-Antoine Coulon (1746–1820) was the former vicar-general of Nevers and chaplain to Queen Marie Antoinette (see S. Clapp, 'Catholic priests exiled in Guernsey after escaping la terreur of the French Revolution', *The Review of the Guernsey Society* (Spring 2015), pp. 20–1).

[362] 'Mr Nico Carey' was probably the Reverend Nicolas Carey (1772–1858), then Rector of St Martin. Reverend Carey, a son of Jurat Jean Carey of 'La Bigoterie' (1740–1810), was to serve as Rector of St Peter Port and Dean of Guernsey between 1832 and 1858.

Mon 4 Apr: to Chief Pleas, which was conducted without disputes between the Bailiff & the Magistrates.

Weds 6 Apr: [...] The new Lieutenant-Governor & Commander, Major-General Sir Hew Dalrymple, was sworn in.[363] He arrived the day before yesterday. Called briefly at la Haye du Puis in the evening.

Thurs 7 Apr: paid my respects to the Governor. I went to town twice & took tea at Mr Gibert's.

Tues 26 Apr: the two Messrs Groult, Messrs le Moine, De la Foidre, De Coulon, le Vatier, Dancel & Bourget (all of them priests) & Monsieur St Jore came to dinner.

Thurs 28 Apr: [...] I attended my cousin James's funeral. He was more than 81 years old.[364] He leaves a widow but no children. His daughter died 19 months ago.

Sat 30 Apr: dined at the Procureur's. The Bailiff was sentenced to 15 days' imprisonment & fined 200 *livres* [£7 2s 10d] for having ill-treated the Prevot when he tried to serve a process on him.

Mon 2 May: l'Abbé Coulon, Messrs Nico Dobrée, Jean Carey, Wm Brock, Mourant, Gibert, de la Haussaye (sen.), de Voscé & Du Campair came to dinner.[365]

Thurs 19 May: Mr Pierre de Jersey took back his old mare & gave me a small 9- or 10-year-old red mare in exchange.

Sun 22 May: to [Castel] church in the morning. Mr Gibert preached (the Revd Mr Mourant having gone to England for a few weeks).

---

[363] General Sir Hew Whitefoord Dalrymple, 1st Baronet Dalrymple of High Mark (1750–1830) was Lieutenant-Governor of Guernsey between 1796 and 1803.
[364] James Le Cheminant, the son of Mollet's aunt Rebecca, *née* Mollet, and Daniel Le Cheminant, had been born in 1714.
[365] 'Monsieur de Voscé' was Guy, Comte de Vossey (1766–1859), a former French naval officer and leading member of Guernsey's *émigré* community. 'Monsieur du Campair' was Paul de Nourquer du Camper (1776–1849), also a former naval officer.

Tues 24 May: called on Mrs Gibert, who arrived from England on Sunday. Picked our first peas.

Sat 4 Jun: to town. Dined at Candie. The people of Guernsey are giving a ball for Lady Dalrymple[366] this evening. I subscribed to it but I am not going.

Fri 17 Jun: Ab. [Machon] & I left for Jersey at nine on board Captn du Feu. We arrived at two.

Sun 19 Jun: dined with le Prince de Bouillon in the old castle where he lives.[367] On my return, I visited Sir Robt Stuart who resides at Grouville Rectory. He is the Colonel of the British Fencibles Regiment.

Mon 20 Jun: called to see Sir Robt Stuart again, & thence to breakfast at Rozel. The Prince & the Marquis de Grego also breakfasted there.

Thurs 23 Jun: left Jersey at 8 o'clock on board Captn Montbrun. Arrived here at six accompanied by my sister Lerrier whom I had gone to fetch.

Mon 27 Jun: to town. Dined at Candie. L'Abbé Coulon took coffee here.

Tues 28 Jun: [...] Called at the Rectory to see Mr Mourant & his young wife who arrived from England on Sunday.[368]

Fri 8 Jul: [...] My two sisters, Mr Mourant, Polly Lerrier, Billy Combs, the two Messrs Brock & their wives, & the two boys came to dinner.

Sat 9 Jul: to town in the morning. Sir Hue [sic] & Lady Dalrymple, Major Ross, Colonel Leggat, the Procureur & his sister, the two Mr & Mrs Brocks, & Miss Caroline Guille (daughter of my friend Nico Guille) took tea here.[369]

---

[366] Frances, *née* Leighton (c.1760–1835).
[367] Captain Philippe D'Auvergne (Prince de Bouillon by adoption – see n. 346) was in charge of the surveillance of enemy activities on the French coast as well as of *émigrés*. In order to facilitate his task, he had made Mont Orgueil Castle, on Jersey's east coast, his headquarters.
[368] The Revd Edward Mourant's new wife was Catherine, *née* Whiskin (1766–1836).
[369] Caroline Guille, who was born in Barcelona in 1777, was staying with her uncle Jean Guille at St George. For her father, Nicolas Guille, see n. 51, above.

Sat 16 Jul: [...] I engaged François des Fontaines, from Mortemart's regiment, to work for me.[370]

Weds 20 Jul: [...] Monsieur De la Roche Vernay has come to live in the upper house.[371] [...] Pierre Lassement, a French soldier from Mortemart's regiment, started working here today.

Thurs 28 Jul: Monsieur de la Roche dined with me. The Revd Mr Mourant took coffee here. All the priests who were here left for England today (about 140, together with some 1600 from Jersey who arrived here yesterday).

Sun 31 Jul: Sir Hue & Lady Dalrymple, Majors Ross, Leighton & Campbell, Captns Macrea & Delancey[372] breakfasted with me, after which we all went to Vazon where there was a Review. Following the Review, we returned here around noon & were joined by le Duc de Mortemart & 3 officers of his regiment, as also the Procureur, l'Abbé Coulon & Mr Pierre Havilland (the last three had breakfasted here after our party had left). After taking refreshments, they all departed at around half past one.

[Charles Mollet turned fifty-four during the course of this month]

Thurs 4 Aug: dined at the Governor's at les Croutes (in the house which once belonged to Billy Brock). There were 15 of us.

Thurs 11 Aug: the Procureur, Major Ross, l'Abbé Coulon, Messrs Jean Carey & Pierre Havilland breakfasted with me. My sister Lerrier left for Jersey.

Fri 26 Aug: [...] The *émigré* gentlemen of Williamson's & Dellonville's companies took ship & departed for England today.[373] There are only a few *émigrés* left here.

---

[370] Mortemart's regiment was composed of Royalist *émigrés* and financed by the British government. It was under the Colonelcy of Victurnien-Jean-Baptiste de Rochechouart, Duc de Mortemart (1752–1812).
[371] Mollet's new tenant was Henri Delaroche-Vernay, a Royalist army officer from Touraine.
[372] 'Captn Delancey' was Oliver De Lancey (c.1749–1822), a military officer of American descent after whom Delancey Barracks (see 2.11.99) were named.
[373] Mollet is referring to two British-financed Royalist corps led, respectively, by Lieutenant-General Marie-Gabriel-Eléonore d'Oilliamson, Comte d'Oilliamson (1738–1830) and Comte Armand-Jean d'Allonville (1732–1811).

Sat 10 Sep: to town in the morning. Dined, in passing, at [the Revd] Mr Mourant's, who returned here with me to take tea. [...] Sam le Page, who has been living here as a farm servant for a year, left my service.

Tues 20 Sep: to town in the morning. The Procureur was married yesterday to Miss Kitty Havilland (daughter of Pierre Havilland).[374] [...] His first wife died 2½ years ago.

[*Owing to the excision of the entry on the other side, entries for 2–7 October 1796 are missing. Subsequent entries show that Charles Mollet had travelled to Jersey on one of the missing days.*]

Tues 11 Oct: accompanied Pierre Havilland to see the Auvergne Tower (la Houguebie) in the morning.[375]

Weds 12 Oct: dined at Rozel. Saw a 106-year-old woman who lives at Rozel Harbour. She was in bed but seemed in reasonable health & quite lucid.

Fri 14 Oct: Ab. & I embarked on board Wm Le Marchant (the same ship as brought us to Jersey) at six in the morning. We arrived in Guernsey at eleven & returned to the Castel in the afternoon.

Tues 18 Oct: [...] On Sunday evening two French *émigrés* (from Mortemart's company of Chasseurs Nobles) were killed by sentries from the Nottingham Fencibles. The Court has exonerated the soldiers.

Mon 14 Nov: Monsieur le Moine & the two Messrs Groult (newly returned from England) came to dinner. [The Revd] Mr Mourant joined us for tea.

Mon 28 Nov: to Candie in the evening. I have taken Elizabeth de la Rue (daughter of Massy de la Rue) on trial as a house servant. She is 14 years old.

Mon 5 Dec: awoke to a frost. Lifted potatoes in the lower garden in the afternoon. Elizabeth de la Rue left my service (see last Monday).

---

[374] HM Procureur Thomas De Sausmarez's bride was Catherine De Havilland (1773–1860), seventeen years his junior.
[375] Philippe D'Auvergne, Prince de Bouillon, had had a gothic tower erected at la Hougue Bie to serve as his new residence.

Fri 23 Dec: [the Revd] Mr Mourant took tea & spent the evening with me. More rain (we have had rain for three consecutive days).

Sun 25 Dec: I did not go out. The weather has been dry but windy these past two days.

Fri 30 Dec: Little Henriette Brock (daughter of Wm Brock & Nancy Mourant) died today.[376]

Sat 31 Dec: to town. Dined at Candie & stayed there until nine. Little Beauvoir Brock died.[377] Wm & Nancy have five children still living.

Notes relating to 1796

Aside from his live-in servants, Charles Mollet gave work to thirteen workmen in 1796. Nine of them were day labourers. As in recent years, the number of man-days worked was comparatively low, since Mollet generally had a complement of three live-in farm servants. Etienne Lihou worked 107 days in 1796. Mollet's other regular labourers were the father and son Jean and Pierre Cateline, Jacques Ozanne, and (after he ceased to be a farm servant) Samuel Le Page. Pierre Cateline (who was only thirteen) worked 182 days and Jean Cateline worked 117 days. Jacques Ozanne and Samuel Le Page worked fewer days. Eleazar Ingrouille did not figure at all among Mollet's day labourers in 1796.

---

[376] Henriette (Harriet) Brock, Mollet's great-niece, was two years old.
[377] Beauvoir Brock was four years old.

1797

Sun 1 Jan: I did not go out. Nine chicks hatched out today, the first of the year.

Tues 3 Jan: brought in the haystack from le Prey. [The Revd] Mr Mourant took coffee with me.

Thurs 5 Jan: [...] The old grey horse I bought from Matth. Tosdevin in September 1776 has become infirm, so I had him slaughtered today. I think he was about 30 years old.

Weds 1 Feb: to town in the morning. Judith Cohu (daughter of Tom) started here as a house servant.

Sun 5 Feb: the Procureur, Mr Jean Carey & Mr Pierre Havilland came to breakfast. [The Revd] Mr Mourant took tea with me.

Mon 13 Feb: [...] Monsieur De Querqueville de l'Oeuvre (who arrived from England yesterday) took tea with me. Wash day. Wm Smith, a soldier in the Durham Fencibles, started working here.

Mon 20 Feb: l'Abbé Groult, Messrs De Querqueville, de Verson, De Voscé, Du Taillas & De Casa Nova came to dinner.[378]

Weds 8 Mar: [The Revd] Mr Mourant took tea & supped with me. I gave him 21 young oaks & 8 ashes to plant around the churchyard at the Forest.

Thurs 16 Mar: dined at Sr Pierre Le Lacheur's in St Andrew with Mr Gibert who was giving a dinner for his farmers. There were 15 of us.

---

[378] The identities of the last two of these gentlemen have not been traced. 'Monsieur De Casa Nova' probably bore the name de Casenave or Cazenave. He was to feature regularly in Mollet's journal, but Mollet never mastered the spelling of his name.

Mon 20 Mar: dug up 200 young elms (from several places) to send to le Prince de Bouillon & the Earl of Leicester in London.[379] We have already taken some of them to town.

Thurs 23 Mar: the Procureur, l'Abbé Groult, Messrs Nico le Fevre, T. Andros, de Verson, de Querqueville, le Moine & de Calbiac came to dinner.[380]

Fri 31 Mar: I have lately been suffering from a cold.

Thurs 6 Apr: to town in the morning. I called at the prison to see the eldest son of Monsieur Du Chevreuil who has been detained here as a prisoner-of-war for the past month.

Tues 18 Apr: Fair Day. To town in the morning. Called on Mr Gibert in the afternoon, as also Mr Pottinger at le Vaubellez.[381]

Sun 23 Apr: Messrs Pottinger, Jean Carey, Pierre De Havilland & the Procureur breakfasted with me. I accompanied the last three gentlemen back to town & dined with them at the Procureur's.

Mon 24 Apr: Nico Roussel sowed barley for us in the strip at the bottom of les Grands Tuzets. He also ploughed part of the northernmost strip at le Courtil Robin. Rain in the evening.

Fri 28 Apr: [...] Ploughed the rest of the barley ground at le Courtil Robin using our own plough, our own horses & Mr Jean Massy's horse. Nico Roussel has refused to finish the work he started on Monday, though, to my knowledge, I have given him no reason for displeasure.

Sat 13 May: to town towards evening. This week's weather has been so changeable that we did not starch the linen until yesterday & only put it out to dry today.

---

[379] Thomas Coke (1754–1842), 1st Earl of Leicester, was a politician and agriculturalist. He was also known as 'Coke of Holkham'.
[380] 'Monsieur de Calbiac' may have been Pierre de Calbiac (1732–1815), a Royalist army officer from the Cévennes, or possibly his son Martial de Calbiac (1757–1870).
[381] 'Mr Pottinger' was Thomas Potenger (1767–1805), a clergyman without cure from Berkshire. Potenger was married to Mary Brock (sister of Daniel De Lisle, Sir Isaac and John Savery Brock) in 1790. He had recently bought les Vauxbelets from Daniel De Lisle Brock.

Mon 22 May: [...] Yesterday I gave 14 one-week-old ducklings to Jean Cateline. He will rear them at home in return for keeping half of them himself.

Mon 29 May: [...] Mr Abraham, Lieutenant & Quartermaster of the 61st Regiment presently stationed here, came to see me with his wife. She is Madelaine Collenette of les Tuzets (daughter of old Abraham Collenette, the father of the present Abraham, & Elizabeth de Mouilpied). Madelaine Collenette is about 55 years old. We were children together. She was married 34 years ago when her husband was a Corporal in the 61st Regiment. They have remained with the Regiment ever since.

Tues 30 May: Mr Mourant, my sister, Peter, Patty, Mary, Nancy, Bon Dobrée, Wm & Hy Brock came to dinner. All the family were here, except Polly Lerrier & the children.[382]

Mon 12 Jun: took tea at Mr Gibert's. Began weeding the parsnips at les Tuzets for the 2nd time. Wash day (it has been 5 weeks since the last).

Thurs 29 Jun: to town in the morning. Yesterday Hy Brock & Mary took up residence at Saumarez for the summer. They took tea with me today.

Sun 2 Jul: Patty's 5 oldest girls & Nancy's 3 girls dined here with their six maids.

Sat 8 Jul: to town. Dined *en famille* at the Procureur's. His mother was buried last Monday.[383]

Mon 24 Jul: the Governor, Sir Thos Saumarez, Major Leighton & Major Carey breakfasted with me. I then accompanied them to Vazon for the Review of the Glen Garry Fencibles, after which they returned here with 7 or 8 other officers.

---

[382] Forty-year-old Polly Lerrier had been living semi-permanently at Candie since January 1795, as a companion to her uncle and aunt.
[383] Marthe De Sausmarez, *née* Le Marchant, born in 1723.

Weds 26 Jul: Lady Saumarez, Mrs Saumarez (the Doctor's wife), Mary Carey,[384] Miss Caroline Guille, Mr & Mrs Josias le Marchant & their two oldest daughters, Hy Brock & Mary breakfasted here. They all then accompanied me to dine at le Chateau des Pezeries, where Captn Geo. de Carteret (who commands the Fort at Roquaine) joined us & provided us with a tent. Very warm weather. We went to les Pezeries in 4 chaises. I drove Lady Saumarez & Miss Guille in the chaise belonging to St George.

Sun 30 Jul: it has been very hot all week. Last night we had thunder, lightning & a little rain. This afternoon we had thunder & heavy rain.

[*Charles Mollet turned fifty-five during the course of August 1797*]

Sun 6 Aug: [...] News reached us of the death of Lord Amherst.[385]

Mon 7 Aug: [...] Danl Ferbrache (son of Jean) started working here. He is 14 years old.[386]

Tues 8 Aug: [...] On Sunday I wrote to Lord Leicester & Mr St Croix. Yesterday & today I wrote to le Prince de Bouillon.[387]

Sat 12 Aug: [...] Dr Saumarez came to lance a boil in Abraham [Machon]'s armpit which has kept him in bed for a week. Hy Brock, Mary & 3 of the children took tea here.[388]

Sun 27 Aug: breakfasted at Mr Pottinger's (le Vauxbellais) with the Procureur, Jean Carey & Pierre De Havilland. Jack Pelley of les Pelleys, Mrs Pelley's eldest

---

[384] For Lady Harriet Saumarez, see n. 300, above. For her sister Judith, the Doctor's wife, see n. 314. For their niece Mary Carey, see n. 313.
[385] This was eighty-year-old Field Marshal Sir Jeffery Amherst, 5th Duke of Amherst and 1st Baron Amherst, who had been Governor of Guernsey since 1770.
[386] For Daniel Ferbrache (1782–1851), who was henceforth to feature frequently in Mollet's journal, see Appendix 4.
[387] Mollet's letter survives at the National Archives (PC 1/115/118C/16). Each incoming Governor appointed his own Receiver, and Mollet was soliciting D'Auvergne's support for his application to become the new Receiver (under Jeffery Amherst's successor). Mollet's letters to Lord Leicester and Nicolas De Ste Croix were probably also written for this purpose.
[388] These were the children of William and Nancy Brock. Henry and Mary Brock never had children of their own.

son, died yesterday evening. He was 44 years old. He leaves 3 brothers. Denis & Nico are ships' captains & away at sea. Thomas is at home. Their sister, Mrs Falla, died ...... years ago.[389] Their father [Jean Le Pelley] died 32 years ago.

Sat 9 Sep: [...] James Toraude's dog killed one of our hens & 8 five-week-old chicks in the Plantation. Etienne [Dancel] shot & killed the dog as it was tearing the hen apart.

Thurs 21 Sep: [...] James Guignon has been here these past two days re-installing the parlour stove.

Sat 23 Sep: to town in the morning. Little John Lerrier (John's eldest son, aged 11) returned here with me to stay until tomorrow, when his father will join us for dinner.[390] They arrived from Jersey yesterday.

Sun 24 Sep: heavy rain all day. None of the guests I was expecting came. I sent little John Lerrier back to Candie in the afternoon.

Thurs 28 Sep: [...] Hy Brock & Mary have spent 3 months at Saumarez & will return to town tomorrow.

Tues 3 Oct: rain in the morning. The 4 boys went home at about 10 o'clock.[391]

Weds 11 Oct: received 2 dozen tulip bulbs from Holland, as also 2 dozen hyacinth bulbs & a box containing 24 potted carnations. Eleazar [Ingrouille] & his wife supped & spent the evening with me.

Fri 13 Oct: [...] had two cartloads of American biscuit (1500lb) which I bought for the pigs from Mr Dan Brock.

---

[389] Susanne, *née* Le Pelley, widow of Daniel Falla of la Ronde Cheminée, had died at the age of forty-four in 1796. See n. 134, above.
[390] 'Little John Lerrier' was Mollet's great-nephew, son of his Jersey nephew John Lerrier (1763–1803).
[391] These were Mollet's day labourers, prevented from working by the bad weather.

Sun 15 Oct: to church in the morning, after which I went briefly to town. News reached us that Admiral Duncan has beaten the Dutch fleet off the coast of Holland & taken ... ships of the line.[392]

Thurs 19 Oct: [the Revd] Mr Mourant called to see me & stayed for dinner.

Mon 23 Oct: [...] I had the mare Mr Pierre de Jersey gave me 2 years ago destroyed.

Thurs 16 Nov: to town in the morning. To the Club at la Haye du Puis in the afternoon.[393]

Sun 19 Nov: the Procureur, Mr Pierre Havilland & Monsieur De Voscé breakfasted with me. L'Abbé Groult took coffee here in the afternoon. He came to visit Etienne Dancel who has been ill.

Sun 26 Nov: to church in the morning. To Mr Mesurier's for the Club in the afternoon.[394]

Tues 12 Dec: strong winds & heavy rain all morning. Mr Pierre le Marchant (brother of Josias) died this morning at la Haye du Puis, where he had been living for several weeks. He was 37 years old.

Mon 18 Dec: [...] Received a box of books (about 20) from London, as also some peas for sowing.

Mon 25 Dec: Eleazar [Ingrouille] & his wife dined here. Mild, dry weather these past three days.

Tues 26 Dec: Fair Day. I sent the brown cow (from Alderney) to the Fair, as also the 3-year-old bullock which I bought as a calf from Pierre Ozanne. They were not sold.

---

[392] Mollet is alluding to what became known as the Battle of Camperdown, at which the British North Sea Fleet under Admiral Adam Duncan defeated the fleet of the Batavian Navy on 11 October 1797. Eleven Dutch warships were captured.
[393] Mollet recorded attending this 'Club' (a social gathering of upper-ranking country parishioners) nineteen times between 1797 and 1801.
[394] 'Mr Mesurier' was Abraham Le Mesurier, for whom see n. 63, above.

Sun 31 Dec: dined at la Haye du Puis. The Club was to meet here, so I returned with Miss Henriette Marchant. Aside from Miss Marchant, only Mr & Mrs le Mesurier & Mr & Mrs Mourant attended. This week has been very wet & windy, but we have so far had neither frosts nor snow.

Notes relating to 1797

Aside from his live-in servants, Charles Mollet gave work to twenty-two men in 1797, including three soldiers. About three-quarters of these men were day labourers. The three men who laboured most regularly for Mollet in 1797 were Sam Le Page (251 days), the teenager Pierre Cateline (245 days), Etienne Lihou (108 days) and the teenager Daniel Ferbrache (105 days).

Mollet's notes show that he used the hide from the mare he had slaughtered on 23 October to make four pairs of heavy-duty hedge-cutters' gloves. He paid the tanner and glove-maker 10 *livres* 4 *sous* for processing the leather and making the gloves. He then sold them on for 5 shillings a pair. This made Mollet a profit of 5 *livres* 11 *sous*.

1798

Mon 1 Jan: to Candie in the morning. Patty, whose health has been fragile for some years, was taken very ill last night & lost the power of speech for seven hours. She has been staying at Candie this past fortnight. When I left at around two, the general opinion was that she would not live much longer.

Tues 2 Jan: to Candie in the morning. Patty Mourant died yesterday at 5 o'clock in the evening. She was not quite 33 years old. She leaves her husband, Bon Dobrée, with seven young children: one boy (the eldest) & 6 girls. A heavy loss for us all.

Weds 3 Jan: to town in the morning. [The Revd] Mr Mourant took tea with me.

Sat 6 Jan: poor Patty was buried. I spent the day at Candie.

Sun 7 Jan: to the Chapel in the morning. Henceforth there will be a sermon in English every fortnight. The first (by Mr Nic. Carey) was today. I called on Mr Gibert in the evening (he arrived back from England this morning).

Tues 9 Jan: [...] I gave Peter [Mourant] 8 ash trees to plant at his property at les Caches in St Martin.

Sat 20 Jan: I have not been out all week. Danl Toraude & his apprentice Danl Mahy have been here since Monday, when we received a delivery of planks. They have planed the wood & made an oval deal table & some chests. They have also started making a bedstead for Ab. [Machon] who told me a week ago that he & Lisabo [Le Ray] are about to get married & will not be here for much longer.

Mon 22 Jan: [the Revd] Mr Mourant took tea & supped with me.

Thurs 25 Jan: [...] Etienne Dancel expressed the wish to leave my service, having been unable to work for some time. He has been here since 4 February 1793. He was taken ill around the 18th or 20th of August, & was scarcely able to work until the beginning of October. He was then taken ill again around the 12th of October, & did no work at all until 20 December, since when he has done very little.

Mon 29 Jan: [...] A ship consigned to Bon Dobrée & loaded with Government wheat was holed near the White Rock & sank to the bottom.

Mon 5 Feb: to town in the morning. Had 4 quarters of wet wheat from the vessel which perished a week ago. It has been under water ever since, with debris scattered all over the rocks.

Sat 17 Feb: [...] Strong winds & wet snow. I fancy I have never found the roads so bad.

Thurs 8 Mar: Mrs Guille (Rachel, the younger of Mr Char. Andros's two daughters, & the widow of Guillaume Guille, eldest son of St George) was buried today.[395] She died on Monday. She had lived with her father-in-law at St George more or less permanently since her husband died on 8 August 1792.

Sat 17 Mar: the old red horse with the white face which the Messrs Brock gave me 6 years ago died yesterday. The only horse I have now is the filly I bought from Danl Gavet on 24 September 1795.

Mon 19 Mar: I went to town today. I had not been there for a month.

Thurs 22 Mar: my farm servant Abraham Machon was married to my house servant Elizabeth Le Rai today. Abraham has lived with me ever since he came to Alderney on 10 August 1789 (except for the two years which I spent at Candie, when he worked for Mr Moullin). Elizabeth Le Rai has lived here since 30 May 1793. They will continue working for me for a while, but they will sleep at the upper house, where they will have two rooms & the eastern side of the garden.

Weds 4 Apr: wind & rain these past two days. [The Revd] Mr Mourant took tea here.

---

[395] Rachel Guille, *née* Andros, was thirty-one years old. See n. 296, above and Appendix 3.

Sun 15 Apr: the Procureur, Mr Jean Carey & l'Abbé de la Motte Rouge breakfasted with me.³⁹⁶

Mon 30 Apr: to town in the morning. Took tea at Mr Gibert's. Billy Brock, Nancy & 4 of their children (Patty, Mary, Judith & baby Beauvoir) left for England with two of their maids. They are going to live near Exeter. Mr Brock is to return here for a time after having settled his family in their new home. Their two older sons will stay in Guernsey with their uncle & aunt (Harry & Mary), who have been living these past few weeks in Mrs Char. Le Marchant's house, which they are renting for seven years.³⁹⁷

Thurs 3 May: [...] At around ten in the evening, the alarm sounded & everyone went immediately to their posts. I went to town, consulted the Governor, & returned here at two in the morning. I then went to Vazon, la Mare de Carteret, &c., and came back home at four. At five, I left again for town, & returned via le Houmet where I gave the order to stand down the militiamen who had been under arms all night. Mr Gosselin (the Colonel) & Anthony Priaulx came here for breakfast.

Fri 4 May: We learned that yesterday's alarm was raised in response to a signal from Jersey which had been made accidentally & without any cause. [...] I think I must have covered 50 or 60 miles on horseback last night.

Thurs 10 May: dined at the Governor's (at Government House, which formerly belonged to Mr Nic. Dobrée). There were 14 of us, including General Whitelock, who has been second-in-command here for about 6 months, but whose acquaintance I had not yet made.³⁹⁸

Thurs 17 May: the Castel Club met here. Mr Guille, Mrs Metivier,³⁹⁹ Mr & Mrs [Josias] Le Marchant, Mr & Mrs [Abraham] le Mesurier, one of the Miss Cocqs & the Revd Mr Mourant attended, as also 5 children.

---

³⁹⁶ The last of Mollet's breakfast guests was the *émigré* Toussaint-François de la Motte Rouge (1755–1823), former Canon of Tréguier cathedral.
³⁹⁷ Charles Le Marchant (see n. 93, above) was married to Elizabeth, *née* Le Mesurier, of the 'College' branch of the family (see n. 54, above).
³⁹⁸ General John Whitelocke (1757–1833), who was court-martialled and cashiered in 1807 after commanding a failed expedition to seize Buenos Aires from the Spanish.
³⁹⁹ 'Mrs Metivier' was Jean Guille's daughter Esther, the widow of former HM Comptroller Jean Carey Metivier (see n. 318, above).

Fri 25 May: weeded & cleaned the driveway. Took tea with Mr Mourant at the Forest Rectory.

Sun 27 May: Mr Pottinger, his father-in-law Lt Col John Brock, Mr Pierre De Havilland, Mr Jean Guille & his brother Nico Guille (my old friend from Barcelona, who has not been to Guernsey for 12 years) breakfasted with me.

Thurs 21 Jun: to [Castel] church to vote in the parish election. Mr Pierre Massy (the eldest son of Mr Massy) was elected a Douzenier to replace his father, & Mr Thos Massy (his youngest son) was elected a Constable to replace Sr James de Garis.

Thurs 28 Jun: this is the time of year for collecting seaweed in sacks,[400] so we had no workmen here today, apart from Ab. [Machon] & Danl Ferbrache (who has been sleeping here for about a month). Polly Lerrier returned from Jersey (where she has been for about 2 months) with Peter Mourant who left on Monday evening to bring her back to Guernsey. My sister is very ill.

Sat 30 Jun: [...] On Wednesday there was a parish meeting called by the churchwardens. About 25 or 28 parishioners attended. We were unanimous (save for Sr Jas de Beaucamp, jun.) that we should take measures to oblige the Revd Mr Dobrée, who has been absent for 5 years, to reside in the parish & perform his parochial duties in person.

Sun 22 Jul: the Revd Mr Mourant, Stephen Mourant, Marie Boulanger & her niece, Peter Dobrée & his 6 sisters,[401] 3 of their maids & a maid from Candie came to dinner. In all, there were 23 of us at table in the parlour & in the kitchen. I accompanied Mr Mourant to Castel church in the afternoon, where he preached.

[*Charles Mollet turned fifty-six during the course of August 1798*]

Sat 4 Aug: [...] Mrs Pottinger died yesterday evening. She had just given birth & leaves 5 children.[402]

---

[400] See n. 99, above.
[401] These were all children of Mollet's deceased niece Patty and Bonamy Dobrée. Peter, the eldest, was thirteen (see n. 270, above). His sisters were Martha, Elizabeth, Mary, Harriet, Sophia and Anne, who was just one year old.
[402] Mary Potenger, *née* Brock, was twenty-seven years old.

Sun 12 Aug: [...] To Candie in the evening. My sister is completely unconscious, but peaceful. She is doubtless nearing her end. May God give her rest.

Sat 18 Aug: [...] My sister Mrs Mourant died at 7 o'clock this morning. She had been ill in bed for 2 months & had suffered recurrent illness for many years. She was about 57 years old. I will feel her loss sorely.

Tues 21 Aug: my sister was buried at the Brothers' Cemetery this evening. Peter [Mourant], Hy Brock, Billy Combs & I were mourners. Messrs Chepmell, Jean Tupper, Matth. De Carteret, Pierre Maingy, Michel Robinson & Tom Lihou were pall-bearers.

Mon 3 Sep: Pierre Cateline (Jean Cateline's son, 15 years old) who has been working here almost every day for quite some time, has told me (without prior consultation) that he wishes to be paid 10 *sous* per day rather than 8 *sous*.[403] I have therefore paid him what I owe him & dismissed him from my service (as I did with Jaques Ozanne, son of Jean Ozanne, for the same reason in April 1796).

Weds 5 Sep: we had 7 extra labourers here today [...] They dug out a pond & fashioned a bank between the top of the meadow at les Tuzets & the bottom of la Daumaillerie garden.

Thurs 6 Sep: [...] I sent 4 dozen Guernsey lilies in 2 boxes to Lord Auckland.[404] [...] The same labourers as yesterday spent the morning working on the pond at the top of the meadow, after which they started fashioning another bank at the lower end of the meadow in order to make a second small pond beyond le Prey du Pomier. Messrs De Verson & de Querqueville took coffee with me.

Sun 9 Sep: [...] Took tea at [the Revd] Mr Mourant's. Rain in the morning – our first, I believe, since 20 July. The weather has been hot & dry this summer (though the grass has grown quite abundantly).

---

[403] Pierre Cateline (1783–1824) would figure prominently in the last volume of Mollet's journal.
[404] William Eden (1745–1814), 1st Baron Auckland, for whom the Reverend Etienne Gibert had worked as a private secretary between 1785 and 1787.

Weds 12 Sep: Mr Jean Guille of St George & [the Revd] Mr Mourant came to dinner. The two Messrs Groult, Monsieur De Querqueville & Monsieur De Verson joined us for coffee.

Weds 10 Oct: […] I visited Mr Pottinger in the evening. His two-month-old son, whose birth occasioned Mrs Pottinger's death, died today.

Sun 14 Oct: Mr Nic. Guille breakfasted with me. To Castel church in the afternoon. The Revd Mr Nico Dobrée (who returned from England on Thursday after a stay of 4 or 5 years) preached there.

Mon 15 Oct: […] I advanced 50 francs to Jean Girard (son of Pierre, son of Zacharie) to finish his house near la Robine.

Thurs 25 Oct: visited Mr Pottinger in the evening. James Guignon has been here these past two days to remove the Blowing Stove in the parlour & replace it with a Bath Stove.

Sun 11 Nov: [The Revd] Mr Mourant came to dinner. It was not to his satisfaction, & he left immediately afterwards. To Castel church in the afternoon. Mr Dobrée preached very zealously against lying.

Weds 14 Nov: […] Attended Mr [William] Chepmell's funeral in the afternoon (I had a hat band). Captn & Mrs Coutart (Mr Chepmell's mother-in-law & father-in-law) both died at Mr Chepmell's house just a fortnight ago. Mr Chepmell's widow & his 7 children stand to inherit *rentes* worth at least £1000 stg.[405]

Tues 11 Dec: Etienne Lihou (who has been too ill to work since 20 September) came to work for us today.

Sat 15 Dec: Mr Gibert took tea with me. I have been incommoded by a cold, headache & rheumatism all week, but I have felt better since yesterday evening, thank God.

---

[405] Forty-three-year-old William Chepmell's parents-in-law were Captain William Coutart and Marie, *née* Bonamy. His widow was thirty-seven-year-old Elizabeth, *née* Coutart, who lived until 1806. See nn. 66 and 178, above.

Mon 24 Dec: awoke to a frost which lingered all day. Mrs [Catherine] Mourant came to dinner (Hy Brock & Mary had also been invited). [The Revd] Mr Mourant joined us for tea in the afternoon, as also Mrs Metivier & Hy Brock.

Tues 25 Dec: snow has been falling nearly all day. There are about 6 inches on the ground.

Mon 31 Dec: Messrs Groult, De Querqueville, Verson, Voscé & Calbiac took tea with me.

Notes relating to 1798

Aside from his live-in servants, Charles Mollet gave work to twenty-one men in 1798 (if we include the seven casual labourers who came to help dig a pond on 5 and 6 September). Unusually at this time, Mollet also recorded work done by a woman (the tailoress Mrs De Mouilpied who came with her husband, Danl De Mouilpied, also a tailor, for a day on 17 December). The bulk of day labour was performed by only four individuals: Samuel Le Page (184½ days), Daniel Ferbrache (126½ days, until 2 July, when he became a live-in farm servant), Pierre Cateline (89½ days, until the beginning of September, when he was dismissed), and Etienne Lihou (79 days, with a gap between September and December, when he was ill).

1799

Tues 1 Jan: fine weather.

Thurs 3 Jan: Messrs De Verson, De Querqueville, De Voscé & De Calbiac came in the morning. After dinner, I went to see [the Revd] Mr Mourant at the Forest & accompanied him to Mr Gibert's for tea.

Thurs 10 Jan: Mr Pottinger & his son Richard,[406] Harry Brock, Nico le Fevre & Peter Mourant came to dinner. They went ferreting & caught a rabbit.

Sat 26 Jan: I did not go out. People are saying that there was a slight earth tremor about 4 o'clock yesterday morning. None of us noticed it here, save Judith [Cohu] who sleeps in the attic & thought she felt her bed shake & heard her table & chairs move.

Sun 27 Jan: [...] My dear old friend Major [John] Waugh died on Friday morning.[407]

Tues 29 Jan: took tea with Mr & Mrs Mourant at the Forest. Called at le Vauxbellais in the evening. Mr & Mrs Wm Brock of London were there.[408] Rain intermixed with wet snow has been falling almost constantly these past two days.

Sat 16 Feb: [...] Danl [Ferbrache] went to offer his services to Captn Nico le Pelley. Apparently (& without my being aware of it) he has long wished to go to sea.

Mon 18 Feb: [...] Pierre Machon (Abraham's brother), who has not worked here since he was apprenticed to a shoemaker 3 years ago, has left shoemaking & returned to my service.

---

[406] Richard Potenger (1792–1860) was to become Rector of St Martin in 1832.
[407] For John Waugh, see n. 192, above.
[408] William Brock (1764–1819) was a brother of Thomas Potenger's recently deceased wife Mary, as also Daniel De Lisle Brock, Major-General Sir Isaac Brock, etc.

Sun 24 Feb: […] [The Revd] Mr Mourant called here around noon. Jean Ferbrache (father of our Danl) dined here. He came to speak to me about Danl's wish to go to sea.

Mon 25 Feb: Danl again attempted to hire himself out as a seaman this morning. His father & mother have refused their permission to such a proceeding, & it has been decided that he will stay here.

Weds 27 Feb: […] Francis Gater (aged 18) & James Radford (12), whom Mr Heathfield engaged in Devonshire to work for me as farm servants, arrived this morning.[409]

Sat 9 Mar: […] 3 soldiers were sentenced by the Court for having robbed & ill-treated Miss Hamlin in the Vale. The Magistrates differed so strongly in their opinions that it was not easy to understand what the final sentences were. Someone told me that the soldiers had been sentenced to death, but that there will be a stay of execution until the King rules whether to reprieve them or banish them.[410]

Mon 25 Mar: the Governor, his son Leighton, Major Leighton & Captn McCrea breakfasted here. Afterwards, I accompanied them to Vazon, where there was a Review of all the militia.

Mon 1 Apr: awoke to two inches of snow on the ground. It continued falling for the first part of the morning, but then started melting, so that by evening there was little left. The weather remains very cold & windy. Thos le Pelley breakfasted with me.

Weds 3 Apr: […] There was a frost last night which left ice half an inch thick in some places.

---

[409] For Anthony Heathfield, see n. 276, above.
[410] The three soldiers were sentenced to hang for burglary but were reprieved on 26.6.1799 (Livres en Crime, Greffe).

Tues 16 Apr: the two Messrs Groult, Messrs De Querqueville, De Verson, De Voscé, De Calbiac, l'Abbé de la Motte & Brother Marie (a Capuchin) came to dinner.[411]

Thurs 18 Apr: [...] Danl de Mouilpied & his wife have been here these past 3 days to do some mending for us, as also to adapt a suit of speckled brown velvet for Danl [Ferbrache].

Sun 21 Apr: to church in the morning. Mr Mourant preached. He called to see me on his way to church. It seems that he has arranged with Mr Dobrée to take the Sunday morning service at the Castel, & will engage a curate to take the service at Torteval.

Sat 4 May: [...] Attended a sale of paper from a prize. Stephen Mourant bought some of the paper for .... per ream, & I am to have 50 reams from him. Ab. brought 10 reams of it home today.

Tues 7 May: Ab. has been to town these past two days to fetch the remaining 40 reams of the paper I had from Stephen Mourant (4 parcels of 10 reams), as also some black parlour chairs (bamboo chairs) I ordered from England (I am giving six of them to Ab). Rain all morning.

Thurs 9 May: [...] Attended another prize sale (*armateur* Mr Jack Carey). Bought 4 tierces of French white table wine at £4 stg per tierce.[412]

Sun 12 May: to church in the afternoon. Mr Mourant preached. Pierre Machon dined here. He has been working for me since 18 February, but I have told him he will not work for me any more, as he is asking too much (1 shilling a day & expenses).

Sun 19 May: the Procureur & Mr Pierre Havilland came to breakfast. I went to St Saviour's church in the afternoon to hear Tom Carey preach.[413] He

---

[411] Frère François Marie, an *émigré*, became a long-term associate of Mollet's and remained in Guernsey for the rest of his life. The Town Church register entry recording his burial (on 29.1.1826) reveals that his actual name was Jean Mortier, and that he was from La Flèche in the Loire Valley.
[412] A tierce contained 35 gallons.
[413] For the Reverend Thomas Carey, Rector of St Saviour, see n. 338, above.

returned here with me for tea. Thick fog nearly all day. Heavy rain in the evening.

Tues 21 May: sent two writs to Sam le Page. The purpose of the first is to make him weed the cleared area on the hillside at le Brulin, which I let him use *gratis* last year on the express condition that he kept it well weeded. The purpose of the second is to make him fulfil his undertaking to weed the half of the parsnip ground which he dug at le Courtil Robin.

Weds 22 May: to town in the morning to see Mr & Mrs Heathfield who are leaving for England. Sam started weeding the parsnips. He will weed the top half (width-wise).

Thurs 23 May: [...] Etienne [Lihou] turned the manure where we will sow cucumbers. Etienne is my only day labourer at present. He is supposed to come two days weekly but he often fails to appear.

Sat 1 Jun: [...] Mr Jean Perchard (the Doctor) was found drowned (or dead from a knock to his head) on the beach at la Pulliaie yesterday morning. Some people believe he killed himself. I saw him at Mr Pottinger's on Tuesday evening. He was speaking rather vaguely, as he usually does, but I noticed no signs of insanity.

Fri 14 Jun: I spent a very agreeable day in Herm at the invitation of Mr Harry Dobrée.

Sun 7 Jul: to church in the afternoon. The Revd Tom Brock preached his first French sermon.[414] He did it well. The text was 'thou shalt not follow a multitude to do evil'. It was a very good sermon.

Tues 23 Jul: Brother Marie came to distil rose water for me. He breakfasted & dined here. Judith le Cheminant & Jemmy Collenette came to eat strawberries & take tea. Wm Brock, his two boys (Wm & Hy), Peter Dobrée, Beauvoir Dobrée & Hy Carey also came here.

---

[414] The Reverend Thomas Brock (1777–1850) was the son of Henry Brock and Susanne, *née* De Sausmarez (see Appendix 3). He was only distantly related to the Henry Brock who had married Mollet's niece Mary Mourant. The Reverend Brock was to become Rector of St Peter in 1803.

Weds 24 Jul: […] On Sunday, Danl Ferbrache, who had been living here for more than a year, left my service, as he & Francis [Gater] do not get on well together. Yesterday, I engaged Pierre Machon as a farm servant. He will start his year here tomorrow.

[*Charles Mollet turned fifty-seven during the course of August 1799*]

Weds 7 Aug: l'Abbé de la Motte, Brother Marie, Messrs Groult, de Querqueville, Verson, Voscé, Calbiac, Carné & Dambreuil breakfasted with me & stayed until 4 o'clock.[415] This is the first time that l'Abbé Groult has been here for 2 months. He has been unwell.

Tues 27 Aug: […] Danl Ferbrache, who left my service on 21 July, offered me his services as a day labourer this morning.[416] […] Francis [Gater], who did not get on with Danl, has also fallen out with Pierre [Machon]. He has asked me if he might leave my service. I have consented on condition that he returns to England. He will seek a passage.

Sat 31 Aug: […] I received a still from London of about 5 gallons capacity, price 5 guineas.

Tues 15 Oct: […] To town in the morning. Heavy rain. The Court convened in the roadway separating my property at la Profonde Rue from that of Messrs Jean de Havilland & Pierre De Lisle. The Bailiff wants me to lower the level of the road & have it paved.

Sun 20 Oct: to Castel church in the morning. Mr Mourant preached. To St Andrew's church in the afternoon. Took tea at Mr Gibert's.

Mon 28 Oct: […] Bought 6 bushels of French salt from a prize at 17 *sous* 6 *deniers* per bushel.

---

[415] The identities of the *émigrés* de Carné and Dambreuil have not been traced. This particular Monsieur de Carné is clearly not the same person as Mollet's earlier visitor Gilles de Carné-Trécesson who died at Quiberon (see 3.8.95).

[416] Daniel Ferbrache re-entered Mollet's service as a farm servant on the 7th of October following.

Thurs 31 Oct: to town in the morning. Took tea at Mr Gibert's. The boys went to pick another 4 bushels of Barbary Muscat apples at les Vallez. This makes 10 bushels in all, for which I am paying 3 shillings per bushel.

Tues 19 Nov: [...] News reached us that William, the only son of Robert Le Marchant, died a week ago at school in England. He was 16 years old & full of promise.

Thurs 21 Nov: I went to fetch Mr Josias Le M[archant] in the morning & we went together to le Moulin des Monts to see the new barracks which are building there (wooden structures, like the ones there already). These barracks will accommodate 5 or 6 thousand Russian troops in the service of England, 1100 of whom, I believe, have already arrived in the island.

Tues 3 Dec: [...] Danl de Mouilpied & his wife have spent two days here mending linen & making a spencer which I will give to James [Radford].[417]

Weds 4 Dec: called on Mr Pottinger (who is leaving for England) after dinner. Mr Gibert took tea here. Wm Le Page slaughtered the two old sows for us.

Sun 8 Dec: to church in the morning. I did not stay for the sermon. Mr St Dalmas was preaching.

Fri 20 Dec: another frost. More snow. Strong winds all day. I went to le Houmet to see a Russian officer & some of the Russian soldiers. I encountered great difficulty getting there & back. The snow was knee-deep most of the way, & in some places up to 5 or 6 feet deep. My former servant Pierre Gavet's wife Marie Nicolle (who was also my servant & the daughter of Hellier Nicolle of la Hougue) died in childbirth, leaving Pierre with six children.

Sun 22 Dec: called briefly at Pierre Gavet's before dinner, then went to la Haye du Puis. Spent a short while at Mrs Pelley's in the evening. The icy conditions persist & the snow is not melting.

---

[417] Spencers were waist-length double-breasted jackets, popular in the 1790s.

Mon 23 Dec: poor Marie Nicolle was buried today. Four of her children were here all day & Pierre came in the afternoon. Thos le Pelley spent the evening with me.

Weds 25 Dec: Eleazar [Ingrouille], his wife & his sister Judith dined here. In the afternoon I went to St George, where I found Mr Mesurier's family & the family from la Haye du Puis.

Sat 28 Dec: […] Last Thursday, when l'Abbé de la Motte, Messrs de Voscé, Calbiac & Carné came to take tea & sup here, they brought with them four Russian officers who speak good French. […] They all stayed here till one o'clock in the morning.

Tues 31 Dec: […] I went to le Houmet in the afternoon & returned with a Russian officer of Polish origin, Mr Gregorius Choroszchec. He supped here & stayed overnight. The snow remains on the ground. It is extremely cold outside & everything is frozen.

Notes relating to 1799

Aside from his live-in servants and piece-rate workers, Charles Mollet gave employment to eleven people in 1799, five of whom were day labourers and six tradesmen or tradeswomen. Mollet's five labourers worked a very low total of 235 man-days between them, there being an average of three farm servants in residence throughout the year. Etienne Lihou worked the largest number of days (85, year-round), Pierre Machon (63, February to May), Sam Le Page (49, January to April), and Daniel Ferbrache (34 days between August and October).

1800

Weds 1 Jan: Mr Richard Ozanne of les Mourants came to breakfast. He speaks good German, as well as some Polish & Russian.[418] Mr Choroszchec can understand him perfectly.

Thurs 2 Jan: [...] To St George in the afternoon, where I joined Mr Mesurier's family & the family from la Haye du Puis. Mrs Metivier's children & the children of the late Mr Guillaume Guille acted out two short French plays, viz., 'Les Etrennes' & 'Le Gouter'. They performed them very well. [...] A thaw set in yesterday evening & has continued all day.

Sun 19 Jan: [...] Thos Le Pelley & Jean Du Maresq came at 4 o'clock to take tea & sup with me. Messrs De Querqueville & De Carné came a little after seven, joined us for supper, & stayed until midnight. Messrs Le Pelley & Du Maresq stayed until one in the morning.

Mon 20 Jan: Pierre Machon (Abraham's brother), who has been living here since 25 July last, greatly displeased me yesterday. He missed church, went out in the evening, & did not return until one in the morning. I dismissed him after breakfast & he left immediately. Took tea at Mr Gibert's.

Tues 21 Jan: [...] Danl Ferbrache, who re-entered my service for a year on 7 October last, left his work at ten without a word & only returned at 7 in the evening. He then told me he wished to leave. I resolutely refused to let him go, & he eventually consented to stay, admitting that he & Pierre [Machon] had made a compact to go to sea together.

Mon 27 Jan: Messrs De Querqueville, Verson, Calbiac & Major Touchienow took tea & supped with me. They stayed until nearly 4 o'clock in the morning.

---

[418] Richard Ozanne (1765–1836) of les Mourains in the Castel had married Catherine Zukowska in Warsaw in 1799.

Weds 29 Jan: [...] Ab. went to fetch 3 quarters of wheat from a foreign vessel driven in to Perelle by a storm 3 months ago which is now selling at 29 shillings per quarter.

Fri 31 Jan: [...] Judith Cohu (daughter of Thos Cohu of les Mourains), who has lived here for 3 years, left my service today with the intention of finding work in town. My only remaining servants are Abraham & his wife, Danl Ferbrache & James Radford.

Weds 5 Feb: [...] Elizabeth Letocq (daughter of Nicolas Letocq, aged 12) began working here.

Sun 9 Feb: the Procureur, Mr Jean Carey, Mr Pierre Havilland & Colonel George Smith breakfasted with me.[419] Messrs De Querqueville & Verson, l'Abbé de la Motte & Brother Marie took coffee here.

Weds 12 Mar: fast day. Took tea with Mr Pottinger who returned from England yesterday.

Fri 14 Mar: Thos le Pelley took tea & spent the evening with me. Yesterday I watched a Review of the Russian troops at l'Hyvreuse. I also attended a parish meeting where it was resolved not to buy new bells for the church but to continue using the old ones.

Thurs 20 Feb: [...] James (Radford) left for England yesterday to visit his mother who is ill.

Tues 18 Mar: [...] Robert Batten, from Sidmouth, started working for me & will sleep here.

Fri 21 Mar: [...] Pierre Machon, who is going to sea & will leave tomorrow, dined here.

Sun 6 Apr: [The Revd] Mr Mourant passed by my house this morning but he did not get off his horse nor request that I be informed he was here.

---

[419] George Smith (1760–1809) was the son of Englishman Thomas Smith and Peter De Havilland's sister Mary. He had married his cousin Carterette (1772–1844), Peter De Havilland's daughter, in 1798. See Appendix 3.

Weds 9 Apr: Ab. & Lisabo went to le Moullin des Monts to buy cloth from the Russian soldiers.

Tues 15 Apr: Mr & Mrs Le Marchant & their three daughters took tea with me.[420] A little later, Major Toustscharinoff arrived & supped with me, staying until nearly midnight.

Fri 18 Apr: I accompanied Mr Josias [Le Marchant] & his two young ladies to le Moullin des Monts after dinner to watch the Russians celebrating the religious ceremony of the Sepulture of our Lord J.C. The weather was fine & warm, & there were many onlookers.

Tues 22 Apr: [...] Mr Eton (the English Commissary for the Russian troops) breakfasted with me. I was also expecting General Sednaratsky & Colonel Toustscharinoff, but the rain prevented their coming. The weather later turned fair.

Weds 23 Apr: [...] Elizabeth Letocq, who has been here since 3 February, left my service.

Thurs 24 Apr: [...] The Russian officers gave a ball last night. I was invited but did not go.

Sun 27 Apr: the Procureur, Messrs Jean Carey, Pierre Havilland & Eton breakfasted here. Not long after they had gone, Lt Col Toustscharinoff arrived (pronounced Turcharinov). He also breakfasted here. He & Mr Eton are leaving for Jersey in a few days' time.

Tues 29 Apr: Mr Ebdon came to tell me that it is likely little James Radford perished (together with a youth whom he was bringing us as a servant) on the night of 18/19 April. A vessel left Beer on Friday 18 April & has not been heard of since. A ship's rowing boat & other flotsam have been found washed up at Chidiock. The vessel had on board a crew of 7 men & two young passengers, one of whom answered young James's description & the other that of the youth travelling with him. James was such a good young fellow that we are all very much afflicted.

---

[420] For the two eldest daughters of Josias and Judith Le Marchant of la Haye du Puits, see n. 339, above. Their youngest daughter was Sophia (1791–1866).

Sun 4 May: yesterday I spoke to some sailors from Beer who arrived here on Thursday. They confirmed that our good little James has indeed perished, along with the young man he was bringing with him & 5 sailors. It happened on Friday 25 April. The weather was fine, but observers on the shore saw the vessel (a smuggler from Beer) capsize in a sudden gust of wind.

Thurs 15 May: [...] Hy Brock, who left Guernsey a week ago, arrived back with Nancy Mourant, who has been in England for 2 years, as also Nancy's 3 youngest children & her servant Rachel.[421]

Sat 17 May: [...] Violent westerly gales overnight & for much of the day. The trees have been seriously damaged. The apple trees were more or less all in blossom. Heavy downpours.

Weds 28 May: Mrs Metivier & Mrs Marchant breakfasted with me. We shared a package containing 102 lb of coffee, a quarter each for the two ladies & the other half for myself. The ladies will pay me the going rate, which is 14d per lb.

Tues 3 Jun: [...] About 3000 (almost half) of the Russian troops who have been here since November & December were embarked on board ship today. It appears that their Emperor has recalled them & has completely detached himself from the coalition against the French Republic. It would scarcely be possible to have been better behaved, or more honest & peaceable than these 6 or 7 thousand soldiers during their sojourn here, both officers & men.[422]

Fri 13 Jun: [...] Colonel Dournovo, Mr Choroszchiek (another Russian Colonel) & Mr Richard Ozanne breakfasted with me.

Tues 17 Jun: to town in the morning. Went to see a Review of a Russian regiment at l'Hyvreuse.

---

[421] Mollet's niece Nancy was being escorted by her brother-in-law.
[422] Records of criminal proceedings contain only one reference to a Russian soldier during the troops' stay in Guernsey. The soldier was accused of rape in January 1800, but the case against him was dropped the following June for lack of evidence, and he was allowed to leave the island with the rest of the Russian contingent (23.1.1800, 7.6.1800, Livres en Crime, Greffe).

Fri 20 Jun: [...] Brother Marie came before breakfast to distil rose water. We made 4 bottles. This is the first time I have used my still.

Tues 24 Jun: to town in the morning. Took tea at Mr Gibert's. Mrs Gibert has returned from Jersey, where she spent a few weeks.

Thurs 3 Jul: [...] I was very displeased with Abraham [Machon] this morning & I dismissed him. His wife Lisabo left in the evening. They have been living in the upper house since 22 March 1798.

Mon 14 Jul: Suzon Collenette of les Tuzets (daughter of Abraham Collenette & Madelaine le Page) started working here as a house servant.

Tues 15 Jul: Thomas Andrews, an English youth of 18 from Devonshire, came to offer me his services yesterday & started working here today. I will pay him 3 shillings a week, including board & laundry. Yesterday Daniel [Ferbrache] delivered two packets of paper (20 reams) to Bon Dobrée (which I sold him for 5s 2d per ream).

Mon 21 Jul: [...] Abraham & Lisabo dined here yesterday & returned this morning (to stay as it seems) without my having asked them to. Pierre Gavet came to speak to me on their behalf on Saturday.

[*Charles Mollet turned fifty-eight during the course of August 1800*]

Fri 8 Aug: [...] went to fetch five 250 lb sacks of buckwheat, split & husked, which I bought for 20 shillings each. These were originally intended for the Russian troops.

Mon 1 Sep: Mr Josias le Marchant has sub-let the tithes of the district of le Nanage to me. Today I collected tithe from Jean Maindonal & Sr Danl Dorey.

Tues 9 Sep: [...] Mr Jean Guille, Miss Guille, the two sons of the late Guillaume Guille,[423] Mrs Metivier & her 4 eldest boys[424] took tea with me.

---

[423] The late William Guille's two sons were John Guille (1788–1845), who later became Bailiff of Guernsey, and William Guille (1792–1869), who later became Dean of Guernsey.
[424] The widowed Esther Metivier, *née* Guille, had five surviving sons: John (1788–1869), George (1790–1881), William (1791–1883), Charles (1793–   ) and Carey (1797–   ). See nn. 317 and 399, above.

Thurs 11 Sep: we have been collecting tithe all this week [...]. It only remains to collect tithe from Nic. Martin, who has some barley above les Niots. To town after dinner. Briefly to Mr Potenger's in the evening. Mr Potenger has recently returned from Jersey & will shortly leave for England, having lately learned of his brother's death there.

Tues 16 Sep: I had no appetite last Sunday & felt weak & off colour. This has continued over the past two days & I have stayed in bed. This evening, thank God, I feel a little better.

Fri 3 Oct: [...] Mr Nat. le Cocq died last night. He leaves 5 children.[425] Mrs Metivier also has 5 children, which – with the 3 children of the late Guillaume Guille – gives Mr Jean Guille a total of 13 orphan grandchildren.

Sun 5 Oct: [...] Danl Ferbrache completed his year as a farm servant & left my service today. He wishes to become a stonemason.

Mon 6 Oct: [...] A dog of Mr Ozanne's from la Porte injured one of our peacocks so badly that we had to kill it. We only have one peacock & one peahen left.

Thurs 23 Oct: [...] Mr Jean la Serre (son of the late Dr la Serre)[426] was elected a Magistrate today, to replace Mr [Pierre] Falla who was found dead in le Braye du Valle on Tuesday.

Sun 26 Oct: the Revd Tom Carey dined with me & I accompanied him to [Castel] church, where he preached. He has just arrived from Bath with his father & sister, where his mother died a fortnight ago.[427]

Mon 27 Oct: [...] Danl Ferbrache, who left me to become an apprentice stonemason at the end of his year's service 3 weeks ago, returned to work for me today, not having found stonemasonry to his liking.

---

[425] Nathaniel Le Cocq (born in 1750) had been married to Jean Guille's daughter Carterette (see n. 311, above). The eldest of their five children was seven at the time of his death and the youngest just a few months old.

[426] Jean La Serre (1759–1835) was the son of Dr William La Serre (1726–74).

[427] Thomas Carey's mother (the wife of Mollet's friend Jean Carey of 'Choisi') was forty-eight-year-old Mary, *née* Brock (see n. 313, above).

Sun 9 Nov: [...] between half past eight & half past ten, we had a violent storm from the west such as we had not seen for several years. A dozen trees came down in the Plantation, & a further dozen in other places (among them the weeping willow at the turning, planted about 25 years ago).

Fri 14 Nov: dined at Mr Rowley's (the doctor)[428] with Mme Labadie, a French lady who is a prisoner here & about to leave for Bordeaux.

Sun 16 Nov: [...] Pierre Machon, who returned from the West Indies yesterday, came to see us.

Sat 29 Nov: I took tea at St George, where I found Monsieur Grimberg.[429]

Weds 17 Dec: [...] I have been weeding the old clover at les Petits Tuzets (where we will sow wheat) these past two days.

Tues 23 Dec: [...] Thos le Pelley took tea & spent *la longue veille* with me.

Thurs 25 Dec: dined alone. Took tea at la Haye du Puis, where the Club met.

Weds 31 Dec: the two Messrs Groult, Messrs de Querqueville, Verson & Calbiac, l'Abbé de la Motte & Brother Marie came to dinner.

Notes relating to 1800

Aside from his live-in servants, Charles Mollet gave work to sixteen people in 1800, eight of whom were day labourers and the rest tradespeople. His most regular labourer in 1800 was Etienne Lihou, who worked 98½ days, distributed throughout the year. Etienne's normal rate was 1 shilling a day. However (switching into *tournois*) Mollet noted that his August rate was 24 *sous* and 6 *deniers* (about 1s 9d). Jean Mauger also did some labouring for Mollet in 1800 – 85 days, concentrated between May and September. Soldier

---

[428] This was Thomas Rowley, who was married to HM Procureur Thomas De Sausmarez's older sister Martha.

[429] Charles de Graimberg (1774–1864) was a Royalist *émigré* who had served in Mortemart's regiment. He remained in Guernsey for several years, earning his living by giving drawing lessons (which may have been what he was doing at St George). Following his return to the Continent, he became quite well-known as a painter and art-collector.

Thomas Franks worked 14½ days for Mollet in July and October. He was paid 17 *sous* and 6 *deniers* per day for his work.

1801

Thurs 1 Jan: we had no visitors. To Mr le Mesurier's for the Club in the afternoon. Mrs Metivier & Miss Guille did not attend. Miss Guille has had a sore throat since Sunday.

Fri 2 Jan: dear sweet-natured Miss Guille died at 11 o'clock yesterday evening.[430] I spent part of the morning at St George, dined at la Haye du Puis, & returned to St George in the afternoon.

Mon 19 Jan: to town in the morning. Chief Pleas today. This is, I believe, eight days earlier than they would have been held, if the old rule had been followed of holding them on the first Monday after St Maurus's day, which is the 19th. […] It was our turn for watch-duty last Monday. Danl did duty on his father's behalf yesterday. Captn Nico le Pelley arrived yesterday after an absence of 16 months.

Fri 23 Jan: […] The St George family came in the afternoon (Mr Guille, young Jean & Wm Guille, Mrs Metivier & her 5 boys).

Sun 25 Jan: […] Ab. & Lisabo [Machon] went to town for the christening of Abraham Marquand's 6th child.[431] Daniel's brother Pierre Ferbrache dined here.

Mon 9 Feb: […] Last week I sent notice of a distraint of goods to Sr Danl Dorey of le Groignet for the wheat *rente* he failed to pay me in 1800. Today he pleaded his case in Court. He refused at first to give me my wheat, but he was sentenced to do so by unanimous decision of the Magistrates.

Thurs 12 Feb: a frost last night & 2 inches of snow on the ground by the morning. Snow fell all day, but the lower layers melted, so that it lay only 4 inches thick at dusk.

---

[430] This was twenty-three-year-old Caroline Guille, daughter of Mollet's Barcelona-based friend Nicolas Guille (see n. 369, above).
[431] Abraham Marquand was married to Lisabo's sister, Marie, *née* Le Ray.

Tues 24 Feb: Mr Gibert called here in the morning. I accompanied him back to St Andrew & took tea with him at the Rectory, where he is alone with two servants, Mrs Gibert having taken up her abode in town.

Tues 3 Mar: Thos Andrews, who has been here since 15 July, left me because I told him he was lazy.

Sat 7 Mar: [...] Donald MacDonald, a soldier from the company of Invalids, started working here.

Mon 16 Mar: to town in the morning to see the Governor (Sir Hew) who returned from England on Tuesday. Also paid a visit to Mr & Mrs Dan Dobrée. Mr Dobrée is a Regulating Captain.[432]

Sun 22 Mar: [...] It has lately been our turn for watch-duty (the last time was on 13 January, 10 weeks ago next Tuesday).

Mon 23 Mar: Danl Toraude came to measure some seasoned & squared elms [...] as also some of the trees brought down by the storm of 9 November which have not been de-barked or squared off. I have sold them all to Mr Alexander T[h]om at 2s per foot. There will be about 140 feet.

Sun 5 Apr: Easter Day. I did not go out. We had no visitors.

Fri 10 Apr: I continued digging le Neuf Courtil. Ab. & Danl continued digging the nursery at les Tuzets. L'Abbé de la Motte, who is leaving for France (via Jersey), came to see me in the afternoon.

Sun 19 Apr: [...] Confirmation reached us of the death of our great enemy, Emperor Paul of Russia.[433] We also learned that the English fleet, under Admirals Parker & Nelson, destroyed part of the Danish fleet off Copenhagen.[434]

---

[432] Captain Daniel Dobrée (1754–1814) was a son of Nicolas Dobrée of 'Bellevue' (see n. 38, above and Appendix 3). Regulating Captains were in charge of Royal Naval press gangs.
[433] Paul I of Russia was assassinated on 23 March 1801.
[434] Mollet is referring to the First Battle of Copenhagen (2 April 1801), in which a British fleet under Admiral Hyde Parker and Vice Admiral Horatio Nelson destroyed a Danish-Norwegian fleet at anchor near Copenhagen.

Tues 28 Apr: […] since Saturday we have been keeping in custody a young man who deserted from the 22nd Regiment in England & from the Tarbert Fencibles in Guernsey. This morning I took him to town with the help of the Constable.

Fri 15 May: […] took tea at Mr Gibert's with Mr Guille, Mrs Metivier & Colonel MacKelcan.[435]

Weds 20 May: Danl Ferbrache left my service as a farm servant, but has offered to labour for me by the day. He had recommenced residing here on 27 October.

Thurs 21 May: […] Daniel supped here, but when I came to pay him his wages, he told me he had changed his mind about leaving & asked if he could stay. I happily consented. We were all very anxious about Abraham [Machon] who – so we thought – had gone missing overnight. He reappeared in the morning.

Fri 22 May: what had happened was that Abraham had gone out to kill rabbits, given up around midnight & returned home to bed. Before his return, however, his wife had got up & left the house to search for him. Eleazar [Ingrouille], Daniel & myself joined in the search, but all the time we were out looking for him, he was sleeping peacefully in bed.

Sat 23 May: […] visited Mr Potenger & his new wife who arrived from England on Thursday.[436]

Sun 24 May: Brother Marie & Mr Davy came to dinner.[437] The Revd Tom Carey also dined here.

---

[435] Lieutenant-Colonel John Mackelcan (1759–1838) was a commander of Royal Engineers at Fort George (see P. Johnston, 'Lt Col John Mackelcan, Commanding Royal Engineer, Fort George, 1797–1809', Part 1, *The Review of the Guernsey Society* (Summer 2005), pp. 60–6; Part 2, (Winter 2005/6), pp. 83–90; Part 3, (Spring 2006), pp. 17–28).
[436] Thomas Potenger had recently remarried in England.
[437] Brother Marie (alias Jean Mortier) was commercially associated with Joseph Davy, who ran a large grocery business in the High Street in partnership with Thomas Bowls (whose name will later be mentioned in tandem with Davy's). A distiller and herbalist, Mortier sold his cordials and remedies through Davy's shop. In all entries after this date, Mollet referred to Brother Marie simply as 'Monsieur' Marie.

Fri 12 Jun: [...] The Court assembled near my property at the top of Berthelot Street & gave the order (having obtained our consent as owners) that the whole road should be paved (carriageway & footpath) with half the cost falling to ourselves. I own about 13 yards of the road at la Profonde Rue (from the bottom corner by Mr Geo. le Fevre's door to the top corner by my warehouse). I believe the road is nearly 8 yards in width. I took tea at St George with Mr Gibert & Colonel MacKelcan.

Thurs 18 Jun: weeded. Worked the hay. I started taking offsets from the carnations. Messrs De Calbiac, Marie & de Luillier came to dinner.[438]

Sat 11 Jul: to town in the morning. Monsieur Grimberg took tea with me. Danl [Ferbrache] has been cutting seaweed for his father these past two days.

Mon 20 Jul: [...] After dinner, I went to ask Mrs Le Marchant of la Haye du Puis why she & her daughters had let it be known that I was offended with them. She admitted having said something to this effect & added some further particulars in clarification, though not to my entire satisfaction. [...] I have called at la Haye du Puis from time to time (see 16 April & 24 June) & never suspected any cooling of relations on their part, as there has been none on mine.

Sun 26 Jul: [...] Two children belonging to Lisabo's eldest sister have been staying here these past few weeks on account of their father's illness.[439] They went home today.

[*Charles Mollet turned fifty-nine during the course of August 1801*]

Tues 4 Aug: [...] News reached us that Admiral Sir James Saumarez, Bart., with 5 ships of the line & a frigate, has attacked 9 French & Spanish ships of the line & 4 frigates, burning 2 Spanish vessels of 112 guns & 1000–1200 men each (of whom only about 30 escaped), & capturing a ship of 74 guns (the rest having sought safety at Cadiz during the night).[440]

---

[438] The *émigré* (de) L'Huillier has not been traced.
[439] These were the children of Abraham and Marie Marquand, *née* Le Ray.
[440] Mollet is referring to the Second Battle of Algeciras, fought on the night of 12 July 1801.

Sat 8 Aug: [...] The whole of the militia was at l'Hyvreuse to fire 3 celebratory volleys in honour of Sir James S's victory.

Weds 12 Aug: little Caroline Guille (aged 11) died this morning of consumption. This was the same illness as took her father (Guillaume Guille, eldest son of St George) & her mother (Rachel Andros, daughter of Charles Andros). She died at her grandfather's (Jean Guille of St George), where her two brothers (John & Guillaume) also reside, together with Mrs Metivier & her 5 sons.

Fri 21 Aug: Daniel [Ferbrache] & I went to gather samphire in the morning, but my horse stumbled when we were nearing le Bourg in the Forest, & I hurt my face so badly that we were obliged to return. Doctor Saumarez came to bleed me & recommended that I apply either vegeto-mineral water or Goulard's Extrait de Plomb to my wounds.

Sat 22 Aug: I have no fever, thank God, but my face is badly injured & the rest of my body is sore.

Sat 29 Aug: we have collected tithe every day lately.

Thurs 3 Sep: collected the last of the tithe. It has been fine, warm & dry since late July, so the grain was harvested & carted in good condition. This year, thank God, has been abundant in everything.

Weds 9 Sep: [...] Daniel Ferbrache, who returned to live here on 27 October last, left my service again today (he also left for one day on 21 May).

Sun 13 Sep: [...] Daniel dined here & I gave him to understand that he could return to work for me if he wished. He spoke of my increasing his wages to 60 *écus*, which I refused to do. I then asked him if he knew & esteemed me enough to trust what I said. Upon his answering 'yes', I told him that I did not wish him to earn any less working for me than he would if he worked elsewhere. Since I was about to go to church, I told him to come back here in the evening after consulting his father & mother. He refused & did not return in the evening.

Fri 25 Sep: [...] Danl Ferbrache (who left me on the 9th) re-entered my service.

Mon 28 Sep: [...] Lady Dalrymple & her three young ladies called here around noon. I had not seen her since her return from England (about a month ago). She had been there over a year.

Sun 4 Oct: [...] News reached us that the preliminary Articles of Peace between England & France were signed last Friday in London.[441]

Sun 11 Oct: [...] I went to church in the afternoon, but I felt very cold about the head, so I left before the sermon.

Tues 13 Oct: [...] There were illuminations in town to celebrate the Peace.

Tues 20 Oct: [...] Mr Guille & Lt Colonel McLeod (commander of the Dutch regiment which has been here since the spring) came to dinner.[442] Mr Gibert came in the afternoon.

Mon 26 Oct: [...] The order arrived yesterday to send all French prisoners to England.

Tues 17 Nov: gathered cider apples for the 4th & last time. We hope to make about 30 barrels of cider this year, which is more than we have ever made in what ought to have been a small-yielding year. Last year, which should have been a year of abundance, we only made 12 barrels.

Thurs 17 Dec: Monsieur De Calbiac & Monsieur Marie breakfasted & dined here. L'Abbé Groult joined us for dinner. Monsieur Marie distilled some cider brandy for us.

Sun 20 Dec: I did not go out. Little Isac [Marquand] returned here.[443]

Weds 23 Dec: Thos le Pelley took tea & spent *la longue veille* with me.

---

[441] On 1 October 1801, Lord Charles Hawkesbury (Chancellor of the Duchy of Lancaster) and the French diplomat Louis-Guillaume Otto signed the Treaty of London preparatory to the Peace of Amiens, which began in March 1802 (and ended in May 1803).
[442] Lieutenant-Colonel Norman Macleod, commander of the King's Dutch Brigade, a unit of the British army which was disbanded under the provisions of the Treaty of Amiens.
[443] Isaac Marquand (1798–1862) was one of the children belonging to Lisabo's sister Marie, *née* Le Ray, who had come to stay at Mollet's in July (see 26.7.01).

Fri 25 Dec: spent the day by ourselves. Only Ab., Lisabo, Daniel & his sister Marie were here. (Marie is working for us while Suzon Collenette is at her father's seeing whether rest will restore her health).

Mon 28 Dec: Mr Ellis (the musician) came in the afternoon & stayed for tea. Rain nearly all day.

Notes relating to 1801

Charles Mollet gave employment to fourteen non-resident workers in 1801, nine of whom were day labourers and the rest tradesmen. The number of man-days worked by the labourers was low – only 229 between the nine of them. Most only worked a total of nine or ten days. Etienne Lihou worked the largest number of days – 102½ year-round. The next was soldier Donald MacDonald who worked 50 days, but only between March and June. Zacharie Girard, who started in October 1801, had worked only 16 days by the end of the year.

1802

Fri 1 Jan: fine weather.

Fri 8 Jan: [...] Jean Bonami, Thomas Paccarin & Anthoine Racinne (Frenchmen from Cherbourg, all married with children) entered my service as farm servants. Pierre Adam, to whom I had written, engaged them for me a fortnight ago.

Mon 11 Jan: icy weather. Snow remains on the ground. Monsieur De Quierqueville, who is about to depart for France, came to take his leave of me in the morning.

Mon 18 Jan: [...] Suzon Collenette, who has been absent for eight weeks owing to her poor health, returned to work today. During her absence we have had (& still have) Marie Ferbrache, Danl's sister.

Thurs 4 Feb: took tea with the Bailiff [Robert Porret Le Marchant] & his wife in their lodgings at Richard Moullin's.[444] The Bailiff has been living there since he fell ill several weeks ago. Their new house at la Rue Piette is nearly finished.

Sun 14 Feb: [...] Antoine Racinne, one of the 3 Frenchmen who arrived on 8 January, left my service to work as a stonemason for Thos Martin of les Niots.

Mon 1 Mar: [...] I received a basket of game & a basket of apples & pears from Mons. Du Chevreuil.

Sat 6 Mar: Ab., Danl & Jean went shore-gathering on yesterday's spring tide. They had 300 ormers.

Tues 9 Mar: [...] I have a very bad cold.

Weds 10 Mar: stayed in bed. Mr Gibert called to see me around noon.

---

[444] Richard Moullin ran a tavern near the Castel church, not far from the Bailiff's new house. For Robert Le Marchant and his wife Marie, *née* Ozanne, see nn. 128 and 226, above.

Sun 21 Mar: I felt better yesterday evening & slept for 7 or 8 hours last night. I had scarcely slept at all for a fortnight. Rain on & off all day.

Thurs 25 Mar: Mr Josias le Marchant called here around noon. He was elected a Magistrate last Thursday to replace Mr Guille, who has obtained his discharge.[445]

Weds 31 Mar: [...] Jaques & George Nicolet (cousins) from Henneville near Cherbourg arrived to work for me & will live here. Mons. du Chevreuil engaged them for me. Another cousin, Joseph le Cocq, came with them in the hope of finding work in Guernsey. I have kept him here on a trial basis.

Mon 19 Apr: the Governor, his 3 aides-de-camp (Leighton, Barkley & Ross), Colonel McKelcan, Dr Walters & Sir Thos Saumarez breakfasted here. There was a Review of all the militia at Vazon.

Sun 2 May: [...] Jean Nicollet, brother of our Jaques Nicollet, arrived from Cherbourg looking for work. I told him he could stay here with his brother & cousin until he has found employment.

Sun 9 May: heard turtle-doves for the first time this year. Started cutting cabbages. Paul Ingrouille, who has been at le Moullin de Bas for about 45 years, was buried today.[446]

Mon 10 May: [...] Pierre Gavet, whose cow died on Saturday after a sickness lasting several weeks (which caused him much trouble & expense), came to fetch our star-marked heifer.

Weds 12 May: Monsieur Du Port, who arrived recently from France, came this morning to bring me letters & compliments from various people. He & his two sons breakfasted with me. Mr Mourant, Peter [Mourant] & Peter Dobrée called here around noon. I had not seen Mr Mourant to speak to since early February.

---

[445] Jean Guille of St George was by this time nearly seventy years old.
[446] Sixty-one-year-old miller Paul Ingrouille was the father of Mollet's neighbour and occasional employee, Eleazar Ingrouille (see n. 210). He was also the uncle of Mollet's farm servant Abraham Machon. 'Le Moulin de Bas' was another name for le Grand Moulin du Roi, the principal mill in the Castel parish, of which Mollet's grandfather had been the tenant in the early eighteenth century.

Sat 15 May: [...] Danl was angry this morning & insisted on settling his accounts with me. I paid him his wages & he went off to town, but he returned here later & asked me to take him back, which I did.

Sun 16 May: [...] It has not rained for many weeks. The days are warm but the nights are cold. Yesterday morning there was a grass frost, & a few icy patches here & there.

Sun 23 May: [...] Monsieur De Calbiac is about to return to France.

Tues 1 Jun: today was a day of thanksgiving for the Peace.

Tues 15 Jun: [...] Jaques Nicollet of Haineville (the same parish as our boys) arrived yesterday from Cherbourg. He is a thatcher by trade. I have undertaken to find him enough work for a month at the rate of 30 French *sous* per day (he will sleep, eat & have his linen washed here). He started re-thatching the barn today.

Thurs 17 Jun: [...] It was the feast of the Holy Sacrament today so our French boys did not work. This is the 5th religious holiday they have observed (by not working) since 1 April.

Weds 23 Jun: Monsieur Marie spent the day here. He rectified the cider spirit & made some liqueurs.

Fri 25 Jun: [...] Lisabo has started distilling roses [to make rose water].

Sat 26 Jun: [...] Judith Marqui, the daughter of Jean Marqui of les Varendes, was banished for 3 years for stealing from her mistress (Jenny Lihou, the widow of young Solomon Lauga).

Sat 10 Jul: [...] Dined & took tea at the Procureur's. In the evening we went to see Monsieur Blanchard, the famous aeronaut. He made invisible young ladies speak.[447]

---

[447] Jean-Pierre-François Blanchard (1753–1809) was a well-known French showman and balloonist. In 1785, he and American John Jeffries had made the first crossing of the English Channel by balloon.

Sun 11 Jul: I went to Castel church in the morning but found the seat of my pew so dirty that I did not stay. [...] I no longer need the services of Joseph le Cocq, who came here on 1 April. He will start work tomorrow for ……… de Garis of Beaubigny.

Sat 17 Jul: [...] went to watch a performance of Monsieur Blanchard's automata at the theatre.

Mon 19 Jul: [...] Jaques Nicolet the thatcher, who has been here 5 weeks, left us today, as there is no more work for him.

Weds 21 Jul: Ab. [Machon] picked the rest of the cherries. They were abundant this year, but we only managed to save those we covered with nets. The strawberries are all finished.

[Charles Mollet turned sixty during the course of August 1802]

Weds 4 Aug: [...] It has been very warm these past few days, & especially warm today. Mr Guille said that the temperature by his thermometer is higher than we have had for several years.

Thurs 19 Aug: Danl Ferbrache, who left my service for one day on 15 May, left me again this morning after I scolded him.

Sun 22 Aug: [...] Daniel came here in the morning. He breakfasted with us & offered to re-enter my service as before. He returned in the evening & slept here.

Tues 24 Aug: the Procureur, Colonel Smith, Mr Pierre Carey,[448] Sir James Saumarez, Mr Richard Saumarez,[449] Mr Jean du Maresq (the Lt Bailiff of Jersey) & his two eldest sons breakfasted with me.[450] (The elder of

---

[448] 'Mr Pierre Carey', also known as Peter Martin Carey (1759–1840) was the brother-in-law of Colonel George Smith (for whom see n. 419, above), having been married to Smith's sister Mary (1758–97). With his second wife, Frances Stafford (whom he married in 1803), Peter Martin Carey had a son, Peter Stafford Carey, who became Bailiff of Guernsey in 1845.

[449] 'Mr Richard Saumarez' (1764–1835), a doctor, was the younger brother of Admiral Sir James Saumarez.

[450] 'Mr Jean du Maresq' was the Jerseyman Jean Dumaresq (1749–1819). Dumaresq became Lieutenant-Bailiff of Jersey in 1820, was knighted in 1803, and resigned from office in 1816.

Mr du Maresq's sons is an Advocate in Jersey & the younger, aged about 21, is the Captn of a Frigate.) The Revd Tom Brock & Miss Mary Carey were married yesterday evening.[451]

Sun 29 Aug: […] Mr Gibert & his wife are in France (at Dinant).

Weds 1 Sep: […] Peter Dobrée is leaving for London tomorrow, where he will join Frederic Brock, with whom he is to reside at Montpellier.[452]

Sat 4 Sep: had a cartload of tithe from Jean Priaulx of Candie & James Lihou of l'Echelle.

Tues 7 Sep: Mr Jean Carey, the Procureur, his wife & two eldest daughters breakfasted here. They were on their way to dine with Sir James Saumarez at les Grands Courtils, where about 50 of the Admiral's friends & relatives had been invited.

Mon 13 Sep: to town in the morning. I had been invited by the Bailiff to dine at Petit Beau in the Forest with his family & the Haye du Puis family. We were thwarted by the rain, & instead ate our dinner (a cold one) at the Bailiff's new house in la Rue Piette, where he has resided since Easter.

Tues 14 Sep: […] collected a cartload of tithe yesterday & another today, which will be the last. There was scarcely any rain during the harvest & carting of the grain this year, so the crop was brought in largely undamaged. This year is one of abundance, thank God, especially as regards barley.

Tues 28 Sep: […] George & Jaques Nicollet, who have been here since 1 April, left this morning to visit their parents in France.

Tues 5 Oct: […] Messrs Pierre Pelley & Hy Brock[453] were elected Magistrates.

---

[451] For Thomas Brock and Mary Carey, see nn. 313 and 414, above.
[452] Seventeen-year-old Peter Dobrée was Mollet's great-nephew, the son of his deceased niece Patty and Bonamy Dobrée (see n. 270, above). Frederick Brock (1768–1806), a merchant, was a younger brother of future Bailiff Daniel De Lisle Brock.
[453] This Henry Brock was the husband of Mollet's niece Mary, *née* Mourant (see n. 196, above).

Thurs 7 Oct: [...] Monsieur le Baron de la Garde took tea with me (for the 1st time & by chance).[454] Four of Bon Dobrée's daughters & two of their maids also took tea here. Captn Denis le Pelley was married today to Miss Falla of les Maisons au Conte.

Weds 13 Oct: [...] Pierre Machon, who has returned from a 15-month voyage to Egypt, visited us.

Thurs 14 Oct: [...] My farm servants George & Jaques Nicollet, who left for France a fortnight ago last Monday, returned this evening. I have re-engaged them for a year, at £8 stg each.

Sat 23 Oct: [...] A shower yesterday afternoon. The roads are a little muddy, but the ground is only wet to a depth of about 3 inches, so that the grass is not re-growing. Some families have already been feeding hay to their cattle for several weeks. Many wells are dry, especially in the Vale.

Thurs 4 Nov: lifted parsnips & potatoes. Received 2000 spring cabbage plants from Cherbourg. I paid 15 shillings for the cabbages & 5 shillings for carriage. I also received 24 potted carnations from Holland.

Mon 22 Nov: to town. Took out a three-months' subscription to Mr Chevalier's Library.

Sat 27 Nov: [...] Theodore du Port, whom Mons. De Verson has sent me as a gardener, arrived today.

Tues 7 Dec: [...] Theodore du Port, who arrived on 27 November, returned to France.

Sun 12 Dec: Jean Ferbrache (Danl's brother) dined here. Eleazar [Ingrouille], his wife & Peter Gavet supped & spent the evening here.[455]

---

[454] Louis-François-Antoine-Maurice de Payen de l'Hôtel, Baron de la Garde (1761–1837), a leading *émigré*.

[455] Peter Gavet was the twelve-year-old son of Mollet's former farm servant Pierre Gavet (see n. 147, above). The boy worked for Eleazar Ingrouille as a labourer.

Fri 17 Dec: to town in the morning. Bought 111 lb of loaf sugar (single refined) at 8d per lb from Messrs Collings & Mauger. 50 lb of it will be for St George.

Thurs 23 Dec: [...] Thos le Pelley took tea, supped & spent *la longue veille* with me.

Sat 25 Dec: spent the day alone (apart from Eleazar, who came for a short while in the afternoon).

Fri 31 Dec: Mr Guille, Mrs Metivier, Mr & Mrs Richard Ozanne & Monsieur Marie took tea here. I was also expecting Mr Gibert, but he did not come. Rain in the evening.

Notes relating to 1802

In 1802, Charles Mollet gave work to twelve men besides his live-in servants. Four of these were tradesmen, and eight were day labourers. Only two of the labourers worked more than seven days: Etienne Lihou (97 days, year-round) and Zacharie Girard (68 days, January to September). The reason for this was that Mollet had four live-in farm servants for most of the year (Abraham Machon, Daniel Ferbrache and two Frenchmen).

1803

Sat 1 Jan: Ab. & Danl put 3 cartloads of seaweed on the parsnip ground at the bottom of the lower field at le Mont de Val (this makes 6 cartloads there so far). Monsieur Marie took tea with me.

Thurs 6 Jan: [...] Between 11 in the morning & noon, 15 eggs were taken from a hen which had been sitting on them for a fortnight under a stack of straw in the stackyard. Part of her tail was pulled out.

Fri 7 Jan: [...] Last night, someone (or something) took a hen which had been sitting for two days on another nest in the cartshed.

Sat 8 Jan: the hen which was taken – or which we thought had been taken – came out of the field at les Eturs around nine in the morning, when I was feeding the other hens at le Marquet. Later in the day, two more eggs were taken from a nest in the cartshed, & at around five o'clock this evening, a further 4 eggs were taken from yet another nest in the cartshed. The hen which was sitting on them was very alarmed & too frightened to return to her nest. The hen which came out of les Eturs in the morning had an injured leg, as if her leg had been tightly bound with a string.

Sun 9 Jan: today another 5 or 6 eggs were taken from two nests in the cartshed. I do not know what to make of this. The theft of the two clutches of eggs on Thursday & the taking of the hen must have been the work of a human being, but the latest egg thefts look as if they were the doing of animals, or at least of someone wishing to make them appear so. Mr Studdart came to settle the lease for the upper house at la Profonde Rue. He will take it for a year at £25 stg, & will move in as soon as Pierre le Tissier leaves it, which will be on 25 March. The wife of Jaques Ozanne (who lives in the upper house at my Castel property) gave birth a week ago to their 2nd son, whom they have named Jean. They also have 4 daughters, of whom the eldest,

Suzon, sleeps in my house. Suzon Ozanne's sisters have also spent two or three days with us this week.[456] Little Isac [Marquand] remains here too.

Fri 21 Jan: Mr Tom de Havilland (son of Pierre), who has been in India for 11 years, called to see me around noon.[457] Mr Gibert took tea with me.

Sun 6 Feb: Lisabo's nephew, little Isac Marquand, who has been here since 22 December, returned home today.

Fri 18 Feb: on Wednesday we found a weasel's nest behind the big barrel in the cartshed. We first saw this weasel a week ago. Over the past 5 or 6 weeks, it has taken between 12 & 15 dozen eggs from under our hens. We found 33 whole eggs in the weasel's nest, together with many empty shells.

Tues 22 Feb: Wm le Page refused to come & slaughter our last two young pigs because he had been asked to do so on a Sunday & said that it was against his principles to give a reply on that day. We therefore asked Danl Trachy, sen., to slaughter them instead. They weighed 391 lb together.

Tues 15 Mar: [...] I have been cutting down the large weeds for the past few weeks, despite suffering from rheumatism. There remain a great many. In general, there is little surface water, & none flowing in the streams. Neither is there very much grass, as none grew in the autumn & winter. Many perennials are half dead owing to last summer's drought.

Sat 19 Mar: [...] No ships have arrived from England since last Sunday, except for a few smugglers. People think there is probably an embargo.

Sun 20 Mar: all the militia were reviewed at Vazon by General Doyle, who is in command here during Sir Hew Dalrymple's absence. When Daniel came back this evening, he told me that his brother Thomas [Ferbrache] had enlisted as a cavalryman.

---

[456] Suzon (Susanne) Ozanne was born in 1795 and was therefore seven years old. Her sisters Judith, Elizabeth and Caroline were born in 1798, 1799 and 1800 respectively. Their mother (Jacques Ozanne's wife) was Marie, *née* Cohu. See Appendix 4.
[457] Lieutenant Thomas Fiott De Havilland (1775–1866) was the eldest son of future Bailiff Peter De Havilland. He had entered the Military Corps of Madras Engineers as a cadet in 1793 and had not been back to Guernsey since.

Mon 21 Mar: immediately after breakfast, Daniel came to tell me that if "I did not increase his wages, he would be off". When I refused, he left without any further discussion. I cannot think of any reason why he might be displeased. He started living here at the age of 15, on 22 July 1798, & has been here continuously since that time (apart from a few absences, after which he always came back). I paid him 25 *écus* for his 1st year, & 40 *écus* for each subsequent year, exclusive of his other perquisites.

Thurs 24 Mar: [...] Thos le Pelley took tea & spent the evening here. He has been living at les Beaucamps for a fortnight. It is 5 weeks since he last came here.

Fri 25 Mar: [...] Daniel came in the evening to fetch some of his clothes. I was most surprised when he asked me "if I would mind if he went to live with Mr Pelley at les Beaucamps?" (Mr Pelley said nothing of this to me yesterday evening, even though we spoke about Daniel). I replied that I could not imagine Mr P. would wish to engage him without consulting me, & that I would certainly not do such a thing in his position. Danl did not ask me for his wages, but I told him that I wished to pay him in the presence of his father or some other person.

Sat 26 Mar: [...] I sent for Eleazar [Ingrouille] in the evening. He supped with me, & in his presence I paid Daniel, who had come to fetch the rest of his clothes. I told Daniel that I would endeavour to forget the manner in which he had left me, & think only of the time he had spent here. I also said that, whenever he established his own household or needed anything, I would do my best to help him – or even, if he preferred, give him a small sum here & now. He thanked me, but said no more. He then got up to leave. I repeated my offer but he went off without speaking. I had planned to give him 5 guineas.

Sun 27 Mar: we had no visitors, aside from Pierre Machon (who has enlisted to serve on the Frigates & came to take his leave of us) & Pierre Gavet who took tea here on his way back from church.

Fri 8 Apr: Good Friday. In the evening I went to see Captn Nico le Pelley at les Beaucamps, where his mother & brother have been living for several weeks. He arrived here on Sunday.

Sat 9 Apr: Eleazar supped with me. Daniel also came here & I confronted him with his wrong-doing.

Mon 11 Apr: all the troops, regulars as well as militia, were under arms & at their alarm posts. The 43rd Regiment was at les Grands Moulins. The greater part of the Black militia regiment entered Eleazar's property & crossed it.[458] [...] I was watching them with Eleazar on the earthbank which separates our two properties, & I only descended from it when I was informed that a company of soldiers was marching through la Daumaillerie (which proved to be untrue). However, shortly afterwards I had an altercation which could have had serious consequences with Mr Lihou of les Prevots. He had entered the top of le Courtil Robin with his company of infantrymen of the Black regiment, & marched them through the Plantation as far as the front of the house, where I stopped them. I insisted that they should go back the way they came & made them turn around under the passage.

Tues 19 Apr: Daniel Ferbrache came here this morning. After leaving me on 21 March, he stayed at his father's for the 1st week, worked for Jean Martel the 2nd week, worked for the Sarchets of le Bouet the 3rd week, & then worked for Sr Pierre le Rai of le Friquet last week (he began eating there yesterday). He told me this morning that he felt better off here than at any of these 3 places, & he offered to come back to me, if it pleased me "to find some arrangement". I refused to have him back save under a written contract. Daniel having consented to this, I nominated Eleazar as my witness & he chose Mr Thos le Pelley. He then went to ask them both to come here this evening. They did so. I explained the matter to them, but as no one had thought to draft a contract, we decided that they would return in a week & settle the business then. For the present, Daniel will stay here on the old footing.

Thurs 28 Apr: the Revd & Mrs Tom Brock took tea with me. [He] has recently been appointed Rector of the parish of St Peter, where he succeeds Mr St Dalmas.

Sat 7 May: the eldest son of Monsieur Colomey (who was formerly in Alderney & is now a merchant at Fleurance & Bordeaux) visited me in the

---

[458] The Fourth or 'Black' militia regiment, so called because of the black facings on their tunics, was composed of men from the western parishes of St Peter, St Saviour and Torteval.

afternoon.[459] He has come here from Paris, where he is at present studying medicine. Sowed more French beans at le Prey.

Thurs 12 May: [...] Took delivery of a blackish-coloured mare which Nico Robilliard purchased for me in Weymouth for 20 guineas. Hy Brock brought her here for me. He came around noon.

Fri 20 May: hoed les Grands Tuzets. Had 3 cartloads of sand. War against France is almost certain.[460]

Sun 22 May: [...] To St Peter's church in the afternoon. Tom Brock took tea here. Sir James Saumarez arrived in Guernsey to take up his command, having been appointed to protect these Islands.

Weds 25 May: [...] Mr Jean Guille of St George sustained a broken leg yesterday. A cart wheel went over it while he was on his way to town.

Weds 1 Jun: [...] Jaques Nicolet, who went out on Monday night to celebrate Whitsun, asked me yesterday if he might go out again. I refused, but he went out nevertheless, leaving the press-house, loft & slaughter-house unlocked. I told him in the morning that, since I could not be sure of his future good conduct, he had better leave. He did so, along with some 40 other Frenchmen who were returning to France. George [Nicolet] is staying here. On Saturday, I had taken them both to Mr Tom Dobrée to be included on the list of Frenchmen who wished to stay in Guernsey. Our new Governor (General Doyle)[461] has expressly permitted this, on condition that those remaining here bear arms [in our defence]. There must be several Frenchmen who are staying.

Thurs 2 Jun: [...] I attended the funeral of my godmother, Mrs Hubert (formerly Rachel Andros of St Saviour).[462] Her first husband was Mr Du Fresne, the Town Rector.

---

[459] For Alderney surgeon Jean Colomez, see n. 243, above.
[460] The Peace of Amiens had come to an end on 18 May 1803.
[461] Lieutenant-General John Doyle (1756–1834) served as Lieutenant-Governor of Guernsey between 1803 and 1816. He was created a Baronet in 1805.
[462] Rachel Hubert, *née* Andros, was seventy-six years old. She was the daughter of Charles Andros, sen. of les Piques (see n. 36, above) and the widow of Jurat James Hubert and the Reverend Elie Du Fresne.

Sun 5 Jun: [...] George told me that the Governor has now ordered all Frenchmen to leave, so he got ready to go & I paid him his wages. He went to town in the morning & again in the afternoon. I went to Candie in the evening. Neither of us could learn whether any particular boat had been appointed to take the Frenchmen away.

Mon 6 Jun: I forbade George from leaving the house before transport has been arranged for the Frenchmen. However, he left after breakfast & did not return in the evening.

Thurs 9 Jun: [...] I paid Mr Guille a short visit between 2 & 3. He is doing as well as can be expected.

Sat 11 Jun: [...] I learned that George has been working in town.

Sun 26 Jun: to Castel church in the morning (for the 1st time this year) & to St Saviour's church in the afternoon. [The Revd] Mr Carey & Miss Maingy took tea with me in my room owing to the strong odour of paint downstairs. So strong has the odour been, that, on Wednesday, I moved out of my usual room to sleep in the bedroom above the cellar, as Daniel has also done.

[*There follows a gap in entries of nearly three months, during which Charles Mollet turned sixty-one, Daniel Ferbrache and Susanne Collenette left his employ, Georges Nicolet returned to work at the farm, and Mollet engaged James Torode as a farm servant.*]

Tues 13 Sep: Mr Mourant, Peter, Polly Lerrier, Nancy Lerrier, Suzanne Lerrier (Dr Lerrier's daughter), Hy Brock, Mary & Mary Brock came to dinner.[463]

Thurs 27 Oct: Monsieur Marie spent the day here. He & Lisabo made liqueurs.

Sat 5 Nov: Daniel came here & supped with me, but he went away without taking his leave of me.

---

[463] Mary Brock (1791–1863) was the daughter of Mollet's niece Nancy and her husband William Brock, who had left the island to live in Exeter. At this time, she seems to have been spending an extended period with her aunt and uncle Mary and Henry Brock in Guernsey.

Tues 8 Nov: heavy rain last night. The ground was wet to a spade's depth. There has been scarcely enough rain to wet the ground more than two inches since before the feast of St John the Baptist, & this summer has been hot. There was nevertheless a reasonable hay harvest, & an abundant, undamaged grain harvest. The bracken was also fairly plentiful. The parsnips & herbage fared badly.

Weds 30 Nov: Messrs Marie, De Voscé, de Grainberg & de Peronne took tea here.[464] The Revd Tom Carey was married to Miss Maingy on Monday.[465] He sent me 6 bottles of mulled wine & a piece of cake.

Tues 6 Dec: a little snow this morning, & more later in the day. The ground is covered to the depth of about an inch.

Weds 7 Dec: frosty weather. I went out riding for a while around noon. Monsieur Marie took tea with me.

Sun 18 Dec: Daniel [Ferbrache] came here with James [Torode] after church. He took tea with the others but he did not come upstairs to see me. [...] James Rouget (Judith Ingrouille's husband) has died at the age of 80. He continued living in his own house after selling it to Eleazar.[466]

Fri 23 Dec: Nico & Thos le Pelley came to take tea & celebrate *la longue veille* with me. Jean Cateline, who called here during the evening, kept the others company in the kitchen. They were all very merry.

Sun 25 Dec: Pierre Machon came here yesterday evening, as also this morning & again this afternoon. He is serving on a frigate which is at anchor in the roads & has not been ashore for 2 months.

Notes relating to 1803

Charles Mollet gave work to thirteen men aside from his live-in servants in 1803. Of these, seven were tradesmen and six were labourers. There were just

---

[464] 'Monsieur de Perone' may have been the *émigré* army officer Charles-Jacques de Péronne, born in 1762 at Saint-Nicolas, near Granville.
[465] 'Miss Maingy' was Mary Rivoire Maingy (1783–1864).
[466] Judith Ingrouille (born in 1735) was Eleazar's aunt. She had married James Rouget late in life and they had no children. Eleazar had bought Rouget's property in 1799.

two labourers whom Mollet paid by the day and four other men who dug, weeded, cut and lifted for a piece-rate. Mollet's most regular day labourer in 1803 was Etienne Lihou. He worked 50 days, but between January and July exclusively. The low number of day labourers was due to the fact that Mollet had a complement of three or four full-time live-in farm servants for much of 1803.

1804

Sun 1 Jan: Pierre Gavet's 3 youngest children spent the day here. Little Judith Collenette, who has spent the whole week with us, left this evening with her father, who took tea here.[467]

Sun 15 Jan: Jean Ferbrache, jun., dined here.[468] He arrived a week ago last Thursday & came to see us the following Saturday. He was captured about a year ago & taken to Cherbourg. He was then sent with 200 other prisoners to Epinal in Lorraine, which is about 200 leagues from Cherbourg. On 9 September he escaped from Epinal with 5 Englishmen. Together they made their way to Shlestat & then to Basel in Switzerland where they crossed the Rhine & followed its course as far as Mayence, afterwards reaching Frankfort & proceeding through Germany as far as the port of Lubeck. They covered a distance of about 250 leagues in 30 or 31 days, & had good weather throughout, except the day before they reached Lubeck. Once arrived at the port, they found an English vessel which took them as far as Newcastle. Jean then continued his homeward journey on a collier bound for Portsmouth.

Thurs 26 Jan: […] There was a lunar eclipse at 8 o'clock this evening.

Sat 28 Jan: the weather has turned wet & stormy. The mail packet arrived, bringing letters & newspapers from 3 weeks ago. There had been no packet for over a month.

Mon 6 Feb: visited le Vauxbellais between midday & 3 o'clock. Mr Potenger, who appeared to have recovered from his gout, was taken ill again last week.

Sun 26 Feb: Pierre Gavet took tea here & spent the evening in the kitchen. Suzon Collenette dined here. Her little niece Judith has been here since Monday, Judith's mother having recently given birth.

---

[467] Judith Collenette, born in 1800, was the daughter of Captain Abraham Collenette and Judith, *née* Nicolle. Her aunts Susanne Collenette and Marie Nicolle (who married Pierre Gavet) were both former servants of Mollet's.
[468] Jean Ferbrache (1777–1811), a sailor, was Daniel Ferbrache's older brother.

Fri 9 Mar: [...] Daniel [Ferbrache] was here on Monday evening & has been coming here morning & evening every day this week. It is because he wants to come back here. He has told Master Elie Mourant that he will not be returning to work for him after this week. He has also dissociated himself from Mr Ozanne's militia company, which I told him he must do before I could consider the conditions under which I will re-engage him.

Mon 12 Mar: [...] Daniel has re-entered my service without discussing his wages. However, I intend to pay him 50 *écus* a year. He appears ready to submit to the conditions I wish to impose on him. I have so far only laid down one of these, which is that I will retain six months of his wages, which he will forfeit if he leaves me before the lapse of two years (unless I dismiss him). I am still considering the possibility of issuing him with a written contract signed by witnesses.

Fri 23 Mar: [...] Monsieur De Peronne, Monsieur De Voscé, his wife & sister-in-law (Mlle de la Bourdonnaye) came here unexpectedly & took tea with me.[469]

Mon 26 Mar: Daniel [Ferbrache] & James [Torode] took a cartload of soil from here to Marie Mauger's. They exchanged it for a cartload of the sandy soil she has in her garden (the sort I fill my carnation pots with) & then delivered this sandy soil to Mrs Daniel Dobrée.

Sun 1 Apr: Easter. Pierre Machon came here in the evening. He is on Admiral Saumarez's vessel presently at anchor in the roads. He has not been ashore since Christmas.

Fri 6 Apr: to town in the morning. I had not been there since September.

Weds 18 Apr: [...] Mr & Mrs Potenger & their children will leave for England on Sunday. They will spend two months there. [...] Suzon Collenette & [her niece] Judith pulled up groundsel in the gardens.

---

[469] Guy de Vossey's wife was the Breton *émigré*'s daughter Félicité, *née* de la Bourdonnaye (1784–1807), whom de Vossey had married in London in 1802. His previous wife, Marie Nourquer du Camper, had died in 1801. Mme de Vossey's sister was Céleste-Octavie de la Bourdonnaye (1787–1863).

Sun 29 Apr: […] Remarkably warm this afternoon. Thunder in the evening.

Mon 30 Apr: […] Yesterday, I went to speak to James [Torode]'s father (taking James with me). I am none too pleased with this boy.

Sun 6 May: the Procureur, Mrs [Catherine] Sausmarez, Miss Betsey & little Kitty Sausmarez,[470] Mr [Jean] Carey, Mr [Pierre] De Havilland & Miss Nancy de Havilland breakfasted with me.[471] Monsieur Marie, Mr Davy & Mr Bowls came to dinner.

Weds 9 May: […] It was our turn to do watch-duty (at le Catiau Roc).

Sat 12 May: Danl [Ferbrache] & James [Torode] took 4 cartloads of gravel from la Profonde Rue to the new cemetery in the morning.[472]

Tues 15 May: […] Captn Nico le Pelley came for breakfast & spent the day here. He shot two magpies & a rabbit (which he took home with him). Ab. also recently shot a couple of rabbits.

Mon 21 May: the Procureur, Mr Jean Carey, Mr Pierre De Havilland & Mr Pierre Carey breakfasted with me. The militia & regular troops assembled at Vazon & marched to the Citadel. They were under arms from 7 o'clock (when they met at Vazon) until half past 3.

[*There is a break in Mollet's journal between 21 May and 26 July*]

Thurs 26 Jul: Mary [Brock], Bon Dobrée's 4 youngest girls, Polly Lerrier & little Dilly Lerrier[473] came to dinner.

---

[470] Twenty-two-year-old Betsey (Elizabeth) and seven-year-old Kitty (Catherine) De Sausmarez were HM Procureur Thomas De Sausmarez's daughters, albeit by different mothers.
[471] Twenty-six-year-old Nancy De Havilland was Pierre De Havilland's daughter, as was also thirty-one-year-old Mrs Catherine De Sausmarez, the Procureur's second wife. For the composition of the De Havilland and De Sausmarez families, see Appendix 3.
[472] The 'new' cemetery to which Mollet refers was the Strangers' Cemetery, opened not far from la Profonde Rue in the early 1780s.
[473] Mollet had two great-nieces named Delicia Lerrier, one born in 1794 (daughter of his nephew Philippe) and one born in 1801 (daughter of his nephew Thomas). 'Little Dilly' is likely to have been Philippe's child.

[*Charles Mollet turned sixty-two during the course of August 1804*]

Mon 6 Aug: George Nicollet, who has been here since 1 April 1802 & whose year should have ended on 15 October, left my service a week ago. He said it was because I had asked him (or Danl) to change his Sunday for going out (so that both of them should not be absent at the same time). I know he wishes to enter Mr De Beauvoir's service & believe he was only looking for an excuse to leave.

Thurs 9 Aug: delivered 107 trusses of straw to the Military General Hospital. I sold it to Sr Jean Dorey for 46 shillings per ton weight. The trusses are all small & together weigh only 1979 lb (which makes a price of 18½d per truss). Jean Cateline, who came last week to fetch 100 trusses for le Vauxbellais, told me that other people are selling straw for 50 shillings per 100 trusses.

Mon 13 Aug: stormy weather. Strong winds & heavy rain from morning until evening.

Fri 14 Sep: breakfasted with Mr Jean Carey at the Revd Tom Brock's in St Peter. Mr & Mrs Tom Carey, Hy Brock & Mary joined us later & we all went to dine on the cliffs at le Creux Mahié in Torteval. About a month ago, I dined in the same company (but with Savary Brock & Mrs Saumarez the Doctor's wife instead of Mr & Mrs Tom Carey) at the farthermost end of Plein Mont point, beyond Fort Peseries. I did not contribute anything to this dinner nor to today's dinner. I breakfasted both times at St Peter's Rectory, where we also all took tea. Daniel accompanied me on both occasions. A fortnight ago, Danl, Ab. & I went to Plein Mont to collect samphire & we also dined on the cliffs.

Sun 16 Sep: Messrs Carey & de Havilland breakfasted here. The Procureur did not come, as one of his children has died.[474] To St Peter's church in the afternoon. Mr & Mrs Tom Brock, Mr & Mrs de Lisle of Plaisance, & Mr & Mrs Tom Carey took tea here. To town in the evening.

[*The journal breaks off here. There are no entries for the rest of 1804.*]

---

[474] This may have been Thomas De Sausmarez's infant son Thomas, born earlier in the year. De Sausmarez had twenty-eight children in all, but never more than fourteen alive at the same time.

Notes relating to 1804

Charles Mollet gave work to eight men aside from his live-in servants in 1804. Three of these were tradesmen, and five were day labourers. Because Mollet always had three or four live-in farm servants during the course of 1804, the day labourers worked only 46 man-days between them. Etienne Lihou worked most (22 days), but he only worked between January and April. On 23 November 1804, Charles Mollet recorded having paid six children a total of £23 9s stg for working 62 man-days gathering cider apples. He paid Etienne Lihou's daughter Betsy 8 *sous* (6¾d) per day, and the other children 7 *sous* per day.

1805

Tues 1 Jan: the Procureur, Mr Pierre De Havilland, Miss Saumarez & Miss De Havilland came to breakfast. Thos le Pelley took tea & spent the evening with me. Light rain almost all day.

Thurs 3 Jan: to the Bailiff's in the morning. To le Vauxbellais for an hour in the afternoon. I called to see Mr & Mrs Gibert, but they were not at home.

Fri 4 Jan: briefly to St George before dinner. Took tea at St Peter's Rectory in the afternoon.

Sun 6 Jan: we had no visitors.

Thurs 10 Jan: Hy Brock, Peter Dobrée, the Revds Tom Brock & Tom Carey came to dinner. Mr Gibert joined us in the afternoon. They all stayed until seven. Last Monday, Messrs Marie, De Voscé, Grainberg & Peter Dobrée took coffee here. Ab. Torode finished thatching the roof above the large kitchen on the southern side of the upper house.

Fri 11 Jan: sowed some Hotspur peas at le Prey yesterday (the first of the year). There are cabbages near the pigsty at la Daumaillerie & to the south of the pigsty at the upper house.

[*The journal breaks off abruptly at this point and does not resume until mid-December, by which time Mollet had reached the age of sixty-three.*]

Mon 16 Dec: paid brief visits to the Bailiff & to Mr Potenger, who is suffering from gout. [...] Daniel Ferbrache told me on the 6th of this month that he wishes to go to sea. I paid him his wages this morning, as he is about to join a ship. He started to work here as a day labourer on 7 August 1797 at the age of 14, & to live here as a farm servant on 22 July 1798. I will miss him greatly, because he is, in general, a good lad, well-affectioned, careful & a good worker. He will join Captn Flere's ship, which is under contract to the Government as a transport vessel, & on which his older brother Jean Ferbrache is serving as boatswain's mate. I have engaged Jean Cateline, who has been working here as a day labourer since 17 September, to replace Daniel as a farm servant.[475] Aside from Jean Cateline, I have Ab. Machon, who has been with me since 23 March 1792 (when he re-entered my service on my return from Candie) & Henry Rouget, who has been here since 19 August last, when I took him on trial for a few weeks. My female servants are Elizabeth le Rai (Ab's wife), who has been here since 30 May 1793, & Marie Ferbrache (Danl's sister), who has been here since 19 August last. […] In the morning I called at St George. I also paid brief visits to the Bailiff & to Mr Potenger, who is suffering from gout.

Tues 17 Dec: […] Daniel has started working on Captn Flere's ship but will continue to sleep & eat here until the ship sails.

Sun 22 Dec: the Procureur & Mr Pierre Havilland breakfasted with me & stayed for a pot-luck dinner.

Mon 23 Dec: […] Nico & Thos le Pelley took tea & celebrated *la longue veille* with me. The party in the kitchen consisted of Daniel, Jean Cateline, Nico Breton,[476] little Judith Collenette (who has been staying with us for a few weeks), Rachel Collenette (who came to help with the laundry & stayed for the evening), Rachel's husband Ab. Torode, & Nico Ferbrache (whose reason for being here I do not know).

Weds 25 Dec: we had no visitors. Daniel is still with us.

Sat 28 Dec: […] Daniel slept here last night but left us in the morning. His ship set sail around noon, seemingly bound for Deptford in the Thames. I gave him as much food & drink as he was able easily to carry, feeling that I owed him this last proof of my good will. I deeply regret that he did not stay here long enough to enable me to benefit him still more.

---

[475] Jean Cateline (1786–1812) was the younger brother of Pierre Cateline, who had worked for Mollet as a day labourer between 1796 and 1798 (see n. 403, above). Their father (also Jean) had frequently done piece-work for Mollet in the past. See Appendix 4.
[476] Nicolas Breton (1763–1829) was a neighbour of Mollet's. A farmer in his own right, he never laboured for Mollet, but he often performed agricultural tasks for him (such as ploughing or carting) in return for reciprocal help from Mollet's labourers when he himself needed it. He was married to Eleazar Ingrouille's sister Anne.

Tues 31 Dec: Mr Potenger died yesterday morning. I spent a few hours with him about a fortnight ago little thinking he was so close to his end (he no doubt thought likewise).

Notes relating to 1805

The number of men Charles Mollet employed in 1805 (aside from live-in servants) had shrunk almost to insignificance. He recorded paying for only 23 man-days, most of them worked by tradesmen.

1806

Weds 1 Jan: Messrs Guille, De Voscé, Marie & Davy came to dinner.

Sun 5 Jan: [...] Jean Cateline began sleeping here this evening. His year as my farm servant started on 1 January.

Fri 17 Jan: [...] The weather has turned fair, after nearly a week of constant gales.

Thurs 30 Jan: [...] I wrote to Daniel, & addressed the letter (on his brother's advice) to 'the ship Reward lying at Deptford or elsewhere in the River Thames'.

Sat 1 Feb: [...] bought 3 quarters of wheat from the 700-ton prize ship 'la Grande' for 16 shillings per quarter.

Sun 16 Feb: [...] Ab. Collenette took home his little daughter, Judith Collenette, who has spent the past two months with us.

Weds 19 Feb: Henry Rouget, who has been here for six months, left my service.

Sat 22 Feb: reasonably fair weather this past fortnight. I have been digging by the upper gate & at the top of the furzebrake garden.

Sun 23 Feb: Jean [Cateline] attended his brother Pierre's wedding yesterday evening.[477]

Tues 25 Feb: [...] Mr & Mrs Poore called here around noon.[478]

---

[477] Mollet's twenty-two-year-old former employee Pierre Cateline had married Margueritte Rougier.
[478] John Poore (1747–1827) was from Redbridge in Hampshire. He had married Guernseywoman Marie De Lisle and established himself as a timber and corn merchant in St Peter Port.

Weds 26 Feb: fast day. My servants went to church in the morning while I stayed here alone.

Weds 5 Mar: Mr Hocart, originally from Jersey but now established at Nova Scotia in North America, dined with me. Messrs Marie & de Voscé joined us for tea. Ab. & Jean went shore-gathering on the low tide & returned with more than 600 ormers.

Weds 12 Mar: awoke to snow this morning. It continued all day, accompanied by strong winds. It is lying more than a foot deep.

Fri 14 Mar: the snow is melting but some remains on the ground. I have stayed in bed most of this week. I have a pain in my finger which has prevented me from sleeping these past 3 or 4 nights.

Sat 15 Mar: most of the snow has gone. Yesterday evening, Sr [Nicolas] du Four of la Rue des Auberts came to see one of our cows who is sick. He stayed here overnight. Ab., Lisabo & Jean also stayed up with the cow.

Fri 21 Mar: the cow which calved yesterday evening has been very sick. Jean went to fetch Sr Nic. du Four around midnight, & he spent the rest of the night with her.

Mon 24 Mar: the cow died during the night. Her calf is doing well.

Weds 26 Mar: Polly Lerrier, Martha Dobrée, Martha, Mary & Judith Brock called here around noon.[479] The Revd Tom Brock took tea with me. Picked stones out of the lucerne at les Petits Tuzets.

Tues 8 Apr: Harry Brock & young Beauvoir Brock called here around noon.[480]

---

[479] Seventeen-year-old Martha Dobrée, Martha Brock (eighteen), Mary Brock (fifteen) and Judith Brock (ten) were Mollet's great-nieces, the last three were daughters of Mollet's niece Nancy and her husband William Brock. Mollet's niece Polly Lerrier, who had been living semi-permanently at Candie since 1795, was now forty-eight.

[480] Beauvoir Brock was a son of Nancy and William Brock. Born in 1797, he was given the same forename as an older brother who had died the previous year. Harry (Henry) Brock was his uncle, the husband of Mary, *née* Mourant.

Thurs 10 Apr: Ab. [Machon] drew off some cider. Jean [Cateline] took some wonders to town.[481]

Sun 13 Apr: very cold weather last week. Sleet & hail nearly every day.

Tues 6 May: Mr Mourant, Peter, Nancy, Polly Lerrier, Miss Roche, Hy Brock, Mary, Bon & Peter Dobrée came to dinner. Mr Billy Brock & his daughters Martha & Mary are in London. Martha Dobrée had toothache & could not come. Etienne [Lihou] sowed cucumber & celery on the old dung.

Thurs 8 May: […] Pierre Langlois came to castrate our two colts (the 2-year-old & the yearling).

Fri 23 May: Mrs Cockell (the General's wife), her sister Miss Hill, Mr & Mrs Harry Dobrée, & Polly Lerrier came to dinner. I had also invited Mrs Daniel Dobrée & her son but the cold wind prevented their coming (young Dan is convalescing from a long & dangerous illness). Captn Dobrée is in England.[482] General Cockell (second-in-command here for several years, although I have never made his acquaintance) has temporarily assumed command of Alderney.[483]

Weds 4 Jun: […] Attended the funeral of Mrs Cohu of les Moulins (the only daughter of Sr Thos le Pelley of les Pedevins in St Andrew).[484] She leaves 8 children, having died while giving birth to the last.

Sun 8 Jun: dined at Sous la Porte with Mr Wm Le Marchant (the former Bailiff), his son (the present Bailiff), the Bailiff's wife & two daughters, & Mr Josias Le Marchant.[485]

---

[481] 'Wonders' (*des merveilles*) were a type of cake.
[482] For Captain Daniel Dobrée, see n. 432, above. His wife was Elizabeth, *née* Du Bois. The couple had two children: Daniel, jun. (1788–1806) and Eliza (1792–1851).
[483] This was Brigadier-General William Cockell (c.1759–1831). His wife was Anne, *née* Hill (1771–1838).
[484] 'Mrs Cohu' was thirty-eight-year-old Marie Cohu, *née* Le Pelley, wife of Jean Cohu.
[485] 'Sous la Porte' in town was the retired Bailiff's home. On his death in 1809, it passed to his son Bailiff Robert Le Marchant, who also had a country residence at la Rue Piette in the Castel parish (see 4.2.1802).

Weds 11 Jun: [...] Lisabo [Machon] has sold 3 quarts of peas at 5 shillings per pot & a pound of strawberries (our first) for 14d.

Sat 14 Jun: [...] To St George towards evening to see Wm Metivier, who is going to sea.[486]

Sun 22 Jun: breakfasted at the Procureur's with Messrs Carey & de Havilland, then accompanied them to dinner at le Cognon in the Vale. Our purpose was to see the works at le Braye du Valle, which the Government has purchased in order to reclaim it from the sea.

Weds 25 Jun: to town in the morning. I sold my English mare to Mr Paul Grut (the Minister's brother) for £20 stg. I will keep her for another week. Young Dan Dobrée (the Captain's son) died this morning at the age of 18. They have only one surviving child – a daughter, Eliza.

Fri 11 Jul: thunder & a little rain in the morning. I breakfasted at [the Revd] Mr Tom Brock's, then accompanied him to le Chateau de la Corbiere in the Forest, where he laid on a dinner for the Procureur, Mr Carey, Hy Brock & Mary, Mr & Mrs Tom Carey, himself, his wife, & me.

Fri 25 Jul: [...] Mr Poore's farm servant, John, drowned yesterday evening. He jumped into their well while under the influence of a fever. They live at les Cordiers, in Mrs McDougal's house.

Sat 26 Jul: [...] Briefly to St George in the evening. John & Wm Guille are leaving for England tomorrow, where Wm will go to school.[487]

[*Charles Mollet turned sixty-four during the course of August 1806*]

Mon 11 Aug: General & Mrs Cockell, Mr & Mrs Hy Brock & Mr & Mrs Harry Dobrée[488] breakfasted here, after which I laid on a dinner for them at Plein Mont, where Mr Wm Brock joined us. Fine weather. I accompanied

---

[486] For fifteen-year-old William Metivier, the grandson of Jean Guille of St George, see n. 424, above.

[487] For fourteen-year-old William Guille and his seventeen-year-old brother John, grandsons of Jean Guille of St George, see n. 423, above.

[488] For Harry Dobrée, see n. 343, above. He was married to Applegarth, *née* Budd (1774–1854).

them back in the evening through the Forest & St Martin as far as Mr Jean Carey's house at les Crouttes.

Sun 17 Aug: our former servants, Marie Robin (who was here at the time of my Dear Father's death) & Marie le Rai (my Dear Mother's maid in the last years of her life) dined here (as they also did about a year ago). They were joined by another of our former servants, Lisabo Nicolle (who has been many years at Candie), an English maid belonging to my niece Nancy, old James Gavet (now an inmate at the Hospital), & Pierre Machon (Ab's uncle & Marie le Rai's husband).

Mon 18 Aug: dined & took tea at Petit Beau courtesy of [the Revd] Mr Tom Carey. His guests (besides his wife & father) were Hy Brock & Mary, the Revd & Mrs Tom Brock, Mr Wm Brock & his children Beauvoir & Judith. Nancy is about to give birth to another child. She is at her father's (where they have been for almost a year). Wash day, which we had postponed for a fortnight.

Thurs 21 Aug: [...] Marie Ferbrache (Daniel's sister), who has worked here as a servant for a year & two days, left us today.

Sun 24 Aug: answered a letter I received on 23 May from Danl Machon, who has settled at Prince Edward Island in the Gulf of St Lawrence with his wife & children & several other Guernsey people.[489] To St Saviour's church in the afternoon, after which the Revd & Mrs Tom Brock returned here with me. Richard Potenger joined us for tea.[490]

Mon 25 Aug: Mr Jean Carey breakfasted with me. Around noon we went to Port Soif (beyond Grandes Roques), where Hy Brock was laying on a dinner. His guests, besides ourselves, were Billy Brock & his son Beauvoir, the Revd & Mrs Tom Brock, & [the Revd] Tom Carey. The Bailiff [Robert Le Marchant] called here while Mr Carey & I were at breakfast. He returned a fortnight ago from England, where he had been very ill. His wife & eldest daughter went to London when they learned of his illness, & stayed there nearly 2 months. Marie Breton (Nico's daughter) has come to help us until we can engage another servant.

---

[489] Daniel Machon (1767–1828) was the older brother of Mollet's farm servant Abraham.
[490] Richard Potenger, son of the late Thomas Potenger, was now fourteen.

Thurs 28 Aug: sent seven small parcels of seeds, spices, Gazettes de Guernesey & other newspapers to Danl Machon via Master Elizée le Page, who is taking his large family to settle at l'Isle St Jean (Prince Edward Island) in the Gulf of St Lawrence.

Sat 30 Aug: [...] Removed the roof from our greenhouse. We will replace it with tiles after the carpenters have installed new rafters & battens.

Sun 31 Aug: called to see Mrs Potenger at St Martin's Rectory in the morning. Not finding her there, I went to the Forest Rectory, where I was told she was staying with Mr Mourant before leaving Guernsey in a few days' time. She is to take up residence in Southampton.[491]

Mon 1 Sep: Mr [Jean] Carey, his son the Revd Tom Carey, Sir Thos & Lady Saumarez, Wm Brock & Mary (Henry's wife) breakfasted here, after which we all went to Lihou, where we were joined by the Revd & Mrs [Thomas] Brock. There, I laid on a dinner for them all, having obtained Mr Eleazar [Le Marchant]'s prior permission to use the house, in which we took tea. I walked to Lihou with Mr Carey in the morning, but I returned home on horseback, since night was approaching (we were late leaving Lihou, as we wished to return from the island by boat). Our servants for this occasion were Lisabo [Machon], Jean [Cateline], Eleazar [Ingrouille] & Leonard (Mr Carey's servant). I had also invited Hy Brock, but he could not come because of an injury he sustained to his face when a soldier struck him yesterday evening.

Weds 3 Sep: [...] received the first tithe (136 sheaves from Sr Danl Dorey).

Fri 19 Sep: Mr Savary Brock & the two Miss de Jerseys (Wm de Jersey's daughters) took tea with me. Mr Brock is to marry the younger daughter (Betsy) next month.[492]

Tues 23 Sep: [...] Thos Priaulx carted [tithe] for us again yesterday. We had only one cartload. Today, we had another cartload. This was Thos Priaulx's last day carting for us.

---

[491] Mrs Potenger was the late Thomas Potenger's second wife, Harriet.
[492] For John Savery Brock, see n. 343, above. Elizabeth (Betsy) De Jersey (1787–1815) was the daughter of William De Jersey (1755–1837) of Ste Hélène in St Andrew. Her older sister and only sibling was Mary De Jersey.

Mon 29 Sep: Wm Brock, Nancy & their children [...] left for England.

Thurs 2 Oct: [...] at around 6 in the evening, I went to Mr Wm de Jersey's in St Andrew to celebrate the marriage of Mr Savary Brock & Mr de Jersey's younger daughter Betsy (aged 20). The Revd Tom Brock blessed the marriage. There were about 25 guests, who only left when supper was over (past 11 o'clock).

Sun 26 Oct: [...] Monsieur Marie came towards evening. We were about to take coffee when he was called to attend the Prévot (Martin de Havilland) who had been taken seriously ill. Our Daniel Ferbrache, who arrived from Virginia a few days ago, paid us a short visit during the morning.

Mon 27 Oct: [...] Marie Fallaize started working here as a house servant.

Mon 3 Nov: an American vessel was lost on the White Rock yesterday. It was a prize ship which had been brought into the roads by the naval vessel which captured it. People are saying that the ship was carrying more than 120,000 Dollars & was worth more than £100,000 stg.

Weds 5 Nov: started cooking parsnips for the Chinese sow & her 3 piglets, which were born in early July. They will not eat parsnips raw.

Weds 26 Nov: Jean [Cateline] & Etienne [Lihou] took the cart to fetch 500 canes from Boucault at 8 shillings per 100 (200 for Etienne & 300 for ourselves). They also brought back 80 lb of Swedish ling (dried fish) at 3½d per lb. Last year we had 100 lb of dried fish from England for 25 shillings.

Sun 7 Dec: [...] Peter Dobrée, who is leaving to establish himself at Buenos Ayres, called to see me.[493]

Weds 10 Dec: [...] The carpenters, who have been here every day since 1 December, finished their work today. They made us a new box-cart, a new cart wheel (which has been fitted with an iron tyre), & a pigeon cage. Drizzle nearly all day.

---

[493] This was Mollet's twenty-two-year-old great-nephew, who had moved to Montpellier to work for merchant Frederick Brock five years earlier (see 1.9.02).

Weds 17 Dec: [...] Lisabo walked to town & brought back little Judith Collenette, who will spend the holidays here.

Thurs 18 Dec: Henry le Tissier & his son came to mend the western gable of la Daumaillerie, where the chimney collapsed 8 or 10 days ago.

Tues 23 Dec: [...] Ab. Toraude has been here these last few days to mend the roofs of the barn, the cartshed & la Daumaillerie (where the chimney collapsed). Thos le Pelley took tea & spent *la longue veille* with me. Nico Breton & his daughter Marie, Daniel [Ferbrache] & Isac Nicolle supped here & stayed until one in the morning. Mr Pelley & I spent the evening by ourselves in the parlour.

Thurs 25 Dec: we had no visitors save Daniel [Ferbrache], who dined here, & Jean [Cateline]'s brother-in-law, who came during the afternoon. The weather was fair & mild, but damp.

Weds 31 Dec: called on [the Revd] Mr Brock at St Peter in the morning. Captn Wm Carey & Peter Mourant (who has lately returned from England) paid me a short visit around noon.[494]

Notes relating to 1806

Mollet recorded employing ten men in 1806. The majority of these were piece-workers, who dug or weeded for him for a set rate per perch. Mollet did not mention tradesmen at all, but we know from his journal that he employed roofers, carpenters, etc., on many occasions in 1806. He also only recorded nine days against Etienne Lihou's name, whereas it is evident from the diary that Etienne worked more days than this. Notes dated 26 January and 5 April 1806 show that Mollet paid Jean Cateline, sen. (the father of his farm servant) partly in wheat for having dismantled an earthbank for him. Another note shows that Marie Breton (daughter of Nicolas Breton) filled in as a house servant between 25 August and 3 November, while Mollet was looking for a permanent house servant. He paid her one guinea for this, together with 2½ yards of cotton fabric and a half-guinea for her share of the flowers the household had sold during this period.

---

[494] Captain William Carey (1776–1808) was a son of Mollet's friend Jean Carey of 'Choisi' (for whom see n. 87, above).

1807

Thurs 1 Jan: lifted potatoes at le Courtil Robin. Fair but dull. We had no visitors.

Fri 2 Jan: the Procureur, Bon Dobrée, Hy Brock, Captn Wm Carey & the Revd Tom Brock came to dinner. I had also invited Peter Dobrée, but he left yesterday for Buenos Ayres where he is to establish himself in business (he was detained here for over a month by contrary winds & bad weather). Daniel [Ferbrache] also left yesterday for Virginia. He is serving on Captn Flere's ship Reward, in which he has already made one voyage. They were ready to leave a full six weeks ago. Fine weather.

Mon 12 Jan: Jaques Ozanne slaughtered our old sow (229lb) & a young pig (131lb). The sow was given me three years ago by Sir Thos S[aumarez]. She was the first sow we reared of the Chinese variety. She had 3 litters. We still have 3 pigs to slaughter.

Weds 14 Jan: Nicolas Gallienne (a cousin of our Jean Cateline aged 17) has come to live here as a farm servant.

Thurs 15 Jan: planted 7 grafts (of which 6 are long-keeping apples) & 7 pear trees (six Chaumontels & one Swan Egg) in two rows between the osier at the bottom of le Neuf Courtil & what was formerly the old nursery.

Mon 19 Jan: [...] Nicolas Gallienne went off in a fit of temper during the morning.

Tues 20 Jan: [...] Nicolas Gallienne came to fetch his clothes & I paid him 3 shillings.

Sat 24 Jan: [...] Jean [Cateline] went to the theatre & did not return until two in the morning.

Sun 25 Jan: [...] It should have been Jean's Sunday off, but I sent him to town on an errand in the morning (where he wanted to go) & to St Andrew in the afternoon. He did not return here until eleven at night, although he was reasonably sober (as he was when he came back in the morning). I saw to the animals myself at 7 o'clock in the evening.

Sat 31 Jan: Jean's younger brother James Cateline, who is about 12 & works in Herm, was sent back to Guernsey because of a bad leg. He came to sleep here last Monday & stayed until today, when he returned to Herm. Rain & hail after dusk.

Weds 4 Feb: Ab. & Lisabo spent last night at Thomas Dorey's bedside. He is the son of David Dorey from near la Hougue du Pomier & has been ill for two months. He has ten children, all of them still at home. The oldest is only 18, & his wife is close to giving birth.

Fri 6 Feb: [...] Towards evening (Jean accompanying me, each of us on his horse) I went to see Mr Gibert. When I left Mr Gibert's house at around 6 o'clock, Jean was nowhere to be found. I waited a few minutes, going from Mr Gibert's stable as far as Mr de Jersey's, & then I walked home alone, amid gales & heavy rain, arriving here at seven. Jean appeared almost immediately, assuring me that he had gone no further than the stream below the churchyard to water the horses. I know this was untrue, because he was seen by Sam Marquand on his way from le Vaubellais.

Weds 11 Feb: [...] I learned of the death of my old friend, Mr Nico Guille of Barcelona.[495]

Weds 18 Feb: [...] A vessel which was in the roads foundered on the Castle Rock. Ten or 12 persons were drowned.

Fri 6 Mar: visited Mr Gibert in the morning. Whilst there, I had words with (almost quarrelled with) his wife.

Tues 17 Mar: [...] Lisabo spent the night at Thos Dorey's. He died yesterday evening.[496]

---

[495] Nicolas Guille, who (like Charles Mollet) was born in August 1742, was sixty-four. See n. 51, above.
[496] Thomas Dorey was forty-two. He was married to Marthe, *née* Le Sauvage.

Weds 18 Mar: [...] I visited Mr Mourant in the afternoon. He has been ill with the gout.

Weds 25 Mar: [...] Lisabo made wonders for the 1st time this year.

Sat 4 Apr: [...] I called to see Thos Martel of les Boulains (he has been ill for some time).

Tues 7 Apr: [...] Little Judith Collenette, who has been here since 28 March, went home yesterday. Our little Suzon (Ozanne) started attending school in town.[497]

Thurs 9 Apr: [...] I called to see Thos Martel. I spoke to his wife, but she did not invite me in.

Mon 13 Apr: [...] I visited Thos Martel of les Boulains after dinner (I have twice seen Thos in person, but on both occasions his wife was not at home & it was his daughter I spoke to.)

Fri 24 Apr: the Procureur, Mr Jean Guille, Hy Brock, the Revds Tom Carey & Tom Brock came to dinner. I had arranged this dinner so that these gentlemen might see Mr Gibert. I went to his house to invite him on the 11th of April & he chose this day himself. He then wrote to me on the 20th of April, saying that he was too weak to come. I went to see him the next day & found him weeding his garden. [...] I believe Mrs Gibert prevented him from coming because she is angry with me for intervening in their disagreement & speaking forcibly to her on the 6th of March (at her husband's request).

Sat 25 Apr: to town around noon. I saw Mr Mourant, who is very weak. [...] I later called on Mr Gibert & found him weeding the paths in his garden.

Sun 26 Apr: [...] Pierre Cohu (son of Nicolas Cohu from near Saumarez) who used to work as a carpenter's labourer for Master Danl Toraude, spent the day here. He is 18 years old & is shortly to accompany his parents, 8 siblings & brother-in-law to settle in America, near New York. They (& 50

---

[497] Suzon (daughter of Jacques Ozanne, one of Mollet's tenants at the upper house) was eleven or twelve years old.

others of our compatriots) are about to leave on an American vessel bound for Norfolk, Virginia.

Mon 27 Apr: [...] Thos Martel, whom I visited again last Monday, was buried today.

Sat 2 May: [...] Called on Mr Guille in the afternoon. His eldest daughter, Mrs Nat. le Cocq, died yesterday evening. She leaves 5 fatherless & motherless children.[498]

Tues 12 May: [...] Ab. has been confined to bed these past two days with boils in his armpits. I wrote to Henry Ingrouille in New York,[499] enclosing a letter for Mr Gibert's nephew, whom Mr Gibert believes is in Georgia.

Thurs 14 May: [...] I went to Candie in the evening but did not see Mr Mourant (though I spent some time in his bedroom with Hy Brock & Mary). Damp, windy weather.

Sat 16 May: [...] Our Daniel Ferbrache, who left on 1 January, has returned from Norfolk, Virginia.

Sun 24 May: to Candie in the morning. Mr Mourant died at 1 o'clock.[500]

Weds 27 May: Mr Mourant was buried at midday. Peter, Hy Brock, Billy Combs & myself were mourners. The pall-bearers were Messrs Matth. De Carteret, André Bonamy, Pierre Maingy, Michel Robinson, Jean Tupper & Tom Lihou. I dined at Candie with Bon Dobrée, Peter Mourant, Polly Lerrier, Hy Brock & Mary.

Thurs 28 May: Daniel [Ferbrache] supped here.

Sat 6 Jun: [...] Mr le Page & Pierre Cateline came to install the large still in the wash-house.

---

[498] The widowed Carterette Le Cocq, *née* Guille, was forty-seven (see nn. 311 and 425, above). Her children were Carterette (born in 1793 and thus fourteen years old), Mary (born in 1795), Peter (1797), Caroline (1798) and John (1800).
[499] Henry Ingrouille was Eleazar's younger brother, born in 1784.
[500] Peter Mourant, sen. was a few weeks short of his sixty-seventh birthday. See n. 7, above.

Tues 16 Jun: [...] Daniel, who will shortly be leaving on his 3rd voyage to Virginia, supped here.

Thurs 2 Jul: Monsieur Marie breakfasted, dined & stayed here until evening to help Lisabo [Machon] distil rose water. This is the first time we have used the large still.

Fri 3 Jul: Mr Guille, John & George Metivier, Monsieur de Voscé & Monsieur le Baron de la Garde took tea here.

Weds 8 Jul: [...] I attended an election for a parochial Douzenier, having been asked by Mr des Vallez to give my vote to his nephew.[501] Mr de Vallez's nephew was duly elected. He is the replacement for Mr [James] Ozanne of la Porte, who has obtained his discharge on the grounds that he is at present residing at St Jaques. Sr Jean Dorey, who was out canvassing for himself this morning, had only about a third of the votes.

Sun 12 Jul: [...] Mr Bon Dobrée left for England yesterday with his daughters Eliza & Henriette. Henriette is to go to school there.[502]

Fri 17 Jul: [...] Little Judith [Collenette] came here with Suzon [Ozanne] to stay until Monday. Little Isac Marquand has been here since 27 June.

[*Charles Mollet turned sixty-five during the course of August 1807*]

Mon 3 Aug: [...] Peter Mourant came at noon to tell me that he has become engaged to Miss Sophie Carey, the youngest daughter of Mr Jean Carey of the High Street.[503]

Tues 4 Aug: [...] Peter Mourant & Miss Sophie Carey took tea with me. I was not previously acquainted with Miss Carey, but she seems very charming. She is 24 years old.[504]

---

[501] 'Mr des Vallez' was Nicolas Moullin, jun. (1777–1824).
[502] Mollet's great-niece Harriet (Henriette) Dobrée was fourteen years old.
[503] Sophia Carey (1784–1862) was the thirteenth of the fourteen children of Jurat Jean Carey and Marie, *née* Le Ray, of 'La Bigoterie' and the High Street.
[504] Peter Mourant was thirty-seven years old.

Sat 8 Aug: [...] Mr Nico le Hurai [the watchmaker] & his family left for America.

Tues 18 Aug: [...] Peter Mourant was married yesterday evening. I was invited, but made my excuses.

Thurs 27 Aug: [...] Received 127 sheaves of tithe barley from Sr Danl Dorey, our first this year.

Tues 1 Sep: [...] We have not grown any grain of our own this year. Peter Mourant & Colonel Le Marchant called to see me around noon.[505]

Tues 8 Sep: [...] Marie Fallaize, who has been here since 27 October, quarrelled with the boys & left the house, taking her clothes with her. She would have completed her year's service in 7 weeks' time.

Sun 20 Sep: [...] A large number of militiamen & regulars armed with bayonets were searching for deserters in the countryside. I saw a young officer from the 87th Regiment & 40 or 50 soldiers from various regiments rummaging through my gardens. They made off with a fair amount of fruit.

Tues 22 Sep: Monsieur Marie, Mr Guille, Monsieur De Voscé & his friends Monsieur De Bottrel & l'Abbé Brajoul came to dinner. Mrs Metivier, young Mary le Cocq & Mrs Frere joined us for tea.[506]

Thurs 1 Oct: [...] Marie Mauger has started coming here to sew for us in place of Rachel Ingrouille who is going to live in town. She is the orphan daughter one of old Jean Mauger's girls.

Tues 6 Oct: [...] Yesterday Lisabo [Machon] distilled 18 bottles of *eau de noyau*. She used Captn Pelley's peach leaves for 12 of them.

---

[505] This was Lieutenant-Colonel John Gaspard Le Marchant (1766–1812), the husband of Peter Mourant's sister-in-law, Mary, *née* Carey (daughter of Jean Carey of 'La Bigoterie').
[506] The 'Monsieur De Botrel' to whom Mollet alludes may have been Constant de Botherel du Plessis (1776–1860), a Royalist army officer and son of René-Jean, Comte de Botherel, a leading member of Jersey's *émigré* community who had died in 1805. 'L'Abbé Brajoul' is likely to have been Charles-Auguste Brajeul (1761–1825), the former Rector of Saint-Quay in Brittany. Mrs Metivier was Jean Guille's widowed daughter Esther (see nn. 318 and 399, above); Mary Le Cocq was Guille's twelve-year-old grand-daughter (see n. 498); and Mrs Frere was the wife (or widow) of his former business associate Pierre Frere.

Sun 18 Oct: […] I had planned to go to St Saviour's church in the afternoon, however Jean [Cateline] did not appear at dinner, & when he did arrive (around one o'clock), he seemed none too sober. As Abraham & Lisabo were going out (to church), I decided to stay here. Messrs Marie & Bowls took tea with me.

Mon 19 Oct: Elizabeth Tosdevin (daughter of Danl Tosdevin of les Vallettes in St Saviour) started here as a house servant. Picked the sweet apples, as also the Chaumontel pears in the stackyard.

Weds 28 Oct: […] attended Mme De Voscé's funeral. She died of a premature labour on Sunday.[507] […] She leaves 3 little girls. Mons. De Voscé has another daughter in France from his 1st wife.

Fri 30 Oct: […] Finished picking the small plums in the lower garden (there was a reasonable amount of them this year, & they were good). Mr Guille, Mrs Frere, young Molly le Cocq, Mrs Metivier, George Metivier & his two youngest brothers took tea with me. A stiff north-westerly breeze.

Tues 3 Nov: […] Mr le Lacheur of the Forest (the merchant) has died. Our Geo. Nicollet has worked for him for several years.

Fri 13 Nov: […] Henry Brock & Mary have returned from England after about 5 months' absence. Young Mary Brock is with them. Henry was ill for about a month (at Bath) & is still quite weak.

Tues 17 Nov: Monsieur Marie, Mr Bertram (the Master of the Town Hospital) & Mr Hermet breakfasted & spent the day here. […] Mr Hermet is a young Spaniard from Cadiz. He was a passenger on the wealthy vessel which sank in the roads a year ago. His leg was broken in the incident & he has been a (paying) patient at the Town Hospital ever since, only having started to walk again in the last month or two.

Sat 21 Nov: […] Lisabo has not been to town these past two Saturdays, having little to sell.

---

[507] Mme de Vossey (Félicité, *née* de la Bourdonnaye), was twenty-three. See n. 469, above.

Sun 22 Nov: [...] Wm Mahy, who used to buy cider from us, was accused of several thefts last spring. He appeared before the Court in May & promised to leave the island [in order to avoid prosecution]. He returned in spite of his promise & was discovered at the beginning of this week stealing peas from the barn of a Mr Lainé. Mahy made his escape, but he was later found drowned at les Grandes Roques. Yesterday, a pilot boat was launched from Perelle in order to guide a larger vessel. The pilot boat has not been seen since & people are beginning to think it must have perished. The boat was crewed by 4 men, 3 from the Brehaut family & one from the de la Rue family. One of the men has 8 children. Another has 2 or 3 children & a pregnant wife.

Thurs 26 Nov: [...] the Bailiff & Mrs Le Marchant left for England on Tuesday. This was doubtless because of the death of our Governor Lord Grey (the Bailiff was his Receiver).[508] [...] I went to see the new tower at Houmet Point in the afternoon.

Mon 30 Nov: [...] On Saturday evening an English frigate, the Boreas, was lost at Hannoi Point. The Captn & about half the crew (of nearly 100) were drowned. Most of the body of the vessel was visible above water on today's low tide.

Thurs 3 Dec: [...] Daniel Ferbrache, who returned from his 3rd voyage to Virginia on Monday evening, came to see us. He supped here & stayed overnight.

Sat 12 Dec: [...] Lisabo went to fetch young Judith [Collenette] to spend the holidays with us.

Mon 14 Dec: [...] Lord Pembroke has become Governor of Guernsey.[509] He has re-appointed the Bailiff as his Receiver.

Thurs 24 Dec: [...] Thos le Pelley took tea here & spent *la longue veille* with me. He has not been here at all this winter. Daniel & our seamstress Marie Mauger also came for *la longue veille*.

---

[508] Lieutenant-General Charles Grey, 1st Earl Grey (1729–1807), had been Guernsey's Governor since 1794.
[509] This was Lieutenant-General George Herbert, 11th Earl of Pembroke (1759–1827). He remained Governor until his death in 1827.

Fri 25 Dec: Christmas. We had no visitors, save Daniel who dined here.

Thurs 31 Dec: […] Rain in the morning & again in the evening, accompanied by gales.

Notes relating to 1807

Charles Mollet gave work to eight men aside from his live-in servants in 1807. Five of these were day labourers. Those who worked the largest number of days were Isac Nicolle (87, year-round), Etienne Lihou (83, year-round) and Isac Le Geyt (88, June–October).

1808

Sun 1 Jan: Daniel [Ferbrache] dined with us.

Mon 2 Jan: [...] Jean [Cateline] went to town in the morning but did not return till 3 o'clock. I reprimanded him, upon which he left the house, taking some of his clothes with him. A wet & windy afternoon.

Sun 3 Jan: [...] Jean arrived just as we were sitting down to breakfast, but he refused to eat anything, even though Lisabo & I invited him to join us. I told him he would be welcome to continue sleeping here until he was better provided for, but he only thanked me & left shortly afterwards.

Mon 4 Jan: Jean returned in the morning & stayed. He said that he had slept in the small cowshed, & that his box, which he had pretended to take away on Saturday, had gone no further than there.

Tues 5 Jan: [...] I received a letter Pierre Machon sent me from Cork on his return from Buenos Ayres. Cut & stripped the osier.

[*Several pages have been torn or cut out of the journal at this point. On the next intact page, we find ourselves in February.*]

Fri 12 Feb: north-westerly gales. [...] Captn Bazin's cutter struck the Castle Rock during the night & was dashed to pieces. Four or five men were drowned. A privateer belonging to Mr Tupper of le Carrefour[510] broke free of its anchor, lost its mast & was carried off towards Jersey.

Mon 15 Feb: a hard frost, with ice about an inch thick. Daniel [Ferbrache] came to see us.

Tues 16 Feb: Daniel left here at five in the morning. [....] He is hoping to leave for Portsmouth today.

---

[510] John Elisha Tupper, sen. (1764–1845), a successful merchant.

Sun 28 Feb: [...] Yesterday I placed advertisements in the newspapers announcing that all my land, houses & buildings are for sale.

Thurs 10 Mar: [...] I took tea at Henry Brock's & accompanied him to see a play performed by some gentlemen for the benefit of Guernsey prisoners-of-war in France. Jean came to fetch me home on foot. It was nearly one o'clock in the morning by the time we arrived back.

Fri 11 Mar: [...] Mrs Le Marchant came to make me a very gracious & liberal offer of pecuniary assistance on the Bailiff's behalf. She said (her own expression) that the Bailiff wished me to 'consider him as a brother'.

Sun 13 Mar: [...] Lisabo took a gallon of cream to Miss S, who is about to leave for India. The Procureur will escort her as far as Portsmouth.[511]

Sat 19 Mar: [...] It has been dry since 13 February (when we last had snow) until today. For about half the intervening weeks, the wind has been north-easterly. This has produced a great deal of dust in the roads.

Sun 3 Apr: Messrs Marie, de Callonne & de Nadailland came here unexpectedly & took coffee with me.[512] We had a few frosts last week & another this morning.

Fri 29 Apr: the Procureur, his sons John & Durrell & twin daughters Rose & Anne,[513] Lady Smith, Mary, Sophie & Nancy Dobrée came to dinner. I had also invited Miss Henrietta Sausmarez, Mary Brock, little Kitty Saumarez, &

---

[511] 'Miss S' was the Procureur's twenty-six-year-old daughter, Elizabeth De Sausmarez (1782–1818), who was on her way to Madras in order to marry Captain Thomas De Havilland (for whom see n. 457, above). She would die there ten years later.

[512] 'Monsieur de Callonne' is likely to have been Captain Jean-Joseph de Calonne. 'Monsieur de Nadailland' was probably Lieutenant Marie-Laurent-Thibéry de Nattes de Nadaillan. Both are listed as members of the Company of French Royalist soldiers based in Guernsey in 1805 (HO 98/28, National Archives).

[513] The children of HM Procureur Thomas De Sausmarez mentioned here and elsewhere in this entry were John De Sausmarez (1790–1870), Durell De Sausmarez (1800–59), Anne De Sausmarez (1802–72), Rose De Sausmarez (1802–41), Henrietta De Sausmarez (1789–1888) and Catherine De Sausmarez (1797–1847).

the elder of Lady Smith's two young daughters, but they were indisposed.[514] Mrs Saumarez (the Procureur's wife) is lying in.

Tues 3 May: [...] I spoke to Mary [Brock] this morning about Mrs Roussel & Mrs Martin, two poor Englishwomen. She gave me 10 shillings for them (5 shillings each) & will also go to see them herself.

Weds 25 May: Daniel Ferbrache came here yesterday between eleven & midnight, having arrived from Jersey (where he did not go ashore) at 5 o'clock in the evening. The master of his ship, Captn Le Cheminant, also came ashore to sleep, as did Mr Le Cheminant's son. They were originally planning to sail for England at five this morning. Jean Ferbrache, the boatswain's mate, left the ship at Jersey. Daniel is a steward on board the vessel.

Sun 29 May: [...] Lisabo Nicolle of Candie dined here. She has recently returned from Jersey, where she spent a few weeks at my sister's. My sister is suffering a great deal with her legs & has not slept in her bed for 7 weeks, spending all day & all night in her armchair.[515]

Weds 15 Jun: [...] Jean [Cateline] is unwell. I went to town towards evening to buy some emetics & purgatives.

Fri 17 Jun: [...] Jean is feeling better. He did a little work today.

Mon 27 Jun: [...] Little Isac Marquand has come to stay for a few weeks. He will do some bird-scaring for us.[516]

Sun 10 Jul: [...] Jean [Cateline] rose at five this morning, but was nowhere to be seen for the next few hours. At nine o'clock, he reappeared & took a horse into town. He returned at one o'clock & was here until six, when he told Betty or Suzon to have his supper ready at seven o'clock precisely (hot soup).

---

[514] Mary, Sophie and Nancy Dobrée (seventeen, fourteen and eleven respectively) were Mollet's great-nieces, daughters of Bonamy and the late Patty. 'Lady Smith' was the former Carterette De Havilland (daughter of Peter De Havilland), who had married her cousin Colonel George Smith in 1798 (see n. 419, above). Smith had been knighted in 1807. Their daughters were Sophia Smith (1800–36) and Mary Smith (1801–74).
[515] Elizabeth (Lisabo) Nicolle was a servant in the Mourant household at Candie. Mollet's Jersey-based sister Marie Lerrier was now a widow of seventy-two.
[516] Lisabo Machon's nephew Isaac Marquand was now ten years old.

This they did, but he went out at half past six (while I was away) & only returned at half past eight. By this time, he was in a bad temper & refused to eat. The only food anyone saw him eat all day was a piece of bread & butter in the afternoon. It was his Sunday to stay in.

Weds 13 Jul: the Procureur, his wife, his son John & daughter Henrietta, Mr Harry Dobrée, Nico le Fevre, Hy Brock, Mary, young Wm Brock & his sister Mary,[517] Peter Mourant & his wife came to breakfast. I then laid on a dinner for them at Plein Mont, after which we all took tea at le Bourg in the Forest, where I left them. We brought all the necessaries with us from here.

Sat 16 Jul: [...] Lisabo took about 50 lb of cherries from the upper garden to market.

Weds 20 Jul: [...] Called at Mr Gibert's (around one o'clock) on my way to les Sometlieuses in the Forest, where Sir Thomas & Lady S[aumarez] were laying on a dinner for the Revd & Mrs Brock, Hy Brock, Mary, Mary Brock & William, the Procureur, his son, & myself. Ab. came to help. Just as we were finishing dinner, a light rain came on & we retreated to the watch-house, where we took tea.

Tues 26 Jul: Mr & Mrs Tom Brock & Mrs Savary Brock breakfasted here. They then accompanied me to le Clos du Valle, where I laid on a dinner for them at Cuhouel (on the hill).[518] We were joined there by Sir Thomas & Lady Saumarez, Hy Brock, Mary, Mary Brock & William. I had also invited the Procureur, his son & Harry Dobrée, but they were unable to come. Savary Brock is at present in Spain.[519] Ab, Lisabo & Eleazar [Ingrouille] came to serve us.

[*Charles Mollet turned sixty-six during the course of August 1808*]

---

[517] 'Young Wm Brock' was one of the twin sons of Nancy and William Brock, born in 1789 (see n. 251, above). He was now a nineteen-year-old medical student. For William's seventeen-year-old sister Mary, see n. 463, above.
[518] Now known as le Mont Cuet.
[519] Thirty-five-year-old John Savery Brock had volunteered for Lieutenant-General Sir John Moore's expedition to Spain, where he acted for several months as one of the General's aides-de-camp.

Weds 3 Aug: Monsieur Marie came to breakfast & stayed all day in order to show Lisabo [Machon] how to separate the oil from the water when distilling peppermint.

Fri 12 Aug: Mr Pierre Le Marchant was giving his yearly dinner at le Groignet.[520] I was expecting the Procureur for breakfast on his way there, but he was prevented from coming by his wife's indisposition, as also a Court Martial.[521] His children (John, Henriette & little Durell de Sausmarez) however did come.

Mon 15 Aug: […] Young Isac [Marquand], who has been here since 27 June, returned home today.

Weds 17 Aug: Henry & Mary Brock, Peter & Sophy Mourant, Mary Brock, Frederick le Messurier & his wife Martha Brock & Mr Charles Bell breakfasted with me.[522] I had also invited Sir Thomas & Lady Saumarez, but they were unable to come. After breakfast, we all went to Lihou Island, where Henry & Mary laid on a dinner for us. We were joined there by Mr & Mrs Tom Brock. It was a neap tide, so we crossed by boat both ways. Nico Marqui, Ab. & Lisabo came to serve us. We supplied the party with fruit, curds, plates, glasses, teacups, &c. We borrowed Eleazar's horse.

Mon 22 Aug: I breakfasted at Hy Brock's with Mr & Mrs Tom Brock, Sir Thos S. & Mr Charles Bell. We then set out for Herm, where Peter & Sophy were laying on a dinner. Their other guests were Mr & Mrs Frederick le M., Martha & Eliza Dobrée, & Nico le Fevre. We all left at 8 o'clock in one boat, & stopped off at Jethou for an hour. We did not return until 9 in the evening.

---

[520] Pierre Le Marchant (born in 1741) was a brother of the former Bailiff William Le Marchant. Afflicted with some form of mental illness, he had been boarded out with the Dorey family of le Groignet, who every year helped organise a dinner for his relatives.
[521] In tandem with his role as HM Procureur, Thomas De Sausmarez also served as military Deputy Judge-Advocate.
[522] Frederick Le Mesurier (1782–1824), the grandson of former Alderney Governor Henry Le Mesurier (see n. 24, above), had recently married Mollet's great-niece Martha Brock (1787–1827). Charles Bell (1767–1844) was the tenth of the twelve children of the Scottish-born merchant William Bell and Marie Le Marchant, whose family Mollet had known for many years.

Sat 27 Aug: [...] Ab. went to fetch 100 lb of coffee which Mr Harry Dobrée put aside for me. Mr Dobrée is charging me 1 shilling per lb, which is what he paid for it himself.

Mon 29 Aug: to town around noon & thence to le Chateau de la Corbiere in the Forest, where the Revd Mr Tom Brock & his wife were laying on a dinner. Their other guests were Sir Thos & Lady S[aumarez], Peter Mourant, Mary & her niece Mary Brock (Hy is in England), Frederick Le Mesurier & Martha, Mr Charles Bell, Mr Wm Brock (the brother of the Revd Tom) & Sir James Saumarez's eldest son.[523] We had very fine weather. [...] Tithe collection has begun.

Thurs 1 Sep: to town after breakfast for the funeral of old Mrs Condomine.[524] I had a hatband.

Sun 18 Sep: [...] Jack Fletcher, a 14-year-old boy who tells me he is from Southampton but has no friends here, came to my door semi-naked to ask me for work. He has spent 3 months at Hy le Tissier's, who fed & lodged him but gave him neither clothes nor money. He says his mother is a poor woman who lives at Broad Lane in Southampton. He has been 7 years at sea & came ashore from the Scout, Captn White, after being maltreated. I will risk keeping him till I know more about him.

Sat 24 Sep: [...] Our seamstress started making some clothes for Jack.

Sat 1 Oct: [...] Jean [Cateline] spent the whole day celebrating his sister Esther's wedding. She married Thos le Tissier, the son of the late Nic. le Tissier of la Mare.

Mon 3 Oct: [...] I went to see James Brehaut at Feu le Comte in St Saviour in order to give him news of his brother Jean Brehaut (who has been at l'Isle Saint Jean for many years) which I received in a letter from Daniel Machon.

Weds 5 Oct: [...] Messrs De Voscé, De Callonne & Nadailland took tea here. Monsieur Marie was busy seeing a patient & could not come. Mr & Mrs

---

[523] Also named James (1789–1863).
[524] 'Old Mrs Condomine' was seventy-six-year-old Marie Condamine, *née* Néel, the widow of former HM Sergeant Jean-Jacques Condamine (see n. 116, above).

Savary Brock came unexpectedly & joined us for tea. Savary has recently returned from Spain & Portugal.

Sat 8 Oct: Jack [Fletcher] accompanied me to town to speak to Captn White, whom he left at Easter.

Mon 10 Oct: […] I dismissed Jack Fletcher this morning.

Weds 12 Oct: […] I went to see Mr Gibert, whom I found quite despondent. His wife returned from Jersey a week ago, bringing with her a maid whom she dismissed yesterday (even though they are without servants & appear to have no prospect of finding any).

Mon 17 Oct: […] Peter Dobrée, who arrived in Guernsey yesterday, called here around noon. He had set sail on 1 January 1807 for the River Plate in America. From there, he made a voyage around the Cape of Good Hope & then returned to Rio Janeiro. He has come here via England.

Weds 19 Oct: […] I reprimanded Jean [Cateline] for having beaten the draught animals excessively on Friday & Saturday. He replied, among other things, that he did not want to be a carter & had come here to work as a gardener. To which I countered that I did not need gardeners but people who could turn their hand to all manner of things, adding that, if he did not wish to do this sort of work, he was free to leave. This is the essence & true import of what passed between us, although much else was said on both sides. After dinner, Jean fetched his clothes & made ready to go, calling first at my room to ask me if I was in a position to pay him. I answered that I was not at present, & I left the room by the other door to avoid further discussion. Jean has worked here for more than 3 years, & has lived here as my farm servant since 1 January 1806. I will undoubtedly miss him, since, when sober, he is a careful & diligent worker & a good & obliging person. However, his fondness for drink & tendency to tell lies greatly detract from his merits.

Thurs 20 Oct: Jean came here in the morning, ostensibly to fetch the rest of his clothes. However, when he had made up his bundle & I had paid him his wages, he noticed that I had mistakenly paid him for a whole year, when his year ends properly on 1 January next. He told me to keep the money, & that he would earn it by working out his full year. I consented, & I think this suited both of us well.

Tues 25 Oct: [...] We learned on Sunday that Wm Carey (son of Jean Carey) had died at Madeira, where he was serving with his regiment.[525]

Thurs 27 Oct: [...] I went to see Mr Gibert. He gave me two 20 shilling notes for Pierre le Page (son of Nicolas) of les Grandes Roques, a poor man who is building himself a small house near le Guet.

Fri 28 Oct: we brought Pierre le Page nearly a cartload of building timber (4 elms & 2 beams made from the spruce trees we felled at the turning).

Fri 4 Nov: the boys picked the Martrenge apples in the morning [...]. I picked one bushel of Permain apples at le Carré. We have had about six bushels of Martrenge apples. Half of them had fallen to the ground, but we were able to save them.

Sat 12 Nov: [...] Nicolas Heaume of le Mont Durand, who was lying drunk at the top of the drive yesterday evening, slept in our barn. We gave him breakfast in the morning.

Thurs 17 Nov: [...] delivered 2 dozen roof rafters we made from the young oaks at the top of le Marquet to Pierre le Page (son of Nicolas).

Sun 20 Nov: [...] To St Peter's church in the afternoon. Mr Brock preached a charity sermon for Guernsey prisoners-of-war in France. Wind & rain all afternoon.

Tues 22 Nov: [...] Le Duc de Bouillon (the Admiral who commands the naval station in these islands) paid me a visit around noon.[526] [...] He has been in Guernsey 3 or 4 weeks without my seeing him.

Mon 28 Nov: I was afflicted with rheumatism all last week, & it has become worse today. It has spread to my stomach & is accompanied by a cough & feeling of oppression which came on yesterday.

---

[525] Captain William Carey (see n. 494, above) was thirty-two years old.
[526] For Admiral Philippe D'Auvergne, see n. 346, above. D'Auvergne had begun styling himself Duc/Duke after the deaths of his patron Duke Godefroy de la Tour d'Auvergne and the Duke's only son in 1794 and 1802 respectively.

Sun 4 Dec: […] I am feeling better, thank God, & rose at nine. Monsieur Marie called here before noon & brought me my newspaper, as also Mr Gibert's newspaper.

Tues 6 Dec: Ab. took the small cart to fetch 3 cases of lemons & one of oranges which Captn Jemmy Collenette brought me from Oporto. I paid Captn Collenette a guinea for their carriage. The others felled twelve 15 ft oaks at the turning, which I am giving to Thomas Collenette (son of Thomas) who is building a house on the coast near le Crocq.

Mon 19 Dec: […] Martha Brock, the wife of Frederick Le Mesurier, has given birth to a daughter in London, where they reside. This is her first child.

Thurs 22 Dec: bitterly cold. […] Messrs Hy & Savary Brock came around midday. They brought me a letter from young Wm Brock in London, to whom I had written concerning Daniel [Ferbrache].[527]

Fri 23 Dec: […] Mr Pelley (Thomas) came here around seven to spend *la longue veille* with me. He has not been here at all so far this winter.

Sun 25 Dec: frosty all day. The ground is partly covered with snow. We had no visitors.

Sat 31 Dec: […] The weather has lately been mild & damp. I do not think I have been to town since 8 October, except for a short time on the 22nd.

Notes relating to 1808

Aside from his live-in servants, Charles Mollet recorded giving work to twelve men in 1808. Five of them were tradesmen, four of them were piece-workers, and there were also three regular day labourers who worked all year round: Isaac Nicolle (111½ days), Jean Blondel (111 days), and Etienne Lihou (93 days).

---

[527] For 'young Wm Brock', see n. 517, above.

1809

Sun 1 Jan: yesterday at ten I reprimanded Jean [Cateline] for having suddenly disappeared for an hour. He told me he had been to the blacksmith's to fetch a fork. He did not eat any dinner, mucked out the cowsheds, then at 4 o'clock he told Lisabo that he would not be returning so she could lock all the doors. He then departed without telling me, even though I had spoken to him not long before. This morning, he returned here between 9 and 10 o'clock, refused breakfast, got dressed in his Sunday clothes, & said he was going to church. [...] He arrived back just as we were sitting down to supper, & gave me my newspaper. I went up to his room to ask him to sup with us, & he refused very brusquely. I then asked him if he would stay the night. He refused again, got dressed in his everyday clothes, & made as if to leave. I asked him again if he would eat something with us when he passed through the kitchen on his way out.

Mon 2 Jan: [...] Jean came here towards noon & went straight to his room. He later came down again & passed through the kitchen while we were having dinner. I asked him twice if he would like to eat with us, but he went off without answering.

Thurs 5 Jan: Pierre Cateline, who has been a roof-tiler for a few years but has no work at present, came to ask me to employ him. I sent him to cut the osier with Etienne & Isac. [...] Jean came yesterday evening to fetch his shoes. I told him he could sleep here, & he stayed overnight.

Mon 9 Jan: [...] Jean [Cateline] will stay in my service. He asked me himself if he could stay here, & he agreed to submit to the conditions I intend to impose on him.

Sat 14 Jan: [...] I received a letter dated 16 November from Mr Thos Lenfesté, the carpenter, who went to America a year ago last May. He has settled in the new town of Cambridge, on the Wells Creek. This is a small but navigable river which flows into the Muskingum river, which itself empties into the Ohio river, & thence into the Mississippi.

Mon 16 Jan: [...] Yesterday evening, as I was feeding the chickens in the cartshed, the old cockerel who has long been in the habit of trying to attack me, pierced my right foot, having pushed down my slipper with his spur. Although the injury seemed only slight, it caused me considerable pain, which has persisted ever since, becoming violent this evening & affecting the whole of my body up to the shoulders.

Tues 17 Jan: [...] I felt ill & did not get up.

Thurs 19 Jan: I am still unwell. Jean carried me to the fireside, where I sat while my bed (which I have not left since Monday) was being changed.

Sat 21 Jan: [...] Monsieur Marie came to see me towards evening. I had my foot bathed & a poultice applied. I am about the same. I am confined to bed, unable to eat or sleep, nor scarcely even to drink. I have a constant fever. Dr Saumarez also came to see me.

Mon 23 Jan: [...] my fever has returned with some force & I feel very weak. Nevertheless, my foot, which started to suppurate on Saturday evening, is less painful.

Tues 24 Jan: [...] Yesterday & the day before, I took a medicine given me by Dr S. which had no effect. This morning I took a draught from Mr Davy, & it worked in the evening. My indisposition has abated. My foot, which continues to suppurate, is less painful (though still very swollen & inflamed).

Fri 27 Jan: [...] I am no worse, but still confined to bed & scarcely eating, save for a little biscuit soaked in milk.

Sat 28 Jan: [...] The Court has ordered people either to chain up their dogs or have them destroyed, because some have been found with rabies.

Fri 3 Feb: I had a bad night. I took some medicine just before 4, but have felt ill all day.

Sun 5 Feb: [...] The packet due a week ago finally arrived. [...] The news remains generally bad: the French have been victorious all over Spain, & our troops are returning from the battlefield in very poor condition. I had my bed changed. Aside from this, I did not get up.

Tues 7 Feb: Betty [Tostevin] injured her arm yesterday evening (on the leg of the soup pot) & went to consult Dr Carey. Suzon [Ozanne] accompanied her & told me afterwards that Daniel [Ferbrache] had entered Guy's Hospital on the 18th of January.

Thurs 9 Feb: [...] I wrote to Wm Brock, & also to Daniel at Guy's Hospital (where he has been since the 18th) care of Wm Brock.

Fri 10 Feb: [...] I went downstairs for the first time since my accident, & sat in the parlour between 3 & 10 o'clock. My foot is still very swollen & painful (as also my leg), even though the wound seems almost healed. We have been applying olive oil to my foot this past week.

Sat 11 Feb: William Johnson, a gunner's mate from the tower at Vazon, started working here as a day labourer.

Thurs 16 Feb: [...] I rose around ten, & went with Jean as far as the nursery at le Prey. I had not been out of the house, nor even downstairs (save once) since 16 January, having been almost constantly confined to my bed. I still have great difficulty walking, though my foot appears almost healed. I have pain in my knee & right hip, which is also very weak.

Sat 18 Feb: Betty & Suzon took the butter to market. Lisabo did not go to town.

Sun 19 Feb: [...] I dined in the kitchen for the 1st time in five weeks.

Thurs 23 Feb: [...] I was up almost all day. I received a letter from Wm Brock informing me that Daniel [Ferbrache] will be returning here in a few weeks' time, as his arm cannot be cured.

Fri 10 Mar: [...] Daniel [Ferbrache] arrived from London this evening. He spent six weeks at Guy's Hospital under the care of Wm Brock. He has almost lost the use of his left arm.

Sun 12 Mar: Daniel dined here. Hy Brock & Nico le Fevre took tea with me. I was also expecting the Procureur, but he was prevented from coming by the news that his brother-in-law, Sir George Smith, has died at Cadiz, where he had been sent by the Government.[528]

Sat 1 Apr: […] Elizabeth Tosdevin, who has been here since 9 October 1807 (one year & 5½ months), left my service today. She has been unwell since Christmas. I sent Ab. to take her home on horseback.

Mon 3 Apr: Easter Monday. The militia was under arms, regiment by regiment. Jean [Cateline] was exempted on account of the problem he has with his hands & did not go. Since last summer, he has had a sort of rheumatism in his finger joints, which, while not particularly painful, is very awkward because it prevents him easily grasping slim things such as spade- or fork-handles.

Sun 9 Apr: […] Jean only changed into his Sunday clothes towards evening, after which he went out. He returned in a drunken state at 10 o'clock. He is upset because he has lost one of his keys.

Sun 30 Apr: […] I have put aside 27 guineas from Jean's wages (10 guineas from his first year, 7 guineas from his second, & 10 guineas when I paid him at the beginning of this year). He has given me his promise that he will turn this money to profit, so today I gave him a note for 400 francs & undertook to pay him a further 500 francs in five years' time. Both Jean & I signed an agreement to this effect, as also Eleazar [Ingrouille] & Daniel le Prevost who witnessed it.

Sun 7 May: […] Margueritte Langlais (daughter of Abraham Langlais of les Chans [Jehans] in Torteval) will begin working here as a house servant tomorrow. I will pay her £6 stg per year.

Sat 20 May: […] Pierre Cateline, who started working here on 5 January, will next week resume his usual occupation as a plasterer & roofer, &c.

Sun 28 May: […] Daniel [Ferbrache] came to breakfast but declined to stay for dinner. As he was leaving, I complained to Daniel that he had not been here for 3 weeks & was less than assiduous in visiting us. […] Gotton Langlais, who started work here on 8 May, left us. I paid her 7s 6d.

---

[528] For Sir George Smith, see nn. 419 and 514, above. For the connection between Smith and HM Procureur Thomas De Sausmarez, see Appendix 3.

Sat 3 Jun: […] Suzon [Ozanne] went to town, but Lisabo [Machon] did not go (we have nothing to sell).

Fri 9 Jun: […] The 2-year-old black (or rather blackish) heifer calved last night. This was her first calf. She was in considerable distress. Ab, Jean & Lisabo were up with her all night. Lisabo went to fetch Eleazar [Ingrouille] around 11 o'clock, & Jean went to fetch Jean du Quemin of St Saviour.

Weds 14 Jun: […] Marie le Page (aged 14) came here to help Lisabo until we can find another house servant. She is the eldest daughter of the late Nico le Page (eldest son of la Roque a Boeuf).

Mon 26 Jun: there was a Review of the whole of the militia & 5 or 6 companies of regular soldiers at l'Ancresse. Two Guernseymen were wounded by small stones which it is believed the regulars put in their rifles.

Sat 8 Jul: […] Lisabo went to sell some produce at the market, which she had not done since 27 May. The produce comprised gooseberries, currants, raspberries, artichokes & potatoes.

Sun 9 Jul: […] Captn Tom Cohu from below l'Aumone is about to leave for Newfoundland. He came to ask me if he could take anything for me, so I am giving him a letter & a chest to take to Danl Machon at l'Isle St Jean.

Tues 11 Jul: […] I took a turn around the Forest in the evening & called to see Nanon Heaume. George [Nicolet], who caught sight of me as I passed le Bourg, ran to catch up with me & spoke to me for several minutes.[529]

Sun 16 Jul: […] Captn Tom Cohu, Eleazar [Ingrouille], Jemmy Colnette & his wife came to dinner, as also Daniel [Ferbrache] & George (Nicollet). Messrs De Voscé, Callonne, Nadaillon & Marie took tea with me.

Weds 19 Jul: […] Young Marie le Page, who has been with us since 14 June, will stay here as our house servant. Her mother came & settled her wages with Lisabo. Marie will have £4 stg per year.

---

[529] Nanon (Anne) Heaume and George Nicolet were both former employees of Mollet's.

Sun 23 Jul: […] I called to see Henry Brock. Henry slipped in the market on Thursday & broke a bone in his shoulder. He is as well as can be expected in the circumstances. He has no fever.

Thurs 27 Jul: […] Distilled 25 bottles of rose water. We have made a total of 126 bottles in 5 batches since 24 June.

[*Charles Mollet turned sixty-seven during the course of August 1809*]

Sun 6 Aug: […] Daniel came for dinner. He accompanied me to St Andrew's church, & afterwards went to town to see his brother Jean who has lately arrived from St Domingue.[530]

Weds 9 Aug: […] We had our bullock shod at Char. Torode's, but we will not use him again, because he insists that he will not shoe oxen anywhere but at his own premises.

Sun 20 Aug: […] In the afternoon I went to St Saviour's church where Mr Carey preached a charity sermon for the benefit of our prisoners in France. The collection yielded £16 stg. Last Sunday, £17 was collected at St Peter's church, & about £19 was collected at St Andrew's a fortnight ago.

Sun 27 Aug: […] The Procureur & Nico le Fevre came to breakfast, & accompanied me to [Castel] church, where Mr Tom Carey preached the same charity sermon he preached at St Saviour's church last Sunday. […] The collection after the sermon yielded £46 stg.

Mon 28 Aug: the carpenters are here to make boxes for our Guernsey lilies. Ab. & Jean Guilbert loaded 5 boxes containing six dozen lilies each & 2 boxes of three dozen each on board Captn Denis for Mr St Croix. They also took six dozen lilies to Mr Moore my shoemaker, six dozen to Mr Wm de Putron & 2 dozen which I am giving to Captn Denis. I sold Ph. Frecker 2 dozen lilies on Saturday.

---

[530] St Domingue was an old name for the former French colony which had recently re-invented itself as Haiti.

Tues 29 Aug: Hy Brock came to tell me that my sister died on Friday morning. She had suffered greatly with her legs for many years.[531]

Tues 5 Sep: […] Sr Danl Dorey carted the first of his wheat. We collected the tithe (144 sheaves). Nico Guignon, jun., (who was here last Sunday morning) fell 40 ft from Mr Pelley's new house at les Beaucamps yesterday. He was carried home, where [his leg] was amputated almost at the top.

Weds 13 Sep: […] Peter Dobrée came to bid me farewell. He is going to establish himself in Gibraltar.[532]

Fri 15 Sep: […] Ab. went to fetch 3 dozen bottles of wine which Mr Savary Brock is giving me. I think there are a dozen of Port, a dozen of Lisbon & a dozen of Albaflor. About two inches of rain fell yesterday between midday & eight in the evening.

Sun 17 Sep: […] Messrs Marie, Bowls, de Callonne, de Nadaillon & de Vossey (who has lately returned from Jersey) took coffee with me. A damp day. Rain in the evening.

Mon 18 Sep: […] Marie Breton, Nico's daughter, who is ill with consumption & has been spending her days here for 5 or 6 weeks, could not come yesterday (nor Friday) because she was too weak.

Tues 19 Sep: […] Fine weather. I pulled out the beans.

Thurs 21 Sep: […] I walked to town, mainly to see two French gentlemen from Caen who arrived here in a ship loaded with grain for Mr Harry Dobrée.[533] I met them at Mr Dobrée's shop. He is to bring them here tomorrow afternoon.

---

[531] Mollet's Jersey-based sister Marie Lerrier was seventy-three years old. See n. 17, above.
[532] Mollet's twenty-five-year-old great-nephew Peter Dobrée had already spent time at counting-houses in Montpellier and Buenos Aires. See nn. 452 and 493, above.
[533] By this time, the so-called 'licence trade' had begun. It was a system whereby permits for the exchange of essential commodities between Britain and France were issued by the British government. Since the beginning of the trade in 1808, St Peter Port had been developing a role as an entrepôt for such commodities. Harry Dobrée (for whom see n. 343, above) was a leading participant in the licence trade.

Fri 22 Sep: the Procureur, his son, Mr Harry Dobrée & Mons. de la Ville from Caen took coffee with me. Mons. de la Ville arrived a week ago & is to leave tomorrow. Daniel worked here in the afternoon.

Sat 23 Sep: Ab. took a dozen Guernsey lilies, 4 pink camellias, 30 roots & a small basket of peony seed to Monsieur de la Ville (to take to Monsieur L'Honoré).

Mon 2 Oct: [...] we put the bracken from les Parcs in the kitchen of the upper house. I am giving it to Margueritte du Quemin to cut up (the mother of our young Marie le Page). There are about 70 bundles, which we are storing here for her, since she has no room where she lives at Albecq. She will also have the bracken from the earthbanks at le Mont de Val.

Thurs 5 Oct: [...] called on Mrs Danl Dobrée & her daughter, who accompanied me to see Harry Dobrée's property & the house he is building to the north of l'Hyvreuse.[534]

Sat 7 Oct: to town in the morning to see Mr Sturmer, the son-in-law of Monsieur du Chevreuil, who has been here since Monday (though I only learned of his presence today).[535]

Sun 15 Oct: a frost this morning, with ice here & there.

Sat 21 Oct: [...] We did not go to market last Saturday, but Suzon went there today to sell 6 lb of butter. [...] Mr Wm Le Marchant, the former Bailiff, died on Monday at the age of 88.

Mon 23 Oct: to town in the morning. I gave Savary Brock (who is leaving tomorrow) a letter & memorandum for Mr St Croix, as also a bill of exchange for £18 stg in payment of various things I have ordered through him.

Weds 25 Oct: [...] Eleazar [Ingrouille] & his wife spent the evening with us. They left at half past ten, as also Ab. & Lisabo. I remained alone in the kitchen with Jean. When Jean made as if to go to bed, I advised him to find himself a

---

[534] Harry Dobrée was having a new house built at what is now known as Beau Séjour.
[535] According to Frederick Lukis, Charles Sturmer became the British Consul at Cherbourg at some point in the early nineteenth century (F.C. Lukis, 'Reminiscences of former days in connection with Guernsey', unpub. MS, Priaulx Library).

candle, & he suddenly flew into a rage, reminding me of what I had said to him in jest at supper (that he would become a drunkard & end up in the Hospital if he left us). This had not seemed to bother him during the evening, when he came twice into my room (to ask for a pack of cards & to fetch some cider for Eleazar). After his outburst, he went upstairs to his bedroom, & I followed him closely in order to light his way. When I later entered his room, he was already in bed. He shouted to me that he would undoubtedly end up in the Hospital, &c., &c., so I said 'you can leave as soon as you like; go tomorrow; go tonight'. He then sprang out of bed & hurriedly put on his clothes. I went into my own room, where he followed me still shouting. I tried to make him sit down & calm himself, but he marched off shoeless, stockingless, hatless & very dirty, leaving the house through the greenhouse.

Thurs 26 Oct: I rose at 4 o'clock & looked everywhere for Jean (at la Daumaillerie, in the haylofts, &c.). I could not find him, but when Suzon [Ozanne] & Marie [Le Page] came downstairs at five, he suddenly appeared. He seemed in good spirits & said he had spent most of the night in the big kitchen at the upper house.

Sat 28 Oct: […] Lisabo went to market. She had only 6 lb of butter to sell.

Sun 29 Oct: […] Messrs De Vossey, Callonne, Nadaillon, Marie, Bowls, Sturmer, Jammart (from Caen), de Fer (from St Malo) & Vonderah (last syllable pronounced 'hay') took tea with me. Mr Vonderah is a Swede established in Spain. Dense wet fog all day.

Weds 1 Nov: […] I visited Sr Danl Dorey of le Groignet, who is unwell (a loaded cart ran over his back a month ago).

Sat 18 Nov: yesterday, Jean [Cateline] went out after supper, returned around eleven, but did not sleep in the house. He reappeared this morning, but did no work. Around one o'clock this afternoon he told Suzon [Ozanne] he was going to town. We have not seen him since.

Sun 19 Nov: Daniel [Ferbrache] dined here. He has been at sea (in a privateer) for ….. weeks, & only returned on Friday.

Mon 20 Nov: […] Jean appeared around nine in the evening to change into his old clothes, but he did not stay. This morning at ten, as I was leaving for town, I came across him in the courtyard. He asked me when I would be ready to pay him his wages. I answered that I did not think it would do him much good to give him a large sum of money. I then asked him to try opening the door of the cider cellar, as I thought I had lost the key. He was unable to do so. I added that he knew where to find me if he wanted to broach this matter with me another time, but that, as he could see, I was about to go out. I then went on my way, & so, apparently, did he.

Tues 21 Nov: Jean returned at nightfall yesterday. I reprimanded him sternly. He promised to behave better & stayed.

Sun 3 Dec: Lisabo, who has already spent a few nights at Marie Breton's bedside, also spent last night there.

Fri 8 Dec: I walked to town in the morning. The roads were full of mud. Mr Sturmer's ship arrived with a cargo of wheat yesterday, but he was not on board. Captn Berg gave me a letter from Monsieur Du Chevreuil, together with 4 turkeys, 2 geese & 4 hens, which Ab. went to fetch.

Mon 11 Dec: [...] Marie Breton died at 3 o'clock this afternoon. They had earlier sent for Lisabo, to whom Marie spoke a few words shortly before she died.[536]

Thurs 14 Dec: [...] Ab. is on watch-duty this evening. It will be my turn tomorrow. The guard is mounted by ten men & an officer from the Castel & two men from the Vale who assemble at a public house near le Grand Pont. They are charged with keeping a watch on 2 or 3 posts manned by the Brunswick Regiment (which has recently arrived & which it seems the Governor distrusts).[537]

Fri 15 Dec: [...] Jean did watch-duty on my behalf at le Grand Pont.

Sat 23 Dec: Thos le Pelley came to spend *la longue veille* with me, but he declined to take tea. He has not been here at all so far this winter. Our

---

[536] Marie Breton, the daughter of Nicolas Breton and Anne, *née* Ingrouille, was seventeen years old.

[537] These were the so-called 'Black Brunswickers', under the command of Friedrich Wilhelm, Duke of Brunswick-Wolfenbüttel, who took refuge in Guernsey after a summer and autumn campaign on the Continent and were accommodated for a few months at Delancey barracks.

seamstress Marie Mauger, who is currently working here, stayed the night. Daniel [Ferbrache], who arrived from Walcheren yesterday, came here in the evening & also stayed the night. Young Isac [Marquand] is spending the holidays here, & young Judith Collenette came here yesterday.

Mon 25 Dec: we had no visitors except Daniel, who dined with us.

Tues 26 Dec: Fair Day. Lisabo took the 4 children there (our Marie & Suzon, little Judith & little Isac). Jean went to town in the morning.

Fri 29 Dec: […] Mrs le Marchant of la H.d.P. paid me a brief visit around two. She had been told I was ill.

Sun 31 Dec: the Procureur, Harry Dobrée, Nico le Fevre, Monsieur de Fer & Captn Berg came to dinner. Fair weather. Mild but damp.

Notes relating to 1809

In 1809, Charles Mollet employed thirteen day labourers, which was more than he had been in the habit of employing in recent years. Some of these labourers only worked a handful of days, but he had six regulars: Jean Blondel (171 days, year-round), Etienne Lihou (90 days, year-round), Thomas Blondel (85½ days, May–December), Isaac Nicolle (78 days, January–September), Pierre Cateline (71½ days, January–May), and the soldier William Johnson (46 days, February–June). Mollet's standard daily rate for male labour at this time was 1s 3d. Mollet also listed three women workers in 1809 – Marie Nicolle (a laundress, 18 days, July–December), Marie Mauger (a seamstress, 14 days, June–December), and Rachel Collenette (8 days, June–August). He recorded paying Marie Nicolle one shilling a day, but did not note what he paid the other women.

1810

Mon 1 Jan: Nico Breton came with his farm servant (young Nico Sauvarin) & his animals, & helped us sow wheat at les Monts de Vaux. Mild, misty weather.

Weds 3 Jan: [...] I paid Mr Ph. Frecker 2½ guineas for his year, as also 5 shillings for having shaved Jean since the feast of St John the Baptist. He will no longer shave me, because he is now asking 3½ guineas per year, which I do not wish to pay.

Sun 7 Jan: I have engaged Billy Caire as my barber.[538] I will pay him the same as I used to pay Mr Frecker – 2½ guineas per year to shave me, 10s a year to shave Jean once a week, & half a guinea per year to buy his apprentice (who will come here to do the shaving) a pair of shoes.

Sun 14 Jan: [...] Towards one o'clock in the afternoon, a bespectacled young man calling himself Monsieur Lainé came here with a young woman he claimed was his sister. He said he had lately arrived from Caen & presented me with a letter of recommendation which was purportedly from young Monsieur St Jore, but was very carelessly written & which I do not intend to honour. The young man said he was a Prussian naturalist settled in Paris, but I think he is French. He may even be a spy.

Tues 23 Jan: [...] Ab. took the cow we had from Candie to town. I have sold her to the Procureur for 20 guineas to provide milk during a sea voyage to India. She was given to me as a calf by Mr Mourant.

Weds 24 Jan: [...] Monsieur De Vossey came unexpectedly about 4 o'clock accompanied by Monsieur De la Ville & Monsieur Gaugain (the son of a Frenchman from Caen, who is living in London). Monsieur Gaugain is on his way to Caen to collect the inheritance of a certain Monsieur Fumée, heir to Madame Lami (des Landes) formerly of la Rue de la Poste. Monsieur G.

---

[538] William Caire (1782–1857).

brought me a letter of recommendation from Monsieur Lami des Vallées, who is at present in London.[539]

Sat 3 Feb: [...] Daniel [Ferbrache] came to bid me farewell in the afternoon. He is leaving this evening on board Captn Thos Moullin (with whom he has already sailed). They are going to Gibraltar & the Straits.

Weds 21 Feb: [...] Lisabo's youngest sister [Marthe Le Ray] has died. She was married to Danl le Pedevin of St Sampson, who rents a property at le Prais [Préel]. She died in childbirth & leaves 3 young children.

Tues 27 Feb: [...] Jean [Cateline] is ill & stayed in bed today. He seems to be suffering greatly. He says he has pain in all his bones & joints. It is rheumatism, no doubt.

Sun 4 Mar: Jean [Cateline] was up almost all day yesterday, but in pain. Around eight in the evening, he & Jean Guilbert,[540] who were in the kitchen with the girls, went outside for a moment, & as they were returning, Jean collapsed just outside the back door. We thought for about an hour that he might be dying. Nico Breton & Eleazar [Ingrouille] came & carried him into the parlour, where Jean Guilbert & I stayed up with him all night. He remained quiet but very weak. Today, he appears somewhat better. His brother Pierre came here for dinner today & only left at seven. Monsieur Marie called here towards evening. [...] Young Isac Marquand has come to live with us.[541]

Thurs 8 Mar: [...] Jean will return to his own bedroom tonight. He has been in the parlour since Saturday. I have spent the last 3 nights with him, sleeping fully dressed on the floor (without undue discomfort).

Mon 12 Mar: [...] Jean seems better. Young Isac Marquand, who came to live here a week ago, has started at St Andrew's school, where Sr Nicolas Naftel is the master.

---

[539] For Monsieur Lamy des Vallées, see n. 273, above.
[540] Jean Guilbert was a young carpenter temporarily lodging at Mollet's.
[541] Lisabo Machon's nephew Isaac Marquand, who had spent short periods at Mollet's since 1801, was now twelve. See n. 443, above.

Tues 13 Mar: Jean has started working again. He has been almost constantly ill since 9 February, having only worked between the 19th & 27th, even though he was unwell. He & Etienne [Lihou] planted onion sets by the upper gate & below the ditch at le Carré.

Thurs 15 Mar: [...] Etienne did not come today, as his eldest son died of consumption yesterday. His two other sons, Thomas & Jean, died some time ago, also of consumption.[542] All three of Etienne's sons had children (the one who died yesterday had a married son). Etienne is now left with just his 4 daughters. They all seem very healthy, but then so did the sons. The late David Doré of la Hougue du Pomier also had 3 sons who died of consumption & left several children, but his daughters are healthy.

Mon 19 Mar: [...] Jean Gavet, Pierre's son (16), started working here as a day labourer.

Thurs 12 Apr: [...] Ab. took some wonders & Perigueux paté (received from Monsieur le Fer on Tuesday) to town in the morning. He returned to town in the afternoon, as the clerk at Mr Bishop's bank had given him 19s 3d too little on the exchange of ten of their notes, as well as charging a premium of 9d for each £1 stg.[543] He spoke to the same clerk as in the morning, but the clerk refused to give him anything more & claimed that Ab. had only brought in 9 notes.

Sat 14 Apr: Ab. went to town again, but Mr Bishop was too busy to go to his bank today.

Tues 17 Apr: [...] Ab. spoke to Mr Bishop in town. Mr Bishop said he would have to raise the matter at the bank.

Fri 20 Apr: Good Friday. Jean helped Ab. dig his ground until midday & again towards evening. [...] I spoke to Jaques Ozanne about Suzon. She will

---

[542] Etienne Lihou's eldest son (also Etienne) was born in 1768 and thus forty-two years old. His younger sons Thomas and Jean were born in 1772 and 1775 respectively.
[543] The draper Abraham Bishop had opened 'The Bank of Guernsey' in partnership with Henry De Jersey in 1804.

stay here on the same basis as previously, but without any formal agreement.[544]

Mon 23 Apr: the militia & regular troops were under arms at l'Ancresse. Thos Langlais from near Baubigny in St Sampson was killed by a cannon ball in one of the forts, & 3 men were injured (though not seriously) by rifle shot, viz., Mr Ozanne from la Porte, John Carrington (Marquand's son-in-law) & Pierre le Page from le Vauquiedor.

Tues 24 Apr: Lisabo took one of our cows to the Fair but was unable to sell her. Daniel [Ferbrache] paid us a brief visit during the morning, & returned here for dinner. Pierre Cateline came to do some work for us. He whitewashed the lower part of the wall in front of the upper house (against which there are two peach trees) & plastered the bottom part of the gable at la Daumaillerie.

Weds 25 Apr: [...] I sold the 5-year-old cow with the star-marked head to Jean Ferbrache (our Daniel's father). She calved for the 4th time on 29 March. The price was supposed to be 18 guineas, but I only asked him to pay £18 stg. He will give the other 18 shillings to I...c N.,[545] whose wife is ill.

Sun 29 Apr: Jean Gavet is doing watch-duty on my behalf this evening. It was Ab's turn last night. We are still required to go to Bourdeaux in le Clos du Valle. Our last turn fell as recently as 7 April. I am paying Jean Gavet 35 *sous* per night for substituting for me.

Sat 5 May: [...] an extensive grass frost yesterday morning. Very cold this evening, with a strong easterly wind.

Sat 12 May: [...] The Bailiff (Mr Robert Le Marchant) & Miss Le Marchant paid me a visit towards evening. Mr Le Marchant is no longer to be Bailiff, having requested & obtained his discharge. Mr Pierre De Havilland is to replace him & was sworn in as Bailiff today. Mr Eleazar Le Marchant was sworn in as Mr De Havilland's Lieutenant-Bailiff (a position he has held under both previous Bailiffs).

---

[544] Suzon Ozanne was now fifteen, no longer at school, and a working member of Mollet's household.
[545] Probably Isaac Nicolle (see 27.8.10).

Sun 13 May: Pierre Cateline dined here. Daniel [Ferbrache] called here on his way to church. Monsieur Marie, Monsieur De Voscé & his sister-in-law, Madame la Vicomtesse d'Alonville, came here unexpectedly & took coffee with me.[546]

Tues 15 May: [...] I called at Hy Brock's in the morning to see his brother Wm who arrived from England on Sunday. I paid Mr Gibert a visit on the way back.

Fri 18 May: [...] Thos Brouard lost a cow yesterday after she swelled up from eating clover. He lost another in an accident only seven months ago.

Thurs 24 May: [...] Daniel [Ferbrache] is expecting to leave for Havana this evening on board Captn Thos Moullin. He was very emotional when saying his farewells, which also made me feel sad. [...] Mr [John Le] Mesurier of les Caches was elected a Magistrate to replace Mr Pierre de Havilland, who is now Bailiff. Mr James Carey (son of Jean Carey) was elected a Magistrate a fortnight ago to replace the late Mr Jean Tupper. A few weeks ago, Mr John Guille (grandson of Mr Guille of St George) was elected a Magistrate to replace Mr James Carey's father, Jean Carey, who has also died.[547]

Mon 28 May: [...] Rachel Colnette & Marie Nicolle washed my bed curtains & blankets (as well as the usual linen). Towards evening, I went briefly to St George, where I had not been since 20 December, not having been out a great deal this past winter (although I did go to town on 8 December & to church at the Castel & St Peter on 5 November).

Thurs 31 May: the Procureur, Mr Wm Brock (sen.), Hy & Mary, Peter & Sophy, Miss Roche & Mr Combs came to dinner.

Weds 6 Jun: [...] The Revd Mr Tom Brock took coffee with me (unexpectedly). He & Mrs Brock are living at [the Revd] Mr Tom Carey's while Mr Carey & his wife spend a few weeks at Mr Pierre Carey's in Taunton.[548]

---

[546] Céleste-Octavie de la Bourdonnaye (see n. 469, above) had married Antoine-Jean-Baptiste d'Allonville (1765–1811) in 1808. Her husband was the son of General Armand-Jean, Comte d'Allonville (see n. 373).
[547] Jean Carey of 'La Bigoterie' (see n. 362, above) had died in February 1810.
[548] For Mr Pierre Carey, see n. 448, above.

Thurs 7 Jun: [...] I visited Mrs Fisher at the Rectory towards noon.[549] She has been living there for several weeks & will continue to live there during the absence of Mr & Mrs Dobrée in England.

Mon 11 Jun: the whole militia was assembled at le Braye du Valle. Ab. [Machon] only returned at six in the evening & went straight to bed. I was told that the men had been stood down at half past one.

Sat 16 Jun: I went to see Wm Brock's 3 sons who arrived a few days ago – Henry (21), Beauvoir (12) & Mourant (8).[550] I also went briefly to town.

Mon 18 Jun: [...] I was in town between 10 o'clock & midday. As I arrived at the post office, I watched a procession of Freemasons on their way to church. I visited Mr Gibert in the afternoon.

Tues 19 Jun: the Revd Mr Grut & two of his children called here around three in the afternoon & took coffee with me.[551] He has never come here before & I do not know him well.

Fri 22 Jun: [...] to town in the morning. Returned via le Clos du Valle, calling at Mr Martinault's[552] & stopping for a while at l'Ancresse. There was a horse race there, but I only saw it from a distance, since I was with Sr Thos Henri on the hill by the druids' altar which was recently discovered after the wind blew away the sand or soil which hid it.

Sat 23 Jun: [...] I attended Miss Le Cheminant's funeral. She was one of the 3 daughters of Captn Pierre Le Cheminant of le Prais [Préel], & died of consumption. I had a hatband & gloves.

Mon 25 Jun: [...] The States Committee in charge of widening the roads (from town to Vazon & from the Citadel to Roquaine) held a meeting at Geo Le Cheminant's public house in les Rohais. I spoke to the Procureur there.

---

[549] Susanna Fischer, *née* Dobrée (see n. 275, above) was the sister of Castel Rector Nicolas Dobrée.
[550] These were Mollet's great-nephews (sons of his Exeter-based niece Nancy, *née* Mourant).
[551] Mollet's visitor was Thomas Grut (1769–1836), who succeeded Etienne Gibert as Rector of St Andrew in 1815.
[552] For the Reverend René Martineau, see n. 111, above.

Tues 26 Jun: [...] Apparently, some soldiers have begun widening the road from les Rohais to the [Castel] church.

Fri 29 Jun: [...] About 160 soldiers are busy widening the road. It is impossible to pass on horseback between les Rohais & the church, & even beyond.

Mon 2 Jul: about 200 soldiers of the 103rd Regiment have been camping in the Fair Field (near le Carrefour des Cailles) since yesterday. They have started removing the earthbanks along le Prais [Préel]. Mr Dan De Lisle (an Inspector of Works appointed by the States) & Mr Savary Brock (an Inspector appointed by the Governor) came to breakfast.

Sun 15 Jul: [...] Colonel Scot of the 103rd Regiment, who was at les Eturs, sent for me to come to him.[553] Colonel Scot has arranged for the new road coming from le Prais [Préel] to pass firstly through land belonging to Mr Bailleul at le Courtil de Charles & le Courtil des Eturs, & secondly through my own property at les Eturs (to the south of the earthbank bordering the old road) & a small portion of Mr Cohu's meadows. After he had shown me this, Colonel Scot returned here with me for half an hour.

Mon 16 Jul: Messrs Tom Brock, Savary Brock & Dan De Lisle (all members of the Roads Committee) came here unexpectedly & breakfasted with me. Colonel Scot, who seems to be in overall charge of the new roads, has set his men to work in Mr Bailleul's fields.

Tues 17 Jul: [...] The soldiers are working in Mr Bailleul's fields. They have also started working in Pierrot le Pelley's Censiere. In the afternoon, Mr Goodwin measured the portion of my field at les Eturs which they are to take for the road (in my presence).[554]

Weds 18 Jul: [...] Towards midday someone came to call me to les Eturs, where work was about to begin. Finding the Governor, the Bailiff & some Roads Committee members there, I objected that no work should be started before compensation had been fixed, but Mr De Havilland (the Bailiff) &

---

[553] Colonel Hercules Scott (1775–1814) of Brotherton, Kincardineshire.
[554] Matthew Pitton Goodwin (1785–1842) was the States' first official architect and superintendent of works.

some others said that no one had the authority to fix compensation until the Court had been granted this power by Order in Council. To me, this seemed sufficient grounds to suspend any work to which I had not expressly consented. After this exchange, the assembled gentlemen continued their inspection of the roads & properties as far as la Hougue (Hellier Nicolle's house), going down la Ruette au Ferré & returning via la Rue de Bas (bordering la Grande Marre), la Rue au Cocq, &c. I accompanied them throughout their tour of inspection, having been requested to do so by some of the gentlemen. On the way back, Mr Harry Dobrée asked me (on Colonel Scot's behalf) if I would be willing after all to allow them to continue the works through my property. Not wishing to be seen to hold up the works, I agreed, on condition that I be given a firm guarantee of full & ample compensation.

Sun 29 Jul: the Revd Tom Carey, Colonel Scott, the Procureur, Nico Le Fevre & Peter Mourant came to dinner. It rained in the afternoon & they stayed until 9 o'clock.

Mon 30 Jul: [...] At 5 o'clock, I was summoned to le Courtil Robin, where I found 6 or 7 soldiers erecting a tent in the south-west corner. I told them to stop, & they took away their tent & baggage. About two hours later, I was called to the top of the drive at la Daumaillerie, where I found Jean Torode of les Moullins with a loaded baggage cart & another person (also named Jean Torode) with Mr du Ponchez's cart, which was also loaded with baggage. With them were several soldiers who had come to put up tents at les Tuzets. I refused to allow them to do so, & they all left.

[*Charles Mollet turned sixty-eight during the course of August 1810*]

Fri 3 Aug: [...] Towards 3 o'clock, I went to les Eturs, where I found Sr James de Beaucamp, Mr Carré of la Couture, Sr Jean Mahy, Sr François le Pelley & Mr Lihou of les Prevosts, who have been sworn in by the Court to assess the compensation due to property-owners in connection with the new roads (i.e., to evaluate the extent of ground taken from them & the damages due them for the demolition of their earthbanks). However, deeming themselves insufficiently authorised to assess the damages (given the potential cost to the public purse of rebuilding these earthbanks should property-owners be unwilling to do so), these gentlemen made no decisions while I was present,

& instead accompanied Colonel Scott to la Houguette. On his return, between 4 & 5 o'clock, Colonel Scott called to see me & partook of some refreshment (cold meat). Ten soldiers, under Corporal Peggy, have started taking stone from le Camp Bailleul at les Grands Tuzets. I have allowed them to do so, on condition that they dig to a depth of 6 or 8 feet across the entire field & take only stone suitable for road-making.

Sun 5 Aug: […] Guillaume le Rai, Lisabo's cousin, dined here. He is a sailor & has been away from Guernsey for 13 years. He is the son of Guillaume le Rai the carpenter & Marie Martel, both of whom are dead.

Mon 6 Aug: […] On Saturday, the soldiers demolished the earthbank at the top of les Eturs to accommodate the width of the new road (which will lie to the south of the existing earthbank). This afternoon, they demolished an equal length of Mr Cohu's earthbank at the bottom of our field. They also took down the wall bordering his field, & started demolishing the earthbank at the bottom of our Censiere (where, on Saturday, they cut the edge off a wheat crop […] & destroyed a patch of parsnips).

Tues 7 Aug: […] This afternoon, the soldiers started to remove turf from my field at les Eturs, where the new road & footpath are marked out. I resolved to raise a *Clameur de Haro*,[555] & sent for Eleazar [Ingrouille] & the Messrs le Pelley of les Beaucamps to act as witnesses. Before they had arrived, however, Colonel Scott came to see me at le Marquet, &, at my request, ordered the men to stop removing the turf.

Weds 8 Aug: […] I gave permission to the soldiers quarrying stone from le Camp Bailleul to pitch their two tents in the south-west corner of le Courtil Robin.

Thurs 9 Aug: Colonel Scott breakfasted with me. […] Mr Robt Le Marchant & Miss Henriette called in to apprise me (confidentially) of the engagement of Miss [Mary] Le M. to Mr Jean Le Marchant, son of James Le M. of Rotterdam.[556]

---

[555] For *Clameur de Haro*, see n. 133, above.
[556] Ex-Bailiff Robert Porret Le Marchant's daughters were Harriet (1793–1877) and Mary (1784–1837). Mary had become engaged to her distant cousin, the merchant and future Jurat John Le Marchant (1785–1862).

Mon 13 Aug: Colonel Scott came to breakfast, after which I accompanied him as far as la Hougue. Hellier Nicolle (jun.) has given his permission for the new road (which will cut across the existing road near Jean Carré's house at le Courtil Fontaine) to pass through his large field at les Ruettes until it reaches the top of Jean Ferbrache's Courtil des Cocqrets, which it will then enter, following the northerly earthbank separating the Courtil from le Petit Guilbert as far as the road which lies opposite Nico Roussel's meadow. Jean Guillard is allowing the soldiers to take the stone they need for this stretch from his quarry at la Hougue, & Colonel Scott has promised to pay him 4 guineas. Colonel Scott told me that Hellier Nicolle, Jean Ferbrache & his tenant Pierre Gavet will be compensated according to the evaluation made by the authorised assessors. Jean Ferbrache & Pierre Gavet only agreed to the passage of the road through their fields on the basis of my assurance that rules made following the objections I raised at les Eturs will be enshrined in law as far as they & others are concerned. Colonel Scott returned here to dine around 4 o'clock.

Weds 15 Aug: [...] We received news on Sunday that the French are massing troops at Cherbourg in preparation for an attack on these Islands, so we are expecting the alarm to be raised at any moment.

Sat 18 Aug: [...] I rode through St Martin as far as le Bourg in the Forest. I later went to Vazon. This was in order to see the new roads in their full length. Ours is now open as far as la Grande Mare.

Tues 21 Aug: [...] Ab. [Machon] carted stone from les Tuzets for the new road. They are paying 11 shillings a day for a cart drawn by 3 animals (such as ours) & 9 shillings a day for a cart drawn by 2 animals. [...] Colonel Scott breakfasted with me. The soldiers pitched another tent at the top of le Courtil Robin, where there are now 3 tents. There are about 20 soldiers digging stone out of le Camp Bailleul.

Sat 25 Aug: Ab. carted stone from le Camp Bailleul. This is our 5th day of carting. [...] Two soldiers of the 103rd Regiment helped us gather in some wheat sheaves in the evening, & supped here.

Mon 27 Aug: [...] Little Pierre Nicolle (aged 5) came to live with us yesterday. He is the son of Isac Nicolle (son of Charles Nicolle) & our Daniel's sister

Rachel Ferbrache. Little Pierre has two younger brothers. He also had an older brother who died a few months ago. His mother is ill, probably with consumption. She is so weak that she has not left her bed this past week.

Tues 28 Aug: [...] Colonel Scott breakfasted with me. By prior arrangement, he then went to my field at les Eturs with one of his labourers & began working on the road there (which has already been opened, the top & bottom earthbanks having been demolished). Also by prior arrangement, I followed the Colonel to the field after a few minutes & interrupted him & his labourer by raising a *Clameur de Haro* (having previously arranged for Eleazar Ingrouille & Messrs Nico & Thomas Le Pelley to come & witness it). Once I had raised the *Clameur* in due form, the Colonel & I went together (as per our agreement) to inform the Procureur & the Bailiff (Pierre de Havilland) about what I had done. I subsequently dined at the Procureur's, & later went to find the Colonel on the new road at St Martin, in order to request his presence in Court at 10 o'clock tomorrow.

Weds 29 Aug: to Court. The Governor was there with Colonel Scott. The Court did not take cognizance of my *Clameur* (on which I did not insist), but decided instead that each property-owner would rebuild his own earthbanks, &c., & that the five sworn assessors (see 3 August) would have the final & binding say on compensation.

Thurs 30 Aug: [...] Rachel Ferbrache died towards noon. She was the wife of Isac Nicolle (son of Charles Nicolle) & the daughter of Jean Ferbrache & Rachel Nicolle (only daughter of Pierre Nicolle of le Rocré). She was my Daniel's sister & the mother of little Pierre (see last Monday).[557]

Sat 1 Sep: [...] Thomas Wilford, a soldier of the 45th Regiment with only one eye, came to offer me his services as a labourer.

Mon 3 Sep: [...] Our Daniel Ferbrache arrived back from Havana yesterday. The voyage took barely 3 months. He supped here. His sister was buried yesterday.

Tues 4 Sep: [...] most of the soldiers who have been camping in 3 tents at the top of le Courtil Robin for the last month have gone to work on the new road

---

[557] Rachel Nicolle, *née* Ferbrache, was thirty-four years old.

through the Forest. There is only one tent left. Three soldiers have stayed to finish reinstating le Camp Bailleul, from which they quarried stone. [...] Thos Wilford (see Saturday) returned here yesterday evening, slept in the hay, & spent another day working for us.

Fri 7 Sep: [...] Colonel Scott came here unexpectedly towards 4 o'clock. We roasted a duck which had already been killed & he dined here. He left again around six.

Tues 11 Sep: [...] Jean Gavet & Thomas (the soldier) started cutting the bracken at le Brulin. Thos Blondel went to collect Nic. Priaulx's tithe. Ab. carted stone for the road until noon.

Fri 14 Sep: [...] Ab. carted stone for the new road for the last time. He began on 21 August & worked 18½ days with 3 animals & one day with 2 animals. I sent in an account last Saturday, on which I specified that we wish to be paid the 11 shillings (or 9 shillings) per day in silver, as the Court has ruled, & not with bills on which we lose 5 per cent when we exchange them. However, Mr Goodwin told Ab. yesterday that those who were unhappy with this form of payment had only to stop doing the work, & that, if I so wished, I could lodge a complaint with the Court.

Sat 15 Sep: weeded the upper garden & collected the last of the tithe (one small cartload from Sr Jean Robert). I went briefly to town & returned via St Martin & the Forest.

Sun 16 Sep: to St Peter's church in the morning. Messrs de Callonne, Nadaillon & Marie took coffee with me. Monsieur De Vossey is in Jersey. George [Nicolet] dined here & Pierre Cateline took tea here.

Mon 17 Sep: [...] Isac [Marquand] has started attending [St Andrew's] school again, the master having closed the school for 4 weeks on account of the harvest.

Weds 19 Sep: [...] There have been six soldiers here for the last fortnight levelling the surface of le Camp Bailleul from which stone has been taken for the road. They finished their work today & left my property, removing the tent in which they were sleeping at le Courtil Robin (see the 4th). They took a fortnight to perform a task which I consider we ourselves could have done in 4 or 5 days. Ab. [Machon] went to the Forest to collect payment for 9 days of carting at 11 shillings, & one day at 9 shillings (£5 8s). Mr Goodwin gave Ab. six bills, & Ab. gave him 12s change. The last time we were paid (for 5 days' work), we were given 3 bills & we returned 5s in change.

Sun 23 Sep: […] Young Wm Brock arrived from England on Friday. Yesterday I accompanied him to see Mr Jemmy le Page of le Mont Durand, who is suffering from a strange illness – a very large swelling in his neck & throat.[558]

Mon 24 Sep: […] I went to inform the Court that Mr Goodwin […] is paying those who carried materials in their carts in banknotes, on the exchange of which they are losing 5 per cent, & that he is moreover forcing them (under threat of not paying them at all) to give him change in silver if the value of the notes exceeds what they are owed. For example, he obliges them to accept a 20 shilling note for one day's work with a cart & two horses (for which the Court has set the price at 9 shillings) & then insists that they give him 11s change in silver, &c. The Court advised me to gather together several people wishing to make the same complaint.

Tues 25 Sep: I went to Court with Ab. & 8 or 10 other people who have carted for the new roads. The Court decided that, although payment in paper bills was not strictly legal, those who had accepted them & still continued to do the work would be obliged to make do with them. They refused to record this decision in a formal act.

Sun 30 Sep: […] Messrs De Vossey, Callonne, Nadaillon & Marie took coffee with me. Colonel Scott joined us as we were finishing but only had one cup. I had not seen him since the 18th. He said he would be in this neighbourhood tomorrow, so I said I would meet him at le Prais [Préel] about 2 o'clock.

Mon 1 Oct: […] At 2 o'clock I went to the top of le Prais to meet Colonel Scott. At half past three, one of his officers (Mr Carney) came to give me the Colonel's excuses, & said that he was unable to come as he was still in Court. I believe this was beyond his control.

Weds 3 Oct: […] Colonel Scott came unexpectedly around 4 o'clock & dined on some sardines Lisabo had just brought back from town.

---

[558] Master plasterer James Le Page died a few weeks later (see 10.11.10).

Fri 5 Oct: [...] Yesterday, the soldiers who are working on the footpath at les Eturs asked permission to pitch their tent at the top of le Courtil Robin (where the other tents used to be). I agreed, & they spent the night there. I believe there are 7 or 8 men & one woman.

Sat 6 Oct: [...] Ab. & Jean dug up 6 Chaumontel pear trees & 3 Swan Egg pear trees, which Sergeant Peggy came to fetch, together with a few other things which Colonel Scott is taking back with him to Scotland.

Tues 9 Oct: [...] Mr Guille of St George, Mrs [Esther] Metivier & her son the Advocate,[559] Miss le Cocq & Monsieur Marie took coffee with me. Mrs Metivier's other sons are away.

Sat 13 Oct: [...] I went to town in the morning & returned via St Martin & the Forest. Work on the roads seems more or less to have finished for the season. The soldiers who were camping out have all returned to barracks.

Sun 14 Oct: [...] I have started having a fire lit in my room. Two years ago I had my first fire on 16 October. In previous years, I have had one towards the beginning of October, & even as early as 28 September.

Thurs 25 Oct: [...] Yesterday we caught a stray horse in the Plantation. An old man named Mr Quick, who is renting this horse & who lives at les Girards, came to fetch it. I made him pay me 5 shillings for having caught it, as also for its food & the damage it has caused. This morning, we caught 9 stray sheep in our field at les Eturs. A young butcher came to fetch them on behalf of John Lye (our butcher). I let him have the sheep without payment.

Thurs 1 Nov: Joseph Renouf came to dinner.[560] I lent him some books (the reason he came).

Sat 10 Nov: rain overnight & throughout the day. The storm has been continuous since 8 o'clock this morning, the winds veering from west to south-west & then north-west. Ab. [Machon] & Ab. Torode went to town to

---

[559] John Metivier (1788–1869) had been admitted to the Guernsey Bar in 1808.
[560] Mollet's young visitor Joseph Renouf (1790–1879) was appointed schoolmaster at the Town Hospital in 1816. He was the father of the renowned Egyptologist Sir Peter Le Page Renouf (1822–97).

repair the warehouse roof, which has sustained much damage. [...] Pierre Cateline came to invite me to the funeral of his employer, Mr James le Page the plasterer.

Sun 11 Nov: [...] Ab. attended Mr le Page's funeral. Pierre Cateline returned here with him & took tea. [...] Charles Andros's widow has died. He himself died 2 or 3 years ago, since which time Mrs Andros has lived in town with her daughter, the widow of Mr Jack Dobrée.[561]

Mon 19 Nov: [...] Daniel [Ferbrache], who has been suffering with his arm, dined here. Rain overnight & nearly all day.

Mon 26 Nov: [...] Jean Guilbert came here today. He will stay with us for the next few months. He arranged his things in the room above the cider cellar where he will sleep from now until Easter. He has slept here occasionally over the past 2 or 3 months, on a bed of bracken in the wash-house.

Mon 10 Dec: rain nearly all day. Young Isac & Pierre [Nicolle] went to Jean Ferbrache's house, where people were gathering in advance of little Thomas Nicolle's funeral (their brother), who died on Saturday. Isac Nicolle has only 3 children left (Isac, our Pierre, & Hellier, the youngest). Another son named Jean died a few weeks before their mother, who died on 30 August.

Weds 12 Dec: yesterday, Monsieur le Fer, who recently arrived from France, sent me a present of a very fine fat goose (dead) & a couple of partridges.

Sat 15 Dec: I stayed in bed all day, more from laziness than necessity.

Tues 18 Dec: [...] Heavy rain today. Young Marie le Page, who has lived here since 14 June 1809, left my service. I gave her notice to leave a month or two ago.

Sat 22 Dec: rain all night & all day. Isac [Marquand] accompanied Lisabo to town, where she delivered a few bottles of rose water, peppermint & *noyau* to Mrs Daniel Dobrée, Mrs Harry Dobrée, Mrs Waugh, Mrs Fisher & Mrs

---

[561] Charles Andros's widow was the former Caroline Le Marchant (born c.1729). She was the aunt of Mollet's neighbour Josias Le Marchant of la Haye du Puits. Charles Andros, who had died in 1805, was Mollet's godfather (see n. 324, above).

Champion. I was up all day & cleaned out the loft over the cartshed. It was *la longue veille* today. Thos le Pelley took coffee with me & stayed until one in the morning. The servants celebrated in the kitchen, but this year they were joined only by Jean Guilbert & Thos Blondel. Jean [Cateline] went to bed early, but he seemed in a good mood. Eleazar [Ingrouille] was busy in the press-house & did not come in.

Sun 23 Dec: incessant rain all night & day, stopping only towards dusk. It fell steadily rather than heavily. The weather has lately been so wet that the linen we washed 4 weeks ago did not dry until Thursday, when we finished drying it in front of the fire.

Tues 25 Dec: I stayed in bed until midday. The only visitor I had today was the barber. Heavy showers overnight & during the day. Strong westerly gales, especially this evening. Stormy.

Mon 31 Dec: a frost this morning. Snow fell during the afternoon & covered the ground to a depth of 3 inches. Brought 361 barley sheaves into the barn.

Notes relating to 1810

In 1810, Charles Mollet employed sixteen men aside from his live-in servants. Of these sixteen men, half were day labourers and the other half tradesmen. Mollet's most regular labourers this year were Thomas Blondel (172 days, year-round), Jean Gavet (171 days, March–November) and Etienne Lihou (80 days, year-round). The soldier Thomas Wilford worked just 21½ days in September and October. Mollet paid Wilford 10d stg per day. Charles Mollet also listed the women and children who performed day labour for him in 1810. The children were employed to gather cider apples. One of the gatherers was young Suzon Breton, who gathered apples on ten days, for which she was paid a total of 7s 6d. Other female workers were Lisabo Collenette (a seamstress), Marie Nicolle, Marie Mauger, Rachel Collenette and Betsy Lihou, who helped with the laundry and filled in around the house as required. Of these, Marie Nicolle worked the most (56 days, year-round). The others only worked intermittently.

1811

Tues 1 Jan: awoke to a frost & 7 or 8 inches of snow. The snow fell until 10 o'clock, when it lay about 15 inches thick. […] I gave Ab, Lisabo, Jean, Suzon, young Isac & young Pierre two guineas each (which came from our sales of flowers, &c., as also from Ab's work carting stone for the new road in August & September).

Thurs 3 Jan: […] About 3 or 4 inches of snow fell last night, & it continued falling all morning. There are now from 20 to 24 inches on the ground.

Fri 4 Jan: extremely cold again last night. The wind, which has been blowing from the north-east all day, became even stronger this evening & filled up the roads with snow.

Weds 9 Jan: young Mr Guillaume Guille (Mr de St George's grandson, who returned from England recently) came to see me in the morning. He is destined for the church & will soon enter Oxford University.[562]

Sat 12 Jan: […] There is still snow in many of the roads – as much as 5 ft in la Rue du Ruquet, which is impassable on horseback. Brought in some hay.

Thurs 17 Jan: […] Snow remains on the ground here & there. It began falling on 31 December. Damp weather. Rain towards evening.

Fri 1 Feb: […] For some time now, Jean [Cateline] has had recurrent bad moods. Over dinner today, he said something which prompted me to reply that, if he was unhappy here, he was free to leave. He rose from the table & asked me to pay him his wages. I did so, up to today, in the sum of £10 19s 5d stg. He then went off with some of his clothes, but returned while the servants were having supper downstairs. Lisabo asked him if he would eat something, but he refused. In the evening, I went to see Mr Gibert, whom I

---

[562] For William Guille, see nn. 423 and 487, above. The Reverend Guille married Mollet's great-niece Judith Brock (daughter of Nancy and William) in 1818. He became Anglican Dean of Guernsey in 1858.

had not seen for a long time, having only gone out twice in several months. He gave me (almost against my will) five £1 notes to pass on to poor people.

Sat 2 Feb: [...] Jean came here around 9 o'clock in the morning. I spoke to him briefly. He said he was going to town. He came back at about 4 o'clock & spent the evening by the kitchen hearth (mostly asleep). He appeared to be drunk. He did not speak to me. I do not think he has eaten this evening, although he drank some cider, as he also did this morning. He seems to be intending to sleep here.

Sun 3 Feb: [...] Jean slept here. He seemed in good spirits during the day & behaved himself well.

Mon 4 Feb: [...] Eleazar [Ingrouille] came to speak to me in the evening. He brought with him Jean Pinchemain who is offering to come here as a farm servant. He is 18 years old. He may (perhaps) start here in a week's time. However, our Jean now appears disposed to stay.

Thurs 14 Feb: [...] Joseph Renouf returned some books & borrowed a few more. He dined with me.

Tues 19 Feb: [...] Jean Pinchemain, who is to be my farm servant, supped & slept here. He is 18 & was born in Guernsey, but his father is French (from Tréguier) & his mother is from Jersey. He himself spent 5½ years in Alderney as a shoemaker's apprentice & then worked for Jean Martel of le Haut Pavé as a farm servant for two years. For the last six months, he has been employed as a journeyman shoemaker by Ab. Letocq.

Thurs 21 Feb: [...] We made 8 bottles of shoe blacking. There are still 4 bottles of the blacking we made two years ago.

Mon 25 Feb: gales, rain & thunder overnight. In the morning I went to see the damage done by the sea when it spilled over the dunes between la Mare de Carteret & la Grande Mare.

Tues 26 Feb: [...] Jean Pinchemain, who came here on Tuesday evening, left my service after supper, for reasons which are not clear to me.

Weds 27 Feb: […] I have been given to believe that Jean Pinchemain left me because Jean Cateline & Thos Blondel put him off working here.

Sat 9 Mar: […] I did a little digging at le Prey. Fine weather. Mary called here around noon with young Henry Brock, who arrived on Monday.[563]

Sun 10 Mar: […] I gave Jean [Cateline] 25 shillings, which he asked me for to pay his mother's rent.

Tues 12 Mar: […] Colonel Scott (of the 103rd Regiment), who arrived here on Saturday, paid me a visit around noon. A light frost. Pierre Cateline came here with his apprentice Jemmy Keane & his young labourer James le Nourry. They plastered the south wall of the big kitchen at the upper house, & made some repairs to the roof of my house.

Tues 26 Mar: […] Mr Ab. Le Mesurier, on behalf of the Committee for the New Roads, sent me a note for £80 10s issued by the Messrs MacCulloch's Bank. I refused to accept it on the grounds that I was not satisfied with the sum accorded for rebuilding the earthbanks, walls, &c., &c.

Mon 15 Apr: […] There is a dense fog this evening – our 4th or 5th such fog in the space of a week or ten days.

Mon 22 Apr: […] Little Pierre Nicolle expressed a wish to leave us.[564] I sent Isac to accompany him home & carry his clothes (which he had packed himself). His grandmother returned here with him almost immediately & stayed for dinner. The child eventually seemed to reconcile himself to staying here.

Sun 28 Apr: Lisabo spent the night at her brother-in-law Abraham Marquand's, which she has done several times since 23 March, when we first learned that he was dying. He died at 10 o'clock yesterday evening.[565] He leaves nine children. The two eldest boys are at sea & the two eldest girls are

---

[563] This was twenty-two-year-old Henry Brock, the twin of Dr William Brock (see nn. 251 and 550, above). He was to die the following year.
[564] Little Pierre was six years old.
[565] Abraham Marquand was forty-seven.

in service. Young Isac [Marquand] is here. Two boys & two girls remain with their mother.

Thurs 2 May: [...] The Bank of Messrs Maccullock, Allaire, Bonamy & Co. stopped payments yesterday on account of difficulties experienced by their agents in London (the successors of the late Messrs Paul & Havilland Le Mesurier).[566] The Bank of Messrs Bishop & de Jersey also stopped payments. We have only these two banks here (& these are two banks too many). It is believed they will honour their commitments & there will be no losses.

Fri 3 May: [...] The seamstress has been here for 8 days making black nankeen suits for Isac & Pierre.

Mon 6 May: [...] Our little Pierre Nicolle has started attending St Andrew's school with Isac. [...] Thomas Blondel has come to live here as a farm servant. I will pay him £15 stg [a year]. He has been working here as a day labourer since the end of May 1809.

Sun 12 May: [...] Young Durell Saumarez came on behalf of his sister Betsy (Mrs de Havilland) to show me the memorial addressed by Captn Tom de Havilland to the East India Company.[567]

Thurs 16 May: [...] Mr John Condomine (the Comptroller's son) came to deliver a letter from Mr St Croix which his daughter Marie Anne St Croix brought with her when she arrived on Monday (Miss St Croix is here for the sake of her health).[568]

---

[566] In 1808, Thomas MacCulloch, John Allaire and John Bonamy had opened 'The Guernsey Bank'. For the Bank of Bishop and De Jersey (otherwise known as 'The Bank of Guernsey'), see n. 543, above.

[567] Captain Thomas Fiott De Havilland had resigned his commission in the EIC army while being court-martialled for having joined a mutiny against the Governor of Madras in 1808. He was campaigning for his rehabilitation and restoration. For De Havilland, see n, 457, above. For his wife, Elizabeth (Betsy), *née* De Sausmarez, see n. 511. For more on this episode, see R. Hocart, *Peter de Havilland: Bailiff of Guernsey. A History of his Life, 1747–1821* (Guernsey, 1997), p. 78.

[568] John Condamine, jun. (1792–1876) was the eldest of HM Comptroller John Condamine's five sons. 'Miss St Croix' was Mary Ann De Ste Croix (1793–1828), daughter of Mollet's second cousin and London agent Nicolas De Ste Croix (for whom see n. 65). John Condamine, sen. was Nicolas De Ste Croix's first cousin (their mothers, both Néels, had been sisters).

Thurs 23 May: [...] Cleaned & tidied the small bedroom.

Fri 24 May: [...] Cleaned & tidied the large bedroom.

Sat 25 May: to town in the morning. Returned via le Braye du Valle. Those who purchased the land there (for £5000 stg) are having it enclosed into fields at what used to be called les Dicqs, where the ground seems fairly [dry], as it was only rarely inundated by the sea.

Sun 26 May: I visited Daniel [Ferbrache] yesterday. He has pain in both arms now. I invited him to breakfast with us this morning & to spend the day here, but he sent little Isac Nicolle to say he could not come. Isac stayed to dinner. Messrs de Callonne, Nadaillon, Vossey, Marie & Bowls took coffee with me, as also a young Englishman by the name of Davy who assists Mr Bowls in his shop.[569]

Mon 27 May: Suzon [Ozanne] went to fetch Miss St Croix before dinner, as she is to spend a few days here. Mr & Mrs Josias Le Marchant, Mrs MacGregor & Miss Sophy Le M. took coffee with us.[570]

Tues 28 May: Miss St Croix was to have breakfasted at la Haye du Puits, but she felt unwell & did not go. Mrs MacGregor dined with us. [...] Mr John Condomine (jun.) & his elder sister arrived as we were taking tea, & took Miss St Croix off with them.

Weds 29 May: [...] Monsieur De Callonne, Monsieur Nadaillon, Miss St Croix & John Condomine breakfasted & dined here. All five of them returned to town in the evening. [...] I have been sleeping in the room above the cellar these past 3 nights.

Fri 31 May: [...] Wm Smith, a soldier in the 103rd Regiment, started working here. I will pay him 1 shilling a day & expenses. [...] I visited Daniel in the evening. The boil at the top of his good arm (the right one) has burst. He has had pain in his left arm for several years (in the elbow & below it).

---

[569] George Davy of Exeter, who though sharing a name with Thomas Bowls' associate Joseph Davy, was not related to him. For Joseph Davy, see n. 437, above.
[570] 'Mrs MacGregor' was Josias Le Marchant's thirty-year-old daughter Harriet (see n. 339), now a widow.

Sat 1 Jun: Lisabo went to town, but had nothing to sell.

Weds 5 Jun: [...] another soldier in the 103rd Regiment, started working here today (see 31 May). Rachel Renouf, daughter of Sr Thos Renouf of le Monée de Bas, entered my service as a house servant. My other house servants are Lisabo [Machon] & Suzon [Ozanne] (who has been receiving wages since Christmas).

Thurs 6 Jun: I went to Court, which – after a long deliberation – at last authorised me to bring an action for the recovery of my costs in erecting an earthbank between my field at les Eturs & the new road, as also in rebuilding the earthbank at the bottom of la Censiere. This follows my refusal to accept compensation of 7 shillings per perch for la Censiere & ... shillings per perch for les Eturs. The Court, however, refrained from specifying the party whom I am to action.

Mon 10 Jun: [...] I brought an action against Mr Matth. Goodwin for the amount still outstanding on Ab's carting of stone for the new road last September. [...] Mr Bishop's Bank has closed down, having stopped payments last Saturday. There are rumours that the house of Brock & Le Mesurier in London is about to become insolvent.

Thurs 13 Jun: to town twice, in the morning & evening. The failure of Messrs Wm Brock & Benjamin Le Mesurier has been confirmed – an unexpected bankruptcy amid deplorable circumstances.[571]

Tues 18 Jun: Lisabo started distilling today & made 25 bottles of rose water. We have 5 soldiers working here at present.

Weds 26 Jun: [...] Barthelemi Henri, a Frenchman from Querqueville, came to offer me his services & spent the day here.

Fri 28 Jun: [...] Captn Thos Cohu came yesterday evening to tell me that he is leaving tomorrow for Newfoundland. I wrote a letter to Danl Machon & filled a small box with various things for him.

---

[571] For William Brock of London, see n. 408, above. Brock's partner Benjamin Le Mesurier (1767–1836) was a son of the former Governor of Alderney Henry Le Mesurier (for whom, see n. 24, above).

Tues 2 Jul: [...] William St Croix, Mr St Croix's eldest son, has come to Guernsey to see how his sister is faring & perhaps escort her home. He paid me a visit in the afternoon.

Sun 7 Jul: to St Peter's church in the morning & St Saviour's church in the afternoon. The Revd Mr [Thomas] Carey returned here with me to take coffee, & I rode back with him as far as les Granges in the evening. This is the first time I have been to church this summer.

Tues 9 Jul: I spent the day at Plein Mont, where I laid on dinner & tea for my guests, who breakfasted here, set off for Plein Mont at eleven & departed from Plein Mont at seven in the evening. The party consisted of Mr & Mrs Robt Le Marchant, Mr & Mrs Jean Le Marchant, Miss Henriette Le Marchant, Mrs MacGregor & her sister Miss Sophie Le Marchant, Colonel Scott, Peter Mourant & his wife. We were attended by Colonel Scott's batman, Ab. & Lisabo [Machon], Jean [Cateline], Suzon [Ozanne], young Isac [Marquand] & little Pierre [Nicolle]. We borrowed a horse from Eleazar [Ingrouille], as also one from le Clos au Comte & one from the Messrs le Pelley. Ab. took most of our necessaries in the small cart, & the other horses carried some in panniers. The horses had difficulty coming back at night & did not arrive here until past eleven o'clock.

Weds 17 Jul: Mr & Miss St Croix breakfasted here at nine, after which Miss St Croix went to la Haye du Puits & I accompanied Mr St Croix along the coast as far as Plein Mont. [...] They both dined here at one, then left immediately to go on board Captn Domaille, bound for Southampton.

Fri 26 Jul: [...] Monsieur De Vauxlandri came unexpectedly yesterday afternoon. [He] is a French gentleman aged over 80 who has been here ..... years, but whom I had never met.[572]

[*Charles Mollet turned sixty-nine during the course of August 1811*]

Weds 7 Aug: Captn [Daniel] Dobrée, Mrs & Miss Dobrée, the Procureur, his son John & daughter Patty, Miss Mary de Havilland & Colonel Scott came to breakfast. After breakfast, all of us except the Colonel went to dine at Plein Mont. It was a very fine day. In the evening, I accompanied them back as far

---

[572] Louis-Joseph-Guy Landry de Vauxlandry (1730–1813).

as the Grange via the Forest & St Martin, the Citadel & Contrée Mansell. […] Ab & Lisabo [Machon], Thomas [Blondel] & Rachel [Renouf] attended us.

Fri 9 Aug: […] I breakfasted at la Haye du Puits. […] On my way there around 9 o'clock, I saw – to my great surprise – 7 or 8 soldiers demolishing the end of the old earthbank at the top of les Eturs, between the new & old roads. I told them I was the landowner & ordered them to stop – which they appeared disposed to do, informing me that it was Mr [Abraham] Le Mesurier who had employed them to do this work.[573] When Thomas brought my horse to la Haye du Puits at one o'clock, he told me that the soldiers had not in fact stopped but had continued to demolish the earthbank. I sent him to les Beaucamps to ask Messrs Nic. & Thos le Pelley to come to les Eturs, & I went myself to summon Eleazar & the Constable (Mr Danl Moullin, jun.). We all went to the earthbank, where I was intending to raise a *Clameur de Haro* if the soldiers refused to stop. However, the Constable pre-empted me by ordering them to cease their work in the name of the King, which they did. In the evening, I went to take tea with the Procureur & tell him all that had happened.

Sat 10 Aug: in the morning, Mr Danl Moullin the Constable came to tell me that Mr Abraham Le Mesurier had been to see him yesterday evening to request his presence in Court today to explain what he (Mr Moullin) had done at my behest. I accompanied him, & the Court resolved that the Committee for the Roads should assemble at les Eturs, &c. From this, I surmise that the matter will be settled in Mr Le Mesurier's favour, since he is acting on behalf of the Committee, which has given him *carte blanche* in this affair – more especially since the Court decided on Thursday that the various strips of land which are now separated by the new roads from the properties to which they used to belong will be offered back to the former proprietors at an assessed price, & if the proprietors refuse to take them at that price, they will then be offered to others. A fine decision! As I see it, the former proprietors are the only legitimate proprietors. Where is the justice in dispossessing them of their own land? What, however, can be done about it? There appears no choice but to submit.

---

[573] For Abraham Le Mesurier, see n. 63, above.

Sat 24 Aug: [...] Thos [Blondel] is doing watch-duty on my behalf.

Mon 2 Sep: Thomas collected tithe until midday. Isac collected it all day. I collected it from 10 o'clock. We had two small cartloads.

Fri 6 Sep: [...] Had a small cartload of tithe. Only James Lihou remains to cart his grain.

Tues 10 Sep: Messrs Marie, de Callonne, Nadaillon, & Vauxlandri came to dinner.

Fri 13 Sep: [...] Young Wm Brock called to see me in the morning. He has been in Guernsey since Monday 2 September & had first come here last Saturday when I was out.

Weds 18 Sep: Sr .... Brouard, the bonesetter from St Peter, came to put back Jean [Cateline]'s knee, which he injured yesterday evening while catching hens which were roosting outdoors.

Thurs 19 Sep: Hy Brock, Mary, Wm Brock (jun.), Miss Roche, Billy Combs, Peter Mourant, Sophy, & their nephew Denis Le Marchant (eldest son of General Le M.) came to dinner.[574]

Fri 20 Sep: [...] Thos fetched the bonesetter for Jean & went to buy him some medicine in town.

Tues 1 Oct: [...] Mr & Mrs Robt Le Marchant, Miss Henriette Le Marchant, Peter Mourant, Sophy, four of General Gaspard Le Marchant's daughters & their governess Miss Baker took coffee with me. The General went to Portugal two months ago, shortly after which his wife (Sophy's sister) died in childbirth. Following her death, the 5 youngest of the 9 surviving Le Marchant children came to live at Candie until their father's wishes could be known.[575]

---

[574] Denis Le Marchant (1795–1874) was the son of Major-General John Gaspard Le Marchant and Sophie Mourant's sister Mary (*née* Carey), who had recently died in childbirth at the age of forty-four (see 1.10.11). Denis was in fact their second son, having an older brother born in 1791.

[575] These were thirteen-year-old Mary, Caroline (eleven), Helen (eight), Anna Maria (seven) and six-week-old baby Thomas.

Sat 5 Oct: at around 5 o'clock Colonel Scott & Colonel De Butts (the chief Engineer)[576] came to ask me if I would sell the remaining elms at the top end of the earthbank between the stackyard & le Marquet to the Government in order to make fascines, as warning has been received of an imminent French attack on the Islands.

Tues 8 Oct: […] Colonel Scott breakfasted with me. Sr Thos Naftel (the Constable), Nic. le Rai, Sr Nic. Dorey & Pierre Torode each provided a cart, & the four carts took away the wood from the earthbank. Eleazar & Mr Thos Pelley valued the wood at 8 shillings per cartload.

Weds 9 Oct: […] Carts belonging to Sr Nico Dorey, Sr Nic. de Garis & Pierre Torode each took away a load of wood from the earthbank.

Fri 11 Oct: to Vazon in the morning. Soldiers & masons are repairing the forts & bulwarks there. I noticed the soldiers removing a large rock at top of the beach west of la Grande Mare. I went to inform Mr Condomine the Comptroller about it, but I did not see him. Colonel Scott (who seems to be supervising the work) told me later that this was by order of the Governor. The Colonel dined here at 2 o'clock & sent two more carts to take away 13 elms from the earthbank at the top of le Marquet.

Sat 12 Oct: […] Two more cartloads of elms & two of branches were taken from here to Vazon.

Mon 14 Oct: […] Jean [Cateline] is unwell & has not worked for more than a week.

Tues 15 Oct: Sr Pierre le Prevost & Sr ……… Girard sent carts which each took a load of quicksets to Vazon. I think this is all I will supply by way of wood. I paid a short visit to St George around noon. Colonel Scott came at 2 o'clock & had a bad dinner on a bad piece of braised beef. I gave him the bill for the wood I have supplied. It amounts to £16 17s 6d (59 ft of 2 in thick elm wood at 3s per foot, & 20 cartloads of elm branches & quicksets at 8s per load). The soldiers who felled the wood have gone.

---

[576] Augustus De Butts (1770–1853) commanded the Royal Engineers in Guernsey from 1809. His son John would later marry Guernsey-born Carterette McCrea.

Sat 26 Oct: I wrote a letter to Polly Lerrier in the morning (to send to Southampton, where she is living at present).

Tues 5 Nov: [...] Last week's mail packet was captured by a French privateer within sight of Alderney.

Fri 15 Nov: [...] Lisabo [Machon], who has never had any children even though she has been married nearly 14 years (since 22 March 1798), has been pregnant for several months. Being about to give birth, she was seized with pains during the night, & Ab. went to fetch Dr le Cocq, who stayed with her until 7 or 8 in the morning. Later (around 11 o'clock) Ab. went to fetch him again. Dr le Cocq dined with me, & towards 11 [in the evening] he finally delivered Lisabo of a daughter.[577]

Sat 16 Nov: [...] The seamstress has finished her work. She spent eleven days here, mending our linen, making great-coats for Isac & Pierre & making two pairs of breeches for me.[578]

Sun 17 Nov: on account of Lisabo's indisposition, I sent word to the Procureur & usual company not to come for breakfast this morning.

Fri 22 Nov: Ab. went to town around noon to fetch some medicine for Jean, who is suffering greatly.

Sat 23 Nov: [...] I scolded Isac [Marquand] this morning & threatened to send him back to his mother's. He replied that he did not care & was ready to leave at any time. I answered that he was free to go when he wished. After breakfast, he packed up his things & left the house, &c., &c.

Sun 24 Nov: Ab's daughter was christened Elizabeth.[579] Ab's father & sister were godfather & godmother, & Suzon (Ozanne) was second godmother. They all dined here, as also Pierre Cateline. James Cateline (Pierre's brother) came in the afternoon.

---

[577] Elizabeth Machon was thirty-six years old and her husband Abraham forty-one.
[578] Mollet used the word *culottes*, which could mean both ankle-length trousers and knee-breeches.
[579] Little Elizabeth Machon remained the Machons' only child. Living until 1868, she was to marry Thomas Sarre (1807–61).

Mon 25 Nov: gathered & stacked brushwood & faggots. Jean [Cateline] tried to help but was unable. He can scarcely stand. He seemed very bad in the evening (but I suspect this was partly because he had drunk too much).

Tues 26 Nov: [...] My suspicions last night were correct. Jean had indeed drunk too much cider, & had even left the spigot of the cider barrel open. [...] Isac [Marquand]'s mother came to ask me to take Isac back.

Weds 27 Nov: [...] Jean stayed in bed. Savary Brock came on his own (as we had agreed) to discuss his brother William's affairs.[580] He took coffee with me & stayed until 9 o'clock. Isac [Marquand] returned here to stay.

Thurs 28 Nov: [...] I went to see Mr Moullin of les Moullins, whose funds are also affected by the bankruptcy of Messrs Brock & Le Mesurier (he is a testamentary executor & heir to one-third of a sum of between £5000 & £6000 in Government securities). I went to ask him to sign their certificate, but he requested time to take advice.

Fri 29 Nov: [...] Jean rose & went down to the kitchen. He has been confined to bed since Monday evening. He needs assistance to dress himself, as also to lift food & drink to his mouth.

Sun 1 Dec: [...] Pierre Cateline came here before dinner to see Jean, who is far from better but nevertheless able to get up. Lisabo went to church (for her churching), & afterwards dined & spent the rest of the day here with her infant. Wind south-westerly, strong towards evening.

Sat 7 Dec: [...] I wrote to the two Jersey printers for a dozen almanacs. I also wrote to Mrs Radford, the mother of our late little James.

Sun 22 Dec: [...] Jean remains unable to work, but he gets out of bed every day. His brother James came to see him in the afternoon & took tea here.

---

[580] This was the William Brock whose banking business, in partnership with Benjamin Le Mesurier, had recently collapsed, causing the failure of the two Guernsey banks. See 13.6.11.and n. 571, above.

Mon 23 Dec: Mr Thomas Pelley borrowed our animals to sow his wheat. He came here in the evening to spend *la longue veille* with me. The others celebrated it downstairs.

Weds 25 Dec: our neighbour Jean Martel (who owns the lower end of the house at the top of les Eturs) died of consumption last night at the age of 24. He was the grandson of old Sr Pierre Martel, & leaves two brothers, Bonami who is at les Jaonets at present, & Daniel who is not yet settled. Colonel Scott paid me a short visit around one o'clock.

Sun 29 Dec: [...] Mr .... le Lacheur (son of Hy le Lacheur from town) came to see me. He has recently arrived from Newfoundland, where he went with Daniel Machon, &c. I had asked him to bring me news of them all, but it seems he has been away from l'Isle St Jean for 15 months, having gone to Halifax.

Tues 31 Dec: finished sowing broad beans at the far end of le Prey (almost 3 perches). Brought in 339 barley sheaves. Ab. took the animals to help Nico Breton sow his wheat. Another light frost.

Notes relating to 1811

In 1811, Charles Mollet employed twenty-six men aside from his live-in workers. Only about ten of these were day labourers or piece-workers. The rest were tradesmen. Etienne Lihou and Thomas Blondel (before he was taken on full-time) were Mollet's most regular day labourers. Etienne Lihou, who was effectively Mollet's gardener, worked 81 days between January and November, when he fell ill. Thomas Blondel worked 70 days between January and May, when Mollet engaged him as a live-in farm servant at £15 stg per year. Mollet also employed six soldiers as day labourers in 1811: Benjamin Collings, William Harrington, William Smith, William Saxon, John Walker and John Hood. Those who worked most were Benjamin Collings (117 days between June and December) and William Harrington (103 days between July and December). The other worked just a handful of days in the summer. Charles Mollet also listed three female workers in 1811: Marie Nicolle (72 days, January to December), Betsy Lihou (19 days, February to October), and Rachel Collenette (24 days, May to December).

1812

Weds 1 Jan: we had no visitors. Fine weather.

Fri 3 Jan: Jaques Ozanne slaughtered our 3 young pigs. They weighed 144 lb, 145 lb & 150 lb. Together with 488 lb from the 2 old sows slaughtered on 3 December, this yields a total provision of 927 lb for the year. We still have 12 or 15 lb of old bacon, as well as two shoulders.

Sat 4 Jan: [...] Jean cannot work & has done nothing since 18 November. He was also scarcely able to work for 10 or 12 days in October.

Sun 12 Jan: [...] There was a charity sermon at Castel church for our prisoners in France. There was also one at St Andrew, St Peter, & the Methodist chapels. The other churches & chapels will have them in the weeks to come. Fine weather.

Tues 14 Jan: [...] Jean started working again yesterday.

Thurs 23 Jan: [...] Yesterday at around one o'clock Thos [Blondel] came to tell me that there were 5 or 6 gentlemen hunting with dogs in our gardens (they were at that time in the nursery at les Tuzets). I went in search of them with Jean [Cateline], Jean Guilbert & Thos, who brought a loaded gun. Finding an unknown Englishman in the furzebrake at le Brulin, I informed him that he had no right to hunt there & asked him to leave. He did not, & seeing that we were surrounded by dogs, I ordered Thos to shoot one which was in le Brulin. Thos did so & killed it. Another man then came up beside the first & started to insult me. I told them my name, but they refused to tell me theirs, so I threatened to call the Constable, shortly after which they left.

Sat 1 Feb: I have been actioned by Captn Thomas Andrews of the ..... Regiment, who claims to be the owner of the dog Thos killed on 22 January. In the morning, I sent word to the Procureur (who is Mr Andrews' Advocate) to let him know that I would come to Court to answer the action if the rain (which began before dawn) stopped before noon, but that I would not go to town if it persisted. In the event, it fell heavily until one or two in the afternoon & prevented me from going to Court.

Sat 15 Feb: Captn Andrews' action against me for the affair of 22 January was determined today. The Procureur acted for him & the Comptroller (Condomine) for me. I was sentenced to pay Captn Andrews 150 francs in damages, besides costs & a fine to the Crown. I was greatly surprised. Given what had passed, I thought that Captn Andrews would be non-suited & charged costs himself. And this indeed is what would have happened if the Court had been better informed. Such a finding would at all events have been but small compensation to me for all the Captn's false & defamatory accusations, only one of which – the fact that I had the dog killed – was true. Alas, however, we must attribute such judgments to the weakness of human understanding & pray to God that the Magistrates will not themselves be judged with too much severity. When the culprit becomes the accuser, or when the criminal accuses the innocent party, the latter's reputation is blackened & the former escapes the censure of justice.

Mon 17 Feb: I sent the Procureur ten one-guinea coins (each worth 23s at current rates, thus a total of £11 10s). Ab brought them to the Procureur in town, as also a note I had written. He returned with a receipt for the fine & costs. I still owe the Procureur 3 shillings.

Thurs 27 Feb: [...] Daniel [Ferbrache] spent the morning here. He arrived from England yesterday. He had set sail with Captn Thos Moullin towards the middle [of October]. They were intending to put in at Havana, but were captured by a French privateer (or rather pirate) off the Cuban coast, whence they were taken to Spain.

Mon 2 Mar: [...] Rachel Renouf of le Monée, who has lived here as a house servant since 5 June, left us today.

Sat 7 Mar: [...] Mr Wm Brock has arrived in Guernsey in order to see his brother Harry.

Tues 10 Mar: [...] Old Charles Nicolle, who was a farm servant here in my father's time & worked here as a day labourer for many years, has once more started working for me by the day. Today, he helped Etienne [Lihou] dig by the gate of the upper house.

Sun 15 Mar: [...] Jean Renouf & his sister Rachel (see 2 March), Daniel Ferbrache, Marie Nicolle, Pierre & James Cateline & their niece Rachel Allez, young Jean Ozanne (Suzon's brother) & Suzon's five youngest sisters (Lisabo, Caroline, Marthe, Ester & Margueritte) dined here today. Jean Ozanne & his five sisters are still living with their father & mother, as also the youngest child, William. The Ozannes have eleven children, of whom the four eldest are in service: Marie (20) who works for Captn du Feu's widow at les Rohais, Jaques (19) who works for Sr ……… Flere in the Vale, Suzon who works here & Judith who works at les Vallez.[581] There were 20 of us at table, not counting Ab's baby girl.

Weds 18 Mar: [...] I have let the upper house at la Profonde Rue to Mrs Rowtell (a young widow, daughter of Susanne le Cras who was sister to Charles le Cras) for £25 a year, payable quarterly. She will move in at the end of May (if she is ready by then).

Tues 24 Mar: Hy Brock died at 9 o'clock yesterday evening. He had been ill for a long time, seemingly with an abscess on the lungs or the liver.[582] I went to see Mary & Mr Wm Brock this evening.

Sat 28 Mar: [...] Harry Brock was buried today. His body was taken to Candie in the morning. Mr Wm Brock, Peter Mourant, Mr Jean Carey & I were mourners. The Procureur, Captn Bourne, Jean Elizée Tupper, Tom Priaulx, Jean Carey of the Grange, & Jack de Lisle of Plaisance were pall-bearers.

Sun 29 Mar: [...] Easter. Pierre Cateline & Daniel [Ferbrache] dined here. Isac [Marquand]'s mother & James Cateline came in the afternoon. Isac's mother, who is the guardian of her children, made an agreement with Pierre Cateline whereby Pierre will employ Isac on a trial basis for a month from next Wednesday, & if all parties are satisfied at the end of the trial month, he will hire Isac for a further 4 years & 4 months, or until he is 18 (Isac is at present 13 years & 8 months old). Pierre Cateline will not clothe, feed or lodge the boy, but will pay him 2s 6d a week for his first year, increasing by a shilling a week each year until the expiry of the agreement. I have undertaken to pay for Isac's lodging, board & clothing for his 1st year. He is to stay at his

---

[581] The children's parents (Jacques and Marie Ozanne) were tenants of Mollet's at the 'upper' house. See also n. 456, above.
[582] Jurat Henry Brock was fifty-one years old. His widow Mary (Mollet's niece) was forty-four. They were childless.

mother's until Michaelmas, after which we will find him a lodging closer to his master.

Sat 4 Apr: [...] Jean [Cateline] was unwell this morning. Pierre Cateline was also unwell, with acute rheumatism.

Weds 8 Apr: [...] I wrote to Polly Lerrier in Southampton & Jean took a small hamper of wonders to the harbour for her.

Mon 20 Apr: Daniel [Ferbrache] started cutting the ivy around the trees on the earthbanks, &c. [...] Colonel Scott called to see me around noon. He anticipates leaving for Canada with his Regiment in a few days' time.[583]

Weds 22 Apr: [...] Monsieur De Vauxlandri came unexpectedly & took coffee with me. Ab. took 70 lb of butter, 18 dozen eggs & 6 hens into town. I have recently bought all these things for Colonel Scott & will pay for them.

Weds 29 Apr: [...] Messrs Wm Brock (father & son) called here towards evening. Young Wm, the Doctor, came specifically to see Suzon who is ill with a sore throat.

Weds 6 May: Mr Wm Brock returned to his home near Exeter. He arrived here a few weeks before the death of his brother Henry. Young Wm Brock left for London on Saturday, but he will soon return, having decided to establish himself here as a medical man. Sir Thos & Lady Saumarez have departed for England on their way to Halifax, the capital of Nova Scotia, where Sir Thomas (at present a Major-General) is to be second-in-command.[584]

Fri 8 May: [...] Our mare was covered by a stallion belonging to Sir John Doyle. This was arranged by Mr Harry Dobrée. The Governor had offered his friends the use of his stallion *gratis* & did not know this was for me. For

---

[583] Colonel Hercules Scott was to be killed at the Battle of Erie in 1814, one of the last engagements of the War of 1812.

[584] For Sir Thomas Saumarez and his wife Harriet, *née* Brock, a sister of William Brock and the recently deceased Henry Brock, see n. 300, above. Saumarez had been Inspector of Guernsey's militia since the beginning of the French Revolutionary War and was to serve as commander of the garrison at Halifax and commander-in-chief of New Brunswick between 1812 and 1813.

this reason the service only cost 5s 6d (which Ab. gave to the Governor's groom).

Fri 22 May: Jean [Cateline] is unwell & did not work.

Fri 29 May: […] I visited Mr Gibert in the afternoon. He is indisposed owing to a fall on Monday. […] I then rode down to Roquaine & along the coast as far as Vazon in order to sow some thorn apple seed.[585]

Thurs 4 Jun: […] I left the house at four in the afternoon & took the new road as far as les Granges. I then went on to l'Hyvreuse through the lanes & thence northwards along the whole length of the road at les Banques. I crossed to le Clos du Valle by the road over le Braye, rode around the barracks at l'Ancresse & then around the bay as far as Cuhouel. I returned along the west coast via Pulias, Grandes Roques, Cobo, Albecq & Vazon, where I turned inland along the road which leads back here. I arrived at my home between 7 & 8 o'clock. My object in all this was to sow thorn apple seed wherever I went.

Sun 14 Jun: […] Nico le Fevre, the Procureur & his sons John & James breakfasted with me, after which we all went to [Castel] church. Mr Tom Carey preached (Mr Dobrée being in England). I went to St Peter's church in the afternoon. Today was the first time I have been to church this year. Last year, I only started going to church on 7 July.

Mon 15 Jun: I visited Mary in the morning. She hopes to move into her new house on Friday or Saturday. I called at St George in the afternoon in order to pass on my newspaper.

Sun 21 Jun: […] I started picking strawberries today – about 2 lb. The ones which ripened earlier were eaten by the birds. The birds are also eating what we have of peas at le Prey.

Weds 24 Jun: the militia & regular troops were under arms at l'Ancresse & staged a mock battle from there to the Citadel, where those representing the

---

[585] Thorn apple (stramonium) was commonly used as a remedy for inflammation, rheumatism, gout and other ailments. Mollet had bought some seed from Messrs Davy & Bowls the previous year.

French chased those representing the English, as usually happens on these occasions. What a way to teach our people, accustoming them to being beaten by the enemy! [...] I visited Mr Gibert in the afternoon. Later, Messrs de Calonne, Nadaillon, Vossey & Marie came here for coffee & strawberries.[586]

Sun 28 Jun: [...] Daniel called here on his way to church. We had not seen him since he finished working here on 2 June.

Mon 29 Jun: I visited Mr & Mrs Etienne in the morning.[587] They arrived from England on Friday, after spending ..... years there. They will now reside here, in Sir Thos Saumarez's house, which they are renting for 3 years. I also visited Mary & went to town, where I had scarcely been since 15 February. [...] Two soldiers from the 14th Garrison Battalion, Frank Macginnis & Pat Murphy, started working here. I will pay them 8s a week, with a pint of cider in the morning, another pint in the afternoon, & half a pint at mealtimes (but no food). Mr Savery Brock recruited them on my behalf from Major Doyle who has commanded this Battalion ever since Sir Thos Saumarez was succeeded as Inspector of the Militia by Colonel Sir Charles Imhoff.[588]

Sat 4 Jul: [...] I visited Mary in the evening. She has been living in her new house at the Grange since Tuesday.

Sun 5 Jul: [...] I was vexed with Ab. [Machon] this morning & I threatened to dismiss him. I even told him he could leave tomorrow if he refuses to do what I order. This was mainly on account of the ox, which I would like to keep permanently indoors, but which he insists on putting outside.

Mon 6 Jul: I wrote letters to Danl Machon & Mr Elizée le Page at l'Isle St Jean. Ab. went to town twice. He took a box for his brother Danl to Captn Thos Cohu (which I am sending Danl care of Mr Elizée le Page). Captn Cohu set sail for Newfoundland later in the day.

---

[586] This is Charles Mollet's last ever reference to French *émigrés*, aside from Monsieur Marie (alias Jean Mortier), the former Capuchin friar who made Guernsey his permanent home.
[587] For Pierre Etienne, see n. 10, above. His wife was Rachel, *née* De Beauvoir.
[588] General Saumarez's replacement, Sir Charles Imhoff (1767–1853), had an unusual and interesting background. Born in Germany of German parents, he had been adopted and brought up by Warren Hastings (the first Governor General of India) after his mother had married Hastings in 1777.

Tues 7 Jul: […] John Guille the Magistrate came to breakfast.[589] Mr Guille (having been authorised to do so by the Court) marked out the line of the wall I am building at the bottom of la Censiere (19 ft from Sr André Cohu's footpath). He also marked out the wall which is to bound my field at les Eturs road (5 ft from the outer edge of the adjacent footpath).

[*This volume of Mollet's journal ends after his entry for 11 July 1812. The next volume is missing.*]

Notes relating to 1812

Mollet's tally of days worked in 1812 extends only to July, when he ran out of space in this volume. Between 1 January and 11 July 1812, Mollet recorded employing 15 men. About half of the men were day labourers and piece-workers, and the rest were tradesmen of various sorts. The labourers worked a total of 191 days between them. The total was low because Mollet had three live-in farm servants in 1812 (Thomas Blondel, Jean Cateline, and young Isaac Marquand until April). Etienne Lihou worked most days (46). Mollet also employed four soldiers as farmhands in the first half of 1812 (Benjamin Collins, John Walker, Pat Murphy and Frank Maginnis). Between them, they worked a total of 69 days. Mollet noted that he paid the elderly Charles Nicolle 1s per day for his labour.

---

[589] For John Guille, grandson and principal heir of Jean Guille of St George, see n. 423, above. Guille had been elected a Jurat in 1810, at the age of twenty-one.

1815

[*There is a three-year gap between the end of the previous surviving volume of Charles Mollet's diary in July 1812 and the start of the next (and last) surviving volume in August 1815. The intervening volume is missing. Much had changed since Mollet's last entries. The Napoleonic Wars were over; Mollet's young farm servant Jean Cateline had died (in October 1812); Mollet had sold the 'upper' house to his long-term servants Abraham and Elizabeth Machon (in May 1815); and Mollet himself had reached the age of seventy-three.*]

Sun 20 Aug: the Procureur, his son John (the Advocate),[590] Monsieur Lamy, Nico le Fevre & Tom Macculloch came to breakfast,[591] after which we all went to [Castel] church, where Mr Tom Carey officiated.

Mon 21 Aug: Judith Machon, Ab's sister (who lives at her father's) has started coming here to help with the laundry, because Suzon Colnette, who started helping us a year ago, can no longer come. She replaced Marie Nicolle, who died on 20 September & Rachel Colnette, who died on 23 October.

Weds 23 Aug: [...] We collected 154 sheaves of tithe. Mr & Mrs Joseph Davy, Mrs & Mrs Bowls, Messrs Vaular, Lamy & Marie took coffee & raspberries with me. A strong south-westerly wind.

Sat 26 Aug: Thos [Blondel] took Lisabo to market & delivered a box to the harbour containing 30 Guernsey lilies for Monsieur Du Chevreuil & Pierre Adam, as also a letter for Mons. Adam.

Weds 30 Aug: Sir Thomas & Lady Saumarez, Mary, Mr [William] Brock & his daughter Judith, Dr & Mrs Brock came to dinner.[592] [...] Thos took a

---

[590] HM Procureur's son John De Sausmarez (for whom see n. 513, above) had been admitted to the Guernsey Bar earlier in 1815. He was to serve as HM Comptroller 1830–45, and became a Jurat in 1847.
[591] Thomas MacCulloch (1771–1852) was the father of future Bailiff Edgar MacCulloch (1808–96). For HM Prévôt Nicolas Lefebvre, see n. 294, above.
[592] Mollet's great-nephew, Dr William Brock, had married Mollet's great-niece (and his own first cousin) Harriet Dobrée (1793–1834) in 1814.

hamper to the harbour containing some butter, 2 cakes & 10 dozen Guernsey lilies for Frederick Le Mesurier & his wife at le Havre de Grace.[593]

Thurs 31 Aug: I visited Mr Gibert in the morning. He has lately resigned his parish in favour of Mr Grut, but he did not mention this to me.[594]

Fri 1 Sep: yesterday I attended the funeral of Mrs le Pelley, who died at les Beaucamps, where she had been living for several years with her sons Thomas & Nico.[595] She survived her husband by 40 years. She had a paralytic stroke about a year ago & was confined to bed for at least ten months. I was not informed of her death nor invited to the funeral. Major Nico de Jersey of les Touillets & I followed the mourners (we were the only ones). Major de Jersey had a hatband. Mrs le Pelley's mourners comprised her 3 sons (Denis, Nico & Thomas) & her grandson (Mr James Le Marchant).

Weds 6 Sep: [...] we collected half a small cartload of tithe from .... Lihou of l'Echelle. This is our last. We have not collected a great deal of tithe this year. The barley has in general been good & abundant, but the wheat has been mediocre. Abraham observes that, this year in le Nanage, it has taken 16 vergees to produce the same amount of tithe which, in other years, we would have collected from just 4 vergees.

Sat 9 Sep: [...] Savery Brock came unexpectedly towards dusk, took coffee here & stayed until 9.[596]

Mon 18 Sep: [...] Daniel [Ferbrache] borrowed the cart, the ox & two horses to cart stone for his brother-in-law James du Quemin who is having a house built to the north of la Grande Mare, not far from the road. One of James's brothers had a house built closer to Vazon earlier this summer. Thos Martel, who used to live at les Boulains, had a house built between le Gelai & the coast. Nic. Martel of les Houmets had a house built in his field (la Croix) near Cobo, & .... Falla (son of Pierre Falla from near les Pins) had a house

---

[593] For Frederick Le Mesurier and his wife Martha, *née* Brock (Mollet's great-niece), see n. 522, above.

[594] Etienne Gibert was seventy-nine years old. He had lost his wife at the beginning of the year.

[595] 'Mrs le Pelley' was Susanne, *née* De Beaucamp. See nn. 83 and 134, above.

[596] John Savery Brock was now a widower. His wife Elizabeth, *née* De Jersey, had died at the age of twenty-eight in April 1815, leaving him with four young children. See n. 627, below.

built between the land belonging to the Castel Rectory & les Varendes. Five new houses will thus have been built in the parish over the course of this year.

Sun 1 Oct: [...] Charles [Ozanne] dined here, as he does nearly every Sunday. He sleeps in the cider cellar & has his linen washed here. It is almost as if he were employed as a farm servant. However, I pay him by the day – 8d daily, which makes 4s per week.

Thurs 5 Oct: [...] Thos [Blondel] & Pierre [Nicolle] delivered a few bottles of our distilled liqueurs to eight different families. While in town, Thos received £15 15s from Mrs Robert in payment of Mrs Newell's rent for the three quarters ending 25 September. He also received £5 5s from Mr Hardy for the current quarter (Mr Hardy having agreed to pay each quarter's rent in advance). Thos later bought us a couple of French turkeys for 6 shillings. Mary called here around noon with Martha, Elizabeth & Anne Dobrée, who have recently arrived from England.[597]

Mon 9 Oct: I visited Mary in the morning & Mr Gibert in the afternoon. Mr Gibert finally told me that he had resigned his parish & that Mr Grut & his family were moving into the Rectory next Monday. I made no comment.

Weds 11 Oct: I called at Mary's before noon. Mr Wm Brock & his daughter Judith returned to England yesterday. I went to St Peter in the afternoon via the new (lower) road. The portion between les Moullins & lower St Saviour is almost finished, & from there it is open (though not finished) as far as les Adams, where it joins the St Peter's road.

Mon 16 Oct: Ab. [Machon] accompanied Master Danl Torode to town, where Master Torode mended the hole in the door of the vault. Ab. received £9 stg from Mr John Brock (son of Henry) for the rent of the vault & warehouse for the six months ending 25 June last.[598] He paid Mr Brock £3 12s for the 2 dozen bottles of Sauternes wine I bought from him in January.

---

[597] Twenty-seven-year-old Martha, Elizabeth (twenty-five) and Anne Dobrée (eighteen) were Mary Brock's nieces and Charles Mollet's great-nieces, daughters of Mary's late sister Patty and Bonamy Dobrée.
[598] John Brock (1769–1841) was an older brother of Mollet's friend the Reverend Thomas Brock, Rector of St Peter.

Tues 24 Oct: [...] Ab. took a few Swan Egg pears & some chestnuts to Mr Gibert & Mr Grut, who are now both occupying the Rectory at St Andrew.

Mon 30 Oct: the wind increased in strength yesterday evening, & as Ab. & Lisabo were getting ready for bed at 9 o'clock, they noticed the thatch lifting off the south-eastern end of the upper house roof. I went to wake Thomas [Blondel], & he & Ab. secured the thatch with some spar gads, which prevented further damage. There was a hole the size of a cider barrel. The storm continued all night & through the day. [...] Sir Thos Saumarez, Peter Mourant & Sophy, who left for France on 13 September, returned at midnight yesterday. They had left Paris on .... , but were detained at le Havre de Grace by an adverse wind & later had to take shelter at Cherbourg.

Sat 18 Nov: a light frost this morning, the first of the season. Thos took Lisabo to market.

Fri 24 Nov: [...] Eleazar [Ingrouille] called here on his way to town. I gave him my newspaper of 15 October.

Mon 27 Nov: [...] Mary [Brock], Sophy [Mourant] & Dr Brock's wife called here around noon. Fair, but dull & very cold. Wind easterly. I subscribed to Mrs Seager's Library for 3 months.

Weds 29 Nov: a hard & extensive frost this morning. The upper pond was covered with ice.

Sat 2 Dec: [...] Savery Brock & his 8-year-old son Julius called unexpectedly at dusk, took coffee with me & stayed until nearly 9 o'clock. Mr Pelley (Thos) sent us some cabbage for the pot.

Sun 17 Dec: the Procureur, his young son James, Harry Dobrée & Nico le Fevre came to breakfast. Isac [Marquand] dined here, as also Pierre Cateline, who left at three. Charles [Ozanne] dines with us every Sunday.

Sun 24 Dec: Isac [Marquand] dined here & shared Charles [Ozanne]'s room overnight.

Mon 25 Dec: Judith Colnette (formerly our little Judith) dined here & left in the evening with Isac.[599]

Sun 31 Dec: the Procureur, his son John, Harry Dobrée, Tom Macculloch & Nico le Fevre came to breakfast. Monsieur Marie & Isac [Marquand] dined with us. Eleazar [Ingrouille] & Mr Cohu (the schoolmaster) took coffee & spent the evening here. I paid Mr Cohu 14s for young Pierre [Nicolle]'s schooling. I had not paid him since 27 March.

---

[599] Judith Collenette was now fifteen years old. Isaac Marquand was seventeen. See nn. 443 and 467, above.

1816

Mon 1 Jan: a frosty morning & fine day. We had no visitors. Thos [Blondel] went to town in the morning. Lisabo & her little girl went to Ab's mother's in the afternoon.[600]

Tues 2 Jan: a hard frost, with ice here & there. It thawed somewhat in the sunshine, but re-froze in the shade from about 3 o'clock. Miss Marina Payne & Monsieur Marie came to dinner & left at eight.[601]

Thurs 4 Jan: Lisabo spent the night at la Lande with Ab's Aunt Judith, who is dying.

Sat 6 Jan: dined at Mary's. Took tea at the Procureur's, then accompanied him to the theatre to see the Italian conjuror Mr Maggioretti. Thos [Blondel], Suzon [Ozanne], Charles [Ozanne], young Pierre [Nicolle] & Isac [Marquand] also went. Neither they nor I thought much of him.

Tues 9 Jan: [...] Ab. attended his Aunt Judith's funeral. She was his father's sister & the widow of the late Jaques Dorey. She was at least 80 years old.[602]

Tues 16 Jan: [...] Isac Nicolle came to pay me £2 stg.[603]

Thurs 18 Jan: today was a day of thanksgiving for the peace which has been re-established between all the nations of Europe within the last few months. Ab, Lisabo, Thos, Suzon, Pierre & Charles went to church, leaving little Betsy with me.

Sat 20 Jan: a certain Mr Adams (an Englishman who I suppose is a painter) came here around 10 o'clock & showed me the contents of his portfolio. I

---

[600] The Machons' daughter, Elizabeth, was now four years old.
[601] Marina Payne has not been traced. She may have been a shopkeeper, possibly in the grocery trade.
[602] Judith Dorey, *née* Machon, had been born in 1735.
[603] This was for the maintenance of his ten-year-old son Pierre, who was living at Charles Mollet's.

declined to purchase any of his work but offered him refreshments. He took coffee here.

Thurs 25 Jan: Monsieur Marie dined with me in the kitchen. Mr Metivier, Miss ……... le Cocq, & the Revd Mr Wm Guille joined us for coffee. Mr Guille has recently taken [holy] orders. He preached his 1st sermon at Castel church last Sunday. It seems he has been engaged as a Curate by Mr [Nicolas] Dobrée, who no longer takes services at the Castel.

Fri 26 Jan: having been troubled by a cough these past 8 days, I stayed in bed until after midday.

Tues 30 Jan: […] Michel Nant had 3000 osier withies for making crab-pots, for which he paid 5s (10d per 100). There was a hard frost this morning which lingered till evening. I stayed in bed all day.

Fri 2 Feb: […] The ash trees have been felled. I think they must have been planted 125 to 130 years ago. The wood will be good for nothing but logs for the fire & faggots.

Sun 4 Feb: Pierre Cateline dined here. His brother [James Cateline] & Monsieur Marie came in the afternoon. I saw all of them, but remained in bed.

Thurs 8 Feb: […] Eleazar [Ingrouille] spent the evening with me. He has been here morning & evening almost every day these past two weeks.

Sat 10 Feb: […] Ab. & Lisabo passed contracts with Mr Moullin for the earthbank separating the area south of the gate of the upper house from Guillaume Girard's field. They bought the earthbank & a narrow strip directly under it for £6. Mr Moullin is to dismantle it & take away the wood.

Weds 14 Feb: Lisabo, Thos, Charles & Hy Ogier went to gather seaweed. Young Pierre accompanied them. They brought back a cartload of seaweed, as also 200 ormers & some crabs. […] Not one of the gatherers has felt cold these past two days in spite of the icy weather. I stayed in bed. Ab. went to town.

Sat 17 Feb: [...] I rose at midday & dined in the kitchen (which I had not done for nearly 3 weeks).

Thurs 22 Feb: [...] Pierre Cateline & Isac [Marquand] came to mend the roofs of the house & greenhouse. Jean Corbet was labouring for them. They ate here.

Thurs 14 Mar: Thos [Blondel] went to dig peat with Danl [Ferbrache] & his team of diggers. There were six diggers in all & they brought up 14 loads.

Fri 15 Mar: [...] Strong westerly or south-westerly winds overnight & for most of the day. The tide came up very high. It broke over the dunes & flowed down the roads towards the houses at le Gellé & la Mare de Carteret. Some damage was done to the coastal fortifications which were built last year. There have been more than 60 carts working the peat at Vazon these past two days.

Thurs 21 Mar: [...] Etienne [Lihou] planted some shallots & onion sets at le Marquet, adjacent to le Ruquet. He had not been here since 19 December owing to illness, & even then he had worked only 4 days since 5 October.[604]

Sat 30 Mar: Danl le Geyt (son of the late Daniel & Oriane Bichard) started working here. He served on board the frigates for many years, but has been at home with his mother & brother these past several months without finding work.[605]

Sun 31 Mar: [...] The Procureur, his sons John & young James, Harry Dobrée & Nico le Fevre breakfasted here. They had not yet come for breakfast this year (except the Procureur & Nico le Fevre who came once).

Fri 12 Apr: [...] I paid Mr Cohu 5s for young Pierre [Nicolle]'s schooling since Christmas (5 *sous* per week). I am thinking of sending Pierre to an English schoolmaster in town.

Mon 15 Apr: awoke to a frost & ice in the bucket under the pump.

---

[604] Etienne Lihou was by this time seventy-three years old.
[605] Daniel Le Geyt was thirty-seven.

Thurs 18 Apr: […] Mr Charles Marquand (youngest son of the late Charles of le Bouet), who left for America in March 1806 with Daniel Machon & 70 or 80 others, called here & took coffee with me.

Mon 22 Apr: […] Pierre [Nicolle] started attending Mr Berry's school in the Bordage (in town).

Fri 26 Apr: […] The seamstress has been here these past 5 days to mend our linen & make a suit for Pierre.

Mon 29 Apr: dined at three o'clock with Mary, Miss Roche, Peter, Sophy, Colonel Octavius Carey (Sophy's younger brother) & Dr [William] Brock (whose wife is in England). They all came in carriages. Mary & Miss Roche had hired a chaise & went for a ride as far as les Adams in St Peter. […] The Governor, Dean, &c., laid the foundation stone of the new Torteval church (the old church having been on the verge of collapse for many years).

Weds 1 May: Daniel Ferbrache will no longer work for me as a day labourer. He came here this morning to pay me for a quarter of barley (18s) & a bushel of potatoes (3s).

Sun 5 May: […] Charles Ozanne will no longer work here. I told him on Monday that I do not wish him to sleep here or eat here on Sundays (although Lisabo told him yesterday that he could have his laundry washed here & that he could dine with us next Sunday). He has not spoken to me, but he told the others he would like me to increase his wages. He began working here on 13 April 1814, & I paid him 10d per day until the following Michaelmas. At that point, he started sleeping here & I reduced his pay to 9d per day. He also ate here every Sunday. When his mother died & he started having his laundry washed here, I reduced his pay further to 8d per day (from 2 January 1815). He went out almost every Sunday evening, as also at other times, &c.

Sun 12 May: the Procureur, his son John, Tom Macculloch, Nico le Fevre & Harry Dobrée came to breakfast. Daniel Ferbrache & his nephews Isac & Hellier Nicolle (brothers of our young Pierre), our laundress Judith Machon, & Nancy le Brocq dined here. Nancy le Brocq is a servant of Mary's from Jersey. She asked Thos if he would show her around the island, so they took our two horses & went for a long ride in the afternoon. I gave Daniel 3 shillings to pay for old Charles Nicolle to be shaved at 1d a week.

Mon 20 May: [...] Jean Simon (a Frenchman) started working here. He is from les Pieux near the port of Dielette, but has lived in Cherbourg (where his wife & 4 children remain) for 10 or 12 years. He has been in Guernsey for 3 months. I have agreed to pay him 9d daily with board & lodging (breakfast & supper only on Sundays). He will sleep in the hayloft.

Mon 3 Jun: very cool for the season, particularly this morning when it was foggy & overcast.[606]

Thurs 6 Jun: [...] [the Revd] Mr Tom Brock & Mrs Brock, their daughters Ann & Mary, Mrs Metivier, her son Charles, Miss Mary le Cocq & the Revd Guillaume Guille came in the afternoon. Lisabo sat up all night with Judith Lihou (wife of Jean Ozanne, the eldest son of Jaques Ozanne of les Deslisles) at Mr Ozanne's house at le Pavé. She has been unwell since giving birth to her 8th child a few days ago.

Mon 10 Jun: [...] I came across James Cateline close to his forge, & he told me he had been married at noon this very day.[607]

Sun 16 Jun: [...] Pierre Cateline & Isac [Marquand] dined here. Lisabo went to see our former servant Marie Robin, who is ill. She must be about 84 or 85 years old.

Mon 17 Jun: [...] In the afternoon, I went to St George to see Mr Wm Metivier who arrived on Friday after ten years' absence.[608] He has established himself as a merchant in Valencia, Spain.

Thurs 20 Jun: the Castel Regiment (Green) & the St Martin's Regiment (Blue) assembled at l'Hyvreuse to be reviewed by the new Lt Governor, Major-General Bayley, who arrived 10 or 12 days ago.[609] The Town Regiment & Artillery were

---

[606] 1816 was the so-called 'year without a summer', when global weather patterns are thought to have been disrupted by the eruption of Mount Tambora in Indonesia the previous year.
[607] Twenty-two-year-old James Cateline had married Jeanne Domaille (daughter of Daniel Domaille) at the Vale church.
[608] See nn. 424 and 486, above.
[609] Major-General Henry Bayly (1769–1846) served as Lieutenant-Governor of Guernsey until 1821. He was knighted in 1834. For the militia regiments and their various colours, see n. 206, above.

reviewed yesterday. The Black Regiment will be reviewed tomorrow. Sir John Doyle remains here, but without function.

Weds 3 Jul: [...] Daniel Ferbrache's wife brought us 150 mackerel for salting at 8s 6d per 100 (whole & ungutted).[610] Large mackerel usually sell for 10s per 100. These were all fairly large.

Thurs 4 Jul: [...] Thomas [Blondel] left at midnight to go fishing with the 3 Ferbrache brothers, who own a boat between them. He returned here at 5 o'clock this evening. He was very seasick.

Fri 5 Jul: young Mr John Condomine & Mr Isac Dobrée came at midday with the news that my friend Mr De St Croix of London died of an apoplectic stroke last Sunday.[611] His death will be a great blow to his numerous family & is a sad loss to me.

Sun 7 Jul: rain yesterday evening & all night, heavy between 4 & 6 in the morning. The Procureur & his wife breakfasted with me, & we went to [Castel] church together. [...] Mr Wm Guille preached & took the service. However, I have become deaf & could not hear him.

Mon 8 Jul: to town with Ab. in the morning. Mr Savery Brock joined us & we took young Pierre [Nicolle] to the National School, which was established (& is maintained) by subscription. The Master is Mr Berry (brother of the Master of the school Pierre has been attending since Easter).

Thurs 11 Jul: Thos almost finished cutting the hay at les Eturs. The others spread it out. We have not yet turned it. Dull weather. Unseasonably cold this evening.

Sat 13 Jul: [...] We sold butter at the market every market day between 1 January & 18 May this year. In all, we have sold 121½ lb, which has yielded £11 9s 5d stg. At present we have 100 lb of butter in pots, & Lisabo has started selling it again. Today she sold 13 lb at 13d per lb.

---

[610] Daniel Ferbrache had married Judith Trachy in 1813.
[611] Jersey-born Nicolas De Ste Croix was sixty-four years old. See n. 65, above.

Thurs 18 Jul: [...] Heavy rain between 8 o'clock & midday. The rest of the day was very damp. The ground is saturated. Water is flowing down the channel in the hillside garden, just as it does in the winter. It has even overflowed into the trees. We have had a stiff, cold south-westerly wind since noon yesterday. It is very rare for us to have such a cold & wet summer as this.

Mon 22 Jul: I called at Mary's in the morning & saw Mr Woolcomb & Elizabeth Dobrée, who were married on Thursday by Mr Brock at St Peter.[612] They are staying with Mary for a few weeks before leaving for England. I went to Mr Crick's garden afterwards, but I found no one there.

Tues 23 Jul: [...] I had a brief visit from Miss de Jersey of les Touillets who has been living in Bristol for 4 or 5 years with her brother Peter, who is a surgeon in Clifton. She is here on account of her mother's illness.[613]

[*Charles Mollet turned seventy-four during the course of August 1816*]

Fri 2 Aug: Dr [William] & Mrs [Harriet] Brock, Sophy Dobrée & Mary Brock (Mrs Jones) called here around one.[614]

Sat 10 Aug: [...] Suzon [Ozanne] attended the funeral of her brother Jaques' wife who died giving birth to her 1st child. The infant survived.

Weds 14 Aug: John Condomine (jun.); Mr George Bell & his wife (formerly Mary Condomine, then Mrs Bowden); Mrs Bell's daughter Mary Bowden (now Mrs Jones, the widow of Mr Jones); Mr Charles Bell of London & his

---

[612] The new husband of Mollet's great-niece Elizabeth Dobrée (1790–1876) was twenty-eight-year-old Lieutenant Robert Woollcombe of Ashbury in Devon. For Elizabeth's birth, see n. 264, above.

[613] Caroline De Jersey (born in 1769) was the only surviving daughter among the eleven children of Jurat Pierre De Jersey of les Touillets (see n. 104). Dr Peter De Jersey (born in 1787) was her youngest brother. Her mother was Pierre De Jersey's second wife, Rachel, *née* De La Mare.

[614] These young people were all great-nieces and -nephews of Mollet's. For Dr William Brock and his wife Harriet, *née* Dobrée, see n. 592, above. Mary, *née* Brock (1791–1863), was William's sister. She had married Pitman Jones of Exeter in 1812. Sophia Dobrée (1794–1874) was the sister of Harriet, *née* Dobrée, and the cousin of William and Mary.

daughter came to breakfast.[615] Monsieur Marie & Miss Marina Payne joined us for coffee & raspberries.

Mon 19 Aug: [...] Daniel le Geyt helped Eleazar cart his hay. Thos [Blondel] cut the hay at the bottom of le Prey (our last grass hay). Jean [Simon] stripped the hemp to make twine, & spread it out.

Sun 25 Aug: [...] to St Saviour's church in the morning. Mr [William] Guille is officiating there in the absence of Mr [Thomas] Carey, who has gone to live in France with his family & his father [Mr Jean Carey].[616]

Sun 1 Sep: [...] Monsieur Marie dined with us in the kitchen. Isac [Marquand] also dined here. George Nicollet & his little boy (7 years old) came in the afternoon. Strong north-westerly winds. Cold. Thos [Blondel] borrowed the two horses to go riding with Mary's servant Lisabo [Le Brocq].

Mon 2 Sep: [...] Ab, Thos & Jemmy Letocq went to gather samphire at Bon Repos. I joined them for a few hours after dinner. [...] We had not gathered any samphire since 16 August 1813, when Ab. & Thos went to gather it with Mr Thos Pelley. I had gone to town that day & was on my way to find them on the cliffs, when my horse (the young filly) took fright, threw me off & trampled on me. I was quite badly hurt but nevertheless went to speak to them at Bon Repos. Once home, I was confined to bed until the end of the month. However, my injuries healed & – thank God – I have not suffered any further ill-effects.

Thurs 5 Sep: I accompanied Thos [Blondel], Lisabo [Machon] & her little Betsey to town in the morning to see an aloe in Mr Geo. Bell's garden at le Bosq. It has produced a flowering spike 25 ft tall.

---

[615] For John Condamine, jun., see n. 568, above. For his aunt Mary, *née* Condamine, see n. 330. This lady, now married to George Bell (1761–   ), had had a daughter, Mary, with her first husband John Bowden in 1785. Mary Bowden had married William Herbert Jones in 1811, but her husband had since died. Charles Bell (for whom see n. 522) was George Bell's younger brother.

[616] For Jean Carey of 'Choisi' and his son the Reverend Thomas Carey, see nn. 87 and 338, above. Though resident in Dijon, the Reverend Carey did not relinquish his living at St Saviour until the end of 1819.

Weds 11 Sep: […] I went to find the Procureur in his garden. On sale in front of the Prevost's office were 21 copies of Berry's History of Guernsey (containing 30 engravings), at 12s 6d each. The Procureur made me a present of a copy. These books had been distrained in order to pay off the author's debts. He himself had been selling them for 3 guineas (2 guineas to subscribers & 5 guineas to those whose houses were represented in the engravings).

Mon 16 Sep: I rode to […] Mr Grut's timber yard. When I was leaving the yard, my filly stumbled & threw me off. I could have been badly hurt, but – thank God – I was relatively unscathed.

Weds 18 Sep: […] I called at Mary's. She is now alone, her guests having left at noon for le Havre de Grace (Mr Wm Brock, Mr & Mrs Pitman Jones, their two little boys aged 3 & 2, & Sophie Dobrée). They are meeting Nancy, her daughter Judith & son Octavius, & Major Winslow at le Havre, whence they plan to go to the south of France or Italy for the winter (for the sake of Mary Brock's health).[617]

Thurs 19 Sep: […] We broached our last barrel of cider on Monday. The workmen have had no cider to drink for the past few weeks (which is the first time such a thing has happened here). I myself have not drunk any cider since Easter.

Sun 22 Sep: […] James Neale dined here. [He] is the 16-year-old son of a blacksmith from la Contrée Mancel who very kindly rushed to help me last Monday when my horse stumbled. Daniel Ferbrache breakfasted with us in the morning. I paid him 33s for weeding 44 perches of parsnips at le Mont de Val (which he had undertaken to weed for 9d per perch). Daniel did not, however, weed them himself, having paid his brother-in-law Jean Trachy to weed them. Mr Thos Pelley told me that Jean Trachy had weeded some of his parsnips for 6d per perch.

---

[617] Nancy was Mollet's niece and 'Mr Wm Brock' was her husband. 'Mrs Pitman Jones' was their twenty-five-year-old daughter Mary (see n. 614, above), who was thought to be consumptive. Judith, the Brocks' third surviving daughter, was twenty-one and Octavius, their youngest son, was eight. Sophia Dobrée (see also n. 614) was their twenty-two-year-old niece.

Tues 24 Sep: [...] Thos collected our first tithe (16 sheaves of wheat & 20 sheaves of barley from Jean le Pelley).

Weds 25 Sep: [...] Jean Simon, the Frenchman who has lived & worked here since 20 May, returned to Cherbourg, having been called back by his wife.

Thurs 26 Sep: [...] News reached us of the death of Admiral D'Auvergne.[618]

Fri 27 Sep: to town before noon. The Newell family has left the upper house [at la Profonde Rue], which is now empty. The Kennedy family remains in the lower house.

Sat 5 Oct: [...] Hy Blondel (our Thomas's brother) has worked here every day since Tuesday, & wishes to continue. Thos told me 8d per day. The boy is 16 years old. On Thursday, I informed Danl le Geyt that I would be reducing his pay from 1s per day (which he has had since starting here) to 9d per day until next August.

Fri 11 Oct: [...] Louis Noel started working here. He is from Saint-Denis-le-Gast, near Gavray (about 5 or 6 leagues from both Coutances & Avranches, & the same distance from the coast). I will pay him 8d per day & he will sleep in the room above the cellar. He is 21 years old. He lost both father & mother at the age of 14, & has no relations save a 15-year-old sister. He came to Guernsey 6 months ago, & has been living & working at Sr Pierre Le Rai's (of le Friquet).

Mon 14 Oct: Ab. [Machon] & Danl le Geyt accompanied Jean le Pelley (the thatcher) to town to begin re-thatching the warehouse roof. I went to see them before noon.

Tues 15 Oct: [...] Ab, Danl & Jean le Pelley went to town to continue their thatching, but they returned here at 3 o'clock, as the Constables ordered them to stop.

---

[618] Sixty-two-year-old Philippe D'Auvergne had died in London (possibly by his own hand) having failed to secure his inheritance as the adopted heir of Godefroy de la Tour D'Auvergne, late Duke of Bouillon. See nn. 346 and 527, above.

Thurs 17 Oct: [...] I went to Court & stayed until 3. The Court gave me permission to re-thatch the part of the warehouse roof which the men left bare on Monday, as also to repair the rest of it.

Sat 19 Oct: [...] Mr Martineau died this morning.[619] Drizzle this evening. Wind south-westerly. I picked a denerel of Mouille Bouche pears.

Mon 21 Oct: [...] Mr & Mrs Robt Le Marchant & their daughter Miss Henriette, Mrs Metivier & her son George & the Revd Wm Guille took coffee with me. We had a wood fire in the parlour.

Thurs 31 Oct: [...] Monsieur Marie & Mr Du Maresq took coffee with me. I had invited them in order to discuss the death of Mr Des Touillets' eldest son, news of which has lately reached us.[620]

Sun 3 Nov: [...] This morning I wrote to the Procureur to enquire whether an Ordinance issued last Tuesday prohibiting the thatching of roofs (or the mending of existing thatched roofs) in certain parts of the town on pain of a 100 *écu* fine would prevent me from finishing the work on my warehouse, as also whether I would be liable to a fine, having continued with the work since Tuesday (although I was unaware of the Ordinance until I saw it in Mr Chevallier's Gazette yesterday evening).

Fri 8 Nov: [...] Thos & Louis picked the apples in the drive at la Daumaillerie & the nursery at le Prey, as also the Artichaux apples. I picked the Permain apples in the furzebrake garden. [...] Mrs Metivier came to bid me farewell.[621] She is going to live near Bristol, where she has 3 sons (Jean, Charles & Carey Metivier). Her son George will go with her, as well as an old servant (Rachel Sauvarin).

Sun 24 Nov: unseasonably hard frosts, both morning & evening.

Tues 26 Nov: [...] James Cateline called here on his way to tell his mother that his wife has given birth to a girl (their 1st child).[622]

---

[619] See n. 111, above
[620] This was Thomas De Jersey, who had died in the West Indies leaving three young daughters. He had left Guernsey in 1787 (see 4.2.87, 6.2.87).
[621] Esther Metivier, *née* Guille, was now fifty-four years old. See n. 318 and 424, above.
[622] They had been married just over five months (see 10.6.16).

Sat 7 Dec: [...] Having been summoned by the King's Sergeant, I went to Court, accompanied by Ab, Pierre Cateline & Jean le Pelley (whom I had asked to come). This was because the Bailiff & some of the Magistrates believed part of the warehouse roof to be contrary to the Ordinance which was issued after the work there had been started, making me liable to a fine of 300 *livres tournois*. However, I informed the Court that I intend to make changes there in due course, & asked their permission to keep the thatch in place for 3 years. The Court granted my request, & might even have granted a longer stay, had I requested it.

Sun 8 Dec: [...] Two Frenchmen came here today. One was a hawker. The other, who called himself Monsieur Du Hallé & was well-dressed & seemingly well-educated, came to ask me for work.

Tues 10 Dec: [...] A ship was wrecked off Lihou last night. It is believed that all on board were drowned, though I do not yet know all the details.

Thurs 12 Dec: [...] the ship which was wrecked on Tuesday was the Samson of London (250 tons), carrying raisins, almonds & juniper from Malaga. Everyone perished. Seven bodies have been found, including those of a lady & a six-year-old girl. They do not appear to have thought themselves in danger, as they all seem to have been in bed (the bodies were not dressed). Monsieur Marie & the young man from Bordeaux who asked me for work on Sunday dined here (in the kitchen).

Fri 13 Dec: [...] Another ship was wrecked off Torteval last night.

Sun 15 Dec: Isac [Marquand] & Hy Blondel dined in the kitchen, as also Monsieur du Hallé, the young man from Bordeaux (see last Sunday & Thursday). Monsieur du Hallé left with Isac before dusk. Wet & windy (as also last night).

Tues 17 Dec: [...] Monsieur du Hallé brought me Mr Bellenger's response to the note I sent him on Sunday (Monsieur du Hallé took Mr Bellenger the note himself).[623] It was short – a refusal. Monsieur du Hallé did not stay (I sent him on his way). Lisabo made some biscuits.

---

[623] This was probably the Reverend Pierre Bellanger, curate of the Forest and Torteval.

Fri 20 Dec: [...] Towards dusk, the oldest daughter of [the Dorey family from] le Groignet came to tell us that our one-year-old bullock was in the pond. She & her brother Daniel stayed with the beast, while her mother, her other brother Hirzel, our Thomas, Louis, Danl le Geyt, Lisabo, young Pierre, Suzon's mother & 2 or 3 of her children all made their way to the pond. With a great effort, they managed to pull the bullock out & brought him home in the cart. I am in hopes that he will recover well.

Mon 23 Dec: [...] Danl le Geyt & Hy Blondel spent the evening here. They had mulled wine with my other servants in the kitchen.

Weds 25 Dec: we had no visitors, save Isac [Marquand] who dined with us.

Sun 29 Dec: [...] Isac [Marquand], Suzon's sisters Esther & Margueritte [Ozanne], & Pierre's brothers Isac & Hellier (Nicolle) dined with us. It started raining at 6 o'clock yesterday evening & continued all night & all day. It is still raining as I write this (at midnight). The rain is moderate but steady. Wind westerly & north-westerly.

Tues 31 Dec: Louis Noel, who has worked, slept & eaten here since 11 October, went to his room above the cider cellar yesterday evening & found his bonnet filled with potatoes (Henry & Pierre were the culprits).[624] He was extremely annoyed, & an altercation ensued in the kitchen before I could come downstairs. As soon as he saw me, he said he was leaving. This he did, taking his clothes with him. [...] Billy Caire brought me the 12 almanacs I had asked him to order from Jersey. The freight cost 6s 3d. I also paid him 2 guineas for shaving me for the last twelve months (as per the agreement we made a year ago, when I persuaded him to reduce his fee by half a guinea). More damp weather. Mr Savery Brock came just before dusk, took coffee with me, & stayed until past 10 o'clock.

Notes relating to 1816

Aside from his live-in servants, Charles Mollet recorded having given work to twenty-two men and two women in 1816. About ten of the men were tradesmen, and the others were day labourers. Mollet's day labourers worked a high number of days in 1816 (713), since Thomas Blondel was his only

---

[624] Henry Blondel was sixteen and Pierre Nicolle was eleven.

permanent live-in farm servant that year. (Charles Ozanne and the Frenchmen Jean Simon and Louis Noël also lived in for a few months, but they were paid by the day and Mollet counted them as day labourers). Daniel Le Geyt worked the largest number of days (200, March–December). Next were Jean Simon (117, May–September), Charles Ozanne (103, January–May) and Henry Ogier (101, January–September). Mollet's old stalwarts Etienne Lihou, Daniel Ferbrache and Eleazar Ingrouille also worked a few days for him in 1816 (Etienne 68 days, Daniel 53 days, and Eleazar 8 half-days). Mollet's female day workers were the laundress Judith Machon (83 days) and the seamstress Olympe Girard (19 days).

In other notes, Mollet listed the recipients of almanacs given as New Year presents in January 1816. These were perhaps the people he considered his closest friends and associates: his niece Mary Brock; the Procureur (Thomas De Sausmarez); John Savery Brock; the Revd Thomas Brock; Monsieur Marie; Master Daniel Torode (a carpenter); Eleazar Ingrouille; Daniel Ferbrache; Pierre Cateline; and Etienne Lihou.

1817

Weds 1 Jan: […] Monsieur Marie & Isac [Marquand] dined with us. […] Dry until 9 o'clock in the morning, after which it started to rain. Around 11 o'clock at night, after Ab. & Lisabo had gone, I noticed that the floor of the dairy was flooded, so I started bailing out the water, & only went to bed around two. None of our people went out to celebrate the New Year, although Lisabo was away for a while in the afternoon.

Sat 18 Jan: […] Lisabo walked to town. She only had butter to sell. […] Sophy Carey & little Tom le Marchant came to see me for an hour around noon.[625] Eleazar [Ingrouille] supped with me.

Fri 31 Jan: […] I had invited Messrs Wm de Jersey & Savery Brock to take coffee with me, but they sent word that they would not be coming owing to the illness of Savery's son.[626] I had also invited Dr [William] Brock. He came alone around two to tell me that Savery's boy, Julius, had died. He had only been unwell for two days. He was Savery's eldest child. Savery's wife died giving birth to her youngest child on 8 April 1815, so he has only his three daughters left.[627]

Sun 2 Feb: Pierre Cateline & his brother-in-law Jack Rougier dined here. The latter arrived in Guernsey on Friday after an absence of 9 years, most of it serving on frigates. I wrote to him for the 1st time last year, after his family was incorrectly informed he had died. Since then I have received a few letters from him.

Mon 3 Feb: […] Mrs Grut sent to tell me yesterday evening that Mr Gibert had grown very weak in both body & mind, so I went to see him this morning. I found him very much changed.

---

[625] Sophia Carey was the wife of Mollet's nephew Peter Mourant (see n. 503, above). Tom Le Marchant was her nephew, the five-year-old son of the late John Gaspard Le Marchant and Sophia's deceased sister Mary (see 1.10.11).
[626] William De Jersey was John Savery Brock's father-in-law (see n. 492, above).
[627] Julius Brock was born in 1808, Elizabeth Brock in 1809, Rosa Brock in 1812, and Betsey Brock in 1815. This last daughter was born the month before her mother died. Her mother's death must have been caused by her subsequent delivery of Betsey's retained twin.

Tues 4 Feb: I attended Mme des Touillets' funeral (without being invited).[628] I arrived rather late & did not join the cortege until it had reached the crossroads at les Cailles. After leaving the cemetery, Nico le Fevre & I went to Mr Wm de Jersey's in order to join the cortege for Julius Brock's funeral. He was 10 years old. I had a hatband.

Weds 5 Feb: [...] Pierre Cateline & his brother-in-law supped in my room & spent the evening with me.

Thurs 13 Feb: [...] Ab. called at St Andrew's Rectory for news of Mr Gibert (as he has done every day lately). Mr Gibert was in bed today, & so feeble that he could not speak to Ab. The day before yesterday, he was still able to shake Ab's hand when he arrived & when he left.

Fri 14 Feb: Mr Gibert died at midday. Ab. had been to see him in the morning. I went to the Rectory at 3 o'clock, then called at Savery Brock's. Savery had gone to St Peter. Later, I spent an hour or so at Mary's. [...] A cold north-westerly wind. Hail showers in the evening. Eleazar [Ingrouille] helped us salt our pork & supped with us.

Thurs 20 Feb: [...] I went to Mr Gibert's funeral (Thos accompanied me). I had a hatband. His funeral was arranged by the Revd Grut & Mr [Nicolas] de Mouilpied (the eldest son of Sr .... de Mouilpied who lives near les Caches in St Martin), to the two of whom Mr Gibert has left all his books, furniture & effects. Mr Gibert also had £1350 stg in Government securities, which he bequeathed to the United Brethren (also known as the Society of Moravians) to be used, as he told me on 3 February, 'for the propagation of the faith'. Fog & drizzle for part of the day, followed by strong winds & hail showers.

Sat 22 Feb: [...] Hy [Blondel] took Lisabo to town. She had 4 hens to sell, as also 7 bottles of rose water.

Thurs 27 Feb: [...] Danl le Prevost took coffee with me. He was here to measure me for a jacket which I am having made out of a brown cloth cloak I bought in London the last time I was there (in 17...), as also for a suit for

---

[628] 'Mme des Touillets' was Rachel De Jersey, *née* De La Mare, born in 1745.

myself & one for young Pierre (from a length of dark brown cotton velvet which I have had for 38 years).

Fri 28 Feb: Messrs Wm de Jersey & Savery Brock came to dinner. Dr Brock joined us for coffee. I was also expecting the Procureur & his son, but they were prevented from coming by the death at midday of the Procureur's youngest child (a one-year-old boy).[629]

Sun 2 Mar: […] Ab. [Machon] shot a dog near the hen-coop in the yard. He had seen it prowling there several times lately. Rain & gales in the evening.

Tues 4 Mar: […] I let the lower house at la Profonde Rue to Mr Christian (an Englishman) for a year at £15 stg annually, payable in quarterly instalments. Mr Christian & his wife keep a public house. They were recommended to me by Mr Jean le Quesne who seems willing to act as their guarantor. Their lease begins on 25 March, but I gave Mr Christian the key today.

Thurs 6 Mar: […] Another stormy night (even more so than Sunday night). I heard thunder, & someone told me that the Vale church was struck by lightning. The storm has done a great deal of damage, not least to the new sea defences at Cobo.

Sat 8 Mar: […] Stormy weather nearly all week. On Wednesday night, the building on the rock named Rousse in the Little Russel was struck by lightning.

Sun 9 Mar: […] Lisabo [Machon] went to see Pierre Priaulx's wife who has become very ill after her recent confinement. She is one of Jean Maindonal's 4 daughters.

Fri 14 Mar: I have had a sort of cramp or rheumatism at the base of my neck for a fortnight. Lately, it has spread to my shoulders & become more painful. At night, I also have a degree of pain in my head & stomach. This afternoon, I went back to bed for a few hours, but I am feeling no better.

---

[629] The little boy was named William. He was the second of HM Procureur Thomas De Sausmarez's sons named William who had died in infancy.

Sun 16 Mar: Mr Savery Brock called here briefly around one o'clock, but I did not see him as I was in bed until three. Monsieur Etienne Gibert (nephew of the late Mr Gibert) came here later with two of the Revd Grut's sons & took coffee with me in my room.

Mon 17 Mar: Ab [Machon], Thos [Blondel] & Danl le Geyt took the two carts to deliver the 60 bushels of potatoes which we have sold to Messrs la Serre & Co. We borrowed a horse & 9 sacks from Eleazar [Ingrouille]. Danl le Geyt & Hy Blondel also brought us some sacks. Pierre Allez's widow & her children have undertaken to clear the furzebrake at le Brulin. They started clearing the part adjacent to the pigs' furzebrake today.

Tues 18 Mar: I rose at noon. I am feeling better, thank God.

Weds 19 Mar: […] John Gardner, the butcher, had previously promised to slaughter our 3-year-old fat bullock this week or next, but he has misled us. He told us today that he was not in a position to buy the bullock from us for the time being, & we have run out of parsnips, &c.

Thurs 20 Mar: Hy Blondel, who has worked here every day since 1 October, came this morning & told his brother Thos that he would not be returning, as he is going to Gaspé. He had given me no warning of this.

Tues 25 Mar: Pierre Allez has started working here. He is 19 years old & the youngest son of the late Pierre Allez of les Hautes Vallez. He is to come here 3 days a week for 10d per day. James Torode also started working here. He is 16 years old & the 2nd son of Jean Torode of les Moullins. He is to come ..... days a week for 8d per day. They are both replacements for Hy Blondel who will only work here for a few more weeks.

Thurs 27 Mar: Ab. [went] to town again, & brought back two ..... lb cases of lemons, which Monsieur Marie bought for me yesterday for 14 shillings each.

Sun 30 Mar: Pierre Catline breakfasted here. He came to tell me that Mr Christian, who rents the lower house [at la Profonde Rue], is willing to rent the upper house on the same terms.

Tues 1 Apr: […] Ab. & Danl le Geyt juiced the lemons we had last Thursday (12 bottles). Each case contained 275 large lemons, but about 50 had rotted in one of the cases, & 75 in the other. Lisabo distilled the rind to make 13 bottles of lemon essence.

Thurs 3 Apr: […] Ab. & Thos took our 3-year-old fat bullock to Mr Croft, an English butcher, to whom we have sold him for 42 shillings per 100 lb. We also sold the pluck for 3s 6d. We are keeping all the other offal, which Ab. & Thos brought back, as also 23 lb of suet for which we paid 7d per lb.

Sat 5 Apr: […] Messrs Wm de Jersey, Daniel Brock, Savery Brock & Dr [William] Brock took coffee with me. We had it in my room, as I was only expecting Savery & William. Savery is leaving for England in a few days' time, whence he will embark for America in order to take possession of 12,000 acres of land in Upper Canada, which have been given to him & his 3 brothers in recognition of the services rendered by their late brother, General Isac Brock, who was killed while securing a 2nd victory against the Americans. In his 1st victory, he took 1000 prisoners & did not lose a single soldier of his own.

Tues 8 Apr: […] I dined at 3 o'clock with Mr Davy & Monsieur Marie. […] Mr Davy gave me 12s & Mr Wm de Jersey sent me 4s 8d. This money is for Jean Torode of les Moullins who had an accident on Friday while digging peat (his foot was injured by the blade of a spade). He has a large family to support.[630]

Weds 9 Apr: a little rain around seven in the morning. Mr Josias Le M[archant] came at eight to alert me to a mistake I made in my tithe payment on Monday. I had paid him what should have been £5 stg in French francs instead of English shillings (French francs are worth only 10d stg). Mary, Mr & Mrs Woolcombe, Martha, Mary & Ann Dobrée came to breakfast. They came at half past nine & stayed until half past twelve.

Sat 12 Apr: […] Savery Brock has left for Southampton. Our Hy Blondel left [for Gaspé] on Wednesday.[631]

Sun 13 Apr: […] Monsieur Marie & Mr Geo. Davy took coffee with me. The latter has spent the last ten months in Rouen but recently returned here to

---

[630] Jean Torode and his wife Rachel, *née* Langlois, had had a total of fourteen children, the youngest of whom had been born the previous year.
[631] Henry was not quite seventeen.

replace Mr Jos. Davy as an associate in Mr Bowls' business.[632] Mr Jos. Davy left yesterday, having received news that his wife & one of his children are ill.

Weds 16 Apr: Lisabo went to town in the morning. In the afternoon, she attended the funeral of Pierre Priaulx's wife. Mrs Priaulx was the daughter of the late Jean Maindonal, & leaves six children.[633] […] I have neckache again. I think it must be rheumatism.

Thurs 17 Apr: Mr Etienne & I had a light breakfast at 10 o'clock. After this, we went to visit Mr Pierre Le Marchant at le Groignet. Later, I took Mr Etienne to Jean Torode's, where he gave Jean Torode a few coins (& left 40s with me for the Torode family). When we returned here, Mr Etienne declined to come in. I had been hoping to keep him for dinner, to which I had invited the Procureur & his son John. They duly came, & the three of us dined alone.

Sun 20 Apr: Pierre Catline dined with us. His sister-in-law (James Catline's wife) took tea here. [She] came to ask me to speak to James (who has deserted her) about maintenance for their child. I had asked him a week ago to be here this morning. He promised me he would, but he did not appear. I fear he is incorrigible.

Fri 2 May: […] We all had sand eels for dinner. Someone came here with some very large sand eels this morning. As well as buying some for ourselves, I bought 3d or 4d worth for the seamstress, as also some for Suzon's people & Jean Torode's family.

Sun 4 May: […] the Procureur, his son John, Mr Tom Macculloch & Mr Harry Dobrée came to breakfast (for the 1st time this year, I think).

Sun 11 May: […] There has been almost constant drought since 4 March (ten weeks ago on Tuesday), apart from a few hours' rain on 25 March (seven weeks ago). The ground is very dry & the grass has scarcely grown. Fortunately, we still have some old hay.

---

[632] For George Davy, Joseph Davy and Thomas Bowls, see nn. 437 and 569, above.
[633] Elizabeth Priaulx, *née* Maindonal, was thirty-four years old.

Tues 13 May: [...] We measured the cleared ground in the furzebrake at le Brulin. There were 27 perches, for which I paid [Pierre Allez's widow] 54s (2s per perch).

Fri 16 May: [...] Pierre Catline brought me his account for the work he has done on my two houses [at la Profonde Rue] during the past two years, & stayed here for supper. The account was for £6 9s stg. I paid him £3 9s, having deducted £3 stg for two years' rent of part of the garden.

Sun 18 May: [...] Rain started falling around 9 in the morning & continued until midday. [...] The butt under the gutter overflowed & the pit in the yard filled up.

Mon 19 May: I did not go to bed until two in the morning. I had a fire lit in my room, bathed my feet, & re-read some of Eleazar's letters.

Sat 24 May: [...] I went to town & passed contracts with Sr Ab. Naftel, from whom I bought 2 bushels & half a denerel of wheat *rente* which I owed him over & above the two quarters which he has owed me since buying, on my advice, the ten bushels & half denerel I owed the late Frederick Price (he bought them from Sr Thos Trachy, an authorised representative of Mr Price's creditors). These two *rentes* are thus now extinguished. The sale was made at the rate of £28 stg per quarter (on both sides). I paid Mr Naftel £14 11s 10d stg. I also paid 3s for the drafting of the contract, 2s 6d for registration, & 6d to the Court. No *congé* was payable, this being the 2nd time the *rente* has been sold in a year.[634]

Weds 28 May: [...] Danl le Geyt & James Torode collected cowpats from the clover at la Censiere.

Weds 4 Jun: Thos took a small hamper to town containing a pot of butter, some wonders & almost a whole lemon cake for Martha Brock at le Havre de Grace. Her brother Dr Brock is on his way to le Havre to fetch Sophie Dobrée, who has spent the winter at Marseilles with Wm & Nancy Brock,

---

[634] *Congé* was a due payable to the seigneur of the fief on which the property associated with a *rente* was situated for permission to transfer its ownership (this due was levied on all sales of real estate).

their daughter Mary Brock, &c. They went there for the benefit of Mary Brock's health, as she is believed to have consumption.[635]

Sat 7 Jun: [...] Lisabo walked to town. She has started selling butter again. We began to put it into pots on 3 May. [...] Lisabo sold today's butter for between 9d & 12d per lb.

Sun 8 Jun: [...] Daniel F[erbrache] whom I had not seen for more than six months, took tea with us on his way back from church. I paid Suzon [Ozanne] her year's wages up to 1 January last (£6 stg).

Mon 9 Jun: yesterday evening, I bathed my feet in my room, where I had a fire lit at nine (I had not had a fire since 18 May). I had stayed up in order to awaken Thos [Blondel] in the early morning, but he rose by himself at a quarter past two. Pierre Allez arrived here soon afterwards, & they both set off with the cart to cut seaweed. They had one cartload, which they put on le Carré. This makes six cartloads in 3 days. There have been a great many people cutting seaweed near le Crocq since Wednesday, most of it for drying. Together with the 86 cartloads we had between 12 November & 11 March, these six make a total of 92 cartloads. [...] Dawn began breaking a little after two this morning.

Tues 10 Jun: Thos & Pierre Allez [...] removed the sediment from the stream at the bottom of the Plantation. [...] They caught a few eels, which Thos later took to Mrs Tom Brock.

Fri 13 Jun: [...] I have lately been loosening the ground around the cucumbers in the hotbed & I have also sowed more cucumbers at the eastern end of the bed. This evening I sowed a few in open ground below the bed. Some of the cucumbers I sowed three weeks ago have come up.

Mon 16 Jun: [...] Lisabo walked to town. In the evening, she & Ab. visited .... du Four near les Grandes Roques. She is the wife of a sailor on the customs boat & has recently given birth to twins. She has had six children in

---

[635] See 18.9.16.

less than 4 years. She has not been married eight years & already has 9 children, of whom 8 are still living.⁶³⁶

Tues 17 Jun: [...] Mr Richard Ozanne came to speak to me in connection with the Agricultural Society which has been set up here by Government.⁶³⁷

Sun 22 Jun: [...] Pierre Catline dined here. His wife told Suzon that she & her husband were not getting on, & that she objected to his coming here. I have long been aware of this, though he has never spoken of it. However, I decided to raise the matter with him today. He told me with some pain & repugnance that his wife had treated him badly for some time, & had treated him particularly badly after the last time he was here (5 June), even though he had returned home before nine.

Mon 23 Jun: I was up from midnight until two o'clock killing the slugs on my dahlias & other plants.

Tues 24 Jun: the whole of the militia was under arms at l'Ancresse. Afterwards, they marched as far as Hougue a la Perre, where they were stood down. The Governor (General Bayley) is in England. He is often absent. Colonel Welch (who I think is Inspector of the Militia) is in command here in the General's absence.⁶³⁸

Weds 25 Jun: [...] Young Tom le Marchant who lives at Candie dined here & stayed until eight, when Peter [Mourant] came to fetch him.

Tues 8 Jul: [...] News reached us of the death of Mrs Nico Carey (Henriette Le Marchant of la Haye du Puits). She died in London, where she was married 4 or 5 years ago.⁶³⁹

---

⁶³⁶ This was the former Rachel Du Four who was married to Customs boatman George Thomas. Their recently born twins were named William and Sophie.
⁶³⁷ The purpose of Mr Ozanne's visit seems to have been to collect information on Mollet's landholdings, livestock and area under cereals for an agricultural census. The information survives at Guernsey's Island Archives in SG 23/43.
⁶³⁸ Colonel Anthony Walsh had been appointed Inspector of Militia in Guernsey in 1816.
⁶³⁹ 'Mrs Nico Carey' was thirty-six-year-old Harriet, *née* Le Marchant (for whom see n. 339, above). Harriet's first husband was a Major MacGregor who had died not long after their marriage. Her second husband was the Reverend Nicolas Carey (see n. 362).

Tues 15 Jul: [...] I attended Mrs Nico Carey's funeral at midday. The cortege assembled at Mr Robt Le Marchant's (I had a hatband). Her body arrived from England on Saturday.

Sun 27 Jul: the Bailiff (Sir Peter de H.), his daughter Nancy, Mr & Mrs Peter Carey & their son, & Lady Smith's youngest daughter came to breakfast. I was also expecting Lady Smith herself, but she is indisposed (rheumatism).[640]

[Charles Mollet turned seventy-five in the course of August 1817]

Weds 6 Aug: tidied up the stackyard. Carted & stacked the hay from le Prey (1½ tons). This is our last hay. There are 14 tons on the stack, & altogether we had about 15 tons.

Thurs 7 Aug: [...] Bought 3 congers weighing 44 lb for salting. I paid 1d per lb for them.

Tues 19 Aug: [...] Pierre Catline took coffee with me. His wife had a miscarriage a week ago & was very ill last night.

Weds 27 Aug: [...] Mary [Brock], Sophy [Mourant], Miss Roche, Martha & Mary Dobrée & Judith Brock came to dinner. Judith Brock arrived from England yesterday with two of the Miss Woolcombes. It rained so much in the night that I hardly expected them to come. I even sent Ab. at eight in the morning to inquire whether they wished to postpone the dinner. It is now dry, but there is a strong, cold westerly wind – so much so that this evening feels more like the end of October.

Sun 31 Aug: fair weather. Monsieur Marie & Mr Bailleul took coffee & raspberries with me. Little Margueritte has been here all week. Her younger brother William spent the day here today.[641]

---

[640] These people were all related. For Lady Carterette Smith, *née* De Havilland, and her daughter Mary Smith, see nn. 419 and 514, above. For Carterette's sister Nancy De Havilland, see n. 471. For Mr and Mrs Peter Carey and their son, see n. 448.

[641] Margueritte Ozanne was ten years old and her brother William six years old. They were the siblings of Mollet's servant Susanne Ozanne. See nn. 456 and 581, above.

Fri 5 Sep: Pierre Catline came after supper yesterday & slept here overnight. His wife, who was better-tempered for a short time while ill (see 19 August), has fallen back into her old ways & is giving him endless trouble.

Sat 6 Sep: a few days ago the Procureur sent Mrs Catline notification that her husband was applying for a separation. This alarmed her, but it was only done to see what effect it would have. Pierre told her afterwards that, if she would only moderate her conduct, he would be willing to continue living with her. I informed the Procureur of this, but I do not think peace will long reign in their household.

Sun 7 Sep: [...] I went to church this morning for the 1st time this year.

Weds 10 Sep: [...] I went to see Mrs Jack Carey in the Grange & we both spoke to Pierre Catline, who is working there.[642] Afterwards, I called at his mother-in-law's, but she was not at home. I was on my way to the Vale to see the Messrs Chepmell (who came here yesterday while I was out) when I chanced upon them in the road. Charles Chepmell is a Captn in the 53rd Regiment. He has lately returned from India after an absence of 14 years.[643]

Fri 12 Sep: [...] In the morning, Thos [Blondel] & Pierre Allez carted the rest of the barley from le Mont de Val. In the afternoon, they collected tithe with Jas Torode & brought back 2 cartloads.

Thurs 18 Sep: [...] the Duke of Gloucester (the King's nephew & son-in-law) arrived this morning, as expected.[644] The whole of the militia was in town, where the men had been ordered to assemble at six. [...] In the evening, Pierre

---

[642] 'Mrs Jack Carey' was Rachel, *née* Dobrée (1775–1849), the wife of John Carey (1769–1847), who served as HM Receiver between 1818 and 1847. She was also the daughter of Mollet's late friend, St Saviour's Rector William Dobrée (for whom, see n. 33, above).

[643] Thirty-three-year-old Reverend William Chepmell and his thirty-one-year-old brother Captain Charles Chepmell were the sons of another of Mollet's deceased friends, William Chepmell (for whom, see n. 66, above). William Chepmell, jun. had been ordained in 1808 and had replaced the late René Martineau as Rector of St Sampson and Vicar of the Vale in 1816.

[644] This was Prince William Frederick, Duke of Gloucester and Edinburgh (1776–1834). He was the son of George III's younger brother William (later William IV) and the husband of George III's daughter Mary.

& Thos went to town to see the illuminations with Ab, Suzon, little Betsy & young Pierre (who had also been to town in the morning).

Fri 19 Sep: those who went to see the illuminations yesterday evening only returned here at midnight. I waited up for them, as did Lisabo.

Tues 23 Sep: [...] I went to see the new Torteval church, whose tower is almost finished.

Weds 24 Sep: [...] collected a cartload of tithe from Jean Priaulx. This is almost the last tithe. The grain is good & the harvest has proceeded well.

Thurs 25 Sep: Fair day. Lisabo sold our 2-year-old red heifer to Captn Towser for £12 5s stg (for export to England), but we have not delivered her yet. We bought her as a calf from Eleazar on 17 April 1815. She is due to calve on 2 November.

Sun 28 Sep: Pierre Catline & his 3 children dined here. I had asked Thos to invite him yesterday, when I learned that his wife has left him. She came to speak to me yesterday evening, but I did not listen to her for long. I believe she left him on Tuesday. She is living at Albecq with her aunt (the wife of Pierre le Page of Enfer).

Tues 30 Sep: [...] The tower under construction at Gerbourg in honour (or rather in memory) of our former Lt Governor Sir John Doyle fell down last night. [...] It was being built at the States' expense.

Thurs 2 Oct: [...] I rode to Gerbourg to see the remains of the tower. I returned via Mary's & spent 2 hours there. In the evening, I learned that Pierre Catline's wife has come back to him.

Tues 7 Oct: [...] Monsieur Gautier from Equeurdreville (a near neighbour of Monsieur Du Chevreuil) dined & supped here.

Fri 10 Oct: [...] I went to town on foot & visited Mary, Mrs Etienne, & Sir Thos & Lady S[aumarez]. I returned here at one, & went to St Peter in the afternoon.

Sat 11 Oct: […] Mrs Moullin of les Vallez died at 3 o'clock. She had only fallen ill at eight in the morning. She was Suzon Nicolle, the daughter of the late Hellier Nicolle of la Hougue.[645] She leaves 3 sons aged between 5 & 12.

Weds 15 Oct: Pierre Catline came here at seven yesterday evening & did not leave until he had breakfasted here this morning. His wife ill-treats him more than I was aware.

Thurs 16 Oct: Pierre Cateline did not come here yesterday evening, so I sent Thos this morning to find out why. At noon I went to the stable & Pierre joined me there. He told me that his wife had admitted she was in the wrong & led him to hope that she would be less violent. He has therefore decided not to proceed with the separation for the time being.

Tues 28 Oct: […] Monsieur Gautier of Equeurdreville (see the 7th) dined & supped here. I received him politely, but I later told him that, having received information he had mistreated his 2nd wife in Jersey, I would no longer be able to receive him as I would have otherwise have done. He denied the allegations, but I do not think he will come here again.

Weds 29 Oct: […] Jean Torode of les Moullins came here to cut out some waistcoats & breeches for Pierre & myself. The seamstress will sew them for us.

Thurs 6 Nov: […] Messrs Josias Le M[archant] & John Guille, representing the States Committee, accompanied the Douzaine to les Eturs in an attempt to sell the old road. I went to see what was afoot, but I told them I did not wish to buy it. Thos Brouard told me this morning that he did not wish to buy it either.

Thurs 20 Nov: […] Ab, Lisabo, Thos & Pierre went sand-eeling, but they did not find many.

Mon 22 Dec: […] In the evening, Thos came to fetch me at Mary's, where I had dined. Sophy [Mourant] joined us in the afternoon, & the three of us were together until past 10 o'clock. I had gone to town on foot at around ten

---

[645] Mrs Moullin was forty-two years old.

in the morning. I spoke to Pierre Catline's wife & visited Mr Robert le Marchant.

Tues 23 Dec: […] Pierre Catline came here at my request, supped with me, & left after 9 o'clock. Our 3 day labourers, &c., stayed until past midnight (they had egg flip, &c.)

Thurs 25 Dec: we dined alone, except for Margueritte [Ozanne], who comes every Sunday. Eleazar [Ingrouille] spent the afternoon & evening with me.

Sat 27 Dec: […] Suzon went to town on foot, having only 7 lb of butter to sell. A heavy hail shower around eight in the morning. Strong westerly winds in the evening.

Sun 28 Dec: Suzon's sisters Marto & Esther & their little brother William came to dinner with a two-year-old cousin who lives with them (the child's mother, a sister of Suzon's mother, also lives with them). The children were here until eight in the evening. Suzon's sister Margueritte who usually stays here from Friday evening to Monday morning, is spending the whole of the Christmas holidays here.

Weds 31 Dec: Thos [Blondel] & Danl le Get fetched a cartload of seaweed which they put on the broad beans we sowed yesterday. The others finished lifting the carrots & parsnips at les Petits Tuzets & brought them here. They also brought a cartload of turnips from among the clover at le Mont de Val. A frosty morning. Wind south-easterly first thing, north-easterly since noon.

Notes relating to 1817

Aside from his live-in servants and occasional piece-workers, Charles Mollet gave work to sixteen men and two women in 1817. The women were the laundress Judith Machon (84 days) and an unnamed seamstress (31 days). Of the men, ten were tradesmen and six were day labourers. Mollet's principal labourers in 1817 were Daniel le Geyt (282 days, year-round), Pierre Allez (204 days, March to December) and James Torode (144 days, March to December). Pierre Allez and James Torode were taken on to replace Henry Blondel (brother of live-in farm servant Thomas Blondel) who left for Gaspé in early April. Etienne Lihou worked 87 days for Mollet in 1817. Eleazar Ingrouille worked 3½ days.

1818

Thurs 1 Jan: Isac & Hellier Nicolle (brothers of our Pierre) dined here, as also Pierre Catline's mother-in-law, his wife & their 3 children. We were not expecting them, as Mrs Catline had declined the invitation I had sent her via Thos last Sunday & via Lisabo on Monday. Pierre Catline came at dusk, took coffee with me & stayed until seven. His family left before he did.

Thurs 8 Jan: [...] Nico le Fevre came to let me know that Savery Brock has arrived in England from America.

Fri 9 Jan: [...] Our Etienne [Lihou]'s daughter Rachel (wife of Nico Roussel) died yesterday evening. She leaves 4 children.[646]

Tues 20 Jan: [...] Mr Wm de Jersey, his son-in-law the Advocate,[647] Mr [Robert] Woolcombe & Dr [William] Brock took coffee with me. I had also invited the Procureur & his son, & the Revd Mr [William] Guille. Mr Guille would have come but for the death of his uncle, Dr Guille, on Saturday.[648] [...] Pierre Machon supped here. He will shortly leave for Havana.

Weds 21 Jan: dined at Candie with the family (Peter, Sophy, the 2 Miss le Marchants & little Tom). Mary joined us for tea. Thos [Blondel] came to fetch me at half past eight. Fine weather. Mr Cohu of les Moullins died today.[649] He was cutting down an elm in his garden which fell on his head. He was a widower. He leaves 8 children, nearly all of them grown up.

---

[646] Rachel Roussel was thirty-eight years old. Her children were aged between four and thirteen. On 15.3.10, Mollet had observed that Etienne Lihou's daughters were all 'healthy' despite the loss of his sons to tuberculosis.

[647] William De Jersey's son-in-law was the Advocate Charles De Jersey (1784–1874), a son of Jurat Pierre De Jersey of les Touillets. Charles, who was to serve as HM Procureur between 1830 and 1851, was married to William De Jersey's only surviving daughter, Mary (see n. 492, above).

[648] The Reverend William Guille's uncle was seventy-two-year-old Dr Richard Guille, a frequent companion of Mollet's in the early days of his diary (see n. 6, above).

[649] This was Jean Cohu, born in 1760.

Fri 6 Feb: […] Captn Denis le Pelley called to see me. He is organising a subscription for Jemmy Ozanne of les Ruettes, whose cow has died, but I declined to donate money in this manner.

Mon 16 Feb: Thos took the animals to help Pierre le Page of le Camp plough for parsnips. This is their 1st day of ploughing.

Tues 17 Feb: […] After Thos brought our animals home following yesterday's ploughing, he went back to le Camp without telling me & supped at Pierre le Page's. I reprimanded him this morning & told him I would reduce his next year's wages by 20 shillings. He expressed his displeasure in terms which shocked me, & I told him (without displaying any anger) that he could either leave straight away, or at the end of his year. I think we both calmed down afterwards.

Thurs 19 Feb: […] I went to see Pierre Gavet around noon. He has been ill & confined to bed for several weeks. He lives at les Truchots, where he bought a small property 6 or 8 years ago.

Sat 21 Feb: […] My former farm servant Pierre Gavet died at 3 o'clock this morning.[650]

Weds 25 Feb: […] Pierre Catline has made a new floor in the kitchen of the upper house. Mrs Christian is renting this kitchen for another year at £4 stg. Thos Allez (jun.) is renting the 2nd floor bedrooms & garret (also for a year) at £7 stg. The 1st floor bedrooms are not yet tenanted. Ab. [Machon] & young Pierre [Nicolle] attended Pierre Gavet's funeral. He was taken to St Andrew's cemetery.

Sun 1 Mar: the Bailiff & his son Charles,[651] the Procureur & his sons John & James, Mr Tom Macculloch, Mr Harry Dobrée & Mr Nico le Fevre came to breakfast. Pierre Catline dined here.

---

[650] Pierre Gavet, who had worked for Mollet in the 1770s and 1780s, was sixty-five years old. See n. 147, above.
[651] Captain Charles De Havilland (1786–1844).

Tues 3 Mar: [...] Mr le Mesurier of le Val in St Peter, who is going to Gaspé to fish for cod [dined with me]. Our Henry Blondel sailed to Gaspé with him last summer. Pierre Catline joined us for coffee.

Weds 4 Mar: ploughed the two middle strips at la Censiere (where we had barley & oats last year) for parsnips. We also ploughed the strip immediately to the west, & planted potatoes there (this is the 2nd strip from the western earthbank, where we had peas last year). The strip immediately adjacent to the western earthbank was under potatoes last year, & we will sow peas there this year. The easternmost strip contains old clover. Our team consisted of Eleazar, his farm servant, his ox & two horses; Hellier Nicolle, his son Pierre, his two oxen & 3 horses; Pierre le Page, his sons Pierre & Sam, his two oxen & two horses; Ab [Machon], Thos [Blondel], Danl le Get, Pierre Allez, young Pierre [Nicolle], our two oxen, our two horses & Nico Breton's horse. Nico Breton also lent us his plough for part of the day, as ours sustained some minor damage. In all, there were 12 men & boys, 8 oxen & ten horses.

Mon 9 Mar: the weather deteriorated yesterday evening, & today was a day of gales & hail. [...] Between 8 o'clock & midnight yesterday, a Dutch ship of about 100 tons sailing from Lisbon to Antwerp was wrecked in Cobo Bay. She had a crew of eight.

Thurs 12 Mar: [...] Stormy, with westerly gales & downpours of rain & hail. The gales have brought down one of the pine trees in la Daumaillerie garden, leaving only two of them there. They have also completely uprooted a large female elm.

Sat 14 Mar: I breakfasted at Mary's then attended Court as a witness in support of Pierre Catline's petition for separation from his wife. No evidence was taken. Instead, they were both sent before a Commissioner to negotiate an agreement.

Sun 15 Mar: [...] Danl le Get & Pierre Allez dined with us. I was expecting Pierre Catline & his children, but they did not come. Monsieur Marie came unexpectedly for coffee.

Weds 18 Mar: I walked to town intending to pay a visit to Mr Brock (Wm), who arrived the day before yesterday, but I did not see him. The Receivers were farming out the King's tithes at Mr Cheminant's in les Rohais. Mr Josias

Le Marchant has for a long time had those of the Castel (at 1600 francs) & has sub-let the district of le Nanage to me. However, Jean Trachy & Danl le Mesurier bid up the price this morning, & the latter secured the Castel tithes for himself for the next 3 years.

Fri 20 Mar: [...] Pierre Catline & his 3 children came here after dinner & stayed until 7 o'clock. The Court has separated him from his wife. She left his house the day before yesterday. Mrs Carey of the Grange,[652] Mr Jean le Cocq & Messrs la Serre & Carré (the Commissioners) oversaw the division of their furniture. Pierre is to give his wife 4s 6d per week. At his request, he is also to keep custody of the children, who will be permitted to visit their mother twice weekly for an hour at a time.[653]

Mon 23 Mar: the Castel Regiment & Black Regiment were ordered to assemble at the Vale church at half past eight prior to a Review. Notwithstanding the threatening weather, they went as instructed, but they were dismissed after a downpour at around 10 o'clock. The Governor never appeared.

Tues 24 Mar: [...] Monsieur Marie, Mr Mesurier of Gaspé (see the 3rd), Eleazar [Ingrouille] & Pierre Catline came to dinner. Pierre brought his 3 children with him. They stayed in the kitchen.

Fri 27 Mar: Jean Roland, a Frenchman from la Hague, started working here today. I will pay him 12s per month, with board, lodging & laundry.

Sun 29 Mar: Danl F[erbrache] came in the morning to bring us 6 lb of cocoa which was damaged by sea water when the ship was wrecked 3 weeks ago. He returned here after church. Later, his nephews Isac & Hellier [Nicolle] (brothers of our young Pierre) brought us another 6 lb of cocoa. His daughter (aged 4) stayed here all day. Danl & the children all dined here & left together around six. I paid them 6d per lb for the cocoa.

---

[652] For 'Mrs Carey of the Grange', see n. 642, above.
[653] Pierre Cateline's wife, Margueritte, *née* Rougier, married another man while only judicially separated from Pierre. In 1821, she was prosecuted for bigamy in the Royal Court. In her defence, she asserted that Pierre had ill-treated her during their marriage, a circumstance corroborated by a number of witnesses (*L'Indépendance*, 27.1.1821).

Mon 30 Mar: [...] Fine, warm weather. Ab's little girl started school today.[654]

Sat 4 Apr: I walked to town, where I bought 2 pairs of English-made shoes at 4s 6d per pair, & a few other small articles to send to the eldest son of Jean B[rehaut] of les Moullins who is in Canso [Nova Scotia]. I also bought some kitchen vegetable seeds to send to Mr O'Hara in Gaspé.[655]

Thurs 9 Apr: [...] Monsieur Marie came to dinner at 5 o'clock with Monsieur Chandepie de Boiviers, an artist from Paris, whom I went to see on Saturday.[656] He is about 50 years old. He was born in Jersey & lived there for a few years. He is the nephew of the late Docteur Chandepie & Mme Girard of Verson near Caen, where I probably saw him when I was there with Peter Mourant in 17....

Sat 11 Apr: Thos loaded the two square cases on board Mr Mesurier's ship which is bound for Gaspé. As well as bottles, the one for Mr O'Harra contains 17 different sorts of kitchen vegetable seeds. Henry [Blondel]'s case contains various small items I thought might be useful to him.

Mon 13 Apr: [...] Jean Roland, who started here on 27 March & has been drunk on our premises several times since, came back exceedingly intoxicated yesterday evening, so I paid him a month's wages after breakfast this morning & dismissed him. Mrs Kinsela sent one of the Miss Du Maresqs to tell me she has learned that Mr Kinsela died 2 years ago at Botany Bay, to which he had been banished.[657]

---

[654] Elizabeth Machon was six years old.
[655] This may have been one of the sons of Felix O'Hara (1732–1805), an early and highly successful settler in Gaspé, who had been involved in the Newfoundland cod fishery and had connections to Channel Islanders similarly engaged.
[656] The artist was Jean-Charles Chandepie de Boiviers (1764–1830), a French miniaturist.
[657] 'Mrs Kinsela' was the former Marie Moullin (sister of Nicolas Moullin of les Vallées). She had married Enoch Kinsella (a twenty-nine-year-old Irishman otherwise known as John Murphy) in 1799. In 1803, Kinsella was convicted of fraud and sentenced by the Royal Court to six years' banishment. Leaving Marie in Guernsey, Kinsella went to serve his banishment in Worcester, where – despite already having a wife – he married an Englishwoman. The first Mrs Kinsella's continued existence in Guernsey eventually came to light and in 1805, Enoch was tried for bigamy at Worcester Assizes. His prior conviction for fraud compounding his conviction for bigamy, he was sentenced to seven years' transportation to Botany Bay (HO 46/37/32, National Archives).

Fri 17 Apr: [...] I breakfasted with Mary & Mr [William] Brock, then paid a long visit to Sophy [Mourant], & returned here at midday.

Sun 19 Apr: Pierre Catline & his 3 children dined here, as also Ed. Masters & his wife (Rachel de la Rue), who were formerly servants at Candie & now lodge at Pierre's house.[658]

Tues 21 Apr: the two-year-old black heifer which should have calved on the 7th showed signs of distress yesterday evening, so we watched her all night. At seven in the morning, Thos went to fetch Sr [Nicolas] du Four from the Forest, but before he could get back with him, the cow calved & seemed to be doing well. Eleazar also came here. Mr Pelley (Thos) called to see me at around 10 o'clock.

Weds 22 Apr: I breakfasted at Mary's, where Monsieur Marie & Eleazar joined me at 10 o'clock. We looked over Mary's garden together, then went to Candie & made a tour of the garden with Peter. Just as we were leaving Candie, the Governor (General Bayley), to whom I had never spoken, arrived. He had come on purpose to meet me, so I was obliged to stay & make his acquaintance. I went to his house with Peter, Sophy, &c., to see the preparations for a party he is giving tomorrow to celebrate the Prince Regent's birthday. I returned here at 2 o'clock feeling very tired & went straight to bed.

Sun 26 Apr: the Procureur & young James, the Bailiff & his son, Messrs Harry Dobrée, Tom Macculloch, Nico le Fevre & Lempriere came to breakfast. I was so tired that I went to bed as soon as they were gone & stayed there until 5 o'clock.

Thurs 7 May: [...] Towards noon I went to le Valet (one of the cherry orchards at St George) to meet an old woman of 95 or 96 who was a servant of my Dear Mother's before I was born. She is in good health & enjoys admirable faculties of both body & mind for her age. I also went to see Mr Guille, whom I found very bent.[659]

---

[658] Pierre Cateline owned a house in Vauvert on the outskirts of town.
[659] Jean Guille of St George was by now eighty-four years old.

Thurs 14 May: [...] Nicolas Brouard (my former farm servant) took tea here.[660] He was in Jersey for many years but has lately moved back to Guernsey with his wife. Their daughter married Mr Dumaresq the printer 3 years ago. She lives with her aunt Mrs Rawlins, who brought her up & from whom she will inherit. Mrs Rawlins has at least £4000 stg in the Funds & life enjoyment of her house in Vauvert.

Sun 17 May: [...] Mary called to see me around noon with Sophie Dobrée & Frederick Le Mesurier, who have lately arrived.[661]

Tues 19 May: [...] Monsieur Marie dined with me. Just as we were taking coffee, Peter, Sophy & little Tom le M[archant] joined us for an hour. Cold, dull weather.

Sat 23 May: [...] Pierre Machon, who returned 8 or 10 days ago from a voyage to Havana, dined with us.

Tues 26 May: [...] Sr .... Brouard, the bonesetter from St Peter, put back one of the hips of the bullock which was castrated on the 18th.

Weds 27 May: [...] Sr .... Brouard came to look at the bullock again & found that his hip was holding well. I paid him 5 shillings. Pierre Cateline dined with us.

Sun 31 May: [...] Pierre Cateline & his son dined with us, as also Isac [Marquand]. Monsieur Marie took coffee here. Pierre Cateline has taken Isac back into his employ (after falling out with him a fortnight ago), but I do not think I can ever fully reconcile them. This is the 4th consecutive week I have also invited James Cateline to dinner. Each time, he has promised to come. I was hoping to confront him with the bad consequences of his behaviour & persuade him to return to his wife, or at least help maintain their child, &c. He has never come & I fear there is no mending him.

Mon 1 Jun: [...] Mr Wm Brock paid me a visit before noon. He will shortly leave for England.

---

[660] Nicolas Brouard had worked for Mollet between 1773 and 1776.
[661] For Mollet's great-nephew by marriage, Frederick Le Mesurier, see n. 522, above. For Mollet's great-niece, Sophia Dobrée, see n. 614.

Weds 3 Jun: […] I rode to town on the young mare this morning [&] paid short visits to Mr Etienne, to Mrs Dan Dobrée (at Harry's), as also to Candie & to Mary (who is lodging at Mr Askew's).

Fri 5 Jun: […] Mr Savery Brock (who arrived on Sunday after 14 months in America & England) took coffee with me.

Mon 8 Jun: […] Cut grass. Picked up cowpats. [The Revd] Mr Tom Brock, his wife, their children Wm & Ann, Mr Wm de Jersey & Mr Savery Brock took coffee with me.

Tues 9 Jun: […] Thos [Blondel] & Pierre Allez cut the hay at the bottom of les Grands Tuzets. Pierre Barbelet (a 22-year-old Frenchman whom I will only employ for a few days) tedded it.

Weds 10 Jun: […] I went to Pierre's school to thank Mr Berry & let him know him that Pierre would be leaving this week.[662] […] Abraham Blondel (Thomas's brother, aged 15) & Jemmy Torode (Suzon Colnette's eldest son) have both started working here.

Fri 12 Jun: […] Thos & young Pierre […] delivered […] a ham, 4 pullets & six bottles of wine to Mr Berry (Pierre's former schoolmaster).

Sat 13 Jun: to town towards noon but I did not stay long. I paid 24s 2d to Mr Poore, Treasurer of the National School which Pierre attended from 8 July 1816.[663] Lisabo walked to town with Thos who went to sell a calf. The calf did not sell well. Thos brought back about 35 lb of meat.

Tues 16 Jun: […] Little Hellier Nicolle (Pierre's brother), little Judith Ferbrache (Danl's daughter) & little Mary Ann le Cheminant dined here & spent the afternoon with little Margueritte [Ozanne] & Betsy [Machon]. Lisabo picked 6 lb of strawberries for them to eat.

Mon 22 Jun: […] Put 14 dozen bottles of the Murviedro wine we bottled on 10 June in the vault (directly on the floor at the top, opposite the door).

---

[662] Pierre Nicolle was now thirteen years old.
[663] For John Poore, see n. 478, above.

Stored another 43 bottles under lock & key in the parlour. Started distilling rose water (24 bottles).

Weds 24 Jun: [...] Yesterday, our neighbour Thos le Prevost (the blacksmith) gave us a young bitch, whom I have named 'Volage'. She came to them by chance. She is .... in colour, with a blackish muzzle. She seems to be what they call a 'pug' or rather a 'Grand's bulldog'. We still have our good little Sapho, but she is old & deaf (perhaps ...... years old), so she will probably not live much longer.

Thurs 25 Jun: [...] Ab's sister (Thos Allez's wife) [...] came to pay me 35 shillings for their first quarter's rent of the two top floors of the upper house at la Profonde Rue. Four quarters at 35s per quarter would amount only to £7 stg, but Pierre Cateline told me he had agreed a rent of £7 10s, together with .... shillings for the small garden by the stable.

Sat 27 Jun: [...] Pierre Cateline came at 9 o'clock yesterday evening & brought me £4 15s from Mrs Christian for her quarter's rent (£3 15s for the lower house & £1 stg for the kitchen of the upper house). I sent 14 fowls to market, which Lisabo sold at 5s for two. She also had some potatoes to sell.

Sun 28 Jun: the Bailiff, Captn [Charles] De Havilland, Miss De Havilland, the Procureur, Mrs De Sausmarez & Captn [Charles] Chepmell came to breakfast. The Procureur's sons John & James are about to leave for Cherbourg, whence they will go to Caen for 3 or 4 months. Pierre Barbelet slept on the hay last night & breakfasted here. He returned in the evening to sleep here again.

Tues 30 Jun: [...] Young Pierre [Nicolle] went mackerel fishing with his uncles Daniel & Thomas [Ferbrache].

Thurs 2 Jul: young Pierre returned from fishing at 10 o'clock after being at sea since Tuesday. He was not sick, & his uncles gave him a dozen mackerel. [...] I went to town in the morning & [...] called at Sous la Porte, having learned of Miss Henriette [Le Marchant]'s engagement to Colonel Octavius Carey.[664]

Fri 3 Jul: [...] I went to see Marthe & Henriette Dobrée at le Frie Baton, where they are staying for a few weeks.[665]

Sat 4 Jul: [...] I went to see Mrs Le M[archant] at la Haye du Puits about organising a subscription for Nico Roussel of les Roussiaux, two of whose horses have recently died.

Weds 8 Jul: [...] Daniel & Thomas Ferbrache sent us 200 fine mackerel for 10 shillings per 100. We gave some of the roe to Etienne [Lihou], Pierre Allez, Suzon Brouard & Danl le Get (who came here today).

Thurs 9 Jul: [...] Pierre Cateline, his apprentice Pierre Tosdevin & his labourer Matth. Tosdevin came to work on the dormer window of the rear garret (they are covering the sides with slates rather than plaster). We also had the seamstress here. Together with Suzon's brother & sister who came here with Betsy at midday, there were 19 of us for dinner.

Sat 18 Jul: Pierre Cateline dined here (as also on Thursday & Friday). Young Pierre [Nicolle] went to le Frie Baton. Mr Robt Le Marchant paid me a visit towards evening. He & his family are residing at the Castel from today. We picked more than 30 cucumbers (our 1st).

Mon 20 Jul: [...] Pierre Cateline dined here. I went to le Frie Baton, where Mary is staying for a few days.

Tues 21 Jul: [...] Lisabo went to le Frie Baton. She baked bread yesterday evening, & made wonders this morning & biscuits this evening.

Fri 24 Jul: Savery Brock & an English botanist named Mr Smith (from London, I believe) breakfasted with me. I escorted them part of the way back

---

[664] Harriet (Henriette) Le Marchant was the twenty-five-year-old daughter of former Bailiff Robert Le Marchant, whose town residence was 'Sous la Porte' at the top of the High Street (see n. 556, above). Octavius Carey (1785–1844) was the younger brother of Mollet's niece by marriage Sophia Mourant.

[665] Mollet's great-niece Harriet (1793–1834) was married to her cousin Dr William Brock (see n. 592, above). Her eldest sister Martha (1788–1848) died unmarried.

& called to see Mr & Mrs Robt Le Marchant before returning home. Mrs Geo. Bell & Mrs Jean took coffee & fruit with me. Mrs Jean (the widow of the painter) is the daughter of my cousin Jean de St Croix & Rachel Cartault. She is also my god-daughter.[666]

Sun 26 Jul: the Bailiff, Captn De Havilland, Miss De Havilland, the Procureur, Mrs De S[ausmarez], Miss Henriette De S[ausmarez], Mr Tom Maculloch, Mr Dan Brock & Mr Smith (see Friday) breakfasted with me. [...] It rained a little in the morning, which prevented the ladies from leaving, so I sat with them until after midday, when the Bailiff's carriage came to collect them. All the gentlemen went to church. Pierre Machon, who arrived on Thursday from Hamburg (see 23 May), dined here. Monsieur Marie took coffee & raspberries here.

Fri 31 Jul: [...] Ab. B[londel] & Jemmy T[orode] gathered up the dry cowpats at les Tuzets & le Courtil Robin.

[*Charles Mollet turned seventy-six during the course of August 1818*]

Sat 1 Aug: [...] I told [Daniel Le Geyt and Pierre Allez] that, after this month, I would reduce their wages by a penny a day. This means that Danl le Get will only have 8d per day, which he appeared to consent to (or at least he said nothing). Pierre Allez, however, said that a reduction of a penny represented 2d less than he could get elsewhere, & that he already considered himself underpaid, having started here at 10d a day. So I told him that he could leave & that I would not expect him back.

Here Charles Mollet's journal ends abruptly. The next eleven pages (twenty-two sides) have been cut out, although the stubs remain, with fragments of Mollet's writing on them. After these eleven stubs, the remaining pages of the volume are blank. Twenty-two sides would typically contain about six months of Mollet's journal at this period. This would bring the diary up to January 1819. Before he began his journal for 1818, Mollet left several blank pages which he filled with occasional notes as the year went on. These notes refer to the whole of 1818, and there is even a note dated 6 January 1819, in which Mollet recorded that he had sowed some rose seed in a flower pot.

---

[666] Marie De Ste Croix was baptised in St Helier in 1763. She had married the miniaturist Philippe Jean in 1788.

Charles Mollet died on Sunday 28 February 1819. He was buried in the Castel churchyard, a mile from his home, on 9 March 1819. Sadly, his precise resting-place is unknown, as inscriptions on the expensive (but soft) stone used for elite monuments have weathered away, and there is no contemporary cemetery plan. In an ironic twist of fate, the humble headstone of his servants Abraham and Elizabeth Machon – plain but robust – still bears its inscription for all to see.

Charles Mollet died without issue, so his property passed, as per Guernsey law, to his collateral male heirs (nephews and great-nephews). They put Mollet's farm up for auction, and in May 1820 it was purchased by the Irish Napoleonic veteran Colonel Ambrose Lane.[667] Colonel Lane, who began the process of extending and modifying the house, lived there with his wife and family until 1844.[668] From 1844 onwards, the property passed through many disparate hands up to the present day. It is now known as 'Woodlands'. The 'upper' house, which Mollet had sold to the Machons in 1815, was handed down through successive generations of the Sarre family (into which the Machons' daughter Elizabeth married) until well into the twentieth century. It is now known as 'Vau des Vallées'.

---

[667] 31.5.1820, Contrats pour Lire, Greffe.
[668] 19.10.1844, Contrats pour Lire, Greffe.

Appendix 1
Mollet family tree, ascending

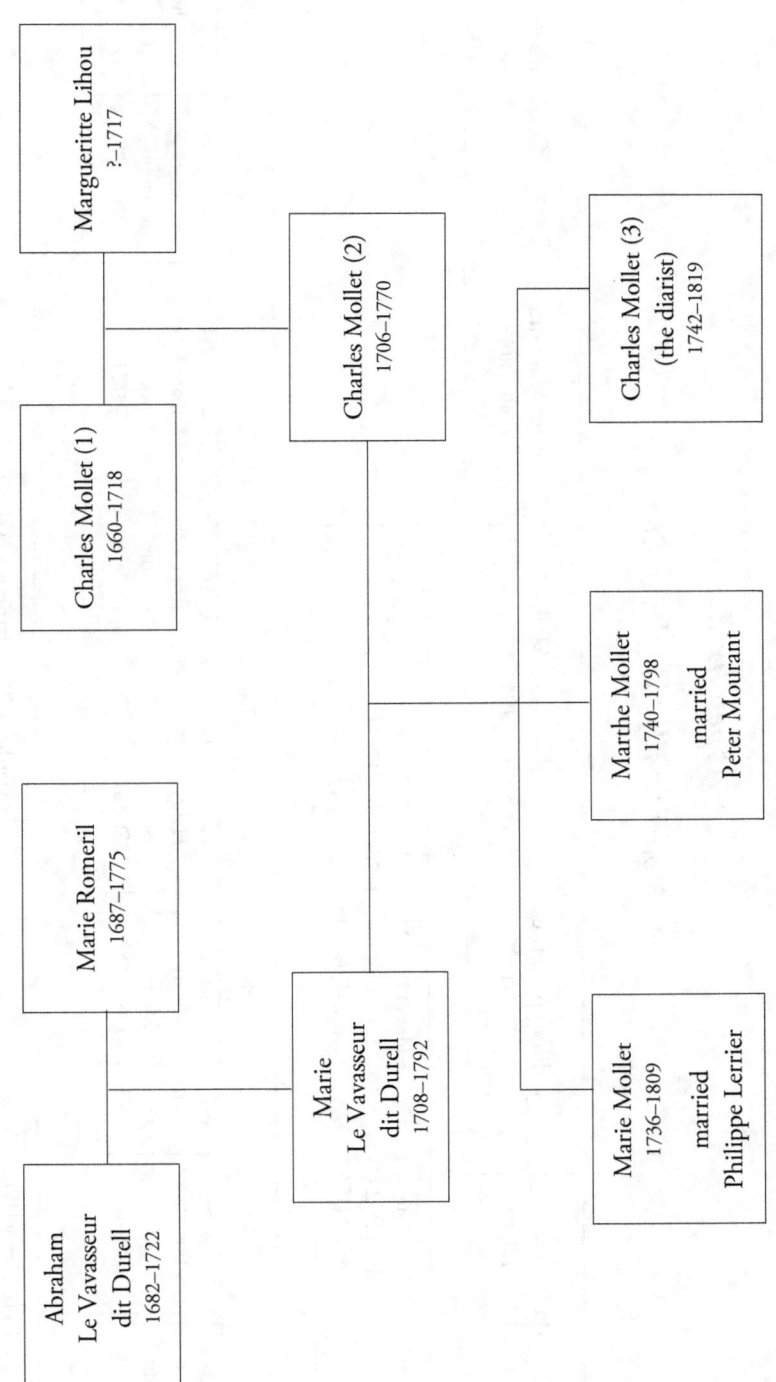

Appendix 2
Mollet family tree, descending

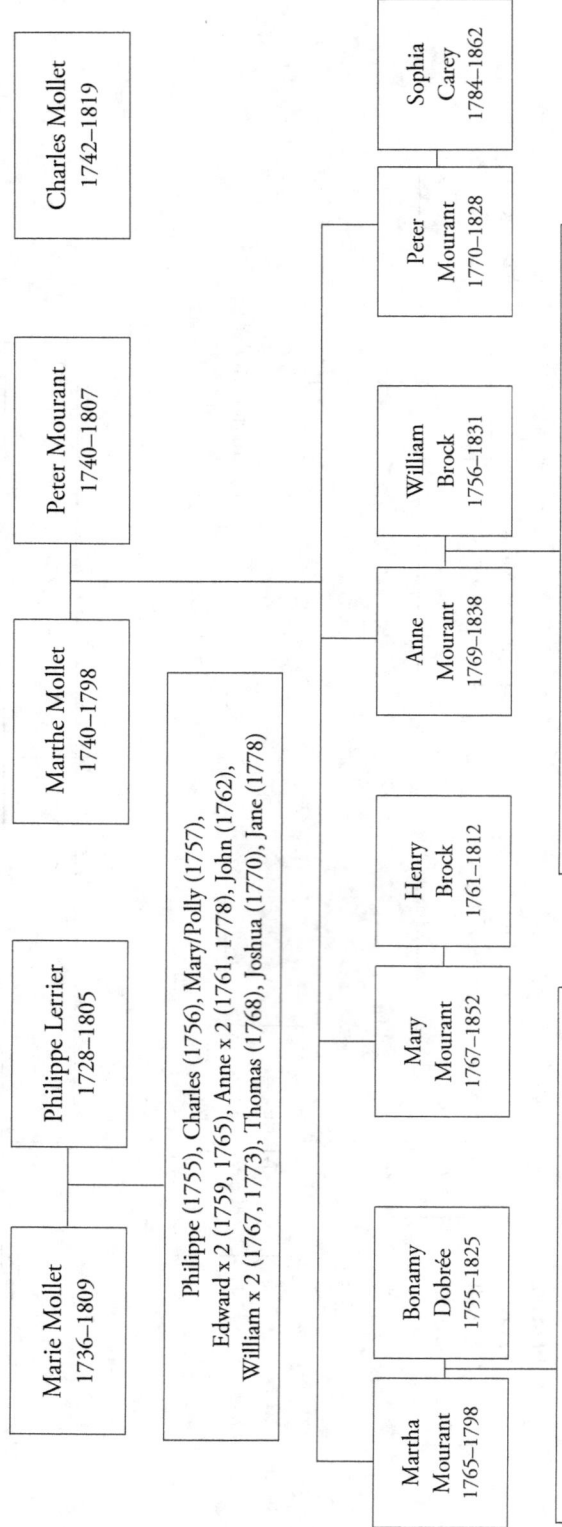

Appendix 3

Composition of principal families associated with Mollet

These outlines are based on Edith Carey's handwritten genealogies held at the Priaulx Library.

Brock

William Brock (1725–1768) married Judith De Beauvoir (1730–1776)

William was a brother of John Brock (1730–1777), father of the large family which included Bailiff Daniel De Lisle Brock, Major-General Sir Isaac Brock, John Savery Brock, Irving Brock and Mary Brock (wife of Thomas Potenger). This made the Brocks who married Mollet's nieces first cousins of the more famous Brocks.

Children of William Brock and Judith De Beauvoir:

Mary Brock (1752–1800) wife of *Jean Carey of 'Choisi'*, for whom see below
Martha Brock (1753–?)
William Brock (1756–1831) husband of Mollet's niece *Anne Mourant*
Judith Brock (1758–1816) wife of *Dr Jean [De] Sau[s]marez*, for whom see below
Henry Brock (1761–1812) husband of Mollet's niece *Mary Mourant*
Harriet Brock (1763–1858) wife of *Sir Thomas Saumarez*, for whom see below
James Brock (1767–1805)

Carey

Jean Carey of 'Choisi' (1748–1821) married Mary Brock (1752–1800)

Jean Carey and Mary Brock had twelve children, including:

Rev. *Thomas Carey* (1772–1849), Rector of St Saviour, husband of Mary Maingy
Captain *William Carey* (1776–1808)
Mary Carey (1779–1864), wife of *Rev. Thomas Brock* (1777–1850),
    Rector of St Peter

Dobrée (of 'Bellevue')

Nicolas Dobrée (1732–1800) married (1) Susanne Le Pelley
                                    (2) Elizabeth Gilchrist

Children of Nicolas Dobrée and Susanne Le Pelley:

Elizabeth Dobrée (1753–1826) wife of *Rudolf Utermarck*
Daniel Dobrée (1754–1814), Captain, RN
Rev. Nicolas Dobrée (1755–1843), Castel Rector
Peter Dobrée (1756–1843)
Charles Dobrée (1757–1780)
Susanna Dobrée (1759–1843), wife of *John Siegfried Fischer*
Augustus Dobrée (1760–1845)
Mary Dobrée (1762–1791), wife of *William Piercy*

Children of Nicolas Dobrée and Elizabeth Gilchrist:

Thomas Godfrey Dobrée (1770–1851), husband of *Mary Waugh*
Harry Dobrée (1771–1851)

Dobrée (of 'Beauregard')

Pierre Dobrée (1722–1808) married Rachel Bonamy (1731–1798)

Children of Pierre Dobrée and Rachel Bonamy:

Mary Dobrée (1754–1825)
Bonamy Dobrée (1755–1825), husband of Mollet's niece *Martha Mourant*
Elisha Dobrée (1756–1844), diarist
Samuel Dobrée (1759–1827), banker in London
Peter Dobrée (1760–1843)
Hellier Dobrée (1761–1847)
Henry Dobrée (1762–1766)
Rachel Dobrée (1764–1842), wife of *Philip Bainbrigge*
John Dobrée (1766–1812)
Elizabeth Dobrée (1777–1845), wife of *Philip Melvill*

De Havilland

Generation 1
Jean De Havilland (1706–1770) married Marie Dobrée (1712–1763)

Jean De Havilland and Marie Dobrée had eight children, including:

Catherine De Havilland (1731–1810), wife of Thomas Dobrée
Mary De Havilland (1732–1820), wife of Thomas Smith, mother of
  George Smith
John De Havilland (1734–1810), husband of Mary Dobrée
James De Havilland (1739–1783), husband of Anne Bonamy
Martin De Havilland (1746–1806), HM Prévôt 1777–1806
Peter De Havilland (1747–1821), Bailiff 1810–1821

Generation 2
Peter De Havilland (1747–1821) married (1) Carterette Fiott
*   (2) Emilia Tupper*

Peter De Havilland and Carterette Fiott had seven children, including:

Carterette De Havilland (1772–1844), wife of *George Smith*, mother of
  Sophia Smith and *Mary Harriet Smith*
Catherine De Havilland (1773–1860), wife of HM Procureur
  Thomas De Sausmarez (for whom see below)
Thomas Fiott De Havilland (1775–1866), Jurat 1846–1856, husband of
  Elizabeth De Sausmarez (daughter of HM Procureur
  Thomas De Sausmarez, for whom see below)
Anne De Havilland (1778–1847)
Charles De Havilland (1786–1844), military officer, husband of
  Martha Saumarez (daughter of Dr Richard Saumarez, for whom see below)
Mary De Havilland (1789–1854)

Peter De Havilland and Emilia Tupper had no children

De Sausmarez/Saumarez

Dr Matthew De Sausmarez (1719–78) married   (1) Susanne Dumaresq
                                                           (2) Carterette Le Marchant

Matthew De Sausmarez and Susanne Dumaresq had only one child:

Susanne De Sausmarez (1743–1830), mother of Rev. Thomas Brock

Children of Matthew De Sausmarez and Carterette Le Marchant:

Anne [De] Sau[s]marez (1752–1846)
Dr Jean [De] Sau[s]marez (1755–1832), husband of *Judith Brock*
Admiral Sir James Saumarez (1757–1832)
General Sir Thomas Saumarez (1760–1845), husband of *Harriet Brock*
Charlotte [De] Sau[s]marez (1763–1860), wife of *Rev. Nicolas Dobrée*
Dr Richard Saumarez (1764–1835)

It is thought that Thomas and James changed their surname from 'De Sausmarez' to 'Saumarez' in order to make it appear less French to the British forces in which they served. Richard, an English-based surgeon, followed his brothers' example, and – by analogy – the name change was sometimes extended to their Guernsey-based siblings.

Dr Matthew De Sausmarez was a brother of HM Procureur Jean De Sausmarez (1706-74), the father of Mollet's friend Thomas De Sausmarez, who became HM Procureur in 1793. Matthew's children were thus all first cousins of HM Procureur Thomas De Sausmarez (1756–1837).

Thomas De Sausmarez (1756–1837) married   (1) Martha Dobrée
                                                     (2) Catherine De Havilland

Thomas De Sausmarez and Martha Dobrée had eleven children, including:

Elizabeth De Sausmarez (1782–1818), wife of *Thomas Fiott De Havilland*
John De Sausmarez (1790–1870), HM Comptroller 1830–1845, Jurat 1847–1870

Thomas De Sausmarez and Catherine De Havilland had seventeen children, including:

Catherine De Sausmarez (1797–1851)
Durell De Sausmarez (1800–1859)
Anne De Sausmarez (1801–1872)
Rose De Sausmarez (1802–1841)
James De Sausmarez (1806–1846)

Guille

Generation 1
Jean Guille, sen. (1711–1778) married Elizabeth Andros (1708–1788)

Jean Guille, sen. and Elizabeth Andros had ten children, including:

Jean Guille, jun. (1733–1820)
Thomas Guille (1737–1796)
Nicolas Guille (1742–1807), merchant based in Barcelona, father of *Caroline Guille* (1777–1801)
Charles Guille (1743–?)
Dr Richard Guille (1745–1818)
Rachel Guille (1751–1803), Mollet's 'Miss Guille', who died unmarried

Generation 2
Jean Guille, jun. (1733–1820) married Marie De Carteret (1737–1792)

Jean Guille, jun. and Marie De Carteret had four children:

Carterette Guille (1760–1807)
Esther Guille (1762–1839)
William Guille (1766–1792)
George Guille (1768–1792)

Generation 3

Carterette Guille (1760–1807) married *Nathaniel Le Cocq* (1750–1800) and had five children

Esther Guille (1762–1839) married *Jean Carey Metivier* (1758–1796) and had six children, including the poet and lexicographer *George Metivier* (1790-1881) and the Jurat *William Metivier* (1791–1883)

William Guille (1766–1792) married *Rachel Andros* (1766–1798) and had three children, including *John Guille* (1788–1845) who became Bailiff in 1843, and *Rev. William Guille* (1792–1869) who married Mollet's great-niece *Judith Brock* and became Dean of Guernsey in 1862

Appendix 4

Frequently mentioned employees of Mollet's

Etienne Lihou (1742–1832)
Son of Thomas Lihou and Judith Breton; husband of Marie Le Page
Day labourer for the entire span of the diaries

Pierre Gavet (1752–1818)
Son of Etienne Gavet and Marthe Cohu; husband of Marie Nicolle (and later Judith Tostevin)
Farm servant 1775–1787

Eleazar Ingrouille (1766–1832)
Son of Paul Ingrouille and Anne Ingrouille; husband of Elizabeth Robert
Day labourer from the early 1780s onwards (latterly only occasionally)

Abraham Machon (1770–1835)
Son of Abraham Machon, sen. and Elizabeth Ingrouille; brother of Pierre Machon and Daniel Machon; husband of Elizabeth Le Ray
Farm servant 1789–1790, 1792 onwards

Elizabeth (Lisabo) Le Ray (1775–1850)
Daughter of Nicolas Le Ray and Marie Le Page; wife of Abraham Machon
Domestic servant from 1793 onwards

Daniel Ferbrache (1782–1851)
Son of Jean Ferbrache and Rachel Nicolle; husband of Judith Trachy
Farm servant 1798–1805

Pierre Cateline (1783–1824)
Son of Jean Cateline, sen. and Thomasse Gallienne; brother of Jean Cateline and James Cateline
Day labourer 1796–1798, January–May 1809

Jean Cateline (1786–1812)
Son of Jean Cateline, sen. and Thomasse Gallienne; brother of Pierre Cateline and James Cateline
Farm servant 1806–1812

Appendix 5

Relatedness of Mollet's employees*
(*employees' names are capitalised)

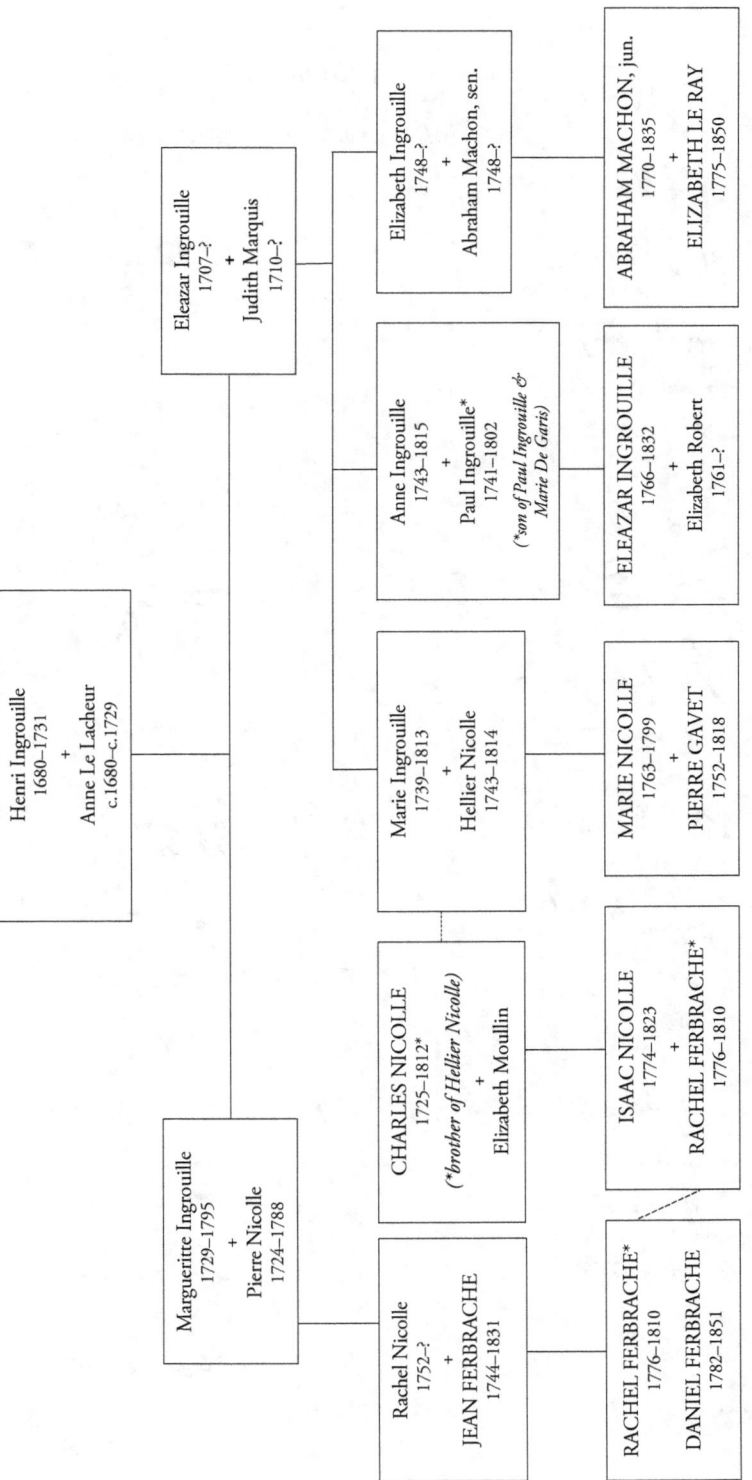

Appendix 6
Mollet's symbols and codes

A. 20 May 1773

B. 19 August 1773

C. 5 May 1776

D. 28 June 1776

E. 9 June 1777

F. 21 October 1778

G. 18 and 19 May 1780

H. 1 September 1780

Mollet's symbols and codes 425

I. 8 December 1780

J. 27 December 1780

K. 11 February 1785

L. 14 November 1794

M. 27 April 1796

N. 7 September 1799

O. 20 April 1802

P. 30 March 1803

Q. 10 February 1804

R. 21 February 1811

426 *The Journal of Charles Mollet (1742–1819): A Selection*

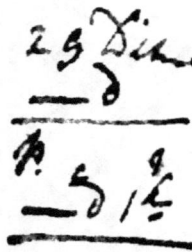

S. 29 March 1812

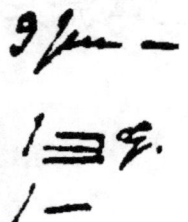

T. 9 November 1815

U. 10 March 1816

V. 9 June 1816

W. 18 July 1817

X. 26 July 1817

Y. 10 April 1818

Z. 9 June 1818

Appendix 7

French émigrés mentioned by Mollet

An effort has been made to identify *émigrés* who socialised with Charles Mollet using online resources, lists preserved at the National Archives (Kew), and the following reference works:

D.A. Bellenger, *The French Exiled Clergy in the British Isles after 1789* (Bath, 1986)
R. de l'Estourbeillon, *Les Familles Françaises à Jersey pendant la Révolution* (Nantes, 1886)
H. Forneron, *Histoire Générale des Emigrés pendant la Révolution Française*, 2 vols (Paris, 1884)
C. Hettier, *Relations de la Normandie et de la Bretagne avec les Iles de la Manche pendant l'Emigration* (Caen, 1885)
J. Vidalenc, *Les Emigrés Français, 1789–1825* (Caen, 1963)

Where it has been impossible to identify an *émigré*, the individual's name is rendered exactly as Mollet gave it. Dates of first mention follow each individual.

1. Paul-Christophe de Robien (1731–99), Marquis de Robien of le Fœil in Brittany **9.8.89**
2. le Comte du Parc **9.4.91**
3. le Comte de Kernel **9.4.91**
4. le Chevalier de Médic **9.4.91**
5. Charles-François du Bot du Grégo, Marquis de la Roche (1741–1812) **12.9.91**
6. Louis-François-Joseph de Bourbon, Comte de la Marche (1734–1814) **4.10.91**
7. Thomas-François de Beaudrap, Seigneur de Biville **17.10.91**
8. Catherine-Vincente Barbier, Comtesse de Lescoët **26.4.92**
9. Marie-Jeanne-Aimée Poulpiquet, Comtesse de Coatlez **26.4.92**
10. Monsieur le Moine, Curé of St Agnan **26.9.92**
11. Monsieur le Moine, Curé of Hubert-Folie **26.9.92**
12. Jean-Charles Dancel (1762–1836), Curé of Valognes **17.2.93**
13. Monsieur Groult, Curé of Néhou **14.3.93**
14. Monsieur Groult (a priest, nephew of the above) **14.3.93**
15. Monsieur d'Urville (probably a member of the Dumont d'Urville family from Urville, near Caen) **16.4.93**
16. Monsieur d'Urville (another member of the same family) **16.4.93**
17. Jean-François Bourdon (born 1744), Seigneur deVerson **7.5.93**

18. Bertrand Faure (1758–95), Seigneur de Saint-Romain-de-Colbosc in Normandy **7.6.93**
19. Joseph-Jean-Baptiste du Trévou, a Royalist executed in Vannes in 1795 **12.6.93**
20. Monsieur Chapel (a priest) **17.6.93**
21. Pierre Bourget, Curé of Noyal-sur-Vilaine in Brittany **17.6.93**
22. Monsieur Vardonne **4.7.93**
23. Monsieur de St Fraquaire **4.7.93**
24. Monsieur de la Valinerie **4.7.93**
25. Monsieur de la Valinerie (son of the above) **4.7.93**
26. Monsieur le Tellier (Mons. de la Valinerie's nephew, who may have been the priest Louis-Sébastien Le Tellier, known to have died in Jersey in 1794) **4.7.93**
27. Ferdinand-Georges-Amable de la Roque, Comte de Ménillet **26.7.93**
28. Jean-Marie-René de Leuvre de Qu[i]erqueville **7.11.93**
29. René-Charles de Percy, Seigneur de Tonneville (1748–95) **2.1.94**
30. Monsieur Sauvegrain, Curé of Secqueville-en-Bessin **22.5.94**
31. Denis Jallobert de Monville (1758–1819) **19.6.94**
32. Dominique Jallobert de Monville (1767–1837) **19.6.94**
33. Monsieur du Sausé **15.7.94**
34. Monsieur de la Foidre, Curé of Moisville **27.7.94**
35. Monsieur de la Foidre, Curé of Boissy-Lamberville **27.7.94**
36. Monsieur Du Fou **25.8.94**
37. Adolphe-Charles de Mauconvenant (1743–1829) **14.9.94**
38. Bonaventure-Corentin de Mauconvenant (1767–95) **14.9.94**
39. Monsieur de Barneville **14.9.94**
40. Gilles de Carné-Trécesson (c.1759–95) **11.11.94**
41. Monsieur de Bergerac **4.12.94**
42. Armand de Chateaubriand (1768–1809) **21.2.95**
43. Monsieur de Belfonds **21.2.95**
44. Gaspard-Pierre de Morel de Than (1760–1843) **5.5.95**
45. Abbé François-Philippe Vattier (1765–1802) of Lisieux **6.5.95**
46. Monsieur de Pirey **16.5.95**
47. Jacques-Louis-Gabriel du Mesnildot (1760–1821) **16.5.95**
48. Anne de Blégier Pierre Grosse, Baronne de la Garde (1767–1836) **26.5.95**
49. Pierre-Henri de Blangy (1756–1823) **7.6.95**
50. Auguste-Pierre de Blangy (1766–1827) **7.6.95**
51. Pierre-Constantin de Blangy (1722–1800) **or** his son Bon-Henri de Blangy (1775–1827) **7.6.95**
52. René-Jean Paris, assistant parish priest of Janzé (diocese of Rennes) **22.10.95**
53. Monsieur Morvan (a priest) **22.10.95**

54. Gabriel-Charles-Marie Levieil de la Marsonnière (1775–1808) **13.11.95**
55. Monsieur de la Cour **11.12.95**
56. Félix-Barnabé Yvetot (1764–1809), parish priest of Saint-Eny (Coutances) **11.12.95**
57. Monsieur de Rouville **11.12.95**
58. Armand-Mériadec Le Gonidec de Traissan (1752–1814) **18.12.95**
59. Balthazar-Hyacinthe Le Gonidec de Traissan (1754–1817) **18.12.95**
60. Monsieur de Blanville **21.12.95**
61. Marie-Pierre-Jean Le Tellier de Vaubadon (1768–1844) **14.1.96**
62. Marc-Antoine Le Bachelier (1751–1816), Seigneur de Saon **20.1.96**
63. Jean-François de Hercé (1776–1849), nephew of Urbain-René de Hercé, Bishop of Dol **23.2.96**
64. Jean-Baptiste Le Vicomte de la Houssaye (1732–1810) **6.3.96**
65. Renaud de la Houssaye (born 1779) **6.3.96**
66. Claude-Antoine Coulon (1746–1820), former vicar-general of Nevers and royal chaplain **13.3.96**
67. Alexandre de Ricouart, Comte d'Hérouville (1761–1842) **13.3.96**
68. Mathurin-René de la Villéon (1752–1806) **18.3.96**
69. Monsieur Marie **18.3.96**
70. Monsieur de Ruvigny **23.3.96**
71. Armand-Louis-Charles de Gontaut-Biron, Marquis de Biron (1771–1851) **23.3.96**
72. le Chevalier Lamberté **3.4.96**
73. Monsieur St Jore **4.4.96**
74. Henri Delaroche-Vernay **10.4.96**
75. Monsieur de la Rosière **10.4.96**
76. Monsieur de Volée **22.4.96**
77. Monsieur du Taillas **22.4.96**
78. Monsieur Denouville **22.4.96**
79. Monsieur de la Valade **22.4.96**
80. Guy, Comte de Vossey (1766–1859) **2.5.96**
81. Paul de Nourquer du Camper (1776–1849) **2.5.96**
82. Monsieur Flambart **15.5.96**
83. Hyacinthe de Folliot de Fierville (1739–1817) **15.5.96**
84. Monsieur le Chevel **5.6.96**
85. Monsieur du Camp **11.6.96**
86. Charles de Péronne (born 1762) from Saint-Nicolas, near Granville **24.6.96**
87. Louis Harscouët de Saint-George (1755–1830) **26.6.96**
88. Monsieur Scelles (surgeon) **19.7.96**

89. Victurnien-Jean-Baptiste de Rochechouart, Duc de Mortemart (1752–1812) **31.7.96**
90. le Chevalier d'Idouville **25.8.96**
91. Jacques de Kerouartz, Vicomte de Kermellec (1761–1844) **8.1.97**
92. Monsieur de Casenave **20.2.97**
93. Pierre de Calbiac (1732–1815), royalist army officer from the Cévennes, **or** his son Martial de Calbiac (1757–1870) **23.3.97**
94. Abbé Toussaint-François de la Motte Rouge (1755–1823), Canon of Tréguier Cathedral **15.4.98**
95. Louis-Quentin Desprez de Montpézat (born in 1747), Seigneur d'Ambreuil **3.10.98**
96. Frère François Marie (Capuchin friar whose civil name was Jean Mortier) **16.4.99**
97. Monsieur l'Huillier **26.5.99**
98. Monsieur du Plessis Pasco **3.1.00**
99. Monsieur de Filleau **26.6.00**
100. Charles de Graimberg (1774–1864) **29.11.00**
101. Monsieur Daucourt **6.8.01**
102. Jean-Marie-Bernard Bégny **15.10.01**
103. Monsieur Doucet (a priest) **15.11.01**
104. Louis-François-Antoine-Maurice de Payen de l'Hôtel, Baron de la Garde **7.10.02**
105. Félicité de la Bourdonnaye, Comtesse de Vossey (1784–1807) **23.3.04**
106. Céleste-Octavie de la Bourdonnaye (1787–1863) **23.3.04**
107. Constant de Botherel du Plessis (1776–1860) **18.9.07**
108. Charles-Auguste Brajeul (1761–1825), Rector of Saint-Quay in Brittany **18.9.07**
109. Jean-Joseph de Calonne **22.3.08**
110. Marie-Laurent-Thibéry de Nattes de Nadaillan **22.3.08**
111. Louis-Joseph-Guy Landry de Vauxlandry (1730–1813) **26.7.11**

Bibliography

Primary Sources

Greffe, St Peter Port, Guernsey

Amerci en Plaids
Contrats pour Lire
Contrats pour Lire et pour la Date
Livres en Crime
Ordonnances

Island Archives, St Peter Port, Guernsey

AQ 1004/01 – St Peter Port Tax Book, 1797–1803
AQ 1017/8 – Castel Parish Register, 1764–1809
AQ 1083/01 – Castel Parish Register, 1664–1764
AQ 1083/03 – Castel Parish Register, 1748–1835
AQ 1572/03 – diary of Elisha Dobrée, 1771–85
AQ 1572/04 – diary of Elisha Dobrée, 1786–99
AQ 1572/05 – diary of Elisha Dobrée, 1800–17
SG 23/43 – Relevé des Propriétaires du Castel, 1817

Priaulx Library, St Peter Port, Guernsey

E.F. Carey's genealogies
F.C. Lukis's 'Reminiscences of former days in connection with Guernsey' (unpub. MS)

Jersey Archive

Book 53, series D/Y/K4 (Public Registry)

National Archives, Kew

HO 46/37/32 – papers relating to transportation of Enoch Kinsella
HO 98/25 – list of French clergy sent from Guernsey to Southampton, July 1796
HO 98/28 – list of Frenchmen in Guernsey, 1805
PC 1/118C/16 – letter from Charles Mollet to Philippe D'Auvergne, 7.8.1797
PROB 11/1248/217 – will of Lieutenant-Colonel William Brown

Bank of England Archives, London

AC27/6731 – Stock Ledger, 1765–71

Guernsey newspapers and magazines

L'Indépendance

Secondary Sources

Pre-1920 publications

Benoît, D., *Les Frères Gibert: Deux Pasteurs du Désert et du Refuge* (Toulouse, 1889)
Carey, E.F., (ed.), *Guernsey Folk Lore from MSS by the late Sir Edgar MacCulloch* (London, 1903)
Clarke, L.L., *The Island of Alderney* (Guernsey, 1851)
de l'Estourbeillon, R.M.J., *Les Familles Françaises à Jersey pendant le Révolution* (Nantes, 1886)
Forneron, H., *Histoire Générale des Emigrés pendant la Révolution Française*, 2 vols (Paris, 1884)
Hettier, C., *Relations de la Normandie et de la Bretagne avec les Iles de la Manche pendant l'Emigration* (Caen, 1885)
Marshall, J., *An Analysis and Compendium of All the Returns made to Parliament Relating to the Increase of Population* (London, 1835)
Metivier, G., *Dictionnaire Franco-Normand ou Recueil des Mots particuliers au Dialecte de Guernesey* (London, 1870)
Robertson, T., *General Outline of the Report upon the Size of Farms* (Edinburgh, 1796)
Tourtel, R.H., 'Words peculiar to our insular dialect not found in any glossary,' *Transactions of the Guernsey Society of Natural Science and Local Research*, 7 (1916), pp. 300–15
Tourtel, R.H., 'List of words, phrases, &c., peculiar to our insular dialect', *Transactions of the Guernsey Society of Natural Science and Local Research*, 8 (1918), pp. 102–9

Post-1920 publications

Balleine, G.R., *The Tragedy of Philippe D'Auvergne* (Chichester, 1973)
Bellenger, D.A., *The French Exiled Clergy in the British Isles after 1789* (Bath, 1986)
Carey, E.F., 'Peter Le Mesurier, Governor of Alderney, 1793–1803', *Transactions of la Société Guernesiaise*, 10 (1926), pp. 45–61

Clapp, S., 'Catholic priests exiled in Guernsey after escaping la terreur of the French Revolution', *The Review of the Guernsey Society* (Spring 2015), pp. 20–3

Crossan, R.-M., *Criminal Justice in Guernsey, 1680–1929* (Benderloch, 2021)

Crossan, R.-M., *Charles Mollet and his World: Daily Life in Georgian Guernsey* (Benderloch, 2024)

Day, A., 'A Russian army on Guernsey and Jersey', *The Review of the Guernsey Society* (Summer 1997), pp. 40–5

De Garis, M., *Dictiounnaire Angllais-Guernesiais* (1967; Chichester, 1982 edn)

Everard, J.A. & Holt, J.C., *Jersey 1204 The Forging of an Island Community* (London, 2004)

Fagan, B., *The Little Ice Age* (New York, 2000)

Fawcett, T., *Bath Commercialis'd: Shops, Trades and Market at the 18th-Century Spa* (Bath, 2002)

Griffin, G., *Who's Who in Gay and Lesbian Writing* (New York, 2002)

Hocart, R., *Peter de Havilland: Bailiff of Guernsey, A History of his Life, 1747–1821* (Guernsey, 1997)

Hocart, R., 'Monsieur de St. George: Jean Guille (1712–78)', *Transactions of la Société Guernesiaise*, 26 (2010), pp. 670–98

Johnston, P., 'Lt Col John Mackelcan, Commanding Royal Engineer, Fort George, 1797–1809', Part 1, *The Review of the Guernsey Society* (Summer 2005), pp. 60–6

Johnston, P., 'Lt Col John Mackelcan, Commanding Royal Engineer, Fort George, 1797–1809', Part 2, *The Review of the Guernsey Society* (Winter 2005/6), pp. 83–90

Johnston, P., 'Lt Col John Mackelcan, Commanding Royal Engineer, Fort George, 1797–1809', Part 3, *The Review of the Guernsey Society* (Spring 2006), pp. 17–28

Le Maistre, F., *Dictionnaire Jersiais–Français* (Jersey, 1966)

Le Mesurier, H., 'The Le Mesuriers who lived at les Beauchamps' [*sic*], *The Quarterly Review of the Guernsey Society* (Spring 1959)

Loveridge, J., *The Constitution and Law of Guernsey* (1975; Guernsey, 1997 edn)

Mills, R.J.W., ' "L'île des bannis": Jersey, Britain and the French emigration, 1789–1815', *European Review of History*, 28 (2021), pp. 99–123

Moore, R.D., *Methodism in the Channel Islands* (London, 1952)

Morley, G., *Smuggling in Hampshire & Dorset, 1700–1850* (1983; Newbury, 1990 edn)

Neeson, J.M., 'Gathering the "humid harvest of the deep": the mid-summer cut vraic harvest in nineteenth-century Guernsey', *Transactions of la Société Guernesiaise*, 26 (2008), pp. 521–38

Priaulx, T.F., 'Cider-making, an old-time Guernsey industry', *Transactions of la Société Guernesiaise*, 15 (1953), pp. 286–292

Priaulx, T.F., 'Some 18th century legal tangles and family squabbles involving le Groignet estate', *Transactions of la Société Guernesiaise*, 15 (1954), pp. 401–3

Vidalenc, J., *Les Emigrés Français, 1789–1825* (Caen, 1963)

Index

References to individual persons, objects, crops, etc., are not exhaustive, as many of them occur simply as mentions. More informative references are highlighted in bold. Names of French *émigrés* have been reconstructed from external sources and are offered as best guesses. The first diary reference to any significant individual is usually annotated with outline biographical information.

Abraham, Madeleine (wife of Lieutenant Abraham) *see* **Collenette, Madeleine**
accidents (sustained by Mollet) 24.12.92, 21.8.01, 22.8.01, 2.9.16, 16.9.16
accidents (sustained by other people) 24.6.76, 10.10.77, 16.5.86, 9.5.87, 12.8.91, 25.5.03, 5.9.09, 1.11.09, 23.4.10, 21.1.18
acorns 9.11.86, 20.11.86, 24.2.91
advertisement (offering Mollet's property for sale) 28.2.08
Agricultural Society 17.6.17
aide-de-camp (Mollet's appointment as) 2.6.90
alarms (of invasion) 3.5.79, 4.5.79, 6.1.81, 7.1.81, 18.3.93, 24.4.93, 3.5.98, 4.5.98, 15.8.10, 5.10.11
Albemarle, Lord *see* **Keppel, George**
Alderney (Court officers in 1789) 2.2.89
Alderney (Mollet's sojourns in) 12.10.87–26.10.87, 1.1.88–6.4.88, 18.4.88–14.5.88, 18.5.88–19.6.88, 22.6.88–31.10.88, 18.11.88–28.12.88, 27.1.89–20.4.89, 21.5.89–1.6.89, 18.6.89–3.8.89, 12.8.89–21.8.89, 26.8.89–5.9.89, 15.9.89–4.10.89, 7.10.89–25.11.89, 2.12.89–1.1.90, 10.2.90–14.2.90, 17.5.90–24.5.90, 25.6.90–4.7.90, 9.9.90–11.9.90, 6.7.94–9.7.94
Algeciras (Second Battle of) 4.8.01, 8.8.01
allegations (concerning Mollet) 18.12.80
Allez, Judith (wife of Pierre Allez) *see* **Machon, Judith**
Allez, Pierre (farm labourer) 25.3.17, 1.8.18
Allez, William (farm servant) 10.11.86, 11.12.86
almanacs 7.12.11, 31.12.16
aloe 5.9.16
America (North) *see* **Cambridge (Ohio), Gaspé, Newfoundland, New York, Nova Scotia, Prince Edward Island, Virginia**
Amherst, Field Marshal Sir Jeffery (Governor of Guernsey 1770–94) 6.8.97
Amiens (Peace of) *see* **Peace of Amiens**
amputation 10.10.77, 5.9.09

Andrews, Thomas (farm servant) 15.7.00, 3.3.01
Andros, Charles, sen. (of les Piques) 7.5.71, 3.12.73
Andros, Charles, jun. (of les Piques, Mollet's godfather, Jurat 1758–1802) 23.9.73, 22.8.74, 5.12.74, 2.1.75, 1.1.79, **26.2.85**, 23.12.85, **8.3.98**, **23.1.06**
Andros, Rachel (Mollet's godmother, wife of Elie du Fresne & James Hubert) 10.4.71, 2.6.03
Andros, Rachel (wife of William Guille, sen., of St George) 8.3.98, 12.8.01
Andros, Thomas (Advocate, son of James Andros) 26.8.75
Andros, Thomas Fouaschin 25.10.71, 11.10.74, 5.12.74
anemones 1.2.91
Anquetil, Jean (farm servant) 7.11.93, 18.10.94
apples 12.10.71, 21.9.86, 20.1.89, 25.11.94, 31.10.99, 17.5.00, 17.11.01, 15.1.07, 19.10.07, 4.11.08, 8.11.16
Arbuthnot (privateer) 29.7.79
Arbuthnot, Vice-Admiral Mariot 3.5.79
area (units of) 19.2.71, 5.1.74
Arfwidson & Sons (Mollet's suppliers of timber & iron) 31.1.88
arrests (of Mollet, in France) 22.10.90, 25.10.90
artichokes 27.5.88, 19.3.89, 8.7.09
asafoetida 6.10.73
ashes (of burnt seaweed) 15.11.71, 31.12.71, 8.3.73
asters 22.4.73, 17.5.1817
aunts (Mollet's maternal) 7.3.71, 8.11.74, 9.1.75, 13.3.76, 19.3.76
Australia *see* **Botany Bay**
Bailiff (dispute with Jurats) *see* **Jurats** (dispute with Bailiff)
Bainbrigge, Rachel (wife of Philip Bainbrigge) *see* **Dobrée, Rachel**
balls (formal) 31.7.86, 4.6.93, 4.6.96, 24.4.00
banks (deposit-taking) 21.10.09, 12.4.10, 14.4.10, 7.4.10, 26.3.11, 2.5.11, 10.6.11, 13.6.11, 28.11.11
Barbelet, Pierre (farm labourer) 9.6.18
barbers 13.10.71, 1.11.71, 2.1.72, 23.1.72, 7.1.10, 31.12.16
Barbet, Etienne (Keeper of King's Weights) 21.1.71, 18.12.71, 18.1.73, 17.1.74
barley 29.1.71, 15.5.71, 6.9.71, 21.4.72, 11.5.72, 28.10.72, 26.12.72, 30.6.73, 11.5.74, 21.5.74, 27.4.75, 13.5.77, 24.4.97, 28.4.97, 27.8.07, 31.12.10, 31.12.11, 6.9.15, 1.5.16, 12.9.17
barracks 21.11.99
barrel (*barrique*) 22.5.73
basket-makers 8.10.74
Bath (Mollet's sojourn in) 30.11.75–4.1.76
Bath stove 25.10.98
Batiste, Marie (domestic servant) 17.5.88, 27.5.88, 3.8.88
Batten, Robert (farm servant) 18.3.00

Bayly, Major-General Henry (Lieutenant-Governor of Guernsey 1816–21) 20.6.16, 24.6.17, 23.3.18, 22.4.18
beans 22.2.71, 26.4.88, 25.2.94, 7.5.03, 19.9.09, 31.12.11, 31.12.17
beech mast 20.11.86
bees 20.10.95
Bellanger, Pierre (Anglican clergyman) 17.12.16
Bell, Charles (merchant) 17.8.08, 22.8.08, 29.8.08, 14.8.16
Bell, George (merchant) 14.8.16, 5.9.16
Bell, William (merchant) 17.8.08
Berry, Elizabeth (wife of Rev. Etienne Gibert) 10.8.91, 27.11.94, 24.5.96, 24.6.00, **24.2.01**, **6.3.07**, 24.4.07, 12.10.08, 31.8.15
Berry, William (author, historian) 11.9.16
Bertram, Jean (Master of the Town Hospital) 17.11.07
Bethel chapel (St Peter Port) 19.9.94, 7.1.98
Bichau, Louis (gardener) 18.5.07, 13.12.07
Billet d'Etat 11.12.71, 14.12.71, 10.4.77, 26.6.77
Bishop & De Jersey (bankers) 12.4.10, 14.4.10, 17.4.10, 2.5.11, 10.6.11
Blanchard, Jean-Pierre-François (French balloonist & showman) 10.7.02, 17.7.02
Blondel, Abraham (farm labourer) 10.6.18
Blondel, Henry (farm labourer, expatriate Newfoundland cod worker) 5.10.16, 20.3.17, 25.3.17, 12.4.17, 3.3.18, 11.4.18
Blondel, Jean (of le Moulin du Milieu) 16.9.76
Blondel, Thomas (farm labourer, farm servant) 6.5.11, 23.1.12, 12.5.16, 4.7.16, 16.2.18, 17.2.18
blowing stove 1.5.80, 25.10.98
Boaz, Herman (conjuror) 3.2.77
boils 12.5.07, 31.5.11
Bonamy, Jean (farm servant) 8.1.02, 7.3.02
Bonamy, Marie (mother of Josias Le Marchant of la Haye du Puits) 13.4.73
Bonamy, Samuel (Bailiff 1758–70) 5.3.71
bonesetters 18.9.11, 20.9.11, 26.5.18, 27.5.18
books 5.3.71, 5.12.89, 18.12.97, 1.11.10, 14.2.11
bornements 20.10.71, 23.2.74, 28.3.75, 26.6.76
Boruwlaski, Jósef (Polish musician & entertainer) 4.5.91, 15.5.91, 27.5.91, 30.5.91, 6.6.91, 17.6.91
botanist 24.7.18
Botany Bay (transportation to) 13.4.18
Bougourd, Esther (sentenced to cage for false accusation) 8.2.72
Bouillon, le Prince/Duc de *see* **D'Auvergne, Philippe**
Boul[l]en, Jacques (Anglican clergyman) 23.6.85, 7.6.93, 12.6.93, 25.7.94
Bourdon, Jean-François (Seigneur de Verson, *émigré*) 7.5.93, 14.9.94, 7.6.95, 6.9.98, 31.12.98, 3.1.99, 16.4.99, 7.8.99, 27.1.00, 31.12.00

Bourget, Pierre (*émigré* priest) 17.6.93, 26.4.96
Bowden, Mary (wife of John Bowden) *see* **Condamine, Mary**
Bowls, Thomas (grocer) 24.5.01, 6.5.04, 18.10.07, 19.9.09, 25.5.11, 23.8.15, 13.4.17
box cart 8.11.71, 10.12.06
bracken 11.10.74, 6.10.77, 27.9.91, 8.11.03, 2.10.09, 11.9.10, 19.11.10
Brackenbury, Robert (Methodist preacher) 27.6.90
Bradby, James (naval officer) 11.4.71, 25.10.71
Brajeul, Charles-Auguste (*émigré* priest) 22.9.07
brandy 14.11.72, 13.2.89, 14.2.89. 16.4.89, 19.11.89, 29.6.90, 3.7.90
Braye du Valle 16.9.76, 23.10.00, 22.6.06, 25.5.11
Brecqhou (l'Isle des Marchands) 16.11.79
breeches 16.11.11, 29.10.17
Brehaut, Jean (emigrant to North America) 3.10.08, 4.4.18
Brehaut, Judith (domestic servant) 26.1.85
Breton, Nicolas (farmer, neighbour of Mollet's) 23.12.05, 23.12.06, 1.1.10, 4.3.10, 4.3.18
Breton, Marie (domestic servant, daughter of Nicolas Breton) 25.8.06, 23.12.06, 18.9.09, 3.12.09, 11.12.09
Bristol (Mollet's visits to) 12.12.75, 28.12.75, 29.12.75
broccoli 11.5.71, 22.7.72, 13.7.74, 8.4.89
Brock & Le Mesurier (banking agents) 10.6.11, 13.6.11, 28.11.11, 18.12.11
Brock, Anne (Mollet's niece, wife of William Brock) *see* **Mourant, Anne**
Brock, Beauvoir (Mollet's great-nephew, son of William Brock) 8.4.06, 16.6.10
Brock, Daniel De Lisle (merchant, Bailiff 1821–42) 11.4.95, 18.4.97, 13.10.97, 5.4.17, 26.7.18
Brock, Frederick 1.9.02
Brock, Harriet (wife of General Sir Thomas Saumarez) 26.1.93, 19.8.93, 26.7.97
Brock, Henry (husband of Mollet's niece Mary Mourant, brother of William Brock, Jurat 1802–12) 27.1.85, 27.3.85, 2.4.86, 20.4.95, 16.10.95, 29.6.97, **5.10.02**, 8.4.96, **1.9.06**, 12.7.07, **13.11.07**, 10.3.08, 12.3.09, **23.7.09**, 31.5.10, **24.3.12**
Brock, Henry (Mollet's great-nephew, son of William Brock) 14.3.89, 20.1.95, 23.7.99, 16.6.10, 9.3.11
Brock, Irving 3.9.97, 11.7.00, 22.3.16
Brock, Major-General Sir Isaac 5.4.17
Brock, James (brother of Mollet's nieces' husbands Henry & William) 5.10.86
Brock, John Savery (merchant) 11.4.95, 20.5.95, 4.8.06, 19.9.06, **2.10.06**, 26.7.08, 5.10.08, 22.12.08, 15.9.09, 23.10.09, 2.7.10, 27.11.11, 29.6.12, 9.9.15, 2.12.15, 8.7.16, 31.12.16, 31.1.17, **5.4.17**, 12.4.17, 8.1.18, **5.6.18**, 24.7.18
Brock, Judith (sister of Mollet's nieces' husbands, wife of Dr Jean [De] Sau[s]marez 19.8.93, 26.7.97

Brock, Judith (Mollet's great-niece, daughter of William Brock, wife of Rev. William Guille) 26.3.06, 27.8.17
Brock, Julius (son of John Savery Brock) 2.12.15, 31.1.17, 4.2.17
Brock, Martha (Mollet's great-niece, daughter of William Brock, wife of Frederick Le Mesurier) 22.8.94, 26.3.06, 17.8.08, 29.8.08, 19.12.08, 30.8.15, 4.6.17
Brock, Mary (Mollet's niece, wife of Henry Brock) *see* **Mourant, Mary**
Brock, Mary (wife of Jean Carey of 'Choisi') 19.8.93, 26.10.00
Brock, Mary (wife of Thomas Potenger) 18.4.97, 4.8.98
Brock, Mary (Mollet's great-niece, daughter of William Brock, wife of Pitman Jones) 13.9.03, 26.3.06, 13.11.07, 2.8.16, 18.9.16, 4.6.17
Brock, Thomas (Anglican clergyman) 7.7.99, **24.8.02**, **28.4.03**, 22.5.03, 26.3.06, 24.4.07, 29.8.08, 6.6.16, 22.7.16, 8.6.18
Brock, William (of London, banking agent, brother of Daniel De Lisle Brock) 29.1.99, 13.6.11, 27.11.11
Brock, William (husband of Mollet's niece Anne Mourant, brother of Henry Brock) 25.5.85, 2.4.86, **5.6.86**, 12.6.92, 1.10.92, 20.4.95, 16.10.95, **30.4.98**, 31.7.99, **18.8.06**, **29.9.06**, 15.5.10, 31.5.10, **7.3.12**, **6.5.12**, 30.8.15, 11.10.15, 18.9.16, 4.6.17, 18.3.18, 17.4.18, 1.6.18
Brock, Dr William (Mollet's great-nephew, son of William Brock) 14.3.89, 20.1.95, 23.7.99, 13.7.08, 22.12.08, 9.2.09, 23.9.10, 13.9.11, 29.4.12, **6.5.12**, **30.8.15**, 5.4.17, 4.6.17, 20.1.18
Brouard, Daniel (miller of les Niots) 5.12.72, 6.12.72, 5.3.74, 15.3.74, 26.3.74, 14.5.74
Brouard, Nicolas (farm servant) 12.9.73, 13.10.73, 17.11.73, 27.12.73, 7.1.74, 15.6.74, 21.1.76, 14.5.18
Brouard, Thomas (thatcher) 22.12.74
Brown, Lieutenant-Colonel William (Lieutenant-Governor of Guernsey 1784–93) 1.1.85, 27.3.85, 1.4.86, 6.6.86, 22.7.86, 13.7.87, 25.7.86, 21.8.86, 1.9.86, 5.10.86, 6.6.87, 4.8.87, 15.8.87, 6.10.87, 26.12.87, 6.4.88, 17.11.88, 29.12.88, 1.1.89, 7.1.89, 18.1.89, 10.6.89, 15.6.89, 6.9.89, **2.6.90**, **11.8.90**, 24.12.90, 9.4.91, 24.6.91, 7.4.92, 14.4.92, **8.9.92**, 1.1.93, 3.5.93, **17.5.93**, 20.5.93
Bruce, Mary (Duchess of Richmond) 24.7.86–26.7.86, 28.7.86, 31.7.86, 3.8.86
Brunswick Regiment 14.12.09
buckwheat 8.8.00
Budd, William (merchant) 28.7.71
Buenos Aires (Argentina) 7.12.06, 2.2.07, 5.1.08
Burhou 17.1.88
Burton, Brigadier-General Napier Christie 4.9.96
bushel (unit of capacity) 29.1.71, 14.11.71
butchers 17.4.71, 25.10.10, 19.3.17, 3.4.17
butter 18.6.88, 21.10.09, 28.10.09, 22.4.12, 30.8.15, **13.7.16**, 18.1.17, **7.6.17**, 27.12.17

cabbages 8.2.71, 8.11.71, 12.3.72, 7.1.74, 13.5.77, 25.9.88, 31.5.92, 10.1.93, 4.11.02, 11.1.05, 2.12.15
cabot (unit of capacity) 29.1.71
Caen (Mollet's visit to) 20.9.90–14.10.90
Caire, William (barber) 7.1.10, 31.12.16
Cambridge, Ohio 14.1.09
camellias 23.9.09
Camperdown (Battle of) 15.10.97
candles 25.10.09
canvassing (for votes) 13.3.74, 10.4.76
Capdion, Pierre (French prisoner-of-war & farm labourer) 1.3.79, 21.8.79
Carey, Caroline (widow of Laurent Carey) *see* **Guille, Caroline**
Carey, Jean (of 'Choisi', Jurat 1772–6) 18.2.72, 30.6.72, 28.11.74, 5.12.74, 24.5.75, 26.6.76, 10.4.77, 13.3.96, 11.8.96, 5.2.97, 15.4.98, 27.4.00, **26.10.00**, 7.9.02, 6.5.04, 14.9.04, 25.8.06, 1.9.06, 25.8.16
Carey, Jean (of 'La Bigoterie', Jurat 1777–1810) 3.8.07, 24.5.10
Carey, Mary, sen. (wife of Jean Carey of 'Choisi') *see* **Brock, Mary**
Carey, Mary, jun. (daughter of Jean Carey of 'Choisi', wife of Rev. Thomas Brock) 24.8.02
Carey, Mary (daughter of Jean Carey of 'La Bigoterie', wife of John Gaspard Le Marchant) 1.9.07, 19.1.11
Carey, Peter Martin 6.6.10, 27.7.17
Carey, Peter Stafford (Bailiff 1845–83) 27.7.17
Carey, Rachel (wife of John Carey of the Grange) *see* **Dobrée, Rachel**
Carey, Sophia (daughter of Jean Carey of 'La Bigoterie', wife of Mollet's nephew Peter Mourant) 3.8.07, 4.8.07, 18.8.07, **19.9.11**, **1.10.11**, 18.1.17, 22.12.17, 17.4.18
Carey, Thomas (Anglican clergyman, son of Jean Carey of 'Choisi') 29.12.94, 26.7.95, 19.5.99, 26.10.00, 24.5.01, **30.11.03**, 27.8.09, 6.6.10, 29.7.10, 14.6.12, 25.8.16
Carey, William (military officer, son of Jean Carey of 'Choisi') 31.12.06, 2.1.07, **25.10.08**
carnations 18.8.74, 25.7.86, 31.12.90, 24.8.91, 7.5.93, 11.10.97, 18.6.01, 4.11.02
carpenters 8.11.71, 28.10.72, 19.3.73, 11.4.74, 23.3.01, 10.12.06, 28.8.09
Carré, Jean (Mollet's Guernsey business partner) 31.3.88, 15.4.88, 6.1.89, 16.5.89, 18.5.89, 2.12.89, 31.1.91, 27.8.91, 25.12.91, 5.3.92
Carré, Thomas (murder victim) 1.6.95
carrots 5.8.88, 31.12.17
Casquets, les (lighthouse at) 13.2.88, 14.2.88, 5.3.88, 4.8.88
Castel Club 7.10.74, 26.2.75, 27.6.77, 16.11.97, 26.11.97, 31.12.97, 17.5.98, 25.12.00, 1.1.01

Castle Cornet 11.7.76, 13.4.78, 13.6.80
Cateline, Esther (daughter of Jean Cateline, sen., wife of Thomas Le Tissier) 1.10.08
Cateline, James (son of Jean Cateline, sen., farm labourer, blacksmith) 31.1.07, 24.11.11, 23.12.11, **10.6.16**, 26.11.16, **20.4.17**, **31.5.18**
Cateline, Jean, sen. (farm labourer, smallholder, blacksmith) 15.1.74, 9.6.80, 23.12.03
Cateline, Jean, jun. (farm labourer, farm servant) 16.12.05, 5.1.06, 24.1.07, 25.1.07, 6.2.07, 2.1.08, 3.1.08, 4.1.08, 15.6.08, 16.6.08, 10.7.08, 1.10.08, 19.10.08, 20.10.08, 1.1.09, 2.1.09, 5.1.09, 9.1.09, 3.4.09, 9.4.09, 30.4.09, 25.10.09–26.10.09, 18.11.09–21.11.09, 27.2.10–13.3.10, 22.12.10, 1.2.11, 2.2.11, 4.2.11, 18.9.11, 20.9.11, 14.10.11, 22.11.11, 25.11.11, 26.11.11, 29.11.11, 23.12.11, 4.1.12, 4.4.12, 22.5.12
Cateline, Jeanne (wife of James Cateline) *see* **Domaille, Jeanne**
Cateline, Margueritte (wife of Pierre Cateline) *see* **Rougier, Margueritte**
Cateline, Pierre (son of Jean Cateline, sen., farm labourer, plasterer, building contractor) 3.9.98, 23.2.06, 6.6.07, 5.1.09, 20.5.09, 4.3.10, 24.4.10, 13.5.10, 16.9.10, 10.11.10, 24.11.11, 1.12.11, 23.9.12, 4.4.12, 17.12.15, 4.2.16, 22.2.16, 16.6.16, 2.2.17, 5.2.17, 30.3.17, 22.6.17, 19.8.17, 5.9.17, 6.9.17, 10.9.17, 28.9.17, 12.10.17, 15.10.17, 16.10.17, 23.12.17, 1.1.18, 25.2.18, 14.3.18, 20.3.18, 24.3.18, 19.4.18, 31.5.18, 25.6.18, 27.6.18, 9.7.18
cattle (accidents sustained by) 20.12.16
cattle (exports of) 8.7.75, 23.1.10, 25.9.17
cattle (general) 17.4.71, 15.12.71, 24.3.72, 19.11.73, 3.12.73, 4.11.74, 27.8.76, 7.4.77, 10.4.92, 19.4.92, 1.1.93, 1.10.94, 1.1.96, 26.12.97, 24.4.10, 25.4.10, 26.5.18, 27.5.18
cattle (illnesses of) 10.5.02, 15.3.06, 21.3.06, 24.3.06, 9.6.09, 18.5.10, 21.4.18
celery 6.5.06
census (agricultural) 17.6.17
census (of St Peter Port, 1790/1) 12.1.91, 11.2.91, 31.3.91
chairs 7.5.99
chaises/gigs 3.4.71, 16.11.75
Chandepie de Boiviers, Jean-Charles (artist) 9.4.18
charity sermons 2.8.72, 20.11.08, 20.8.09, 27.8.09, 12.1.12
Château des Marais, le 1.4.86, 6.6.87, 6.10.87, 15.6.89, 12.9.89, 6.6.91
Chefs de Famille 12.5.71
Chepmell, Anne (wife of Philip Chepmell & William Fergusson) *see* **Lerrier, Anne**
Chepmell, Charles (military officer, son of William Chepmell, sen.) 10.9.17, 28.6.18
Chepmell, Elizabeth (wife of William Chepmell, sen.) *see* **Coutart, Elizabeth**

Chepmell, William, sen. (merchant) 18.8.71, 22.7.74, 24.7.74, 15.8.74, 4.7.76, 17.7.76, 22.7.76, 20.4.77, 11.5.77, 9.7.77, 27.7.77, 8.9.77, 21.8.77, 10.1.79, 3.1.80, 15.12.85, 16.5.89, 21.8.98, 14.11.98
Chepmell, William, jun. (Anglican clergyman) 10.9.17
Cherbourg (Mollet's visits to) 21.6.86–26.6.86, 15.10.88–20.10.88, 21.8.89–26.8.89, 11.9.90–18.9.90
Cherbourg (mutiny at) 22.7.89
cherries 21.7.02, 16.7.08
chestnuts 24.10.15
Chevauchée de St. Michel 7.6.86
chicks (*see also* **poultry**) 3.2.72, 18.7.72, 11.6.85, 5.8.94, 3.1.97, 9.9.97
chicory 18.9.71, 18.8.88, 28.8.88, 24.8.91
Chief Pleas 21.1.71, 30.9.71, 20.1.72, 5.10.72, 18.1.73, 17.1.74, 3.10.74, 6.10.77, 19.1.78, 18.1.96, 7.3.96, 4.4.96, 19.1.01
chocolate 26.1.93
christening 24.11.11
Christian family (tenants of Mollet's) 4.3.17, 30.3.17, 25.2.18, 27.6.18
churching (after childbirth) 1.12.11
churchwardens (Castel parish) 21.10.72, 25.3.75, 20.5.75, 27.5.75
cider 3.1.71, 4.2.71, 12.10.71, 7.9.72, 31.12.72, 22.5.73, 12.7.73, 3.5.74, 26.10.77, 25.2.85, 21.9.86, 31.5.92, 28.7.94, 16.5.95, 1.1.96, 17.11.01, 10.4.06, 26.11.11, 19.9.16
clameurs de haro 26.7.74, 7.8.10, 28.8.10, 29.8.10, 9.8.11
clocks 1.11.71, 15.11.80, 21.12.91
clover 6.4.72, 4.7.76, 13.5.77, 17.12.00, 31.12.17, 4.3.18
club *see* **Castel Club**
coasts (storm/sea damage to) 13.1.89, 25.2.11, 15.3.16, 6.3.17
Cockell, Brigadier-General William 23.5.06, 11.8.06
cocoa 29.3.18
cod-fishing 3.3.18
coffee 28.11.72, 28.5.00, 27.8.08
Cohu, Jean (Castel *Procureur des Pauvres*) 7.1.72
Cohu, Jean (of les Moullins, accident victim) 21.1.18
Cohu, Judith (domestic servant) 1.2.97, 31.1.00
Cohu, Pierre (emigrant to North America) 26.4.07
Cohu, Captain Thomas (of L'Aumone) 9.7.09, 16.7.09, 28.6.11, 6.7.12
Coke, Thomas (1st Earl of Leicester) 20.3.97, 8.8.97
Collenette, Captain Abraham 1.1.04, 16.2.06
Collenette, Abraham (farm servant) 12.2.87, 1.1.88, 8.2.88
Collenette, Judith (daughter of Capt. Abraham Collenette) 1.1.04, 26.2.04, 18.4.04, 23.12.05, 16.2.06, 17.12.06, 7.4.07, 17.7.07, 12.12.07, 23.12.09, 25.12.15

Collenette, Madeleine (wife of Lieutenant Abraham of the 61st Regiment) 29.5.97
Collenette, Marie (domestic servant) 27.2.87
Collenette, Susanne (domestic servant, subsequently wife of James Torode) 14.7.00, 25.12.01, 18.1.02, 26.2.04, 18.4.04
Colomez, Jean (Alderney surgeon) 23.2.88, 5.5.88, 8.4.89, 7.5.03
Combs/Combes, William (merchant) 22.11.72, 1.1.73, 25.12.73, 22.4.86, 10.8.91, 8.7.96, 21.8.98, 27.5.07, 31.5.10, 19.9.11
Compton, Spencer (8th Earl of Northampton) 4.7.73
Condamine, Elizabeth (wife of HM Comptroller John Condamine) *see* **Coutart, Elizabeth**
Condamine, Jean-Jacques (HM Sergeant, 1744–64) 30.6.73
Condamine, John, sen. (HM Comptroller 1797–1821, son of HM Sergeant Jean-Jacques Condamine) 10.4.91
Condamine, John, jun. (son of HM Comptroller John Condamine) 16.5.11, 28.5.11, 29.5.11, 5.7.16
Condamine, Marie (wife of HM Sergeant Jean-Jacques Condamine) *see* **Néel, Marie**
Condamine, Mary (daughter of HM Sergeant Jean-Jacques Condamine, wife of John Bowden & George Bell) 22.8.94, 14.8.16
congé 24.5.17
conger eels 7.8.17
conjuror 6.1.16
Constables (elections of, Castel parish) 27.2.71, 30.4.72, 7.6.75, 17.6.75, 17.10.76, 13.1.79, 21.6.98
consumption *see* **tuberculosis**
cooper 6.10.86
Copenhagen (First Battle of) 19.4.01
Corbet, Major Moses (Lieutenant-Governor of Jersey 1771–81) 9.3.71, 6.1.81, 7.1.81
Costin, Dom Jérôme-Jean (French ecclesiastic) 14.10.90, 17.10.90
Coulon, Claude-Antoine (*émigré* priest) 13.3.96, 20.3.96, 25.3.96, 3.4.96, 26.4.96, 27.6.96, 31.7.96, 11.8.96
Courtenay, William (3rd Viscount Courtenay of Powderham) 31.12.90
Coutances (Mollet's visit to) 15.10.90–18.10.90
Coutart, Elizabeth (wife of William Chepmell, sen.) 10.1.79, 14.11.98
Coutart, Elizabeth (wife of John Condamine, sen.) 22.8.94
Coutart, Jeanne (wife of Captain Robert McCrea) 12.9.93
Coutart, Marie (wife of Pierre Coutart, HM Comptroller 1796–7) *see* **Roche, Marie**
Coutart, Pierre (HM Comptroller 1796–7) 1.3.71, 16.4.71, 23.7.72, 30.6.73, 24.2.92
cowpats (collection of) 28.5.17, 8.6.18, 31.7.18

crab-pots 30.1.16
crabs 7.1.06, 14.2.16
Craig, General Sir James (Lieutenant-Governor of Guernsey 1793) 9.11.93
cream 13.3.08
Crescent (ship commanded by Capt. James Saumarez) 8.6.94
Crespin, Elie (Dean of Guernsey 1765–95) 18.6.95
cress 7.12.80
Croft, Thomas (butcher) 3.4.17
Cuba 27.2.12
cuckoos 28.4.88, 21.4.93, 21.4.94, 11.4.95
cucumbers 1.5.71, 17.5.76, 21.8.93, 23.5.99, 6.5.06, 13.6.17, 18.7.18
curds 17.8.08
Curtis, William (of the London Botanic Garden) 11.11.93
dahlias 23.6.17
dairy 18.5.78, 1.1.17
d'Allonville, General Armand-Jean (Comte d'Allonville, *émigré*) 26.8.96
d'Allonville, Céleste-Octavie (wife of Antoine d'Allonville) *see* **de la Bourdonnaye, Céleste-Octavie**
Dalrymple, Lady Frances (wife of Sir Hew Dalrymple) *see* **Leighton, Frances**
Dalrymple, Lieutenant-General Sir Hew (Lieutenant-Governor of Guernsey 1796–1802) 6.4.96, 7.4.96, 9.7.96, 31.7.96, 24.7.97, 3.5.98, 10.5.98, 25.3.99, 16.3.01, 19.4.02, 20.3.03
Dancel, Etienne (farm servant) 4.2.93, 19.11.97, 25.1.98
Dancel, l'Abbé (*émigré* priest) 17.2.93, 17.6.93, 22.5.94, 25.7.94
Daumaillerie, la *see* **Domaillerie, la**
D'Auvergne, Philippe (British naval officer, Prince/Duc de Bouillon) 26.5.95, 19.6.96, 20.6.96, 10.10.96, 27.3.97, 8.8.97, 22.11.08, 26.9.16
Davy, George (grocer) 26.5.11, 13.4.17
Davy, Joseph (grocer) 24.5.01, 6.5.04, 1.1.06, 24.1.09, 23.8.15, 13.4.17
deafness (Mollet's) 7.7.16
deaths, perinatal (of infants) (*see also* **stillbirths**) 18.5.87, 19.5.87, 10.10.98
deaths, perinatal (of mothers) 4.8.98, 4.6.06, 21.2.10, 10.8.16, 31.1.17, 16.4.17
deaths (of children) 5.7.88, 30.12.96, 31.12.96, 19.11.99, 25.6.06, 31.1.17, 28.2.17
De Beaucamp, Susanne (widow of Jean Le Pelley) 15.11.71, 18.8.74, 4.1.89, 25.4.91, 31.12.91, 27.8.97, 22.12.99, 1.9.15
de Beaudrap, Thomas-François (Seigneur de Biville, *émigré*) 17.10.91, 16.5.95
de Blangy, Pierre-Henri (*émigré*) 7.6.95
de Blangy, Auguste-Pierre (*émigré*) 7.6.95
de Blégier Pierre Grosse, Anne (Baronne de la Garde, *émigrée*) 26.5.95
de Bourbon, Louis-François-Joseph (Comte de la Marche, *émigré*) 4.10.91
De Butts, General Augustus (military engineer) 5.10.11

de Calbiac, Pierre (*émigré*) 23.3.97, 31.12.98, 3.1.99, 14.4.99, 7.8.99, 27.1.00, 31.12.00, 18.6.01, 23.5.02
de Calonne, Jean-Joseph (*émigré*) 3.4.08, 5.10.08, 16.7.09, 17.9.09, 29.10.09, 16.9.10, 10.9.11, 24.6.12
de Carné-Trécesson, Gilles (*émigré*) 11.11.94, 3.8.95
de Chateaubriand, Armand (*émigré*) 21.2.95
de Coatlez, Marie-Jeanne-Aimée Poulpiquet (Comtesse de Coatlez, *émigrée*) 26.4.92
deer 2.11.74
De Garis, Elizabeth (domestic servant) 17.5.80
de Graimberg, Charles (*émigré*) 29.11.00, 11.7.01, 30.11.03, 10.1.05
De Havilland, Carterette, sen. (wife of Peter De Havilland) *see* **Fiott, Carterette**
De Havilland, Carterette, jun. (daughter of Peter De Havilland, wife of Sir George Smith) 29.4.08, 27.7.17
De Havilland, Catherine (daughter of Peter De Havilland, wife of Thomas De Sausmarez) 20.9.96, 29.4.08
De Havilland, Charles (military officer, son of Peter De Havilland) 1.3.18, 28.6.18, 26.7.18
De Havilland, Elizabeth (daughter of Thomas De Sausmarez, wife of Thomas Fiott De Havilland) *see* **De Sausmarez, Elizabeth**
De Havilland, Martin (HM Prévôt 1777–82, brother of Peter De Havilland) 13.3.74, 10.4.76, 26.10.06
De Havilland, Peter (Bailiff 1810–21) 4.5.71, 28.7.71, 13.3.74, 5.12.74, 14.12.74, 24.5.75, 27.5.75, 10.4.76, 22.5.76, 31.12.79, 24.2.85, 17.10.86, 21.11.95. 28.11.95, 12.12.95, 18.1.96, 13.3.96, 3.4.96, 31.7.96, 11.8.96, 5.2.97, 23.4.97, 27.5.98, 19.5.99, 6.5.04, 1.1.05, 22.12.05, **12.5.10**, 18.7.10, 21.7.17, 1.3.18, 26.4.18, 28.6.18, 26.7.18
De Havilland, Thomas Fiott (military officer, engineer, Jurat 1842–56, son of Peter De Havilland) 21.1.03, 13.3.08, 12.5.11
De Jersey, Caroline (daughter of Jurat Pierre De Jersey of les Touillets) 23.7.16
De Jersey, Charles (son of Jurat Pierre De Jersey of les Touillets, HM Procureur 1830–51) 20.1.18
De Jersey, Elizabeth (daughter of William De Jersey of Ste Hélène, wife of John Savery Brock) 19.9.06, 2.10.06, 9.9.15, 31.1.17
De Jersey, Hellier (of le Groignet) 27.2.71, 13.10.71, 13.3.72, 12.4.72
De Jersey, Marie (wife of Hellier De Jersey) *see* **Roland, Marie**
De Jersey, Pierre (of les Touillets, Jurat 1771–1822) 21.10.72, 22.10.72, 24.10.72, 25.3.75, 23.2.87, 10.3.87, 2.5.87, 3.5.87, 7.5.87, **20.4.95**
De Jersey, Rachel (wife of Jurat Pierre De Jersey of les Touillets) *see* **De La Mare, Rachel**
De Jersey, Thomas (son of Jurat Pierre De Jersey of les Touillets) 4.2.87, 31.10.16

De Jersey, William (of Ste Hélène) 19.9.06, 2.10.06, 31.1.17, 4.2.17, 5.4.17, 20.1.18, 8.6.18

de la Bourdonnaye, Céleste-Octavie (sister-in-law of Guy de Vossey, wife of Antoine d'Allonville, *émigrée*) 23.3.04, 13.5.10

de la Bourdonnaye, Félicité (wife of Guy de Vossey, *émigrée*) 23.3.04, 28.10.07

de la Foidre, Monsieur (Curé of Moisville, *émigré* priest) 27.7.94

de la Foidre, Monsieur (Curé of Boissy-Lamberville, *émigré* priest) 27.7.94

de la Garde, le Baron de *see* **de l'Hôtel, Louis-François**

de la Houssaye, Jean-Baptiste (Seigneur de la Houssaye, *émigré*) 6.3.96

de la Houssaye, Renaud (*émigré*) 6.3.96

De La Mare, Rachel (daughter of Jurat Jean De La Mare, wife of Jurat Pierre De Jersey) 23.7.16, 4.2.17

de la Motte Rouge, Toussaint-François (*émigré* priest) 15.4.98, 16.4.99, 27.6.99, 7.8.99, 9.2.00, 31.12.00, 10.4.01

Delaroche-Vernay, Henri (tenant of Mollet's, *émigré*) 20.7.96

De La Rue, Elizabeth (domestic servant) 28.11.96, 5.12.96

de Lescoët, Catherine-Vincente Barbier (Comtesse de Lescoët, *émigrée*) 26.4.92

de l'Hôtel, Louis-François-Antoine-Maurice de Payen (Baron de la Garde, *émigré*) 7.10.02, 3.7.07

de Mauconvenant, Adolphe-Charles (Marquis de Sainte-Suzanne, *émigré*) 14.9.94

de Mauconvenant, Bonaventure-Corentin (Vicomte de Sainte-Suzanne, *émigré*) 14.9.94

De Mouilpied, Daniel (tailor) 18.4.99, 3.12.99

de Nadaillan, Marie-Laurent-Thibéry de Nattes (*émigré*) 3.4.08, 5.10.08, 16.7.09, 17.9.09, 29.10.09, 5.1.10, 16.9.10, 26.5.11, 10.9.11, 24.6.12

denerel (unit of capacity) 29.1.71

de Percy, René-Charles (Seigneur de Tonneville, *émigré*) 2.1.94, 22.5.94, 22.6.94, 14.9.94, 3.8.95

de Péronne, Charles-Jacques (*émigré*) 30.11.03, 23.3.04

de Peyster, Lieutenant-Colonel Arent (British military officer) 6.6.90

depradations 11.12.80, 14.12.80

de Qu[i]erqueville, Jean-Marie-René de Leuvre (*émigré*) 13.9.90, 7.11.93, 16.5.95, 13.2.97, 9.9.98, 31.12.98, 3.1.99, 16.4.99, 7.8.99, 27.1.00, 31.12.00, 11.1.02

de Robien, Paul-Christophe (Marquis de Robien, *émigré*) 9.8.89

de Rochechouart, Victurnien-Jean-Baptiste (Duc de Mortemart, *émigré*) 16.7.96, 31.7.96

de Rullecourt, Baron Philippe (French military officer) 13.1.81

de Saint-Dalmas, François Emeric (Anglican clergyman) 9.6.76, 8.12.99, 28.4.03

De Sausmarez *see also* **Saumarez**

De Sausmarez, Catherine (daughter of HM Procureur Thomas De Sausmarez) 6.5.04

De Sausmarez, Elizabeth (daughter of HM Procureur Thomas De Sausmarez, wife of Thomas Fiott De Havilland) 6.5.04, 13.3.08, 12.5.11, 17.5.11
De Sausmarez, Jean (HM Procureur 1744–74, father of HM Procureur Thomas De Sausmarez) 13.3.72
[De] Sau[s]marez, Dr Jean (son of Dr Matthew De Sausmarez) 3.1.80, 30.7.80, 21.9.80, 9.5.87, 24.12.92, 22.3.93, 10.7.95, 12.8.97, 21.8.01, 21.1.09, 24.1.09
De Sausmarez, John (HM Comptroller, 1830–45, son of HM Procureur Thomas De Sausmarez) 20.8.15
[De] Sau[s]marez, Judith (wife of Dr Jean [De] Sau[s]marez) *see* **Brock, Judith**
De Sausmarez, Martha (wife of HM Procureur Thomas De Sausmarez) *see* **Dobrée, Martha**
De Sausmarez, Dr Matthew 8.4.71, 1.1.72, 1.10.75, 18.9.76
De Sausmarez, Thomas (HM Comptroller 1777–93; HM Procureur 1793–1830) 2.9.77, **9.11.93**, 29.12.94, 20.5.95, 7.6.95, 13.3.96, **20.9.96**, 5.2.97, 23.4.97, **8.7.97**, 19.5.99, 16.5.02, 6.5.04, **16.9.04**, 1.5.05, 24.4.07, 13.3.08, **12.8.08**, 20.8.15, 31.3.16, 11.9.16, **28.2.17**, 1.3.18, 26.4.18, 28.6.18, 26.7.18
deserters (naval & military) 23.8.80, 28.4.01, 20.9.07
des Fontaines, François (farm labourer) 16.7.96
De Ste Croix, Marie (Mollet's god-daughter, wife of miniaturist Philippe Jean) 24.7.18
De Ste Croix, Mary Ann (daughter of Nicolas De Ste Croix) 16.5.11, 27.5.11, 28.5.11, 17.7.11
De Ste Croix, Nicolas (Mollet's cousin and London agent) 1.8.71, 6.10.71, 13.2.90, 10.4.91, 8.8.97, 28.8.09, 23.10.09, 16.5.11, 5.7.16
des Vallées, Michel-Louis Lamy (French merchant and politician) 21.9.90, 24.1.10
de Vauxlandry, Louis-Joseph-Guy Landry (*émigré*) 26.7.11, 10.9.11, 22.4.12
de Vossey, Félicité (wife of Guy de Vossey) *see* **de la Bourdonnaye, Félicité**
de Vossey, Guy (French Royalist naval officer, *émigré*) 2.5.96, 19.11.97, 31.12.98, 3.1.99, 16.4.99, 7.8.99, 30.11.03, 23.3.04, 10.1.05, 20.3.07, 22.9.07, 5.10.08, 16.7.09, 17.9.09, 13.5.10, 16.9.10, 26.5.11, 24.6.12
Dinan (France) 29.8.02
Dobrée, Bonamy (son of Pierre Dobrée of 'Beauregard', husband of Mollet's niece Marthe Mourant) 26.1.85, 27.3.85, 2.4.86, 7.12.86, 10.4.87, 13.2.89, 9.9.89, 16.7.90, 25.3.95, **2.1.98**, **6.1.98**, 29.1.98, 15.7.00, 6.5.06, 2.1.07, 25.5.07, 12.7.07
Dobrée, Daniel (naval officer, son of Nicolas Dobrée of 'Bellevue') 24.8.85, 10.5.99, 16.3.01, 23.5.06, 25.6.06, 7.8.11
Dobrée, Elizabeth (Mollet's great-niece, daughter of Bonamy Dobrée, wife of Robert Woollcombe) 12.7.07, 5.10.15, 22.7.16
Dobrée, Elisha (diarist, brother of Bonamy Dobrée) 2.4.86, 7.12.86

Dobrée, Harriet (Mollet's great-niece, daughter of Bonamy Dobrée, wife of Dr William Brock) 12.7.07, 30.8.15, 3.7.18

Dobrée, Harry (son of Nicolas Dobrée of 'Bellevue', merchant, Jurat 1836–57) 11.4.95, 14.6.99, 23.5.06, 11.8.06, 13.7.08, 27.8.08, 21.9.09, 22.9.09, 5.10.09, 18.7.10, 8.5.12, 17.12.15, 31.3.16, 4.5.17, 1.3.18

Dobrée, Martha/Patty (Mollet's niece, wife of Bonamy Dobrée) *see* **Mourant, Martha**

Dobrée, Martha (Mollet's great-niece, daughter of Bonamy Dobrée) 26.3.06, 6.5.06, 5.10.15, **3.7.18**

Dobrée, Martha (daughter of Isaac Dobrée, wife of HM Comptroller Thomas De Sausmarez) 1.4.94

Dobrée, Mary (daughter of Nicolas Dobrée of 'Bellevue', wife of William Piercy) 1.4.94

Dobrée Nicolas (of 'Bellevue', merchant & shipowner) 14.4.71, 1.3.79, 17.9.91, 24.2.92

Dobrée, Nicolas Peter (Anglican clergyman, son of Nicolas Dobrée of 'Bellevue') 14.4.71, 3.6.85, 29.1.95, 30.6.98, 14.10.98, 21.4.99, **7.6.10**, 14.6.12, **25.1.16**

Dobrée, Peter (brother of Bonamy Dobrée) 22.7.87, 11.8.90

Dobrée, Peter (merchant, Mollet's great-nephew, son of Bonamy Dobrée) 1.9.02, 7.12.06, 2.1.07, 17.10.08, 13.9.09

Dobrée, Pierre (of 'Beauregard', familiarly known as 'the Cardinal', merchant, father of Bonamy Dobrée) 2.4.86, 24.2.92

Dobrée, Rachel (sister of Bonamy Dobrée, wife of Philip Bainbrigge) 10.4.87

Dobrée, Rachel (daughter of Rev. William Dobrée, wife of John Carey of the Grange) 20.3.18

Dobrée, Samuel (banking agent, brother of Bonamy Dobrée) 2.4.86, 14.9.89, 8.5.90

Dobrée, Susanna (daughter of Nicolas Dobrée of 'Bellevue', wife of John Siegfried Fischer) 24.12.90, 7.6.10

Dobrée, William (Anglican clergyman, father of Prof. Peter Paul Dobrée) 3.4.71, 6.10.71, 25.8.72

dogs 13.5.75, 10.3.87, 12.9.94, 9.9.97, 6.10.00, 21.1.09, 23.1.12, 1.2.12, 15.2.12, 2.3.17, 24.6.18

d'Oilliamson, Lieutenant-General Marie-Gabriel-Eléonore (Marquis de Courcy, *émigré*) 26.8.96

Domaille, Jeanne (wife of James Cateline) 10.6.1816, 20.4.17, 31.5.18

Domaillerie, la (property purchased by Mollet) 14.8.73, 30.11.73, **3.12.73**, 11.9.74, 18.12.06

Don, Lieutenant-General Sir George (Lieutenant-Governor of Jersey 1806–14) 2.8.07

Dorey, Daniel (of le Groignet) 9.2.01, 1.11.09

Dorey, Judith (wife of Jacques Dorey) *see* **Machon, Judith**

Douzaine (Castel, meetings of) 26.4.71, 7.11.71, 14.12.71, 7.9.72, 21.10.72, 16.3.73, 21.3.75, 19.9.76, 10.4.77, 26.6.77, 14.5.78, 6.4.79, 14.6.79
Douzaine (Castel, members of) 19.1.87, 21.6.98, 8.7.07
Doyle, Lieutenant-General Sir John (Lieutenant-Governor of Guernsey 1803–16) 20.3.03, **1.6.03**, 18.7.10, 29.8.10, 8.5.12, 20.6.16
Doyle Column (Jerbourg) 30.9.17, 20.10.17
drought 15.6.75, 8.7.75, 20.7.78, 18.4.85, 5.9.85, 9.9.98, 23.10.02, 15.3.03, 8.11.03 19.3.08, 11.5.17, 18.5.17
drownings 16.9.76, 18.6.87, 10.7.93, 23.10.00, 22.11.07
'druid's altar' (L'Ancresse) 22.6.10
du Camper, Paul de Nourquer (brother-in-law of Guy de Vossey, *émigré*) 2.5.96
Duchess of Kingston (privateer) 1.4.91, 11.4.91, 15.4.91
ducks (*see also* **poultry**) 18.6.88, 11.5.93, 28.5.94, 26.12.94
duel (between Mollet & Alderney Lieutenant-Governor Peter Le Mesurier) 23.9.89–7.10.89
Du Four, Nicolas (cattle doctor) 15.3.06, 21.3.06, 21.4.18
Du Four, Rachel (wife of George Thomas) 16.6.17
du Grégo, Charles-François du Bot (Marquis de la Roche, *émigré*) 12.9.91, 20.6.96
Dumaresq, Sir John (Lieutenant-Bailiff of Jersey 1802–16) 24.8.02
du Mesnildot, Jacques-Louis-Gabriel (*émigré*) 16.5.95
Dundas, Colonel Thomas (military commander & Lieutenant-Governor of Guernsey 1793) 26.1.93, 26.5.93, 29.6.93, 9.11.93
Dundas, Lady Elizabeth Eleanor (wife of Colonel Thomas Dundas) *see* **Home, Elizabeth**
dung 15.11.71, 3.3.73, 3.3.74, 16.2.76, 31.12.78, 28.5.17, 8.6.18, 31.7.18
du Plessis, Constant de Botherel (*émigré*) 22.9.07
Du Port, Judith (domestic servant) 18.4.80
Du Port, Théodore (gardener) 27.11.02, 7.12.02
Duppa, Richard (English artist) 27.5.89
Durand, François (Anglican clergyman) 8.5.71
Durell, Thomas (Jersey Vicomte 1743–85) 19.3.76
D'Urville, Messrs (*émigrés*) 16.4.93, 7.5.93, 7.6.93, 12.6.93, 17.6.93 2.1.94, 3.4.94, 25.5.94, 14.9.94
Dutch brigades 20.10.01
du Trévou, Joseph-Jean-Baptiste (*émigré*) 12.6.93, 3.8.95
earthbanks 6.6.11, 9.8.11, 10.2.16
earth tremors 15.4.73, 17.4.73, 23.4.73, 26.1.99
eau de noyau 6.10.07, 22.12.10
eclipse (lunar) 26.1.04
Eden, William (1st Baron Auckland) 6.9.98
Edgcumbe, George (1st Earl of Mount Edgcumbe) 31.12.90

eels (freshwater) 10.6.17
eels (sand) *see* **sand eels**
egg flip (alcoholic beverage) 23.12.17
eggs 1.1.03, 6.1.03, 7.1.03, 8.1.03, 9.1.03, 18.2.03, 22.4.12
Egypt 13.10.02
elections (for Constable) *see* **Constables** (elections of)
elections (for Jurat) *see* **Jurats** (elections of)
'electrification' (for health) 27.3.76
embargo 5.5.79, 8.5.79, 19.3.03
emigration (from Guernsey to North America) 24.8.06, 28.8.06, 26.4.07, 8.8.07, 3.10.08, 14.1.09, 18.4.16
émigré **priests** 26.9.92, 17.2.93, 17.6.93, 4.7.93, 22.5.94, 27.7.94, 22.10.95, 11.12.95, 13.3.96, **28.7.96**, 15.4.98, 22.9.07
émigrés (general) *see also under individual surnames* 9.8.89, 9.4.91, 19.9.91, 28.9.91, 19.7.95, 3.8.95, 11.1.96, 13.1.96, 16.1.96, 4.2.96, 6.2.96, 28.7.96, 26.8.96, 18.10.96
England (Mollet's visits to the south-west of) 30.11.75–4.1.76, 31.10.88–15.11.88, 21.4.89–20.5.89, 17.2.90–28.4.90, 11.10.92–23.12.92, 6.10.93–7.11.93
epidemic (local) 14.9.80, 16.9.80, 17.9.80, 21.9.80
Etienne, Pierre (also known as Peter Stephens) 14.1.71, 25.10.71, 29.6.12, 17.4.17, 3.6.18
Exeter 7.11.88, 8.11.88, 9.11.88, 31.12.90, 30.4.98, 6.5.12
fair (quarterly, for sale of livestock) 26.9.71, 21.4.72, 10.4.87, 18.4.97, 26.12.97, 26.12.09, 24.4.10, 25.9.17
Falla, Pierre (early Methodist) 8.11.87
Falla, Pierre (accident victim, Jurat 1777–99) 23.10.00
Falla, Thomas (of les Moullins, Castel Douzenier) 8.11.77, 15.11.77, 6.3.78, 16.5.78, 23.5.78, 20.6.78
Fallaize, Marie (domestic servant) 27.10.06, 8.9.07
Faro (Portugal) 17.7.76
fascines 5.10.11
fast days 12.3.00, 26.2.06
Faure, Bertrand (Seigneur de Saint-Romain, *émigré*) 7.6.93
Favourite (privateer) 29.12.79
Fenien, George (butcher) 17.4.71, 26.4.71
Ferbrache, Daniel (farm labourer, farm servant, sailor, fisherman, smallholder) 7.8.97, 28.6.98, 16.2.99, 24.2.99, 25.2.99, 24.7.99, 27.8.99, 21.1.00, 5.10.00, 27.10.00, 20.5.01, 21.5.01, 9.9.01, 13.9.01, 15.5.02, 19.8.02, 22.8.02, 21.3.03, 25.3.03, 26.3.03, 9.4.03, 19.4.03, 5.11.03, 9.3.04, **12.2.04**, **16.12.05**, 17.12.05, 28.12.05, 26.10.06, **2.2.07**, 16.5.07, 16.6.07, **3.12.07**, 15.2.08, 16.2.08, **25.5.08**, 22.12.08, **7.2.09**, 9.2.09, **23.2.09**, **10.3.09**, **28.5.09**, 22.9.09, **19.11.09**, **23.12.09**,

25.12.09, 3.2.10, **24.5.10**, **19.11.10**, **26.5.11**, **31.5.11**, **27.2.12**, 18.9.15, 14.3.16, **1.5.16**, **3.7.16**, **4.7.16**, **22.9.16**, 8.6.17, 29.3.18, 8.7.18
Ferbrache, Jean, sen. (farm labourer, smallholder, father of Daniel Ferbrache) 25.4.10
Ferbrache, Jean, jun. (sailor, brother of Daniel Ferbrache) 12.12.02, **15.1.04**, 16.12.05, 25.5.08, 6.8.09
Ferbrache, Marie (domestic servant, sister of Daniel Ferbrache) 25.12.01, 18.1.02, 16.12.05, 21.8.06
Ferbrache, Rachel (sister of Daniel Ferbrache, wife of Isaac Nicolle) 27.8.10, 30.8.10
Fergusson, Anne (wife of Dr William Fergusson) *see* **Lerrier, Anne**
Fergusson, John (naval officer, son of Dr William Fergusson) 3.6.75, 6.6.75, 7.6.75, 20.6.75, 22.6.75
Fergusson, Philip (son of Dr William Fergusson) 6.10.89, 7.10.89, 15.10.89
Fergusson, Dr William (of Dundee, resident in Jersey) 8.3.71, 23.6.71, 13.3.80
Fermain 23.7.72, 28.6.73, 4.10.78, 16.11.79
ferrets 28.1.73, 10.1.99
fine (handed down to Mollet by the Royal Court) 15.2.12
Fiott, Carterette (wife of Peter De Havilland) 4.5.71
fires (accidental) 11.11.74, 10.10.77, 26.5.79, 10.6.79, 18.11.86
Fischer, Susanna (wife of John Siegfried Fischer) *see* **Dobrée, Susanna**
fish (dried) 26.11.06
fishing 22.8.74, 4.7.16, 3.3.18, 30.6.18, 2.7.18
Fletcher, Jack (destitute cabin-boy from Southampton) 18.9.08, 24.9.08, 8.10.08, 10.10.08
flour 20.1.89
flowers (general) 12.3.74, 7.1.88, 5.4.88, 22.4.88, 1.1.11
Floyd, Edward (farm servant) 3.6.80, 11.6.80
fortifications 7.4.73, 6.5.73, 11.9.75, 13.9.75, 18.6.78, 27.1.80, 24.2.80, 25.2.93, 26.2.93, 26.11.07, 11.10.11, 15.3.16
fowls *see* **poultry**
France (Mollet's visits to) 21.6.86–26.6.86, 15.10.88–20.10.88, 21.8.89–26.8.89, 11.9.90–25.10.90
Frecker, Philip (barber) 3.1.10
Freemasons 18.6.10
French Revolutionary War (start of) 26.1.93
funerals 18.9.76, 13.5.78, 26.5.79, 14.9.80, 7.10.91, 20.5.93, 17.7.93, 31.10.94, 26.2.96, 28.4.96, 14.11.98, 2.6.03, 4.6.06, 28.10.07, 1.9.08, 23.6.10, 11.11.10, 10.12.10, 1.9.15, 9.1.16, 10.8.16, 4.2.17, 20.2.17, 16.4.17, 15.7.17, 25.2.18
furze 26.4.71, 8.2.72
Gallienne, Nicolas (farm servant) 14.1.07, 19.1.07, 20.1.07
Gardner, John (butcher) 19.3.17

Gaspé (North America) 20.3.17, 12.4.17, 3.3.18, 4.4.18, 11.4.18
Gater, Francis (farm servant) 27.2.99, 24.7.99, 27.8.99
Gauvain, Jean (Judge of Alderney) 6.10.88, 2.2.89
Gavet, Marie (wife of Pierre Gavet) *see* **Nicolle, Marie**
Gavet, Pierre (farm servant, smallholder) 8.5.75, 26.11.75, 3.1.76, 2.4.76, **10.9.76**, **12.9.76**, 18.6.78, 4.7.80, **20.10.80**, **23.10.80**, 13.1.81, 16.1.81, 15.2.85, 6.6.86, **23.8.86**, **6.3.87**, 29.9.87, 30.9.87, **1.12.87**, 6.12.87, 7.1.88, 23.10.91, 22.12.91, 10.5.92, **20.12.99**, 22.12.99, 23.12.99, 21.7.00, 10.5.02, 27.3.03, 26.2.04, 19.3.10, 13.8.10, **19.2.18**, **21.2.18**
geese (*see also* **poultry**) 22.6.71, 1.1.95, 8.12.09, 12.12.10
George III (King of England) 4.6.85, 31.3.89
geraniums 22.4.88, 1.2.94
Gibert, Cécile (daughter of Rev. Etienne Gibert) 10.8.91, 25.10.94, 31.10.94
Gibert, Elizabeth (wife of Rev. Etienne Gibert) *see* **Berry, Elizabeth**
Gibert, Etienne (Anglican clergyman) 1.8.85, 10.8.91, 15.8.91, 1.6.94, 9.6.94, 30.6.94, 22.8.94, 25.10.94, 11.11.94, 27.11.94, 29.12.94, 24.11.95, 4.3.96, 22.5.96, 24.5.96, 18.4.97, 7.1.98, 30.4.98, 15.12.98, 4.12.99, 20.1.00, 24.6.00, 24.2.01, 10.3.02, 29.8.02, 10.1.05, 6.2.07, 6.3.07, 24.4.07, 20.7.08, 12.10.08, 27.10.08, 18.6.10, 1.2.11, 29.5.12, 31.8.15, 9.10.15, 3.2.17, 13.2.17, 14.2.17, 20.2.17
Gibert, Etienne (nephew of Rev. Etienne Gibert) 12.5.07, 16.3.17
Gibraltar 13.9.09, 3.2.10
gin 29.1.88, 12.9.88, 3.7.90, 20.11.90
Girard, Olympe (domestic servant) 30.1.71, 9.2.72, 28.9.78, 15.12.79
Girard, Rachel (domestic servant) 6.9.95
Girard, Zacharie, sen. (farm servant) 12.1.71, 19.1.71
Glategny (St Peter Port) 13.1.89, 12.1.91
Glasgow Regiment (83rd Regiment of Foot) 26.5.79, 6.1.80
Godefroy, Jean (Anglican clergyman) 12.4.72, 25.8.72, 12.9.73, 11.9.74, 2.1.75, 19.5.75,
god-daughter (Mollet's) *see* **De Ste Croix, Marie**
godfather (Mollet's) *see* **Andros, Charles, jun.**
godmother (Mollet's) *see* **Andros, Rachel**
Goodwin, Matthew (States' architect & surveyor) 17.7.10, 14.9.10, 19.9.10, 24.9.10, 10.6.11
gooseberries 18.6.88, 24.8.91, 25.2.94, 8.7.09
Gosselin, Joshua (Greffier 1768–92) 1.1.71, 27.2.71, 14.4.71, 25.5.71, 12.9.71, 10.5.72, 25.4.73, 8.8.73, 17.10.74, 2.11.74, 5.12.74, 13.1.75, 5.3.75, 24.5.75, 17.6.75, 22.5.76, 13.1.89, 26.4.92, 3.5.98
Gosselin, Sarah (daughter of Joshua Gosselin) 26.4.92
Gosselin, Thomas (naval officer, son of Joshua Gosselin) 10.9.88
Gothenburg (Sweden) 9.6.89, 2.8.89, 29.7.90

Gounon dit Pradon, Antoine-Charles-Frédéric (Anglican clergyman) 29.8.73, 16.2.76
gout 9.7.77, 28.10.90, 6.2.04, 16.12.05, 18.3.07
government stocks *see* **securities** (government)
grafting (of trees) 10.9.71
grain (parochial imports of during dearth) 8.5.71, 12.5.71, 15.5.71, 18.5.71, 28.10.72, 18.11.72, 26.12.72, 27.4.75
Grand Pont (St Sampson) 14.12.09, 15.12.09
Green, Major-General Sir William (military engineer) 13.7.87
greenhouse 2.11.74, 30.8.06, 14.3.16
Greffier (of Alderney) 17.1.88, 2.2.89
Grey, Lieutenant-General Charles (1st Earl Grey, Governor of Guernsey 1797–1807) 26.11.07
Groignet, le (farm adjoining Mollet's) 12.4.72
Groult, Monsieur (Curé of Néhou, *émigré* priest) 17.6.93, 25.5.94, 19.6.94, 14.11.96, 12.9.98, 31.12.98, 16.4.99, 31.12.00
Groult, Monsieur (nephew of Curé of Néhou, *émigré* priest) 17.6.93, 25.5.94, 19.6.94, 14.11.96, 12.9.98, 31.12.98, 16.4.99, 31.12.00
Grut, Thomas (Anglican clergyman) 19.6.10, 31.8.15, 9.10.15, 20.2.17
Guernsey lilies *see* **lilies (Guernsey)**
Guignon, James (thatcher) 2.11.74
Guilbert, Jean (carpenter & painter) 4.3.10, 26.11.10
Guilbert, Thomas (farm servant) 3.11.77, 26.12.77
Guille, Caroline (widow of Laurent Carey of la Brasserie) 8.4.75, 13.7.75
Guille, Caroline (daughter of Nicolas Guille of Barcelona) 9.7.96, 26.7.97, 1.1.01, 2.1.01
Guille, Caroline (daughter of William Guille, grand-daughter of Jean Guille, jun.) 12.8.01
Guille, Carterette (wife of Nathaniel Le Cocq, daughter of Jean Guille, jun.) 6.7.93, **3.10.00**, **2.5.07**
Guille, Charles (son of Jean Guille, sen.) 19.5.71, 6.6.73, 6.6.73, 20.6.73, 21.4.75
Guille, Esther (wife of Jean Carey Metivier, daughter of Jean Guille, jun.) 17.5.98, **9.9.00**, 23.1.01, 31.12.02, 9.10.10, 6.6.16, 21.10.16, 8.11.16
Guille, Jean, sen. (1712–78, Seigneur of St George) 22.2.71, 2.11.74, 3.12.74, 7.2.75, 13.5.78
Guille, Jean, jun. (1734–1820, Seigneur of St George) 6.10.71, 30.6.73, 24.4.74, 3.5.74, 3.6.78, 17.10.86, 12.12.86, 5.3.92, 18.10.97, 8.3.98, 27.5.98, 12.9.98, 9.9.00, **3.10.00**, 15.10.00, 23.1.01, **12.8.01**, 20.10.01, **25.3.02**, **25.5.03**, 9.6.03, 24.4.07, 2.5.07, 6.5.07, 3.7.07, 22.9.07, 9.10.10, 7.5.18
Guille, John (1788–1845, Seigneur of St George, grandson of Jean Guille, jun.; Bailiff 1843–5) 9.9.00, 26.7.06, **24.5.10**, 7.7.12, 6.11.17

Guille, Judith (widow of Jurat Jean Ozanne of la Houguette) 6.9.72, 13.4.73, 3.5.74, 22.12.86, 22.4.87, 9.5.87, 7.10.91
Guille, Nicolas (Barcelona-based merchant, son of Jean Guille, sen.) 19.5.71, 25.8.71, 30.8.71, 12.9.71, 14.11.72, 8.12.74, 14.12.74, 17.12.74, **10.6.75**, 27.5.98, 14.10.98, 11.2.07
Guille, Rachel (daughter of Jean Guille, sen.) 8.6.72, 24.4.76
Guille, Richard (surgeon, son of Jean Guille, sen.) 6.1.71, 16.1.71, 20.1.71, 27.3.71, 19.5.71, 25.8.71, 8.8.73, 21.6.74, 24.6.74, 24.4.76, 2.9.77, 20.1.18
Guille, Thomas (son of Jean Guille, sen.) 28.10.71, 24.3.73, 6.5.73, 2.6.73, 28.1.74, 31.12.74
Guille, William, sen. (son of Jean Guille, jun.) 8.8.92, 12.8.01
Guille, William. jun. (Anglican clergyman, son of William Guille, grandson of Jean Guille, jun.) 9.9.00, 26.7.06, 9.1.11, 25.1.16, 6.6.16, 7.7.16, 25.8.16, 21.10.16
gunpowder 10.6.71, 18.6.72, 19.6.72, 13.4.78
Guy's Hospital 7.2.09, 9.2.09, 10.3.09
Haiti 6.8.09
Halifax (Nova Scotia) 29.11.11, 6.5.12
Hamburg (Germany) 26.7.18
Hampton Court 4.8.71
harbour dues (farm of) 21.1.71, 20.1.72, 18.1.73, 17.1.74
Haslar Hospital (Portsmouth) 11.7.71
hats 28.10.71, 3.11.71, 8.11.71, 27.1.78
Havana (Cuba) 24.5.10, 27.2.12, 20.1.18, 23.5.18
haws 28.10.72, 12.3.74
hay 15.12.71, 18.7.72, 14.7.75, 15.7.75, 9.6.80, 6.7.95, 3.1.97, 18.6.01, 23.10.02, 8.11.03, 12.1.11, 11.7.16, 19.8.16, 6.8.17, 9.6.18
Heathfield, Anthony (of Lympstone, Devon) 31.12.90, 27.2.99, 22.5.99
heatwave 19.7.93
Heaume, Anne (domestic servant) 17.5.88, 27.5.88, 18.8.89, 18.11.89, 16.7.90, 19.12.91, 19.6.92, 27.9.93, 11.7.09
Heaume, Pierre (farm servant) 6.4.72, 7.2.73
Hemery, Jacques (Jersey Lieutenant-Bailiff 1809–14) 4.2.71, 25.3.96
hemp 19.8.16
Herbert, General George (11th Earl of Pembroke, Governor of Guernsey 1807–27) 14.12.07
Herm 1.6.89, 14.6.99, 31.1.07, 22.8.08
Hero (privateer) 26.1.78, 24.11.80
History of the Island of Guernsey (W. Berry) 11.9.16
Holland (*see also* **Rotterdam**, **Walcheren**) 19.9.91, 8.12.94, 3.2.95, 11.10.97, 4.11.02
holly berries 12.3.74

Home, Elizabeth Eleanor (wife of Lieutenant-Governor Colonel Thomas Dundas) 27.7.93, 9.8.93, 9.9.93, 12.9.93
horse-racing 5.10.86, 20.10.86, 22.6.10
horses 15.1.71, 25.10.73, 27.10.73, 8.11.73, 12.5.74, 17.5.74, 17.5.76, 10.9.76, 19.4.92, 14.7.92, 11.9.92, 12.10.92, 25.3.93, 12.6.93, 6.11.95, 19.5.96, 5.1.97, 23.10.97, 17.3.98, 12.5.03, 8.5.06, 25.6.06, 25.10.10, 8.5.11, 2.9.16, 16.9.16
Hospital, Country 16.1.71, 26.4.71, 1.5.71, 30.10.71, 8.2.72, 1.3.72, 20.6.72, 19.9.76, 1.12.80, 6.6.91
hospital (military) 2.12.94, 9.8.04
hospital (naval) 22.3.93
Hospital, Town 17.11.07
houses (Mollet's, at la Profonde Rue) (*see also* **warehouses**) 23.5.91, 5.11.91, 30.4.92, 22.3.93, 9.1.03, 18.3.12, 5.10.15, 27.9.16, 4.3.17, 30.3.17, 16.5.17, 25.2.18, 1.4.18, 29.4.18, 25.6.18, 27.6.18
houses (newly-built in the Castel parish) 18.9.15
Hunter (privateer) 26.1.78
hunting 18.1.73, 28.1.73, 17.10.74, 2.11.74, 23.1.12
hyacinths 3.2.95, 11.10.97
Ile Saint-Jean *see* **Prince Edward Island**
illnesses (serious, suffered by Mollet) 28.3.71–8.4.71, 1.10.75–22.11.75, 4.12.93–4.1.94, 16.1.09–16.2.09
illuminations (celebratory) 31.3.89, 17.4.89, 13.10.01, 18.9.17, 19.9.17
Imhoff, Lieutenant-General Sir Charles (Inspector of Militia) 29.6.12
India 21.1.03, 13.3.08, 23.1.10, 10.9.17
Ingilby, Robert (farm servant) 9.6.80, 11.6.80
Ingrouille, Eleazar (farm labourer, farmer) 15.2.85, **15.1.86**, 1.1.87, **1.12.87**, 6.12.87, 13.3.88, 25.3.88, **17.9.88**, 24.12.91, 23.8.92, 20.12.95, 11.10.97, 25.12.99, 22.5.01, 12.12.02, 26.3.03, **18.12.03**, 26.7.08, 25.10.09, 4.3.10, 4.2.11, 31.12.15, 8.2.16, 18.1.17, 19.5.17, 25.12.17, 21.4.18, 22.4.18
Ingrouille, Elizabeth (wife of Eleazar Ingrouille) *see* **Robert, Elizabeth**
Ingrouille, Henry (brother of Eleazar Ingrouille, emigrant to North America) 12.5.07
Ingrouille, Judith (aunt of Eleazar Ingrouille, wife of James Rouget) 18.12.03
Ingrouille, Judith (sister of Eleazar Ingrouille) 25.12.91, 25.12.99
Ingrouille, Paul (miller, father of Eleazar Ingrouille) 3.11.85, 15.1.86, 9.5.02
Ingrouille, Rachel (domestic servant) 9.9.76
insurance (of Mollet's houses) 24.11.91
Irving, Lieutenant-Colonel Paulus Aemilius (Lieutenant-Governor of Guernsey 1770–83) 23.8.71, 10.5.72, 23.6.72, 19.6.73, 8.8.73, 17.10.74, 21.12.74, 28.6.79, 21.8.79, 30.7.80, 29.6.93
Isle of Wight 25.10.89
Ivy Castle *see* **Château des Marais**

Jallobert de Monville, Denis (*émigré*) 19.6.94
Jallobert de Monville, Dominique (*émigré*) 19.6.94
Jean, Marie (wife of Philippe Jean) *see* **De Ste Croix, Marie**
Jean, Philippe (miniaturist) 24.7.18
Jehan, Leonard (farm servant) 21.3.74, 12.6.74
Jerbourg 1.5.79, 16.2.90, 30.9.17, 2.10.17
Jersey (French attacks on) 2.5.79, 6.1.81, 7.1.81, 13.1.81
Jersey (Mollet's mother's sojourns in) 26.5.72–22.7.72, 29.7.73–29.9.73, 10.4.74–31.5.74, 12.11.74–17.10.75, 14.4.76–23.3.77, 4.7.80–?
Jersey (Mollet's visits to) 6.3.71–3.4.71, 12.6.71–4.7.71, 12.10.73–17.11.73, 11.3.76–2.4.76, 3.3.80–24.3.80, 27.7.86–4.8.86, 26.10.90–28.10.90, 20.5.95–28.5.95, 17.6.96–23.6.96, 2.10.96–14.10.96
Jethou 22.8.08
Johnson, William (soldier & farm labourer) 11.2.09
Jones, Pitman (husband of Mollet's great-niece, Mary Brock) 2.8.16
Jurats (dispute with Bailiff William Le Marchant) 18.2.75, 1.4.75, 1.6.76, 15.6.76, 3.8.76, 29.3.77, 10.4.77, 16.4.77
Jurats (elections of) 30.6.72, 15.6.76, 16.4.77, 3.6.78, 23.10.00, 25.3.02, 5.10.02, 24.5.10
kale 4.1.71, 17.4.71, 2.9.74, 31.12.76, 13.5.77, 10.1.93
Keeper (Mollet's dog) 17.3.92
Kennedy family (tenants of Mollet's) 27.9.16
Keppel, George (3rd Earl of Albemarle, Governor of Jersey 1761–72) 12.6.71, 18.6.71, 23.6.71
Kew Gardens 4.8.71
King's Dutch Brigade *see* **Dutch Brigades**
King's Weights (farm of) 21.1.71, 20.1.72, 18.1.73, 17.1.74
Kinsella, Enoch (convicted fraudster & bigamist, transportee) 13.4.18
Kinsella, Marie (wife of Enoch Kinsella) *see* **Moullin, Marie**
Kite (privateer) 18.12.79
Langlois, Margueritte (domestic servant) 7.5.09, 28.5.09
Langlois, Marie (domestic servant) 21.11.80
larkspur 4.3.76, 8.4.79
Lassement, Pierre (farm labourer) 20.7.96
La Serre, Elizabeth (wife of Dr Guillaume La Serre) *see* **Perchard, Elizabeth**
La Serre, Dr John (son of Dr Guillaume La Serre; Jurat 1800–35) 28.6.73, 24.2.92, 23.10.00
La Serre, Dr Guillaume 23.7.71, 23.10.00
Le Beir, Rachel (domestic servant) 28.9.78, 18.10.78
Le Cheminant, Daniel (Mollet's first cousin once removed) 5.5.71, **30.10.71**, 13.8.74, 28.5.75, 13.8.77, 12.10.78, 14.6.79, 23.12.80

Le Cheminant, James (Mollet's first cousin) 28.2.71, 3.3.71, 5.5.71, 25.12.71, 13.9.73, 25.12.73, 25.12.74, 15.7.75, 10.5.78, 25.9.94, 25.12.94, 28.4.96
Le Cheminant, Nicolas (Mollet's first cousin) 3.3.71, 5.5.71, 2.1.72
Le Cheminant, Pierre (Mollet's first cousin) 3.3.71, 28.3.75, 12.2.77
Le Cocq, Carterette (wife of Nathaniel Le Cocq) *see* **Guille, Carterette**
Le Cocq, Joseph (farm labourer) 31.3.02
Le Cocq, Nathaniel 6.7.93, 3.10.00
Le Cornu, Hellier (sentenced to pillory for using false measure) 19.9.11
Le Cras, Charles (master stonemason) 26.11.72, 21.3.77, 23.10.95
leeks 23.7.77, 5.4.88, 7.5.93
Lefebvre, George, sen. (Seigneur of Blanchelande) 3.1.75, 13.3.75
Lefebvre, George, jun. (HM Greffier 1792–1835) 17.5.95
Lefebvre, Nicolas (son of George Lefebvre, sen.; HM Prévôt 1806–51) 26.4.92, 4.7.93, 11.4.95, 20.5.95, 10.1.99, 13.7.08, 12.3.09, 29.7.10, 20.8.15, 31.3.16, 8.1.18, 1.3.18, 26.4.18
Le Geyt, Daniel (farm labourer) 30.3.16, 5.10.16, 8.7.18, 1.8.18
Le Geyt, Elizabeth (domestic servant) 14.12.79, 9.2.80
Le Geyt, Henry (farm labourer, farm servant) 8.2.73, 20.7.73, 19.11.73
Le Gonidec, Armand-Mériadec (*émigré*) 18.12.95
Le Gonidec, Balthazar-Hyacinthe (*émigré*) 18.12.95
Le Havre de Grâce (France) 30.8.15, 30.10.15, 18.9.16, 4.6.17
Le Huray, Nicolas (watchmaker, emigrant to North America) 8.8.07
Leighton, Frances (wife of Sir Hew Dalrymple) 4.6.96, 9.7.96, 31.7.96, 28.9.01
Le Lievre, Elizabeth (domestic servant) 19.6.92, 30.5.93, 10.7.93
Le Lievre, Pierre (tenant of la Daumaillerie) 11.9.74, 13.12.85, 14.12.85
Le Marchant, Caroline (aunt of Josias Le Marchant, wife of Charles Andros) 11.11.10
Le Marchant, Caroline (daughter of Josias Le Marchant) 7.1.95
Le Marchant, Charles (merchant) 10.5.72
Le Marchant, Denis (son of John Gaspard Le Marchant) 19.9.11
Le Marchant, Eleazar (Jurat 1778–1832, Lieutenant-Bailiff 1800–32) 12.5.10
Le Marchant, Elizée (of la Haye du Puits) 4.1.71, 22.9.79
Le Marchant, Harriet (daughter of Josias Le Marchant, wife of Major McGregor & Nicolas Carey) 7.1.95, 31.12.97 27.5.11, 8.7.17, 15.7.17
Le Marchant, Hirzel (son of Bailiff William Le Marchant; HM Procureur 1774–93) 2.11.74, 17.10.86, 27.5.87, 17.8.93
Le Marchant, John (Rotterdam-based merchant) 9.8.10
Le Marchant, Major-General John Gaspard 1.9.07, 19.9.11, 1.10.11
Le Marchant, Josias (of la Haye du Puits, Jurat 1802–31) 11.10.74, 17.10.74, 18.12.74, 24.4.76, 2.9.77, 9.5.78, 4.10.78, 4.5.79, 21.2.80, 17.10.86, 5.3.92, 2.1.94, 7.1.95, 26.7.97, 21.11.99, 18.4.00, 1.9.00, **25.3.02**, 8.6.06, 27.5.11, 9.4.17, 6.11.17, 18.3.18

Le Marchant, Judith (wife of Josias Le Marchant) *see* **Ozanne, Judith**
Le Marchant, Marie (mother of Josias Le Marchant) *see* **Bonamy, Marie**
Le Marchant, Mary (daughter of Robert Porret Le Marchant, wife of John Le Marchant of Rotterdam) 9.8.10
Le Marchant, Pierre (brother of Josias Le Marchant) 12.12.97
Le Marchant, Pierre (brother of Bailiff William Le Marchant) 12.8.08, 17.4.17
Le Marchant, Robert Porret (son of Bailiff William Le Marchant; Bailiff 1800–1810) 24.4.74, 11.5.77, 3.9.79, 17.10.86, **25.1.87**, 6.1.89, **24.11.91**, 17.4.94, **19.11.99**, **4.2.02**, 13.9.02, 8.6.06, **25.8.06**, **26.11.07**, 14.12.07, **11.3.08**, **12.5.10**, **9.8.10**, 9.7.11, 1.10.11, 21.10.16, 22.12.17, 18.7.18
Le Marchant, Thomas (son of John Gaspard Le Marchant) 18.1.17, 25.6.17, 21.1.18, 19.5.18
Le Marchant, William (Bailiff 1771–1800) 26.4.71, 18.12.71, 7.10.74, 18.2.1775, 18.1.77, 25.1.77, 8.9.77, 6.6.91, **21.11.95**, **28.11.95**, 5.12.95, 12.12.95, 30.4.96, 8.6.06, 21.10.09
Le Marchant, William (of la Haye du Puits, uncle of Josias Le Marchant) 4.1.71, 1.5.71, 8.2.72, 15.2.72, 20.6.72, 7.1.73, 11.2.73
Le Messurier, Jean (farm servant) 22.1.71, 11.2.71
Le Mesurier, Abraham (of les Beaucamps, merchant) 28.7.71, 24.6.74, 26.11.97, 26.3.11, 9.8.11, 10.8.11
Le Mesurier, Frederick (son of Alderney Governor Henry Le Mesurier, husband of Mollet's great-niece Martha Brock) 17.8.08, 22.8.08, 29.8.08, 19.12.08, 30.8.15, 17.5.18
Le Mesurier, Havilland (son of Alderney Governor Jean Le Mesurier) 30.4.88
Le Mesurier, Henry (Alderney Governor 1729–43) 27.2.71, 18.2.72, 25.4.73
Le Mesurier, Jean (Alderney Governor 1744–93) 12.12.86, 31.12.87
Le Mesurier, Mary (wife & cousin of Alderney Governor Peter Le Mesurier) 4.2.88, 30.5.88, 1.7.88, 22.11.88
Le Mesurier, Nicolas (son of Alderney Governor Henry Le Mesurier) 8.6.71
Le Mesurier, Peter (Alderney Governor 1793–1803) 27.2.71, 17.7.71, 23.7.71, 12.10.87, 31.12.87, 1.1.88, 30.5.88, 14.7.88, 29.7.88, 22.11.88, 17.4.89, **23.9.89**, 24.9.89, 25.9.88, 27.9.88, **7.10.89**, 16.11.89
Le Mesurier, Paul (son of Alderney Governor Jean Le Mesurier; MP for Southwark) 4.9.90
Le Moine, Monsieur (Curé de Hubert-Folie, *émigré* priest) 26.9.92, 22.5.94, 9.6.94
Le Moine, Monsieur (Curé de Saint-Agnan, *émigré* priest) 26.9.92, 22.5.94, 9.6.94
lemon cake 4.6.17
lemon essence 1.4.17
lemons 22.4.86, 6.12.08, 23.3.17, 1.4.17
Lemprière, Charles (Lieutenant-Bailiff of Jersey 1750–81) 18.10.73

Lenfestey, Thomas (carpenter, emigrant to North America) 14.1.09
Lennox, Charles (3rd Duke of Richmond) 15.5.85, 22.7.86–26.7.86
Le Page, Anne (domestic servant) 28.6.86, 1.1.88, 24.3.88, 5.5.88, 17.6.88, 31.7.88, 1.1.90, 16.1.90, 16.7.90
Le Page, Elizée (militia bandmaster, emigrant to North America) 28.8.06, 6.7.12
Le Page, James (master plasterer & roofer) 6.6.07, 10.11.10
Le Page, Jean (farm servant) 15.12.91, 21.3.92
Le Page, Marie (domestic servant) 14.6.09, 19.7.09, 18.12.10
Le Page, Nicolas (Mollet's manservant in Alderney) 17.5.88, 27.5.88, 10.12.88
Le Page, Pierre (of les Grandes Rocques & le Guet) 27.10.08, 28.10.08, 17.11.08
Le Page, Samuel (farm labourer, farm servant, smallholder) 7.9.95, 10.9.96, 21.5.99, 22.5.99
Le Page, Susanne (wife of Nicolas Le Page) *see* **Trachy, Susanne**
Le Pelley, Captain Denis 20.1.79, 29.7.79, 25.12.79, **27.8.97**, **7.10.02**, 1.9.15, 6.2.18
Le Pelley, Hellier (Mollet's manservant in Alderney) 21.12.88, 18.8.89
Le Pelley, Jean (farmer, Mollet's neighbour) 20.1.79, 22.12.85, 1.1.86, 22.12.86, 4.2.87, 2.12.89, 10.4.91, 25.2.94, 27.8.97
Le Pelley, Captain Nicolas 20.1.79, 27.8.97, 19.1.01, 8.4.03, 23.12.03, 15.5.04, 1.9.15
Le Pelley, Susanne (mother of Captains Denis & Nicolas Le Pelley, & farmers Jean & Thomas Le Pelley) *see* **de Beaucamp, Susanne**
Le Pelley, Thomas (farmer, Mollet's neighbour) 20.1.79, 31.12.80, 22.12.85, 25.12.85, 18.11.86, 22.12.86, 18.6.89, 17.7.89, 10.4.91, 1.4.99, 23.4.99, 19.1.00, 14.3.00, 23.12.00, 23.12.01, 23.12.02, **24.3.03**, **25.3.03**, 19.4.03, 23.12.05, 23.12.06, 24.12.07, 23.12.08, **23.12.09**, 22.12.10, 23.12.11, 1.9.15, 21.4.18
Le Prevost, Daniel (tailor) 27.9.16
Le Ray, Elizabeth/Lisabo (domestic servant, wife of Abraham Machon) 30.5.93, **20.1.98**, **22.3.98**, 3.7.00, 21.7.00, 3.12.09, 11.12.09, 26.12.09, 28.4.11, **15.11.11**, **1.12.11**, 6.6.16
Le Ray, Guillaume (sailor, cousin of Elizabeth Le Ray) 5.8.10
Le Ray, Jeanne (domestic servant) 6.1.94
Lerrier, Anne (mother of William Chepmell, sen., wife of Philip Chepmell & Dr William Fergusson) 4.7.76
Lerrier, Anne (Mollet's niece, daughter of Philippe Lerrier, sen.) 13.6.85, 10.10.91, 11.12.91
Lerrier, Charles (Mollet's nephew, son of Philippe Lerrier, sen.) 13.7.71, 23.8.71, 6.10.72, 10.4.74
Lerrier, Delicia (Mollet's great-niece, daughter of Philippe Lerrier, jun.) 26.7.04
Lerrier, Edward (Mollet's nephew, son of Philippe Lerrier, sen.) 21.7.74, 7.9.74
Lerrier, John (Mollet's nephew, son of Philippe Lerrier, sen.) 23.9.97
Lerrier, Marie (Mollet's sister) *see* **Mollet, Marie**

Lerrier, Philippe, sen. (Mollet's brother-in-law, husband of Mollet's sister Marie) 4.2.71, 2.7.71, 2.8.71, 4.8.71, 23.8.71, 6.10.72, 16.6.74, 2.9.74, 7.9.74, 4.12.74, 5.12.74, 8.12.74, 14.12.74, 15.12.74, 12.6.87, 31.3.92
Lerrier, Philippe, jun. (surgeon, Mollet's nephew) 16.6.74, 21.6.74, 24.6.74, 21.8.77, 2.9.77, 13.1.80
Lerrier, Polly (Mollet's niece, daughter of Philippe Lerrier, sen.) 26.1.85, 23.6.85, 7.4.92, **18.6.92**, 23.6.93, 25.3.95, 8.7.96, **30.5.97**, 28.6.98, 13.9.03, 26.3.06, 27.5.07, **26.10.11**, 8.4.12
Le Tellier, Louis-Sébastien (*émigré* priest) 4.7.93
Le Tocq, Elizabeth (domestic servant) 5.2.00, 23.4.00
lettuce 28.8.88, 27.2.89, 8.4.89, 24.8.91
Le Vavasseur dit Durell, Jean (Mollet's uncle) 2.7.71, 24.8.71, 17.1.72, 23.1.72, 23.6.72, 8.3.76, 13.3.76, 17.5.93, 19.5.93
Le Vavasseur dit Durell, Marie (Mollet's mother) 29.1.71, 31.12.71, 1.1.72, 26.5.72, 22.7.72, 29.7.73, 29.9.73, 10.4.74, 31.5.74, 12.11.74, 17.10.75, 14.4.76, 23.3.77, 4.5.77, 4.7.77, 5.12.77, 9.7.78, 18.10.78 13.12.78, 11.9.79, 26.10.79, 9.2.80, 14.5.80, 4.7.80, 13.10.80, 8.5.85, 20.7.85, 16.8.85, 2.10.85, 31.3.86, **16.5.86**, 4.7.86, 30.8.86, 27.10.86, 18.4.87, **9.5.87**, 22.11.87, 18.6.88, 19.6.88, 16.11.88, **1.1.92**, 18.1.92, 5.2.92, 8.2.92, **19.2.92**, 24.2.92
Level, Jean (French prisoner-of-war & farm labourer) 7.4.79, 21.8.79
Liberty (pleasure yacht) 21.6.86, 20.5.95, 28.5.95
libraries (circulating) 22.11.02, 27.11.15
'licence trade' 21.9.09
Lihou, Etienne (farm labourer, gardener, smallholder) 14.1.71, 14.9.73, 10.12.87, 16.10.95, 11.12.98, 23.5.99, 6.5.06, 26.11.06, 13.3.10, **15.3.10**, 10.3.12, **21.3.16**, **9.1.18**, 8.7.18
Lihou, James (Mollet as executor of) 23.9.80, 4.10.80
Lihou, James (miller of L'Echelle) 5.12.72
Lihou, Rachel (daughter of Etienne Lihou, wife of Nicolas Roussel) 9.1.18
Lihou Island 22.8.74, 24.4.76, 1.9.06, 17.8.08
lilies (Guernsey) 6.8.98, 28.8.98, 28.8.09, 23.9.09, 26.8.15, 30.8.15
lime 14.11.71, 29.7.73
lime-pit 7.12.71
limpets 15.12.94, 26.12.94
loans (money borrowed by Mollet from others) 10.6.71, 13.8.74, 28.5.75, 15.7.75, 12.10.78
loans (money lent by Mollet to others) 10.5.78
London (Mollet's visit to) 16.7.71–19.8.71
longue veille 22.12.85, 22.12.86, 21.12.87, 23.12.00, 23.12.01, 23.12.02, 23.12.03, 23.12.05, 23.12.06, 24.12.07, 23.12.08, 23.12.09, 22.12.10, 23.12.11, 23.12.16, 23.12.17
Lorani family (of Alderney) 8.1.88

Louis XVI (King of France) 22.6.86–26.6.86, 23.8.89
lucerne 18.9.71, 26.3.06
Ludlam, Peter (merchant) 1.6.89
Lye, John (butcher) 25.10.10
MacCulloch, Allaire, Bonamy & Co. (bankers) 2.5.11
MacCulloch, Thomas (merchant) 20.8.15, 31.12.15, 12.5.16, 4.5.17, 1.3.18, 26.4.18, 26.7.18
Macdonald, Donald (soldier & farm labourer) 7.3.01
Machon, Abraham (farm servant, smallholder) 7.8.89, 24.1.90, 22.3.92, 31.8.95, 6.9.95, 14.9.95, 17.6.96, 14.10.96, 12.8.97, 20.1.98, **22.3.98**, 3.7.00, 21.7.00, 21.5.01, 22.5.01, 12.5.07, **15.11.11**, **5.7.12**, 10.2.16
Machon, Daniel (brother of Abraham Machon, emigrant to North America) 24.8.06, 28.8.06, 3.10.08, 9.7.09, 28.6.11, 6.7.12, 18.4.16
Machon, Elizabeth (wife of Abraham Machon) *see* **Le Ray, Elizabeth**
Machon, Elizabeth (daughter of Abraham Machon, subsequently wife of Thomas Sarre) 15.11.11, **24.11.11**, 18.1.16, 5.9.16, 18.9.16, 30.3.18
Machon, Judith (wife of Jacques Dorey) 4.1.16, 9.1.16
Machon, Judith (wife of Pierre Allez) 17.3.17, 13.5.17
Machon, Pierre (brother of Abraham Machon, farm labourer, farm servant, shoemaker, sailor) 18.2.99, 12.5.99, 24.7.99, 27.8.99, 20.1.00, 21.1.00, 22.1.00, 21.3.00, 16.11.00, **13.10.02**, **27.3.03**, 25.12.03, 1.4.04, 5.1.08, 20.1.18, 23.5.18, 26.7.18
Mackelcan, Lieutenant-Colonel John (military engineer) 15.5.01, 25.5.01, 19.4.02, 14.10.06
Mackenzie, Lieutenant-General Francis (Lord Seaforth) 19.11.78
Mackenzie, Major-General John (Lord Macleod) 1.3.78, 19.11.78
mackerel 15.6.76, 4.7.16, 2.7.18, 8.7.18
Macleod, Lieutenant-Colonel Norman 20.10.01
Madeira 27.1.78, 25.10.08
Madras (India) 24.9.91, 19.7.93, 21.1.03, 13.3.08
Maggioretti, Mr (conjurer) 6.1.16
magnifying glass 6.10.71
magnolia 30.3.72
magpies 15.5.04
Mahy, William (early Methodist) 18.11.87
Mahy, William (publican, suspected thief) 22.11.07
mail packet 28.1.04, 5.2.09, 5.11.11
Maindonal, Elizabeth (wife of Pierre Priaulx) 9.3.17, 16.4.17
Maingy, Mary (wife of Rev. Thomas Carey) 30.11.03
Mare de Carteret, la (hostelry at) 25.5.71, 3.1.75, 2.7.76, 8.9.77

Marett, Thomas (Mollet's business partner in Alderney) 14.11.87, 23.11.87, 18.1.88, 4.3.88, 18.7.88, 28.8.88, 26.8.89, 24.9.89, 16.11.89, 8.5.90, 18.5.90, 16.3.91, 27.6.91, 26.2.96
Marie, Frère François see **Mortier, Jean**
market (new) 7.11.71, 9.11.71, 14.12.71, 11.1.72, 23.1.73
Marquand, Abraham (brother-in-law of Elizabeth Machon née Le Ray) 25.1.01, 26.7.01, 28.4.11
Marquand, Charles (emigrant to North America) 18.4.16
Marquand, Isaac (nephew of Elizabeth Machon, fosterling of Mollet's) 20.12.01, 6.2.03, 17.7.07, 27.6.08, 15.8.08, 23.12.09, **4.3.10**, 12.3.10, 17.9.10, **23.11.11**, **26.11.11**, 27.11.11, **29.3.12**, 17.12.15, 24.12.15, 22.2.16, 16.6.16, 9.8.16, 1.9.16, 25.12.16, **31.5.18**
Marquis, Judith (convicted thief) 26.6.02
Marseilles (France) 4.6.17
Martel, Jean (of les Eturs) 25.12.11
Martel, Nicolas (farm servant) 22.4.87, 2.5.87. 1.1.88, 5.5.88, 20.5.88
Martel, Thomas (of les Boulains) 4.4.07, 9.4.07, 13.4.07, 27.4.07
Martineau, René (Anglican clergyman) 31.1.73, 26.12.74, 25.12.77, 25.12.78, 22.6.10, 19.10.16, 10.9.17
Martinique 28.11.72
Mauger, Thomas (tenant of Mollet's) 19.1.95
Mauritius 23.9.91
McCrea, Jeanne (wife of Robert McCrea) see **Coutart, Jeanne**
McCrea, Robert (military officer) 12.9.93, 31.7.96, 25.3.99
measures (of volume) 29.1.71
medicine 16.9.80, 24.1.09, 3.2.09, 20.9.11, 22.11.11
melons 6.4.72, 9.8.73
Melvill, Philip (military officer) 16.7.90
messier (of Castel parish) 4.5.75
Methodists 19.8.87, 1.9.87, 11.11.87, 8.12.87, 22.5.88, 6.9.89, 22.2.03
Metivier, Esther (wife of Jean Carey Metivier) see **Guille, Esther**
Metivier, George (poet & lexicographer, son of Esther Metivier) 9.9.00, 3.7.07, 30.10.07, 21.10.16, 8.11.16
Metivier, John (Advocate, son of Esther Metivier) 9.9.00, 9.10.10
Metivier, Jean Carey (HM Comptroller 1793–6, husband of Esther Guille) 9.11.93, 11.1.96, 17.5.98
Metivier, William (merchant, Jurat 1845–81, son of Esther Metivier) 9.9.00, 14.6.06, 17.6.16
Migault, André (Anglican clergyman) 1.1.71, 11.1.71, 22.2.71, 25.2.71, 3.5.72, 30.6.73, **31.10.73**
militia (general) 4.1.71, 10.6.71, 8.6.72, 19.6.72, 4.7.73, 24.6.74, 24.6.76, 24.6.77, 8.4.78, 30.7.80, 17.7.85, 24.7.86, 24.6.91, 31.7.96, 24.7.97, 3.5.98,

25.3.99, 19.4.02, 20.3.03, **11.4.03**, 21.5.04, 20.9.07, 3.4.09, 26.6.09, **23.4.10**, **20.6.16**, 24.6.17, 23.3.18
militia (mutiny of) 11.6.80–13.6.80, 8.7.80
milk 27.1.09, 23.1.10
mill *see* **Moulin**
millers 13.10.71, 5.12.72
miscarriage 28.10.07, 19.8.17
Mitchell family (tenants of Mollet's) 22.3.93
Mollet, Charles (Mollet's father) 19.1.87, 19.2.92
Mollet, Marie (Mollet's mother) *see* **Le Vavasseur dit Durell, Marie**
Mollet, Marie (Mollet's sister, wife of Philippe Lerrier, sen.) 4.2.71, 27.7.71, 2.8.71, 4.8.71, 6.10.72, 21.7.74, 17.8.74, 7.9.74, 13.6.85, 28.7.85, 28.5.86, 30.5.86, 3.7.86, 12.6.87, 24.7.87, **28.7.87**, 10.10.91, 11.12.91, 23.6.96, 11.8.96, 29.5.08, 29.8.09
Mollet, Marthe (Mollet's sister, wife of Peter Mourant, sen.) 9.1.71, 20.1.71, 7.4.71, **5.10.71**, 25.12.71, 3.5.72, 22.11.72, 1.1.73, **20.5.73**, 25.12.73, 1.1.74, **23.3.74**, 22.5.74, 9.10.74, 6.6.75, **29.1.76**, 3.7.76, 24.10.76, 12.11.76, 27.7.77, **10.7.78**, 7.1.79, 28.8.79, 23.10.79, 3.6.85, 16.5.86, 30.5.86, 9.5.87, 26.10.90, **12.8.91**, 15.8.91, 23.11.94, 30.5.97, 28.6.98, 12.8.98, **18.8.98**, 21.8.98
Mont d'Aval, le (Mollet's fields at) 26.9.73, 19.10.79
Mont Saint-Michel (Mollet's visit to) 19.10.90–20.10.90
Moravians 25.12.75, 20.2.17
Mortemart, le Duc de *see* **de Rochechouart, Victurnien**
Mortier, Jean (*émigré* Capuchin friar also known as Frère François Marie) 16.4.99, 23.7.99, 7.8.99, 9.2.00, 20.6.00, 31.12.00, 24.5.01, 17.12.01, 23.6.02, 31.12.02, 27.10.03, 7.12.03, 1.1.06, 2.7.07, 3.8.08, 21.1.09, 16.7.09, 4.3.10, 26.5.11, 23.8.15, 25.1.16, 13.4.17, 23.5.17, 31.8.17, 15.3.18, 22.4.18, 26.7.18
Morvan, Monsieur (*émigré* priest) 22.10.95
Moulin de Bas (also known as le Grand Moulin du Roi or King's Mill) 10.10.77, 9.5.02
Moulin de l'Echelle 5.12.72
Moulin du Milieu 16.9.76, 3.11.85
Moulin des Monts 1.11.99, 9.4.00, 18.4.00
Moulin des Niots 5.12.72
Moullin, James (basket-maker) 8.10.74
Moullin, Marie (wife of Nicolas Moullin & Richard Moullin) *see* **Tourgis, Marie**
Moullin, Marie (of les Vallées, wife of Enoch Kinsella) 13.4.18
Moullin, Nicolas (of le Ponchez) 22.12.85
Moullin, Nicolas, sen. (of les Vallées) 20.2.71, 28.10.71, 8.9.87
Moullin, Nicolas, jun. (of les Vallées) 8.7.07
Moullin, Richard (cooper & publican) 12.9.72, 14.5.78, 11.6.80, 4.2.02

Moullin, Susanne (wife of Nicolas Moullin, jun., of les Vallées) *see* **Nicolle, Susanne**

Mourant, Anne/Nancy (Mollet's niece, wife of William Brock) 9.10.74, 2.4.76, 7.1.79, 25.2.85, 5.6.86, 8.3.87, 14.3.89, 12.6.92, **30.12.96**, **31.12.96**, 30.4.98, 18.8.06, 29.9.06, 18.9.16

Mourant, Catherine (wife of Rev. Edward Mourant) *see* **Whiskin, Catherine**

Mourant, Edward (Anglican clergyman) 7.6.93, 27.7.94, 29.1.95, 6.2.95, 19.4.95, 13.6.95, 10.7.95, 15.8.95, 30.8.95, 19.9.95, 29.9.95, 22.10.95, 28.11.95, 20.12.95, 22.5.96, **28.6.96**, 10.9.96, 14.11.96, 23.12.96, 3.1.97, 19.10.97, 3.1.98, 4.4.98, 25.5.98, 22.7.98, 12.9.98, 11.11.98, 21.4.99, 6.4.00

Mourant, Martha/Patty (Mollet's niece, wife of Bonamy Dobrée) 9.10.74, 18.9.76, 24.10.76, 12.11.76, 7.1.79, 28.8.79, 26.1.85, 15.5.85, 3.10.85, 29.10.85, 30.10.85, 1.11.85, **18.5.87**, 19.5.87, 15.8.87, 15.2.90, **28.5.91**, 1.1.98, **2.1.98**, 6.1.98

Mourant, Marthe (Mollet's sister) *see* **Mollet, Marthe**

Mourant, Mary (Mollet's niece, wife of Henry Brock) 9.10.74, 7.1.79, 27.1.85, 25.2.85, 1.10.92, 29.6.97, 13.9.03, 13.11.07, 3.5.08, 31.5.10, 9.3.11, **24.3.12**, **15.6.12**, **4.7.12**, 30.8.15, 9.10.15, 29.4.16, 22.7.16, 18.9.16, 22.12.17, 21.1.18, 17.4.18, 22.4.18, 20.7.18

Mourant, Peter, sen. (Mollet's brother-in-law, husband of Marthe Mollet) 11.171, 12.1.71, 20.1.71, 7.4.71, 14.4.71, 25.12.71, 3.5.72, 22.7.72, 6.9.72, 22.11.72, 1.1.73, 6.6.73, 25.12.73, 1.1.74, 13.3.74, 3.5.74, 24.6.74, 18.12.74, 25.12.74, 6.6.75, 13.7.76, 26.1.78, 28.1.78, 9.5.78, 28.8.79, 23.10.79, 3.6.85, 15.12.85, 9.5.87, 20.12.88, 16.1.89, 22.7.90, 17.3.92, 8.7.96, 18.3.07, 14.5.07, 25.4.07, 24.5.07, 27.5.07

Mourant, Peter, jun. (Mollet's nephew) 9.10.74, 7.1.79, 28.7.89, 1.8.89, 21.8.89–26.8.89, 5.9.89, 9.9.90, **1.10.90**, **22.4.92**, 1.10.92, 8.12.94, **9.1.98**, 28.6.98, 21.8.98, 13.9.03, 31.12.06, **3.8.07**, 4.8.07, **18.8.07**, 31.5.10, 9.7.11, 19.9.11, **30.10.15**, 29.4.16, 25.6.17, 21.1.18, 22.4.18

Mourant, Sophia (wife of Peter Mourant, jun.) *see* **Carey, Sophia**

Mourant, Stephen (brother of Peter Mourant, sen.) 2.4.86, 24.12.92, 22.7.98, 4.5.99, 7.5.99

Mouriaux House (Mollet's home in Alderney) 31.12.87, 1.1.88, 4.1.88

Mouton, Marie (flogged for theft) 8.2.72

murders 3.4.75, 5.4.75, 1.7.75, 14.7.75, 1.6.95

muskets 18.6.72, 13.8.77, 8.4.78

myrtle 30.3.72

Nant, Michel (crabpot-maker) 30.1.16

Naftel, Nicolas (master of St Andrew's school) 12.3.10

National School (St Peter Port) 8.7.16, 10.6.18, 13.6.18

Neale, James 22.2.16

Néel, Marie (wife of Jean-Jacques Condamine) 30.6.73, 7.8.74, 1.9.08

New Street (St Peter Port) 22.7.90
New York (USA) 26.4.07, 12.5.07
Newell family (tenants of Mollet's) 5.10.15, 27.9.16
Newfoundland 29.10.73, 9.7.09, 28.6.11, 6.7.12
newspapers 19.8.89, 28.1.04, 28.8.06, 28.2.08, 4.12.08, 1.1.09, 15.6.12, 24.11.15
Nicolet, Georges (farm servant) 31.3.02, 28.9.02, 14.10.02, 1.6.03, 5.6.03, 6.6.03, 11.6.03, 6.8.04, 3.11.07, 11.7.09, 16.7.09, 1.9.16
Nicolet, Jacques (farm servant) 31.3.02, 28.9.02, 14.10.02, 1.6.03
Nicolet, Jacques (thatcher) 15.6.02
Nicolet, Jean (farm labourer) 2.5.02
Nicolle, Charles, sen. (of Albecq, farm labourer, smallholder) 10.3.12, 12.5.16
Nicolle, Isaac (son of Charles Nicolle, jun., farm labourer, smallholder) 27.8.10, 30.8.10, 10.12.10, 16.1.16
Nicolle, Marie (domestic servant, subsequently wife of Pierre Gavet) 29.5.86, 23.8.86, 6.3.87, 30.9.87, 8.2.90, 20.12.99
Nicolle, Pierre (son of Isaac Nicolle, fosterling of Mollet's) 27.8.10, 22.4.11, 6.5.11, 12.4.16, 22.4.16, 8.7.16, **10.6.18**, 30.6.18, 2.7.18
Nicolle, Rachel (wife of Isaac Nicolle) *see* **Ferbrache, Rachel**
Nicolle, Susanne (wife of Nicolas Moullin of les Vallées) 11.10.17
Nicolle, Thomas (dispute with his brother William Nicolle) 19.6.77, 1.10.77, 13.1.79
Noël, Louis (farm labourer) 11.10.16, 31.12.16
Nova Scotia 5.3.06, 6.5.12, 4.4.18
noyau (*eau de*) see ***eau de noyau***
oats 19.9.71, 8.3.73, 27.7.80, 4.3.18
Ogier, Henry (farm labourer) 28.8.15, 2.9.15, 3.11.15
O'Hara, Mr (of Gaspé) 4.4.18, 11.4.18
Ohio (USA) 14.1.09, 6.2.11
onions 12.3.72, 17.5.80, 5.4.88, 13.3.10, 21.3.16
Oporto (Portugal) 6.12.08
oranges 6.12.08
Ordinances (of the Royal Court) 21.1.71, 5.10.72, 18.1.73, 13.5.75, 19.1.78, 5.10.78, 21.1.09, 3.11.16
ormers 19.2.72, 11.3.85, 6.3.02, 5.3.06, 14.2.16
osier 8.2.71, 24.2.74, 5.1.08, 5.1.09
oven 26.11.72
oxen 15.12.71, 26.4.72, 20.5.73, 21.11.76, 9.8.09, 5.7.12, 4.3.18
Oxford University 9.1.11, 16.4.11
Ozanne, Charles (farm labourer) 1.10.15, 17.12.15, 24.12.15, 5.5.16
Ozanne, Jacques (farm labourer, tenant of Mollet's) 9.1.03, 21.1.07, 3.1.12, **15.3.12**, 31.8.17

Ozanne, James (of la Porte) 14.11.71, 17.12.85, 10.7.93, 8.7.07, 23.4.10
Ozanne, Judith (widow of Jurat Jean Ozanne of la Houguette) *see* **Guille, Judith**
Ozanne, Judith (daughter of Jurat Jean Ozanne, wife of Josias Le Marchant) 6.8.72, 24.8.72, 24.4.76, 18.10.78, 25.12.78, 1.1.79, 21.2.80, 27.1.95, 19.7.97, 26.7.97, **20.7.01**, 29.12.09, 4.7.18
Ozanne, Marie (daughter of Jurat Jean Ozanne, wife of Robert Le Marchant) 8.6.72, 25.1.87, 11.4.08
Ozanne, Richard (of les Mourains) 11.6.80, **1.1.00**, 31.12.02, 17.6.17
Ozanne, Susanne (daughter of Jacques Ozanne, fosterling of Mollet's, domestic servant) 9.1.03, 7.4.07, 20.4.10, 24.11.11, 10.8.16, 8.6.17
Paccarin, Thomas (farm servant) 8.1.02, 7.3.02
paper (writing) 4.5.99, 7.5.99, 15.7.00
'Paradis' (Mary Brock's new house in the Grange, St Peter Port) 15.6.12, 4.7.12
Paris (France) 14.1.10, 30.10.15, 9.4.18
Paris, René-Jean (*émigré* priest) 22.10.95
parish meetings (Castel) 15.5.71, 7.1.72, 28.10.72, 30.6.98, 14.3.00
parlour 1.5.80, 21.9.97, 22.7.98, 25.10.98, 23.12.06, 10.2.09, 4.3.10, 8.3.10, 21.10.16, 27.6.18
parsnips 20.2.71, 18.9.71, 1.3.72, 16.2.76, 21.11.76, 30.1.86, 12.6.87, 28.2.92, 6.3.94, 12.6.97, 21.5.99, 22.5.99, 4.11.02, 1.1.03, 8.11.03, 3.11.06, 19.3.17, 31.12.17, 16.2.18, 4.3.18
Patriarche, David (Jersey Jurat) 19.10.73
Paul I (Tsar of Russia) 3.6.00, 19.4.01
Peace of Amiens (1802–3) (*see also* **Treaty of London**) 4.10.01, 13.10.01, 20.5.03
Peace of Paris (1815) 18.1.16
peacocks (& peahens) 11.6.85, 12.9.94, 6.10.00
pears 15.1.07, 19.10.07, 6.10.10, 24.10.15, 19.10.16
peas 22.2.71, 1.5.71, 11.5.71, 8.3.73, 3.5.74, 23.12.85, 26.4.88, 27.2.89, 19.3.89, 3.5.92, 6.3.94, 15.8.95, 24.5.96, 18.12.97, 11.1.05, 11.6.06, 21.6.12, 4.3.18
peat 24.5.77, 31.5.77, 31.3.86, 10.5.92, 14.3.16, 15.3.16, 8.4.17
Perchard, Elizabeth (wife of Dr Guillaume La Serre) 23.7.71, 2.8.71
Perchard, Dr Jean (suspected suicide) 1.6.99
Perchard, John (of London, banking agent & silversmith) 24.7.71
Perchard, Matthew (of London, banking agent & silversmith) 24.7.71, 27.7.71
perche (unit of area) 19.2.71
Perrin, Judith (domestic servant) 23.2.85, 11.1.87
Perron, Paul (farm servant) 4.1.85, 16.1.85
pews (owned by Mollet) 19.9.94
Phoenix Insurance Co. 24.11.91

picnics (& pleasure trips) 6.6.73, 20.6.73, 9.5.75, 24.5.75, 6.8.75, 24.4.76, 6.8.76, 13.9.02, 26.7.97, 14.9.04, 11.7.06, 11.8.06, 18.8.06, 25.8.06, 1.9.06, 13.7.08, 20.7.08, 26.7.08, 17.8.08, 22.8.08, 29.8.08, 9.7.11, 7.8.11
Piercy, Mary (wife of William Piercy) *see* **Dobrée, Mary**
pigeons 16.12.76, 10.12.06
pigs 18.9.71, 13.3.73, 10.9.76, 16.12.80, 1.1.87, 27.5.88, 27.9.91, 31.12.92, 28.5.94, 4.12.99, 22.2.03, 3.11.06, 12.1.07, 3.1.12
pigsties 27.9.91, 23.10.95, 11.1.05, 25.9.16
pilot boat (lost) 22.11.07
Pinchemain, Jean (farm servant) 4.2.11, 19.2.11, 26.2.11, 27.2.11
Pipon, Thomas (HM Procureur, Jersey) 23.6.71, 26.3.76
Pleinmont 4.10.78, 3.9.79, 14.9.04, 11.8.06, 13.7.08, 9.7.11, 7.8.11
plums 2.9.88, 30.10.07
polyanthus 4.3.76
ponds 17.10.85, 19.10.85, 5.9.98, 6.9.98, 20.12.16
Poore, John (timber & corn merchant) 25.2.06, 13.6.18
Portsmouth 10.7.71, 13.7.71, 29.7.71, 15.1.04, 16.2.08, 13.3.08
potatoes (export of) 15.3.17, 17.3.17, 3.5.17
potatoes (general) 30.1.71, 24.2.72, 19.6.77, 7.12.80, 5.12.89, 20.11.90, 19.4.92, 3.5.92, 6.3.94, 20.2.95, 25.2.95, 19.9.95, 5.12.96, 4.11.02, 1.1.07, 8.7.09, 1.5.16, 4.3.18, 27.6.18
Potenger, Harriet (wife of Thomas Potenger) 23.5.01, 31.8.06
Potenger, Mary (wife of Thomas Potenger) *see* **Brock, Mary**
Potenger, Richard (son of Thomas Potenger, Anglican clergyman) 10.1.99
Potenger, Thomas (of les Vauxbelets, Anglican clergyman without cure) 18.4.97, 23.4.97, 27.8.97, 27.5.98, 4.8.98, 10.10.98, 25.10.98, 4.12.99, 12.3.00, 11.9.00, 6.2.04, 18.4.04, 16.12.05, 31.12.05
poulage 30.9.71
poultice 21.1.09
poultry 18.11.72, 1.1.80, 7.1.88, 11.5.93, 28.5.94, 22.5.97, 1.1.03, 6.1.03, 7.1.03, 8.1.03, 9.103, 18.2.03, 16.1.09, 8.12.09, 22.2.17, 27.6.18
Pradon, Antoine (Anglican clergyman) *see* **Gounon dit Pradon, Antoine**
Préel, le (Mollet's house at) 14.12.85, 28.12.87, 26.11.91
pregnancy (outside wedlock, Anne Le Page's) 5.5.88, 17.6.88, 31.7.88
Priaulx, Elizabeth (wife of Pierre Priaulx) *see* **Maindonal, Elizabeth**
Prince Edward Island 24.8.06, 28.8.06, 3.10.08, 9.7.09, 29.12.11
Prince William Frederick (Duke of Gloucester) 18.9.17
Prince William Henry (later William IV) 4.2.86, 6.6.86
prisoners-of-war (French) 1.3.79, 7.4.79, 21.8.79, 10.4.95, 6.4.97, 14.11.00, 26.10.01
prisoners-of-war (Guernsey) 15.1.04, 10.3.08, 20.11.08, 20.8.09

privateers 26.1.78, 28.1.78, 19.4.78, 4.5.78, 5.5.78, 8.5.78, 9.5.78, 16.8.78, 21.9.78, 5.10.78, 7.10.78, 12.10.78, 16.10.78, 10.11.78, 5.7.79, 29.7.79, 15.9.79, 16.11.79, 18.12.79, 29.12.79, 1.4.91, 11.4.91, 15.4.91, 19.11.09, 5.11.11, 12.1.12, 27.2.12

Procureur des Pauvres 7.1.72, 13.12.85

Profonde Rue, la (*see also* **houses**; **warehouses**) 31.12.79, 30.5.86, 5.11.91, 22.3.93, 15.10.99, 12.6.01, 18.3.12

public houses (inspection of) 5.5.71, 6.10.71, 3.5.72, 7.9.72, 3.1.73, 25.12.73, 26.12.73, 5.7.77, 14.9.77, 26.10.77, 6.12.78, 2.2.79, 23.12.80

Quakers 31.12.75

quarter (unit of capacity) 29.1.71

quarrying 7.4.73, 11.9.75, 10.11.78

quay (new, St Peter Port) 2.4.74

Queripel, Elizabeth (domestic servant) 29.5.86, 8.6.86

Quiberon peninsula (French Royalist attack on) 3.8.95

quicksets 12.3.74, 28.2.92

quint (unit of capacity) 29.1.71, 6.2.72

rabbits 28.1.73, 16.12.76, 10.1.99, 22.5.01, 15.5.04

Rabey, Richard (farm servant) 27.6.92, 8.9.92

rabies 28.1.09

Racine, Antoine (farm servant) 8.1.02, 14.2.02

Radford, James (farm servant) 27.2.99, 3.12.99, 20.2.00, 29.4.00, 4.5.00, 7.12.11

Rambler (privateer) 29.12.79

raspberries 20.2.71, 8.3.76, 31.12.95, 8.7.09, 23.8.15, 14.8.16, 31.8.17, 26.7.18

Receiver, HM (Mollet's application for appointment as) 8.8.97

Renouf, Joseph (Town Hospital schoolmaster) 1.11.10, 14.2.11

Renouf, Rachel (domestic servant) 5.6.11, 2.3.12

rentes 10.2.71, 7.1.72, 17.12.85, 23.2.87, 25.2.94, 9.2.01, 24.5.17

Resolution (privateer) 5.7.79, 15.9.79

rheumatism 10.7.95, 15.12.98, 15.3.03, 28.11.08, 3.4.09, 27.2.10, 4.4.12, 14.3.17, 16.4.17, 27.7.17

rhubarb 1.11.71

Richmond, Duke of *see* **Lennox, Charles**

Richmond, Duchess of *see* **Bruce, Mary**

roads (general) 5.5.71, 6.10.71, 22.10.71, 24.3.71, 5.10.72, 22.10.72, 9.6.74, 3.4.77, 28.6.79, 30.5.86, 17.2.97, 8.12.09

roads (new) 25.6.10, 26.6.10, 29.6.10, 2.7.10, 15.7.10, 16.7.10, 17.7.10, 18.7.10, 30.7.10, 3.8.10, 4.8.10, 6.8.10, 7.8.10, 13.8.10, 18.8.10, 21.8.10, 4.9.10, 14.9.10, 13.10.10, 9.8.11, 10.8.11, 6.11.17

robberies (from the person) 27.6.95, 9.3.99

Robert, Elizabeth (wife of Eleazar Ingrouille) 17.9.88

Robert, Joseph (Castel parish *messier*) 4.5.75

Robin, Marie (domestic servant) 9.1.71, 29.1.71, 17.8.06, 16.6.16
Roche, Anne (daughter of HM Sergeant Jean Roche) 16.4.71, 3.6.85, 25.7.94, 22.8.94, 6.5.06, 31.5.10, 19.9.11, 29.4.16, 27.8.17
Roche family 7.4.71
Roche, Marie (daughter of HM Sergeant Jean Roche, wife of HM Comptroller Pierre Coutart) 16.4.71, 3.6.85, 25.7.94
Rocquaine 10.6.89, 2.6.90, 6.6.90, 12.9.93
Roland, Jean (farm labourer) 27.3.18, 13.4.18
Roland, Marie (wife of Hellier De Jersey of le Groignet) 12.4.72
Roman Catholics (*see also émigré* **priests**) 31.12.75
Romeril, Marie (Mollet's maternal grandmother) 9.1.76
roses 10.1.73, 13.3.85, 25.7.86, 31.12.90
rose water 23.7.99, 20.6.00, 25.6.02, 2.7.07, 27.7.09, 18.6.11, 22.2.17, 22.6.18
Ross, Lieutenant-Colonel Andrew 9.1.11, 27.1.11, 4.2.11, 9.2.11
Rotterdam 25.7.94, 9.8.10
Rouget, Henry (farm servant) 16.12.05, 19.2.06
Rouget, James (farmer) 8.12.03
Rouget, Judith (wife of James Rouget, aunt of Eleazar Ingrouille) *see* **Ingrouille, Judith**
Rougier, Jean (sailor, brother of Margueritte Rougier) 2.2.17
Rougier, Margueritte (wife of Pierre Cateline) 23.1.06, 22.6.17, 19.8.17, 5.9.17, 6.9.17, 28.9.17, 2.10.17, 15.10.17, 16.10.17, 22.12.17, 1.1.18, **14.3.18**, 20.3.18
Rougier, Nicolas (murderer) 3.4.75, 5.4.75, 1.7.75, 14.7.75
Roussel, Elizabeth (domestic servant) 7.4.94, 14.5.94
Roussel, Rachel (wife of Nicolas Roussel) *see* **Lihou, Rachel**
Rowley, Dr Thomas 14.11.00
rum 16.1.89, 3.7.90, 20.11.90, 9.12.90
Russians (in Guernsey) 21.11.99, 20.12.99, 28.12.99, 31.12.99, 1.1.00, 27.1.00, 14.3.00, 9.4.00, 15.4.00, 18.4.00, 22.4.00, 24.4.00, 27.4.00, 3.6.00, 13.6.00, 17.6.00, 8.8.00
sales (of wines & spirits, etc., in Alderney) 29.1.88, 1.2.88, 19.2.88
salt 28.10.99
salting bench 19.3.73
samphire 20.7.73, 21.8.01, 14.9.04, 2.9.16
sand 3.3.73, 26.3.74, 3.5.74, 2.11.74, 27.5.75, 20.5.03
sand eels 2.4.17
Sappho (Mollet's dog) 24.6.18
sardines 3.10.10
Sark 5.9.89, 2.11.91
Saumarez *see also* **De Sausmarez**
Saumarez, Admiral Sir James 27.3.85, **8.6.94**, **4.8.01**, 8.8.01, 24.8.02, 7.9.02, 22.5.03, 29.8.08

Saumarez, General Sir Thomas (brother of Admiral Sir James Saumarez) 14.6.87, 26.1.93, 24.7.97, 19.4.02, 1.9.06, 12.1.07, 20.7.08, 26.7.08, 29.8.08, **6.5.12**, 30.8.15, 30.10.15, 10.10.17

Saumarez, Lady Harriet (wife of General Sir Thomas Saumarez) *see* **Brock, Harriet**

Saumarez, Lady Martha (wife of Admiral Sir James Saumarez) *see* **Le Marchant, Martha**

Sauvegrain, Monsieur (*émigré* priest) 22.5.94, 19.6.94, 27.7.94

scarlet fever 3.4.71

Scott, Colonel Hercules (of the 103rd Regiment) 15.7.10, 16.7.10, 29.7.10, 3.8.10, 7.8.10, 9.8.10, 13.8.10, 28.8.10, 29.8.10, 7.9.10, 30.9.10, 1.10.10, 3.10.10, 6.10.10, 12.3.11, 9.7.11, 7.8.11, 5.10.11, 8.10.11, 11.10.11, 15.10.11, 25.12.11, 20.4.12, 22.4.12

sea-bathing 15.7.75, 17.7.79, 27.7.80, 9.7.85, 18.6.87

seamstresses 1.10.07, 24.12.07, 24.9.08. 23.12.09, 3.5.11, 16.11.11, 26.4.16, 2.5.17, 29.10.17, 9.7.18

seaweed (as fertiliser) 4.1.71, 10.9.71, 15.11.71, 3.3.73, 13.2.75, 13.7.75, 2.3.89, 14.2.94, 28.6.98, 1.1.03, 14.2.16, 31.12.17

seaweed (permitted times for cutting) 8.5.71, 1.7.72

securities (government) 26.7.71, 28.11.11, 20.2.17, 14.5.18

separation (marital) 14.3.18, 20.3.18

Seward, Philip 14.6.73, 11.5.77

sheep 25.10.10

shipwrecks 11.10.71, 28.11.72, 25.10.78, 16.11.79, 25.1.89, 29.1.98, 5.2.98, 29.1.00, 29.4.00, 4.5.00, 3.11.06, 18.2.07, 17.11.07, 30.11.07, 12.2.08, 10.12.16, 12.12.16, 13.12.16, 9.3.18

shirts 6.2.96

shoe blacking 21.2.11

shoes 4.4.18

shore-gathering (*see also* **crabs**, **ormers**) 19.2.72, 11.3.85, 23.9.86, 6.6.92, 6.3.02, 5.3.06, 14.2.16

shrub (fruit liqueur) 9.12.90

sick people (bedside vigils & visits) 4.2.07, 17.3.07, 3.12.09, 28.4.11, 4.1.16, 6.6.16

Simon, Jean (farm labourer) 20.5.16, 25.9.16

Skinner, George (illegitimate son of Lieutenant-Governor William Brown) 8.9.92

Skinner, Mary (servant of Lieutenant-Governor William Brown, mother of his sons) 8.9.92

Skinner, Richard (illegitimate son of Lieutenant-Governor William Brown) 8.9.92

sloes 5.11.87, 6.11.87

slugs 11.5.93, 23.6.17

Small, Major-General John (Lieutenant-Governor of Guernsey 1793–6) 2.12.94, 21.3.96, 3.4.96

Smith, Lady Carterette (wife of Colonel Sir George Smith) *see* **De Havilland, Carterette**
Smith, Colonel Sir George 9.2.00, 24.8.02, 12.3.09
Smith, William (soldier & farm labourer) 31.5.11
snipe (bird) 13.2.71, 31.12.85
snow (significant falls of) 9.1.71–19.1.71, 24.1.71, 9.2.71, 11.2.71, 16.4.71, 10.2.73, 22.1.76, 31.12.76–11.1.77, 25.2.86–18.3.86, 15.1.95–4.2.95, 20.12.99–2.1.00, 12.3.06–16.3.06, 1.1.11–11.1.11
snuff 27.7.02
soldiers (British) 24.6.76, 1.6.78, 3.6.78, 17.9.78, 19.11.78, 5.5.79, 26.5.79, 30.10.79, 6.1.80, 20.1.80, 19.4.80, 10.6.80, 10.8.80, 13.10.80, 1.12.80, 2.12.80, 13.12.80, 18.2.93, 21.8.93, 12.9.93, 25.2.95, 26.2.95, 27.6.95, 1.9.06, 20.9.07, 26.6.09
Solier, Pierre (Anglican clergyman) 3.2.88
Southampton (Mollet's stays in) 67.71–12.7.71, 2.11.88–6.11.88, 14.5.89–20.5.89, 12.10.92, 24.12.92
Spain (*see also* **Valencia**) 26.7.08, 5.10.08, 5.2.09, 29.10.09, 17.6.16
spy (suspected) 14.1.10
spyglasses 16.5.89
St Croix, Nicolas *see* **De Ste Croix, Nicolas**
St Andrew's church 8.11.71, 3.1.73, 5.6.86, 6.8.09
States (meetings of) 7.11.71, 9.11.71, 18.12.71, 11.1.72, 9.5.72, 23.1.73, 2.4.74, 3.6.78, 2.12.94
Stephens, Peter *see* **Etienne, Pierre**
stills (alembic) 31.8.99, 20.6.00, 6.6.07
stillbirths 5.10.71, 20.5.73, 23.3.74, 29.1.76, 10.7.78
stockings (silk) 19.5.71
Stonehenge 22.8.71
stonemasons 26.11.72, 13.7.74, 23.10.95
storekeeper 24.9.85, 22.4.86
storms 28.11.72, 22.2.73, 23.2.73, 26.2.73, 19.8.73, 17.5.00, 9.11.00, 10.11.10, 30.10.15, 6.3.17, 8.3.17, 12.3.18
stoves 1.5.80, 21.9.97, 25.10.98
St Peter's church 25.4.73, 8.8.73, 24.7.74, 5.3.75, 6.8.75, 22.5.03, 16.9.04, 20.11.08, 28.5.10, 16.9.10, 7.7.11, 14.6.12
stramonium (herbal remedy) 29.5.12, 4.6.12
Strangers' Cemetery (St Peter Port) 12.5.04
straw 9.8.04
strawberries 19.9.71, 15.5.76, 12.6.87, 4.6.88, 18.6.88, 22.6.88, 31.5.92, 29.9.95, 23.7.99, 21.7.02, 11.6.06, 21.6.12, 24.6.12, 16.6.18
stray animals 10.3.87, 9.9.97, 25.10.10, 2.3.17
strokes (paralytic) 23.11.94, 1.9.15, 5.7.16

St Saviour's church 8.11.71, 26.2.75, 19.5.99, 26.6.03, 24.8.06, 20.8.09, 7.7.11, 25.8.16
Studdart family (tenants of Mollet's) 9.1.03, 25.3.06, 1.3.12
Sturmer, Charles (British Consul at Cherbourg) 7.10.09, 29.10.09, 8.12.09
subscriptions (to charitable causes) 11.1.96–16.1.96, 6.2.18, 4.7.18
subscriptions (to circulating libraries) 22.11.02, 27.11.15
sugar 17.12.02
suicides (suspected) 1.6.99, 26.9.16
summer of 1816 (weather disturbances) 3.6.16, 11.7.16, 18.7.16
swallows 28.4.88, 16.4.89, 5.5.93, 21.4.94, 22.4.95
swede (vegetable) 3.5.74
Swift (privateer) 26.1.78
tailors 18.4.99, 22.7.17, 29.10.17
target practice 8.2.74
Tartar (privateer) 9.5.78, 25.8.78, 5.10.78
Taunton 6.6.10
tax 26.4.71, 29.4.71, 30.10.71, 8.2.72, 15.2.72, 20.6.72, 12.12.72, 19.9.76, 14.6.79, 11.11.79
teeth (Mollet's, extractions of) 2.1.72, 21.3.78
thatched roof (difficulty over in St Peter Port) 15.10.16, 17.10.16, 3.11.16, 7.12.16
thatchers 2.11.74, 22.12.74, 28.2.92, 10.1.05, 14.10.16
theatre 4.11.74, 23.11.74, 28.11.74, 5.12.74, 14.12.74, 21.12.74, 28.12.74, 13.1.75, 20.1.75, 25.1.75, 27.1.75, 13.2.75, 26.12.75, 29.10.87, 7.11.87, 17.11.87, 24.11.87, 3.11.88, 23.8.89
thefts 15.9.71, 16.9.71, 13.3.72, 19.10.72, 18.1.77, 22.12.77, 20.2.79, 11.12.79, 1.12.80, 7.12.80, 13.12.80,14.12.80, 20.2.95, 25.2.95, 26.2.95, 27.6.95, 26.6.02
Thom, Alexander (shipwright) 28.7.94, 23.3.01
Thomas, Rachel (wife of George Thomas) *see* **Du Four, Rachel**
thorn apple *see* **stramonium**
tithes (collection of) 12.9.73, 13.9.73, 14.9.73, 20.9.73, 23.9.73, 11.9.74, 26.9.74, 31.8.75, 28.9.75, 11.9.76, 12.9.76, 18.9.76, 19.9.76, 14.9.77, 15.9.77, 1.9.78, 5.9.78, 25.8.79, 6.9.79, 5.9.80, 10.9.80, 29.8.85, 24.8.86, 1.9.86, 4.9.87, 8.9.87, 1.9.00, 11.9.00, 29.8.01, 3.9.01, 4.9.02, 14.9.02, 3.9.06, 23.9.06, 27.8.07, 29.8.08, 5.9.09. 11.9.10, 15.9.10, 2.9.11, 6.9.11, 23.8.15,6.9.15, 24.9.16, 12.9.17, 24.9.17
tithes (farm of) 7.1.73, 26.2.85, 17.4.94, 1.9.00, 18.3.18
tobacco 19.4.78, 27.7.02
Torode, Daniel (master carpenter) 20.1.98, 23.3.01, 24.6.07, 16.10.15
Torode, James (farm labourer, farm servant) 30.4.04
Torode, James (farm labourer, son of Jean Torode of les Moullins) 25.3.17
Torode, Jean (of les Grands Moullins, tailor) 8.4.17, 29.10.17

Torteval (new church at) 29.4.16, 23.9.17
Tostevin, Elizabeth (domestic servant) 19.10.07, 7.2.09, 1.4.09
Tourgis, Marie (wife of Nicolas Moullin & Richard Moullin) 28.10.71, 12.4.72, 12.9.72
Trachy, Judith (wife of Daniel Ferbrache) 3.7.16
Treaty of London (1801) 4.10.01
trees 20.2.71, 28.10.71, 29.11.71, 22.2.73, 26.2.73, 3.3.74, 16.2.76, 31.12.90, 1.2.91, 24.8.91, 28.2.92, 25.2.94, **17.3.94**, **28.7.94**, 8.4.97, 20.3.97, 9.1.98, 17.5.00, **9.11.00**, 23.3.01, 15.1.07, 6.12.08, 5.10.11, 15.10.11, 2.2.16, 12.3.18
Trinity House 4.8.88
tuberculosis 12.8.01, 15.3.10, 23.6.10, 27.8.10, 25.12.11, 4.6.17
tun 16.12.74, 18.11.86
tulips 2.9.88, 3.2.95, 11.10.97
Tupper, Daniel (of Hauteville, merchant) 30.7.80
Tupper, Elizée (Jurat 1771–98) 18.5.71
Tupper, John (Jurat 1798–1810) 20.1.72, 21.8.98, 25.5.07
Tupper, John Elisha, sen. (of le Carrefour, merchant) 12.2.08
Tupper, John Elisha, jun. 28.3.12
turkeys 8.12.09
turnips 20.2.71, 31.12.73, 3.3.74, 13.5.77, 7.12.80, 13.12.80, 18.8.88, 18.7.94, 31.12.17
turtle feast 21.8.86
turtle-doves 5.5.93, 9.5.02
Tuzets, les (Mollet's fields at) 15.1.85, 6.12.87
twine (from home-grown hemp) 19.8.16
'upper' house (bought by Mollet from Jean Batiste) 19.7.80, 29.7.85, 27.9.91, 28.2.92, 8.2.94, 19.1.95, 22.3.98, 30.10.15
Valencia (Spain) 17.6.16
Vallat, Isaac (Anglican clergyman) 25.4.73, 3.1.75, 5.3.75, 24.5.75, 16.2.76, 20.7.78, 27.3.85
Vallat, Jeanne (wife of Isaac Vallat) *see* **Allez, Jeanne**
Vau des Vallées *see* **'upper' house**
vergee (unit of area) 5.1.74
vines 28.2.92
vingtaines (of the Castel parish) 29.4.71
vingtième 8.10.76
Virginia 26.10.06, 2.2.07, 26.4.07, 16.5.07, 16.6.07, 3.12.07
Volage (Mollet's dog) 24.6.18
vue de justice 7.5.71
Vulture (privateer) 26.1.78
Walcheren (Holland) 23.12.09
Walsh, Colonel Anthony (Inspector of Militia) 24.6.17

Walters, Dr Robert 30.7.80, 19.4.02
warehouse(s) (Mollet's, at la Profonde Rue) 31.12.79, 8.2.86, 23.5.91, 5.9.91, 16.10.15, **14.10.16**, 15.10.16, 17.10.16, 7.12.16
War of American Independence (France's entry to) 2.4.78
wasps 28.9.85
watch-duty 2.5.79, 3.9.79, 19.1.01, 22.3.01, 9.5.04, **14.12.09**, 15.12.09, **29.4.10**, 24.8.11
Watkins, Daniel (merchant) 22.2.71, 10.4.71
Waugh, John (military officer) 16.12.80, 27.3.85, 24.9.85, 12.1.91, 11.2.91, 31.3.91, 6.7.94, 27.1.99, 28.1.99
weasels 11.10.85, 18.2.03
weather vane 21.3.77
Wesley, Rev. John (Methodist preacher) 19.8.87, 1.9.87
West Indies 4.2.87, 1.7.88, 16.11.00
wheat 19.9.71, 28.10.71, 14.11.71, 7.12.71, 10.12.71, 2.1.72, 6.4.72, 26.4.72, 18.11.72, 8.3.73, 3.5.74, 31.5.74, 15.12.74, 27.8.76, 12.12.86, 23.8.92, 5.8.94, 5.2.98, 29.1.99, 17.12.00, 1.2.06, 1.1.10, 23.12.11, 6.9.15
Whiskin, Catherine (wife of Rev. Edward Mourant) 28.6.96
Whitelocke, General John 10.5.98
Whyte, General Richard 10.6.80
wig 1.11.71
Wilford, Thomas (soldier & farm labourer) 1.9.10, 4.9.10
Williams, Thomas (of Alderney) 17.1.88, 31.1.88, 15.2.88, 17.2.88, 5.3.88, 30.5.88, 3.6.88, 1.7.88, 14.7.88, 28.8.88, 22.9.88, 25.9.88, 28.9.88, 30.9.88, 2.10.88, 7.10.88, 9.10.88, 15.10.88, 9.11.88, 25.11.88, 3.12.88, 25.12.88, 25.2.89, 8.4.89, 21.4.89, 11.5.89, 16.5.89, 28.5.89, 2.6.89, 22.6.89, 27.6.89, 25.7.89, 26.8.89, 23.9.89, 24.9.89, 30.9.89, 13.2.90, 8.5.90, 22.7.90, 1.8.90, 28.10.90, 30.10.90, 11.11.90, 10.4.91, 24.9.91
windows (Mollet's, smashed by mob in Alderney) 31.3.89
wine 4.7.76, 24.11.80, 10.12.87, 5.12.91, 1.2.96, 9.5.99, 30.11.03, 15.9.09, 16.10.15, 23.12.16, 12.6.18, 22.6.18
wonders (cakes) 10.4.06, 25.3.07, 12.4.10, 8.4.12, 4.6.17, 21.7.18
Woollcombe, Elizabeth (wife of Robert Woollcombe) *see* **Dobrée, Elizabeth**
Woollcombe, Lieutenant Robert (husband of Mollet's great-niece Elizabeth Dobrée) 22.7.16, 20.1.18
wrynecks (birds) 21.4.93
'year without a summer' (1816) *see* **summer of 1816**
Yvetot, Félix-Barnabé (*émigré* priest) 11.12.95

www.ingramcontent.com/pod-product-compliance
Lightning Source LLC
Chambersburg PA
CBHW070521010526
44118CB00012B/1041